The Philosophy of Language in Islamic Legal Theory

Handbook of Oriental Studies

Handbuch der Orientalistik

SECTION ONE

The Near and Middle East

Edited by

Maribel Fierro (*Madrid*)
M. Şükrü Hanioğlu (*Princeton*)
D. Fairchild Ruggles (*University of Illinois*)
Florian Schwarz (*Vienna*)

VOLUME 201

The titles published in this series are listed at *brill.com/ho1*

The Philosophy of Language in Islamic Legal Theory

On the Avicennian Classification of Signification in Faḫr ad-dīn ar-Rāzī (d. 1210)

By

Nora Kalbarczyk

BRILL

LEIDEN | BOSTON

This work has been edited by Andrew Wigman on the basis of an English draft translation generated by DeepL.

ISSN 0169-9423
ISBN 978-90-04-73602-3
ISBN 978-90-04-73601-6 (PDF)
DOI https://doi.org/10.1163/9789004736016

Library of Congress Control Number: 2026940668

Brill and Koninklijke Brill BV are part of De Gruyter Brill.
www.degruyterbrill.com

Questions about General Product Safety Regulation: productsafety@degruyterbrill.com

Cover illustration: Faḫr ad-dīn ar-Rāzī: Šarḥ al-Išārāt wa-t-tanbīhāt. Ms. or.oct. 1802, BERLIN STATE LIBRARY—Prussian Cultural Heritage, Oriental Department.

In memory of my beloved father
who passed away far too soon
Burkhard Wothe
(1962–2009)

It is in this language that their exchanges on science take place, their conversations, their teachings, and discussions; it is in it that their quills drip onto the page, in it that the documents and decisions of their judges are written. They are thus clothed in the Arabic language—no matter where they go, they do not part themselves from it.

> ABŪ L-QĀSIM AZ-ZAMAḪŠARĪ: *al-Mufaṣṣal*. Ed. by J.P. Broch, 1859, p. 2, last line–p. 3, line 2

•••

Vielmehr ist die Sprache das universale Medium, in dem sich das Verstehen selber vollzieht. Die Vollzugsweise des Verstehens ist die Auslegung.
(Language is rather the universal medium in which understanding itself takes place. The manner in which understanding occurs is interpretation.)

> HANS-GEORG GADAMER: *Wahrheit und Methode: Grundzüge einer philosophischen Hermeneutik*. In *Gesammelte Werke*. Tübingen: J.C.B. Mohr, 1999, vol. 1, p. 392

∴

Contents

Preface

The present study was written as part of the German-British research project "Major issues and controversies of Arabic logic and philosophy of language" (Ruhr-University Bochum and Cambridge University, funded by the German Research Foundation and the Arts and Humanities Research Council, 2011–2015) and was accepted as a dissertation by the Faculty of Philology at Ruhr-University Bochum in spring of 2016 under the title *"Die Klassifikation sprachlicher Bezeichnung im islamischen Rechtsdenken: Faḫr ad-dīn ar-Rāzīs Synthese zwischen Logik, Grammatik und Jurisprudenz in seinem Werk* al-Maḥṣūl fī ʿilm uṣūl al-fiqh."

It has benefited in every respect from the intellectual, critical acuity of my doctoral supervisor Prof. Dr. Cornelia Schöck, to whom I owe a great debt of gratitude, and it would not have been conceivable without her initiative and without her inlcusion of it into the research project for which she was responsible.

I would like to thank Prof. Dr. Asad Q. Ahmed (University of California, Berkeley), who supervised this thesis as second reader, for all his valuable comments and remarks during my doctoral studies.

My sincere thanks go also to Prof. Dr. Gerhard Endreß, who always lent me a sympathetic ear during my time in Bochum and read my work with a critical eye.

Annual joint workshops have given me the opportunity to present my work from different perspectives to a knowledgeable audience. I would therefore like to thank all those who have participated in these workshops and supported my work: In addition to my two supervisors, these include in particular our project co-leader Dr. Tony Street as well as (in alphabetical order) Dr. Rachel Friedman, Prof. Dr. Dimitri Gutas, Dr. Alexander Kalbarczyk, Dr. Joep Lameer, Prof. Dr. James Montgomery, Dr. Reza Pourjavady, Prof. Dr. Khaled el-Rouayheb, Prof. Dr. Riccardo Strobino, and Prof. Dr. Paul Thom. My communications with Prof. Dr. Peter Adamson, Prof. Dr. Dag Hasse, Dr. Andreas Lammer, and the other participants of the Würzburg and Munich reading groups as well as with Prof. Dr. Robert Gleave and Dr. Ayman Shihadeh have been and continue to be particularly fruitful for my reflections. My special thanks go to the anonymous reviewer, whose thorough corrections were extremely helpful. I would also like to thank the editors of the *Islamic Philosophy, Theology and Science* series as well as Teddi Dolls and Wilma de Weert from the Brill publishing house for their wonderful cooperation.

I would like to take this opportunity to thank my husband, Alexander Kalbarczyk, for our constant discussions about my dissertation project, for thinking and rethinking through ideas with me, and for his patient, loving support. My grandfather Lothar Wothe and my grandparents Bernd and Hella Schmid I thank for their unfailing love and support. To my parents-in-law Johanna and Hendrik Kalbarczyk, too, without whose care and support many things would not have been possible, I give my special thanks. My children Elias and Sophia, whose daily life from the very beginning has been shaped by my involvement with Islamic intellectual history, have taught and continue each day anew to teach me to wonder and ask questions. Their shining eyes have shed light on many things.

Sankt Augustin, April 2018
Nora Kalbarczyk

Addendum to the English Edition

The English translation of my German book from 2018 was carefully prepared by Andrew Wigman. I am very grateful to him for this wonderful and enriching collaboration. I would also like to thank Paulina Bastian from Brill, who always supported us with advice and assistance.

Sankt Augustin, Oktober 2025
Nora Kalbarczyk

Figures and Tables

Figures

Tables

Introduction

1 Interdisciplinary Arabic Philosophy of Language: Islamic Legal Hermeneutics (*uṣūl al-fiqh*), Grammar (*naḥw*), and Avicennian Logic (*manṭiq*)

This study focuses on one of the "meta-interpretive questions that lurk just beneath the surface of the legal theory manuals,"[1] namely the fundamental question of how the relationship between word and meaning is conceived of in Islamic legal theory against the background of the interdisciplinary context in which Arabic hermeneutics is embedded. The answers that Arabic legal scholars give us to questions about the philosophy of language in general and about the theory of signification in particular are difficult for us to understand if we look only at the traditions of legal theory and practice without taking into account the other disciplines in which the same scholars were also active or by which they were intellectually influenced.[2] The diverse and highly sophisticated linguistic contemplation that permeates Islamic works of legal theory is a direct indication of the essential connection between the two disciplines of legal theory and grammar—there was a fruitful and, above all, *reciprocal* rela-

1 David R. Vishanoff, *The Formation of Islamic Hermeneutics: How Sunni Legal Theorists Imagined a Revealed Law* (New Haven, CT: American Oriental Society, 2011), p. xvii.

2 This should be self-evident for the Islamic disciplines like *kalām*, *fiqh*, *uṣūl al-fiqh*, *naḥw*, and *tafsīr* that must be thought of as "holistic enterprise[s]," cf. Reinhart, "'Like the Difference between Heaven and Earth': Ḥanafī and Shāfiʿī Discussions of *Farḍ* and *Wājib* in Theology and Uṣūl," in *Studies in Islamic Legal Theory*, ed. by Bernard G. Weiss (Leiden [et al.]: Brill, 2002), p. 205; I include philosophy and logic in this as well. The fact that these different disciplines have all developed their own hermeneutical foundations has been pointed out by Gregor Schwarb in an investigation into the mutual influence of *uṣūl al-fiqh* and *uṣūl at-tafsīr*, see Gregor Schwarb, "Capturing the Meaning of God's Speech: The Relevance of *uṣūl al-fiqh* to an Understanding of *uṣūl al-tafsīr* in Jewish and Muslim Kalām," in *A Word Fitly Spoken: Studies in Medieval Exegesis of the Hebrew Bible and the Qurʾān Presented to Haggai Ben-Shammai*, ed. by Meir M. Bar-Asher, Simon Hopkins, Sarah Stroumsa and Buno Chiesa (Jerusalem: Ben-Zvi Institute, 2007), pp. 111–156, esp. pp. 111–112. With regard to theological, logical, and grammatical questions, this interrelationship has been analyzed by Cornelia Schöck, see Cornelia Schöck, *Koranexegese, Grammatik und Logik. Zum Verhältnis von arabischer und aristotelischer Urteils-, Konsequenz- und Schlusslehre* (Leiden [et al.]: Brill, 2006) and id., "Name (*ism*), Derived Name (*ism mushtaqq*) and Description (*waṣf*) in Arabic Grammar, Muslim Dialectical Theology and Arabic Logic," in *The Unity of Science in the Arabic Tradition. Science, Logic, Epistemology and their Interactions*, ed. by Shahid Rahman, Tony Street and Hassan Tahiri (Dordrecht: Springer, 2008), pp. 329–360.

 | DOI:10.1163/9789004736016_002

tionship between the two disciplines, in which the terminology, questions, and methods of one discipline diffused into the other and vice versa.[3]

At the same time, the passages on the philosophy of language in the works on legal theory of the post-formative period[4] are characterized by intensive engagement with the writings of Arabic logic and philosophy of language.[5]

---

3 On the mutual influence of the two disciplines, see for example Ulrich Haarmann, "Religiöses Recht und Grammatik im klassischen Islam," in *Zeitschrift der Deutschen Morgenländischen Gesellschaft*, suppl. vol. 2 (1974): pp. 149–169; Versteegh also refers to this mutual exchange in his comprehensive introduction to Arabic theories of signification, see Cornelis Versteegh, "The Arabic Tradition," in *The Emergence of Semantics in four Linguistic Traditions: Hebrew, Sanskrit, Greek, Arabic*, ed. by Wout J. van Bekkum, Jan Houben, Ineke Sluiter, and Kees Versteegh (Amsterdam [et al.]: John Benjamins, 1996), pp. 225–284, esp. pp. 266ff.; on the significant influence of legal theory on grammar, see Michael G. Carter, "Les origines de la grammaire arabe," *Revue des Études Islamiques*, vol. 40 (1972): pp. 69–97; on the modes of argumentation shaped by legal theory that appear in grammatical works, see id. "A Missing Link between Law and Grammar: The Intiṣār of Ibn Wallād," *Arabica*, vol. 48, no. 1 (2001): pp. 51–65; on the influence of legal theory on grammar, see Gerhard Endreß, "'This is Clear Arabic Speech': God's Speech and Prophetic Language in Early Islamic Hermeneutics, Theology and Philosophy," in *Transcending Words: The Language of Religious Contact Between Buddhists, Christians, Jews and Muslims in Premodern Times*, ed. by Görge K. Hasselhoff and Knut Martin Stünkel (Bochum: Winkler, 2015), pp. 27–42, esp. pp. 27–30; on the dependence of legal theory on Arabic linguistics, see esp. Bernard G. Weiss, "Language and Law: The Linguistic Premises of Islamic Legal Science," in *In Quest of an Islamic Humanism: Arabic and Islamic Studies in Memory of Mohamed al-Nowaihi*, ed. by A.H. Green (Cairo: The American University in Cairo Press, 1984), pp. 15–21. Arabic-language research literature also deals with this interrelationship, see for example Muṣṭafā Ǧamāl ad-dīn, *al-Baḥṯ an-naḥwī ʿinda l-uṣūliyyīn* (Baghdad: Dār ar-Rašīd li-n-našr, 1980).

4 The term 'post-formative' usually refers to "the settling down of the four Sunnī *madhhabs* around the end of the fifth/eleventh century"; see Sherman A. Jackson, "*Taqlīd*, Legal Scaffolding and the Scope of Legal Injunctions in Post-Formative Theory *Muṭlaq* and *ʿĀmm* in the Jurisprudence of Shihāb al-Dīn al-Qarāfī," *Islamic Law and Society*, vol. 3, no. 2 (1996): p. 168.

5 Questions relating to the philosophy of language, such as the relationship between linguistic expression, meaning, and extramental matters, were treated in the texts on logic. The term 'logic' is used in the Peripatetic context to classify the six books of the *Organon*, comprising (1) *Categories*, (2) *On Interpretation* (*Peri Hermeneias*, *De Interpretatione*), (3/4) two *Analytics* (i.e. the *Analytica Priora*, in which syllogistics is developed, and the *Analytica Posteriora*, which focuses on considerations of scientific theory), (5) *Topics*, and (6) *On Sophistical Refutations*. The *Organon* was supplemented in the Arabic tradition by the Neoplatonic introductory treatise on logic, the *Eisagoge* (*Εἰσαγωγή*/*Īsāġūǧī*) by Porphyrios (d. 301–305). In its entirety, the *Organon* deals with the fundamentals of linguistics, logic, and epistemology, i.e. with terms and concepts, semantics, declaratives, conditionals, argumentation theory, proof theory, philosophy of science, etc. In the Peripatetic tradition, logic is regarded as an instrument of correct thinking and thus as the propaedeutic for each individual science; a brief introduction to the *Organon* and its reception history can be found in Dominik Perler and Ulrich Rudolph, in the introduction to *Logik und Theologie. Das Organon im Arabischen und*

The influence of *Aristotelian* or *Greek* logic on works of legal theory has readily been suspected or denied,[6] but in my opinion the question of such influence is relevant mainly to early legal theory, not to works written after the time of al-Ġazālī[7] (d. 505/1111).[8] These are indeed clearly influenced, although not by a logic that can be declared as *Aristotelian*, *Peripatetic*, or as *Greek*—even if that influence remains to a certain extent tied to the Peripatetic tradition and Arabic Aristotelianism—but by an *Avicennian* logic. With the work of the polymath Ibn Sīnā (d. 428/1037), the study of Aristotelian texts and the commentaries based on them became virtually obsolete; instead, Ibn Sīnā's writings became the reference texts for subsequent generations, which, due to Ibn Sīnā's immense influence, are called "post-Avicennian."[9] Ibn Sīnā, who adapted

---

im Lateinischen Mittelalter, ed. by Dominik Perler and Ulrich Rudolph (Leiden [et al.]: Brill, 2005), pp. 1–16; additional comprehensive studies are found in the works of Rescher, including Nicholas Rescher, *The Development of Arabic Logic* (Pittsburgh: University Press, 1964); see also Henri Hugonnard-Roche, *La logique d'Aristote du grec au syriaque: Études sur la transmission des textes de l'*Organon *et leur interprétation philosophique* (Paris: Vrin, 2004).

6 See for example van Ess's remark (*Die Erkenntnislehre des ʿAḍudaddīn al-Īcī. Übersetzung und Kommentar des ersten Buches seiner Mawāqif* [Wiesbaden: Harrassowitz, 1966], p. 382): "Aristotelian logic enters theology; the field of jurisprudence remains closed to it [...]"; Haarmann ("Religiöses Recht und Grammatik," pp. 155 and p. 160) builds on van Ess's remark: "al-Ġazzālī (d. 505/1111), who introduces Aristotelian logic into legal doctrine as well—albeit without lasting effects"; similar remarks can be found in Bernard G. Weiss, *The Search for God's Law. Islamic Jurisprudence in the Writings of Sayf al-Dīn al-Āmidī* (Salt Lake City: University of Utah Press, ²2010) [1st edition 1992], p. 23 and in Birgit Krawietz, "Zum Verhältnis von Sprache, Recht und Theologie in der islamischen Rechtstheorie von Sayf al-Dīn al-Āmidī," *Der Islam*, vol. 72 (1995): p. 144. Ulrich Rudolph takes the opposite position: "The fact that Ġazālī significantly contributed to establishing Aristotelian logic as the methodology of Islamic theology and jurisprudence has long been undisputed," Ulrich Rudolph, "Die Neubewertung der Logik durch al-Ġazālī," in *Logik und Theologie*, ed. by Dominik Perler and Ulrich Rudolph (Leiden [et al.]: Brill, 2005), p. 73.

7 On the spelling of the name *al-Ġazālī*, see Griffel's remarks, in which he argues that there are good reasons for both the spelling *al-Ġazālī* and *al-Ġazzālī*; in line with his conclusion, the spelling al-Ġazālī is used here, see Frank Griffel, "Al-Ghazālī or al-Ghazzālī? On a Lively Debate Among Ayyubid and Mamluk Historians in Damascus," in *Islamic Thought in the Middle Ages: Studies in Transmission and Translation in Honour of Hans Daiber*, ed. by Anna Akasoy and Wim Raven (Leiden: Brill Academic Publishing, 2008), pp. 101–112.

8 Since al-Ġazālī's logic is influenced not only by Ibn Sīnā, but just as much by al-Fārābī, the term 'Aristotelian' could still be appropriate in this context, see for example Tony Street, "Arabic Logic," in *Handbook of the History of Logic. Volume 1: Greek, Indian and Arabic Logic*, ed. by Dov M. Gabbay and John Woods (Amsterdam [et al.]: Elsevier North Holland, 2004), p. 559 and Jules Janssens, "Al-Ghazzālī's *Miʿyār al-ʿilm fī fann al-manṭiq*. Sources Avicenniennes et Farabiennes," *Archives d'histoire doctrinale et littéraire du Moyen Âge*, vol. 69 (2002): pp. 39–66.

9 Cf. Tony Street, "Arabic and Islamic Philosophy of Language and Logic," *Stanford Encyclopedia*

the content and terminology of philosophy and logic to the needs of Islamic disciplines,[10] forms the culmination of earlier and the starting point of later scholarship:[11]

> […] he reviewed the old canon of the theoretical sciences, he created a new encyclopedia of the method and matter of philosophy—of the classical *curriculum studiorum* of ethical propaedeutics, logical hermeneutics, demonstrative logic, physics and metaphysics, including the elementary matter of mathematics and astronomy, and adding—outside the philosophical canon proper—a manual of theoretical and practical medicine. It was through him that the *Falsafa* came to be and to stay an integral and living part of Arabic Islamic thought—in the scientific community, both Muslim and non-Muslim, as a universal religion for intellectuals, and then also in the religious community, where grammarians, jurists and theologians adopted from demonstrative science the guidelines of their *uṣūl*.[12]

His immense influence can be seen on the one hand directly in the number of commentaries, summaries, refutations, and quotations that refer to him by name, and on the other hand in indirect references. It is precisely the latter which—because they have gone unrecognized—may have led to the erroneous assessment that al-Ġazālī's project of introducing logic into legal her-

of Philosophy, 2008, p. 7; on the difference between Ibn Sīnā's logic and Avicennian logic, see Robert Wisnovsky, "Avicenna's Islamic Reception," in *Interpreting Avicenna: Critical Essays*, ed. by Peter Adamson (Cambridge: Cambridge University Press, 2013), pp. 190–213, esp. pp. 199–203.

10 Cf. Dimitri Gutas, "The Heritage of Avicenna: The Golden Age of Arabic Philosophy, 1000–ca. 1350," in *Avicenna and his Heritage*, ed. by Jules Janssens and Daniel De Smet (Leuven: Leuven University Press, 2002), pp. 81–97, esp. pp. 84–85 and id., "Avicenna's philosophical project," in *Interpreting Avicenna: Critical Essays*, ed. by Peter Adamson (Cambridge: Cambridge University Press, 2013), pp. 28–47, esp. pp. 33–35; the direct compatibility with Islamic disciplines is especially noted of Ibn Sīnā's *Išārāt wa-t-tanbīhāt*, see (in the form of an exemplary content analysis) Schöck, "Name (*ism*), Derived Name (*ism mushtaqq*) and Description (*waṣf*)," pp. 329–360 and Frank Griffel, "Al-Ghazālī's Concept of Prophecy: The Introduction of Avicennan Psychology into Aš'arite Theology," *Arabic Sciences and Philosophy*, vol. 14 (2004): pp. 101–144; also cf. for example Wisnovsky's overview article cited above ("Avicenna's Islamic Reception," pp. 193–194).

11 Gutas, "The Heritage of Avicenna," p. 80.

12 Gerhard Endreß, "Reading Avicenna in the Madrasa: Intellectual Genealogies and Chains of Transmission of Philosophy and the Sciences in the Islamic East," in *Arabic Theology, Arabic Philosophy. From the Many to the One: Essays in Celebration of Richard M. Frank*, ed. by James E. Montgomery (Leuven: Peeters, 2006), p. 379.

meneutics had remained "without lasting effects."[13] In fact, a reappraisal of the influence of Avicennian logic on the Arabic Islamic sciences—in the context of the larger question of "to what extent the *maʿqūlī* tradition penetrated the hermeneutical boundaries of the *manqūlī* tradition"[14]—remains a desideratum:[15]

> The great historical task is working out the precise clashes between the Islamic disciplines and philosophy which left the logical treatises as narrowly focused as they are, and finding the genres which took over treatment of these previously logical topics. This is really the key point for future research [...]. And if ever we can appreciate those changes, we can speak not only of the contributions of Muslim scholars to logic, but also of the contributions of logic to Islamic culture.[16]

This study aims to contribute to the reappraisal of indirect references to the Avicennian tradition within Islamic scholarship, in particular *uṣūl al-fiqh*, beginning with the works of the important post-Avicennian scholar Faḫr ad-dīn ar-Rāzī (d. 606/1210). Faḫr ad-dīn ar-Rāzī, who was well versed in the fields of theology, legal theory, philosophy, logic, and grammar among others, and who is said to have been a grumpy critic of Ibn Sīnā, played a major role in bringing it about "that Ibn Sīnā entered the madrasa," i.e. that Avicennian philosophy and logic became part of the curriculum for the training of legal scholars and theologians.[17]

---

13 Haarmann, "Religiöses Recht und Grammatik," p. 155.

14 Asad Q. Ahmed, "Systematic Growth in Sustained Error: A Case Study in the Dynamism of Post-Classical Islamic Scholasticism," in *The Islamic Scholarly Tradition*, ed. by Asad Q. Ahmed, Behnam Sadeghi and Michael Bonner (Leiden [et al.]: Brill, 2011), pp. 343–378, esp. p. 345.

15 There are, however, important works of research that treat the influence of Avicennian philosophy on the structure and methods of the Arabic Islamic sciences, such as Robert Wisnovsky, "One Aspect of the Avicennian Turn in Sunnī Theology," *Arabic Sciences and Philosophy*, vol. 14 (2004): pp. 65–100; Heidrun Eichner, *The Post-Avicennian Philosophical Tradition and Islamic Orthodoxy: Philosophical and Theological Summae in Context*, unpublished habilitation thesis, Halle, 2009; Ayman Shihadeh, "From al-Ghazālī to al-Rāzī: 6th/12th Century Developments in Muslim Philosophical Theology," *Arabic Sciences and Philosophy*, vol. 15 (2005): pp. 141–179; and Frank Griffel, "Between al-Ghazālī and Abū l-Barakāt al-Baghdādī: The Dialectical Turn in the Philosophy of Iraq and Iran During the Sixth/Twelfth Century," in *In the Age of Averroes: Arabic Philosophy in the Sixth/Twelfth Century*, ed. by Peter Adamson (London: The Warburg Institute, 2011), pp. 45–75.

16 Street, "Arabic Logic," p. 585.

17 Endreß, "Reading Avicenna in the Madrasa," p. 398; cf. Gutas, "The Heritage of Avicenna," p. 92. Tony Street is particularly active in the field of the logic of Ibn Sīnā and Faḫr ad-dīn ar-Rāzī, cf. Street, "Faḫraddīn ar-Rāzī's Critique of Avicennan Logic," in *Logik und Theolo-*

Recent research has suggested that Faḫr ad-dīn acted as a kind of "master synthesizer"—as one "who had successfully digested and integrated all that had preceded him";[18] he combined methods, structures, and content from different disciplines and in turn had a formative influence on the scholars of subsequent generations and centuries.[19]

---

gie, ed. by Dominik Perler and Ulrich Rudolph, pp. 99–116, id., "An Outline of Avicenna's Syllogistics," *Archiv für Geschichte der Philosophie*, vol. 84 (2002): pp. 129–160, and id., "Avicenna on the Syllogism," in *Interpreting Avicenna: Critical Essays*, ed. by Peter Adamson (Cambridge: Cambridge University Press, 2013), pp. 48–70; the influence of Ibn Sīnā's metaphysics on Faḫr ad-dīn ar-Rāzī is analyzed by Jules Janssens in his essay "Ibn Sīnā's Impact on Faḫr ad-dīn ar-Rāzī's *Mabāḥiṯ al-Mašriqiyya*, with particular regard to the section entitled *al-Ilāhiyyāt al-maḥḍa*: An Essay of Critical Evaluation," *Documenti e studi sulla tradizione filosofica medievale*, vol. 21 (2010): pp. 259–285; post-Avicennian philosophy in general and that of Faḫr ad-dīn in particular is also treated by, among others, Bilal Ibrahim in his essay "Faḫr ad-Dīn ar-Rāzī, Ibn al-Hayṯam and Aristotelian Science: Essentialism versus Phenomenalism in Post-Classical Islamic Thought," *Oriens*, vol. 41 (2013): pp. 379–431, this being a summary of the main arguments developed in his dissertation; id., *Freeing Philosophy from Metaphysics: Fakhr al-Dīn al-Rāzī's Philosophical Approach to the Study of Natural Phenomena*, unpublished doctoral dissertation (Montreal: McGill University, 2013).

On Faḫr ad-dīn's life, works, and impact, see, among others, Ǧamāl ad-dīn ibn al-Qifṭī, *Taʾrīḫ al-ḥukamāʾ*, ed. by Julius Lippert (Leipzig: Dietrich'sche Verlagsbuchhandlung, 1903), pp. 291–293; Tāǧ ad-dīn as-Subkī, *Ṭabaqāt aš-Šāfiʿiyya al-kubrā*, ed. by Maḥmūd M. Ṭanāḥī and ʿAbd al-Fatāḥ M. al-Ḥulw (Cairo: ʿĪsā l-Bābī l-Ḥalabī, 1964–1976 [1324]), vol. VIII, pp. 81–96; Aḥmad b. Muḥammad Ibn Ḫallikān, *Wafayāt al-aʿyān wa-anbāʾ abnāʾ az-zamān*, ed. by Iḥsān ʿAbbās (Beirut: Dār aṯ-ṯaqāfa, 1968–1972), vol. 4, pp. 248–252; for research literature on Faḫr ad-dīn ar-Rāzī's life and the historical context in which he worked, see Roger Arnaldez, *Fakhr al-Dîn al-Râzî: Commentateur du Coran et philosophe* (Paris: Vrin, 2002), esp. pp. 15–52; see further Georges Anawati, Fakhr al-Dīn al-Rāzī, *EI*[2] and id., *Fakhr al-Dīn al-Rāzī: tamhīd li-dirāsat ḥayātihī wa-muʾallafātihī*, in *Mélanges Taha Hussein*, ed. by ʿAbd ar-Raḥmān al-Badawawī (Cairo: Dār al-Maʿārif, 1962), pp. 193–234; a comprehensive introduction to his life and especially to his work is given by Ṭahā Ǧābir al-ʿAlwānī's *al-Imām Faḫr ad-dīn ar-Rāzī wa-muṣannafātuhū* (Cairo: Dār al-Islām, 2010); see also Frank Griffel, "On Fakhr al-Dīn al-Rāzī's Life and the Patronage He Received," *Journal of Islamic Studies*, vol. 18, no. 3 (2007): pp. 313–344; and Tony Street, "Concerning the Life and Works of Fakhr al-Dīn al-Rāzī," in *Islam: Essays on Scripture, Thought and Society. A Festschrift in Honour of Anthony H. Johns*, ed. by Peter G. Riddel and Tony Street (Leiden [et al.]: Brill, 1997), pp. 135–146. The dictionary of Faḫr ad-dīn ar-Rāzī's technical terminology—Samīḥ Duġaym, *Mawṣūʿāt Muṣṭalaḥāt al-imām Faḫr ad-dīn ar-Rāzī* (Beirut: Maktabat Lubnān Nāširūn, 2001)—is a valuable introductory resource.

18 Sherman A. Jackson, *Islamic Law and the State: The Constitutional Jurisprudence of Shihāb Al-Dīn al-Qarāfī* (Leiden [et al.]: Brill, 1996), p. 8. See also Tariq Jaffer, *Rāzī: Master of Qurʾānic Interpretation and Theological Reasoning* (Oxford: Oxford University Press, 2014).

19 Shihadeh, who ascribes the same rank to Faḫr ad-dīn ar-Rāzī in theology as to Ibn Sīnā in philosophy, elaborates on "his gradual synthesis of kalām and falsafa," Shihadeh, "From al-Ghazālī to al-Rāzī," pp. 178–179.

He wrote commentaries on Ibn Sīnā's works, amongst which his commentary on the *Išārāt wa-t-tanbīhāt* must be regarded as one of the most important. This is because it is a commentary that—at least in the field of logic—had a decisive impact on the further history of the reception of and commentary on the *Išārāt* thanks to the questions it poses and the topics it addresses. Later commentaries, such as those by Naṣīr ad-dīn aṭ-Ṭūsī (d. 672/1274) and Sayf ad-dīn al-Āmidī (d. 631/1233), built on Faḫr ad-dīn's commentary to such an extent that they are often difficult to understand without it.

Faḫr ad-dīn's logic itself is, in turn, thoroughly characterized by intensive engagement with Ibn Sīnā's logic, to such an extent "that Rāzī's logic is incomprehensible apart from Avicenna's system."[20] This applies not only to Faḫr ad-dīn's logical commentaries, logical compendia, and the chapters on logic in his philosophical summae, but also to the logical passages not explicitly labelled as such in works dedicated to other disciplines—such as those in Faḫr ad-dīn's *uṣūl al-fiqh* work *al-Maḥṣūl fī ʿilm uṣūl al-fiqh*, which is the subject of this study. The *Maḥṣūl* proved to be an influential work, much commented upon, "which was to represent the authoritative foundation of the discipline for many centuries"[21]—"if there is one book that concludes the formative phase of Islamic legal theory, then it is the *Maḥṣūl* of ar-Rāzī,"[22] writes Thomas Bauer. The work also generated commentaries from scholars of other schools of law. In fact, it should be emphasized that some of the *Maḥṣūl* commentators[23]—such as Sirāǧ ad-

20 Street, "Faḫraddīn ar-Rāzī's Critique of Avicennan Logic," p. 101.

21 Thomas Bauer, *Die Kultur der Ambiguität. Eine andere Geschichte des Islams* (Berlin: Verlag der Weltreligionen, 2011), p. 160.

22 Ibid., p. 161.

23 For an overview of the commentators of the *Maḥṣūl*, see Kātib Çelebī, *Kašf aẓ-ẓunūn ʿan asāmī l-kutub wa-l-funūn* (Istanbul: Maarif Matbaasi, 1941–1943), vol. 2, pp. 1615–1616; see also the very valuable overview of extant, previously edited commentaries existing in manuscript form in the introduction to the edition of the *Maḥṣūl* mainly used here, namely *Maḥṣūl fī ʿilm uṣūl al-fiqh* by Faḫr ad-dīn ar-Rāzī, ed. by Ṭaha Ǧābir Fayyāḍ al-ʿAlwānī (Riyāḍ: Ǧāmiʿat al-Imām Muḥammad b. Suʿūd al-Islāmiyya, 1979), pp. 52–57. Al-ʿAlwānī's edition is the reference text of this study except where otherwise stated. The following commentaries were consulted for this study: (1.) Ismāʿīl al-Wārānī at-Tabrīzī (621/1224), *Tanqīḥ Maḥṣūl Ibn al-Ḫaṭīb fī uṣūl al-fiqh*, ed. by Ḥamza Zuhayr Ḥāfiẓ (Mecca: Umm al-Qurā University, s.d.); (2.) Abū ʿAbd Allāḥ al-Iṣfahānī (the editor of the *Kāšif* gives his year of death as 653, while Kātib Çelebī gives the year as 678), *al-Kāšif ʿan al-Maḥṣūl fī ʿilm al-uṣūl*, ed. by ʿAdil Aḥmad ʿAbd al-Mawǧūd and ʿAlī Muḥammad Muʿawwaḍ (Beirut: Dār al-Kutub al-ʿilmiyya, 1998); (3.) Tāǧ ad-dīn al-Urmawī (d. 656, according to Kātib Çelebī), *al-Ḥāṣil min al-Maḥṣūl fī uṣūl al-fiqh*, ed. by ʿAbd as-Salām Maḥmūd Abū Nāǧī (Beirut: Dār al-Madār al-Islamī, 2006); (4.) Sirāǧ ad-dīn al-Urmawī (d. 682/1283), *at-Taḥṣīl min l-Maḥṣūl*, ed. by ʿAbd al-Ḥamīd ʿAlī Abū Zunayd (Beirut: Muʾassasat ar-risāla, 1988 [1408]); (5.) Šihāb ad-dīn al-Qarāfī (d. 684/1285), *Nafāʾis al-uṣūl fī šarḥ al-Maḥṣūl*, ed.

dīn al-Urmawī—also wrote commentaries or meta-commentaries on Ibn Sīnā's logical writings. If we take the commentaries on later works of legal theory that refer directly or indirectly to the *Maḥṣūl* (such as Bayḍāwī's *Minhāǧ al-wuṣūl* and Ibn al-Ḥāǧib's *Muḫtaṣar*) into consideration, then we see form before us a network of scholars that we encounter again and again.

2 The Tripartition of Signification into Congruence (*muṭābaqa*), Containment (*taḍammun*), and Implication (*iltizām*): Introduction and State of the Research

This work will focus on, as its source text and starting point, the logical chapter of the *Maḥṣūl*, which will be located within its Avicennian context and investigated in the form of an analytical commentary. At the same time, the analysis of this chapter is also intended to contribute to research into the Tripartition of Signification, which is the actual focus of the content of this study. This is a classification scheme that developed in Arabic logic that categorizes the types of semantic signification into congruence (*muṭābaqa*), containment (*taḍammun*), and implication (*iltizām*). The following citation from one of al-Ġazālī's logic textbooks will help give a first impression of this classification:

> [§1] Know—may God grant you success—that the discourse in this discipline (*fann*) can grow protracted, but I will not devote myself to that which I believe you can grasp on your own. I shall confine myself to providing a note (*tanbīh*) on classifications whose neglect (*ihmāl*) evokes many errors (*aġālīṭ*).
> [§2] The first part (*qism*): The signification of meaning through linguistic expression is limited to three manners, namely [1.] congruence (*muṭābaqa*), [2.] containment (*taḍammun*), and [3.] implication (*iltizām*).
> [§3] For the linguistic expression 'house'
> [*ad* 1] signifies the meaning 'house' by way of congruence and
> [*ad* 2] signifies 'roof' only by way of containment; for [*the linguistic expression*] 'house' contains 'roof' because 'house' is an expression (*'ibāra*) for 'roof' and 'walls' (*ǧudrān*, sg. *ǧidār*). This is just like how the linguistic expression 'horse' signifies 'body,' since a horse is nothing other than a

by Muḥammad 'Abd al-Qādir 'Aṭā (Beirut: Dār al-kutub al-'ilmiyya, 2000 [1421]) as well as id., *Šarḥ Tanqīḥ al-fuṣūl fī iḫtiṣār al-Maḥṣūl fī l-uṣūl*, ed. by Ṣidqī Ǧamīl al-'Aṭṭār (Beirut: Dār al-fikr, 2004 [1424]); id., *Muḫtaṣar at-Tanqīḥī al-fuṣūl fī l-uṣūl*, ed. by Aḥmad Muḥammad Walīd an-Naššār (Damascus: Dār al-farfūr, 2007 [1428]).

> body, since every time we say 'horse,' we find corporeality in the equineness.—So let us use the term (*tasmiya*) 'containment' for this manner [*of signification*] and [*the term*] 'congruence' for the first manner.
> [§ 4] [*ad* 3] As for the way of implication, this is like how the linguistic expression 'roof' signifies the wall (*ḥā'iṭ*); for it [*i.e. the linguistic expression 'roof'*] was not imposed for the [*meaning*] 'wall' in the manner that the linguistic expression 'wall' was imposed for it—namely, in such a way that it is congruent in relation to it.
> [§ 5] Beware, in investigations based on reasoning (*naẓar al-ʿaql*), of using linguistic expressions that signify by way of implication; otherwise you will strengthen your opponent (*aw tumakkinu ḫaṣmaka*). Limit yourself instead to [*the linguistic expressions*] that signify by way of congruence or containment.[24]

This quotation comes from a logic textbook and already clearly shows that the Tripartition of Signification needed a certain amount of explanation. As I will show in detail in this study, this classification scheme developed in Arabic logic throughout the course of various treatments into a general classification of signification and was introduced into Islamic legal theory by al-Ġazālī and Faḫr ad-dīn ar-Rāzī. Both scholars developed it further and made it useful for questions in the field of legal hermeneutics, after which it also gained importance for other Islamic disciplines like Arabic rhetoric (*ʿilm al-balāġa*).

Thomas Bauer has commented on the significance of this connection:

> The corresponding passage [*in the Maḥṣūl*] in turn essentially goes back to Ibn Sīnā (Avicenna)'s commentary on Porphyrios's ⟨Isagoge⟩, which forms the first part of Ibn Sīnā's commentary on Aristotle. Thus, starting in philosophy, this theory of reference finds its way into legal methodology and from there, through as-Sakkākī, into r[*hetoric*], where it provides the semiotic-theoretical basis for *ʿilm al-bayān*.[25]

The development of this classification of signification will be traced here both in the writings of the field of Arabic logic and in those of *uṣūl al-fiqh*. Such an investigation is necessary, firstly, because the aforementioned Tripartition

24 Abū Ḥāmid Muḥammad al-Ġazālī, *Kitāb Miḥakk an-naẓar*, ed. by Rafīq al-ʿAǧam (Beirut: Dār al-fikr al-lubnānī, 1994), pp. 73–74, line 1.

25 Thomas Bauer, "Rhetorik der arabischen Kultur," in *Rhetorik: Begriff, Geschichte, Internationalität*, ed. by Gert Ueding (Tübingen: Niemeyer, 2005), pp. 283–300, here: p. 292; see also Udo G. Simon, "Majāz," *EALL*, vol. 3, p. 120.

develops into an important classification—one might even call it a theory—and into an important component of various Arabic Islamic sciences, the relevance of which has not yet been adequately recognized due to a lack of research interest. Secondly, we can use this classification to investigate the intellectual-historical development of Islamic legal theory and Arabic (especially post-Avicennian) logic.

A research publication focusing on this classification has yet to be written, although it is being recognized as relevant in more and more works and is often dealt with in passing:

In his fundamental study *Islam and Literalism: Literal Meaning and Interpretation in Islamic Legal Theory*,[26] Robert Gleave devotes a section to the Tripartition of Signification, in which he explores what was and is actually understood by "literal meaning" in the history of Islamic legal theory. Based on the work the *Nihāyat al-wuṣūl* by the Šīʿite jurist Ǧamāl ad-dīn al-Ḥillī (d. 726/1325), Gleave treats the question of the relationship between word and meaning, noting that the Tripartition of Signification represents a classification that is used "in most works of *uṣūl al-fiqh*,"[27] but which has so far remained "obscure."[28] Gleave's brief discussion unintentionally gives the impression that this classification is a strange answer, limited to the minds of the "Uṣūlīs," to what are actually fundamental questions in the philosophy of language; it therefore seems unnecessarily exoticizing.

Characterized by a similar lack of understanding is the treatment of the Tripartition in Muḥyī ad-dīn Muḥassab's monograph entitled "Semantics among the Arabs using the example of Faḫr ad-dīn ar-Rāzī" (*ʿilm ad-dalāla ʿinda l-ʿarab: Faḫr ad-dīn ar-Rāzī namūḏaǧan*). Although he recognizes the Tripartition's Avicennian origins to an extent, he has no explanation as to why it might have developed or from which sources Ibn Sīnā might have drawn.[29] Moreover,

26 Robert Gleave, *Islam and Literalism: Literal Meaning and Interpretation in Islamic Legal Theory* (Edinburgh: Edinburgh University Press, 2013).

27 Ibid., p. 33.

28 Ibid., p. 34.

29 Muḥyī ad-dīn Muḥassab, *ʿIlm ad-dalāla ʿinda l-ʿarab: Faḫr ad-dīn ar-Rāzī namūḏaǧan* (Beirut: Dār al-kitāb al-ǧadīd al-muttaḥida, 2008), pg. 104, fn. 45; however, he erroneously attributes the coining of the term *dalālat al-iltizām* to al-Ġazālī. Regarding the origin of the Tripartition, he writes that nothing more is known about it than what Ibrāhīm Madkūr wrote in his introduction to Ibn Sīnā's *Madḫal*. Madkūr in turn refers to an alleged influence of the Stoics on the development of the Tripartition, especially the *dalālat al-iltizām*, cf. Ibrāhīm Madkūr, introduction to Ibn Sīnā's *Kitāb aš-Šifāʾ, al-Manṭiq, al-Madḫal*, ed. by Ibrāhīm Madkūr and Ǧurǧ Qanawātī et al. (Cairo: al-Hayʾa al-ʿĀmma li-Šuʾūn al-Maṭābiʿ al-Amīriyya, 1952), p. 62. Madkūr also gives a short paraphrase of the Tripartition else-

Muḥassab considers the terminology and examples in the context of this classification to be enigmatic (*ġāmiḍ*) and believes that this enigmaticness (*ġumūḍ*) is the reason why Faḫr ad-dīn leaves the classification out of his *Tafsīr* and only paraphrases it in his rhetorical work, bypassing the technical terms.[30]

With regard to Islamic legal theory, another brief paraphrase of the classification can be found in Hadi Ensar Ceylan's essay "Ghazali's Account of Signification,"[31] in which he deals cursorily with some aspects of al-Ġazālī's most important *uṣūl al-fiqh* work *al-Mustaṣfā min ʿilm al-uṣūl* and—through a rather arbitrary reference to the logical commentary the *Taḥrīr al-qawāʿid al-manṭiqiyya* by Quṭb ad-dīn ar-Rāzī at-Taḥtānī (d. 766/1365)—recognizes the connection between this passage and works of Arabic logic.[32]

Mohamed M. Yunis Ali's study *Medieval Islamic Pragmatics: Sunni Legal Theorists' Models of Textual Communication*[33] discusses Arabic approaches to linguistic theory, particularly in the context of Islamic legal theory, from the perspective of modern semantics and pragmatics. Here, the Tripartition of Signification also receives mention.[34] But it is not his intention to trace the development of the Tripartition or to analyze the functions it fulfilled. Although his approach occasionally leads to original criticism[35] and certainly reveals inspiring connections, it is anachronistic with regard to intellectual-historical coherence and is in part terminologically misleading, particularly because the author ignores the logical background[36]—of which he is well aware.[37] Despite these objections, Yunis Ali's *Medieval Islamic Pragmatics* is, on the whole, a significant contribution to research and it forms an important point of reference for the present work.

---

where (using the translations concordance/contenance/consécutif), see Ibrāhīm Madkūr, *L'Organon d'Aristote dans le monde arabe* (Paris: Vrin, 1969), pp. 60–61.

30 Muḥassab, *ʿIlm ad-dalāla ʿinda l-ʿarab*, p. 103.

31 Hadi Ensar Ceylan, "Ghazali's Account of Signification," *Journal of Islamic Research*, vol. 3, no. 2 (Dec. 2010): pp. 98–114; the Tripartition is discussed on pp. 101–102.

32 Ceylan, "Ghazali's Account of Signification," p. 101, fn. 13.

33 Mohamed M. Yunis Ali, *Medieval Islamic Pragmatics: Sunni Legal Theorists' Models of Textual Communication* (Richmond, Surrey: Curzon Press, 2000).

34 Ibid., pp. 149 ff. Here, Yunis Ali translates the three terms as follows: "equivalence-signification" (*dalālat al-muṭābaqa*), "incorporational signification" (*dalālat at-taḍammun*), and "implicational signification" (*dalālat al-iltizām*).

35 See, for example, ibid., p. 150, where he discusses the definition of containment (*taḍammun*) from the perspective of modern semantics and pragmatics. Vishanoff arrives at a similar assessment of this study, describing Yunis Ali's monograph as "an ahistorical but creative work," see Vishanoff, *The Formation of Islamic Hermeneutics*, p. xiv, fn. 18.

36 Cf. for example Yunis Ali, *Medieval Islamic Pragmatics*, p. 157.

37 Cf. ibid., p. 158.

Some research articles on Arabic rhetoric also occasionally refer to the Tripartition of Signification.[38] Udo Simon, for example, gives a concise explanation of the Tripartition in connection with as-Sakkākī's *Miftāḥ al-ʿulūm*:

> Theorists distinguish between three types of *dalālāt*: *dalālat al-muṭābaqa* is used when the word refers to its complete meaning. *Dalālat at-taḍammun* is used when it refers to a part of the whole. If the word refers to something outside of the concept that is nevertheless in a conditional relationship to the original concept, the term *dalālat al-iltizām* is used. While the first type of interpretation is solely based on the lexical establishment of the word (*waḍʿī*), the other two are inferred through activity of the intellect (*ʿaqlī*).[39]

This explanation corresponds to Faḫr ad-dīn ar-Rāzī's understanding, whereas most of the thinkers who came after him also regarded the second type of signification and later even the third type as *waḍʿī*, as will be explained later.[40]

In his aforementioned handbook article, Thomas Bauer also addresses the Tripartition of Signification—he calls it a theory of reference—and refers to the individual types of signification with the terms 'equivalence reference' (*Äquivalenzreferenz*), 'containment reference' (*Inklusionsreferenz*), and 'implication reference' (*Implikationsreferenz*).[41] Bauer's excellent presentation makes reference both to the logical background and to the fundamental role played by the classification of signification in the context of a rhetorical "standard theory."[42]

Even in the research literature focusing on traditions of logic, the Tripartition of Signification is repeatedly paraphrased in passing, without much

---

38 Thus, for example, in passing—with the translations "symmetry" (*muṭābaqa*), "inclusion" (*taḍammun*), and "implication" (*iltizām*)—in Versteegh, "The Arabic Tradition," p. 264; also—with the translations "congruence" (*muṭābaqa*), "implication" (*taḍammun*), and "concomitance" (*iltizām*)—in Wolfhart Heinrich, "Naḳd," *EI*²; also (without translation of the technical terms) Miklos Maróth, "The Changes of Metaphor in Arabic Literature," *Arabic Sciences and Philosophy*, vol. 12, no. 2 (2002): pp. 251–252; as well as Versteegh, "The Arabic Tradition," p. 264—Versteegh writes of "signification of symmetry," "signification of inclusion," and "signification of implication."

39 Udo G. Simon, *Mittelalterliche arabische Sprachbetrachtung zwischen Grammatik und Rhetorik: ʿilm al-maʿānī bei as-Sakkākī* (Heidelberg: Heidelberger Orientverlag, 1993), p. 63, fn. 7 and pp. 38–39; cf. Simon, "Majāz," *EALL*, vol. 3, p. 120.

40 See Chapter 2, Section 3.2.

41 Bauer, "Rhetorik der arabischen Kultur," pp. 294–295.

42 Cf. ibid., pp. 291–292 and pp. 294–295.

insightful value. Shams Inati, for example, in the context of Ibn Sīnā's logical introductions, and in this case in the particular context of the treatment of simple linguistic expressions, briefly discusses the Tripartition of Signficiation. I quote the paragraph in full because it is a good example of the sort of casual, paraphrased presentation that the Tripartition of Signification tends to receive:

> 'Essential signification' is what Ibn Sina also refers to as 'signification by correspondence,' namely, the total parallelism between the signifying expression, such as 'human being' and the concept signified, such as 'rational animal.' This is to be distinguished from signification by implication (*'ala sabil-l-tadamun* [*sic*!]) and signification by necessity of following (*'ala sabil-l-istitbāʿ wa-l-iltizām*). In signification by implication, the signifying expression indicates a part of the concept for which the expression stands, as 'human being' signifies 'animal.' And in the signification by necessity of following, the signifying expression indicates neither the whole nor the part of the concept, but an external element that necessarily accompanies the concept, as 'human being' signifies 'capacity for laughter.'[43]

Like this one, most presentations of the Tripartition of Signification are limited to a brief paraphrase. But this classification scheme requires a thorough and in-depth analysis, one that focuses on the reconstruction of the origin of the Tripartition.[44]

This study aims to contribute to this reconstruction, starting from a linguistic and linguistic-philosophical chapter of Faḫr ad-dīn ar-Rāzī's work on legal the-

43 Shams C. Inati, "Ibn Sina on Single Expressions," in *Islamic Theology and Philosophy: Studies in Honor of George F. Hourani*, ed. by Michael E. Marmura (Albany: State University of New York Press, 1984), pp. 148–159, esp. p. 154.

44 After the present study was completed, a very valuable work on the Tripartition of Signification was published, namely Riccardo Strobino's "Per Se, Inseparability, Containment and Implication. Bridging the Gap between Avicenna's Theory of Demonstration and Logic of the Predicables," *Oriens*, vol. 44 (2016): pp. 181–266. This article examines, on the one hand, how Ibn Sīnā, in his theory of proof ("Posterior Analytics complex"), thinks about *per se* predication, so important for the Aristotelian history of science, and on the other hand, how this thinking is linked to his theory of predicables ("Isagoge complex"). The Tripartition of Signification illustrates, through the underlying relationships of its necessary components, a connection between the *Burhān* and *Madḫal* complexes. Among other things, Strobino's findings were helpful in the critical examination of some of the connections that my work draws to the *Burhān*. Wherever it seemed useful, I have referred to this article in the footnotes and indicated the results that are relevant to the context at hand.

ory, *al-Maḥṣūl*. Faḫr ad-dīn's—and not al-Ġazālī's—work was chosen as the starting point for this study because it gives special treatment to the Tripartition of Signification; nevertheless, al-Ġazālī's work forms an important point of reference, as will be shown.

My goal is, in the form of an analytical commentary on the concept's historical development: to [a] highlight Faḫr ad-dīn's own systematization and his efforts towards synthesis, [b] to work out the context of the original problems and questions from which the Tripartition of Signification emerged, and [c] to trace the issue that it becomes in the later *uṣūl al-fiqh* literature. In order to be transparent on the one hand, avoiding ahistorical and anachronistic conclusions, and on the other hand to appeal to Islamic scholars specializing in both Islamic law as well as philosophy and logic, this analysis will be as detailed and "close to the text" as possible. This means that—as far as possible—an attempt will be made to leave out the "associations that modern scholars may detect" and instead to work out "those associations perceived by the theologians and legal theorists"[45]—an endeavor in which rigid textual work and the constant tracing of theorems, questions, and exact wording back to earlier and earlier texts is unavoidable. This leads to the contextualization of the previously "disembodied text," the text torn from its scientific-historical and genealogical environment, which is how we should consider our object of research.[46]

Before examining the logical background underlying the creation of the Tripartition in detail in Chapter 2, I will introduce the genre of *uṣūl al-fiqh* literature, the *Maḥṣūl*, and the textual tradition of which it is a part in Chapter 1.[47] This chapter has two focal points. Firstly, it will present how Faḫr ad-dīn derives the overall structure of the *Maḥṣūl* in general and the structure of its chapter on language in particular from his definition of *uṣūl al-fiqh*. Secondly, it will provide an overview of the topics treated in the chapters that clearly deal with linguistics. After this follows a translation of a chapter of the *Maḥṣūl* that is particularly exemplative of Faḫr ad-dīn's synthesis of logical, grammatical, and legal-theoretical methods and content and in which the Tripartition of Signification fulfills an important function. This chapter of the *Maḥṣūl* is then divided into sections, which are analyzed in Chapters III, IV and V of this study.

---

45 Aron Zysow, "Muʿtazilism and Māturīdism in Ḥanafī Legal Theory," in *Studies in Islamic Legal Theory*, ed. by Berhard G. Weiss (Leiden [et al.]: Brill, 2002), p. 235.

46 Jonathan E. Brockopp, "Early Islamic Jurisprudence in Egypt: Two Scholars and their Mukhtasars," *International Journal of Middle East Studies*, vol. 30, no. 2 (1998): p. 168.

47 This contributes to answering the question "as to whether developments in *uṣūl* were influenced by Arabic translations of and commentaries on Porphyry's Isagoge," see Ahmad Pakatchi, "Alfāẓ," *Encyclopaedia Islamica*, vol. 3, p. 468.

Chapter 2—which together with Chapter 3 represents the core of the work—will first deal with the question of the logical context in which the aforementioned chapter of the *Maḥṣūl* (sections §1–11) is to be classified and the extent to which its contents correspond to the Avicennian *Madḫal* genre. A second chapter will examine the development of the Tripartition of Signification in the logic of al-Fārābī and, above all, Ibn Sīnā and explain the conceptual development of this classification scheme. The third chapter of Chapter 2 treats the modifications and further development of this classification in Faḫr ad-dīn's logical writings, also tracing the influence that these modifications, which are accompanied by the creation of new technical terms, have on later, so-called post-Rāzian logical compendia and debates. Chapter 3 analyzes Faḫr ad-dīn's transfer of logical structures to classifications and theorems of grammatical and legal theory. This chapter also investigates the question of how the concept of figurative language (*maǧāz*) relates to the individual types of signification.

Chapter 4 is devoted to the question of the relevance of the Tripartition of Signification to inquiry in the *uṣūl al-fiqh* genre. A first step will involve the examination of which legal-theoretical functions Faḫr ad-dīn himself assigns to the Tripartition of Signification—in particular to implication (*iltizām*)—and which genuine legal-theoretical types of implication he associates with this originally logical classification. A second step then involves the reconstruction of the independent life that the combination of logical and legal-theoretical implication leads in post-Rāzian *uṣūl al-fiqh* compendia and commentaries.

Since few if any of the works used in this study are available in European languages, it seemed essential to treat, translate, and analyze the source material in detail when writing this book. The translations are my own, unless otherwise stated. The transcription follows the system of the German Oriental Society with slight modifications.

CHAPTER 1

Starting Point of the Study of Faḫr ad-dīn ar-Rāzī's *al-Maḥṣūl fī ʿilm uṣūl al-fiqh*

This chapter will provide an introduction to Faḫr ad-dīn's *uṣūl al-fiqh* work *al-Maḥṣūl fī ʿilm uṣūl al-fiqh*, beginning with a brief contextualization of the work within its genre and tradition as well as an outline of its structure and main themes. This will allow us to then transition to the actual focus of this study, namely the chapter of the *Maḥṣūl* that provides a hermeneutical toolkit through its presentation of the fundamentals of linguistic theory and linguistic philosophy.

1 Introduction to the Work and Its Structure

1.1 *The Tradition of the* Maḥṣūl

The tradition to which Faḫr ad-dīn's *Maḥṣūl* belongs is aptly described by Ibn Ḫaldūn in a passage that has often been used to outline the broader tradition of the formative period of *uṣūl al-fiqh* but which I cite here in order to focus on this particular tradition:

> The best that the theologians (*mutakallimūn*) have written about it [*i.e. about legal methodology* (uṣūl al-fiqh)] include: the *Kitāb al-Burhān*[1] by Imām al-Ḥaramayn [al-Ǧuwaynī, d. 478/1085] and the *Mustaṣfā*[2] by al-Ġazālī [d. 505/1111]—they both belong to the Ašʿariyya school; as well as the *Kitāb al-ʿumad*[3] by ʿAbd al-Ǧabbār [d. 415/1025] and its commentary, the *Kitāb al-Muʿtamad*[4] by Abū l-Ḥusayn al-Baṣrī [d. 436/1044]—they both belong to the Muʿtazila school. These four [*works*] constituted the foundations (*qawāʿid*) and the pillars (*arkān*) of this discipline (*fann*).

1 Imām al-Ḥaramayn al-Ǧuwaynī, *al-Burhān fī uṣūl al-fiqh*, ed. by Ṣāliḥā b. Muḥammad b. ʿUwayḍa (Beirut: Dār al-Kutub al-ʿilmiyya, 1997 [1418 H]).

2 Abū Ḥāmid Muḥammad al-Ġazālī, *al-Mustaṣfā min ʿilm al-uṣūl*, ed. by Ḥamza b. Zuhayr Ḥāfiẓ (Medina: Šarikat al-Madīna al-munawwara li-ṭ-ṭibāʿa wa-n-našr, 1993 [1413 H]).

3 This work unfortunately no longer survives.

4 Abū l-Ḥusayn al-Baṣrī, *Kitāb al-Muʿtamad fī uṣūl al-fiqh*, ed. by Muḥammad Ḥamīd Allāh (Damascus: al-Maʿhad al-ʿilmī l-faransī li-d-dirāsāt al-ʿarabiyya, 1964–1965 [1384–1385 H]).

 | DOI:10.1163/9789004736016_003

> These four works were summarized by two greats (*faḥlān*) amongst the later theologians—namely Imām Faḫr ad-dīn [*ar-Rāzī*] ibn Ḫaṭīb in the *Kitāb al-Maḥṣūl* and Sayf ad-dīn al-Āmidī [d. 631/1233] in the *Kitāb al-Iḥkām*.[5]

Here Ibn Ḫaldūn outlines the tradition of the "theologians" (*mutakallimūn*) who had a fundamental and lasting influence on the genre of *uṣūl al-fiqh*. With regard to methodology, he contrasts it—in his terminology—with the tradition of the "jurists" (*fuqahā'*), by which he primarily alludes to the Ḥanafites.[6] Not mentioned in this list is, among others, the influence of the Aš'arite Mālikite scholar Abū Bakr al-Bāqillānī (d. 403/1012–1013) and his *uṣūl al-fiqh* work *at-Taqrīb wa-l-iršāda*.[7] It fits into the tradition of those who came to prominence through their influential *uṣūl ad-dīn* and *kalām* works.

Of all the works mentioned, it is the *Kitāb al-Mu'tamad* that proved to be particularly influential for the *Maḥṣūl*, both in terms of structure and content. Ibn Ḫallikān (d. 681/1282) alluded to its great influence when he said that "Faḫr ad-dīn ar-Rāzī took his *Kitāb al-Maḥṣūl* from it" (*wa-minhū aḫaḏa Faḫr ad-dīn*

5 'Abd ar-Raḥmān b. Muḥammad ibn Ḫaldūn, *al-Muqaddima* (Beirut: Maktabat Lubnān, 1970) [reprint of the edition by Benjamin Duprat, Paris, 1858], vol. 3, p. 22, lines 2–9. According to Hallaq, the fifth/eleventh century is "[t]he earliest period for which we have an extensive record" and "which can claim a special status in the field of legal theory," Wael B. Hallaq, *A History of Islamic Legal Theories: An Introduction to Sunnī uṣūl al-fiqh* (Cambridge: Cambridge University Press, 1997), p. 36. For works that provide overviews of (or at least mention) this tradition, see for example Norman Calder, "Uṣūl al-Fiḳh," *EI*²; cf. Wael B. Hallaq, "The Primacy of the Qur'ān in Shāṭibī's Legal Theory," in *Islamic Studies Presented to Charles J. Adams*, ed. by Wael B. Hallaq and Donald P. Little (Leiden [et al.]: Brill, 1991), p. 70; Devin J. Stewart, *Islamic Legal Orthodoxy: Twelver Shiite Responses to the Sunni Legal System* (Salt Lake City: University of Utah Press, 1998), pp. 36 f.

6 The topos of the theologian-*uṣūlīs* and the jurist-*uṣūlīs* is rather reductive and has accordingly been frequently criticized—especially by Ahmad, see Ahmad A. Ahmad, *Structural Interrelations of Theory and Practice in Islamic Law. A Study of Six Works of Medieval Islamic Jurisprudence* (Leiden: Brill, 2006), pp. 31 ff. and p. 72; see also Zysow's remark "that the standard representation of the *uṣūl* of the Ḥanafis as peculiarly legal in contrast to the theological *uṣūl* of the other schools is without foundation," Aron Zysow, *The Economy of Certainty: An Introduction to the Typology of Islamic Legal Theory* (Atlanta: Lockwood Press, 2013), p. 73; as well as Reinhart's criticism of this topos, cf. Reinhart, "'Like the Difference between Heaven and Earth,'" p. 206 and p. 231; Schwarb on the other hand sees Ibn Ḫaldūn's distinction as consistent with the "evidence of tenth- and eleventh-century manuals of *uṣūl al-fiqh*" and the approaches prevalent therein, see Schwarb, "Capturing the Meaning of God's Speech," p. 126.

7 Qāḍī Abū Bakr al-Bāqillānī, *at-Taqrīb wa-l-iršād*, ed. by 'Abd al-Ḥamīd b. 'Alī Abū Zunayd (Beirut: Mu'assasat ar-Risāla, 1998 [1418 H]); on this work, see Vishanoff, *The Formation of Islamic Hermeneutics*, pp. 161–189.

ar-Rāzī kitāba l-maḥṣūl).[8]—A separate work could and should be devoted to comparing the *Kitāb al-Muʿtamad*[9] (of Ḥanafite, Muʿtazilite influence) to the *Maḥṣūl* (of Šāfiʿite, Ašʿarite influence) along with a study on what Faḫr ad-dīn incorporated into his *Maḥṣūl*, what he distanced himself from, and how theological differences influenced legal methodology. This is unfortunately beyond the scope of the present work; however, occasional comparisons and references will serve to indicate avenues for further research.[10]—The *Maḥṣūl* cites the other scholars that Ibn Ḫaldūn mentioned as well. But one of the tasks of the present work is to reveal the clear influence in the *Maḥṣūl* of a scholar whom Faḫr ad-dīn does not cite by name in this work—unlike, for example, in his *Tafsīr* and works on logic—namely Ibn Sīnā.

1.2 *Understanding the Discipline:* fiqh *and* uṣūl al-fiqh *in the Introduction of the* Maḥṣūl

With the context of the *Maḥṣūl*'s tradition in mind, we can now move on to a brief overview of the topics it treats and its structure. By starting with Faḫr ad-dīn's definition of *uṣūl al-fiqh*, the systematization underlying the structure of the work will become readily apparent.

The introduction of the *Maḥṣūl* begins—just like that of the *uṣūl al-fiqh* works of al-Bāqillānī, al-Baṣrī, al-Ǧuwaynī, and al-Ġazālī that came before it—with a definition of the term *uṣūl al-fiqh*, in both its lay and technical uses.[11] Since the compound word can only be understood once the meanings of its individual components have been explained,

> it behooves us to give the definition (*taʿrīf*) of *aṣl* and *fiqh*, furthermore the definition of *uṣūl al-fiqh*:

---

8 Ibn Ḫallikān, *Wafayāt al-aʿyān*, vol. 2, p. 1616, lines 4–6—I owe the reference to this passage to a conversation with Gregor Schwarb.

9 On this work and the history of its reception, see Hassan Ansari and Sabine Schmidtke, "The Muʿtazilī and Zaydī-Reception of Abū l-Ḥusayn al-Baṣrī's *Kitāb al-Muʿtamad fī Uṣūl al-fiqh*: A Bibliographical Note," *Islamic Law and Society*, vol. 20, no. 1–2 (2013): pp. 90–109 and Wilferd F. Madelung, "Abū l-Ḥusayn al-Baṣrī," *EI*².

10 On the relationship between the works of al-Bāqillānī (still under the assumption that the *Kitāb al-Taqrīb* was no longer extant), al-Ǧuwaynī, and al-Ġazālī, see Eichner, *The Post-Avicennian Philosophical Tradition and Islamic Orthodoxy*, pp. 232–233.

11 Makdisi attributes to this definition, which first emerged in the works of the late tenth and early eleventh centuries together with the use of the term 'uṣūl al-fiqh' for this discipline, the ability to 'finally' distinguish between the different disciplines of *fiqh* and *uṣūl al-fiqh*, "and thus put an end to the equivocal use of the latter term," see George Makdisi, "The Juridical Theology of Shāfiʿī: Origins and Significance of *Uṣūl al-Fiqh*," *Studia Islamica*, vol. 59 (1984): pp. 5–47, esp. pp. 8–9.

> [1.] As for *aṣl* ('root,' 'foundation,' 'origin'), it is 'that which one needs' (*fa-huwa l-muḥtāǧu ilayhi*).
> [2.] As for *fiqh* ('understanding,' 'insight'), it is [2.1] in the basic linguistic meaning (*fī aṣli l-luġa*; lit. 'in the origin of language') an expression for 'understanding the intention of the speaker from his speech' (*ʿibāratun ʿan fahmi ġaraḍi l-mutakallimi min kalāmihī*); [2.2] in the parlance of the scholars (*iṣṭilāḥ al-ʿulamāʾ*) it is an expression for [2.2.1] the knowledge of the applied legal rulings (*ʿibāratun ʿani l-ʿilmi bi-l-aḥkāmi š-šarʿiyyati l-ʿamaliyya*), [2.2.2] whose concrete [*formulations*] are deduced (*al-mustadalli ʿalā aʿyānihā*), [2.2.3] provided that this fact [*i.e. the legal rulings on the particular actions*] is not necessarily known from religion[12] [*itself*] (*bi-ḥayṯu lā yuʿlamu kawnuhā mina d-dīni ḍarūratan*).[13]

While according to al-Baṣrī, the term *fiqh* was used both in everyday language and in the parlance of jurists/scholars (*fuqahāʾ*), Faḫr ad-dīn's explanation suggests that the word was limited to its narrower, technical meaning.[14] In comparison to earlier works, Faḫr ad-dīn's definition of the technical term *fiqh* proves to be markedly detailed; al-Baṣrī, al-Ǧuwaynī, and al-Ġazālī had essentially limited their definitions of *fiqh* to "the knowledge of the rulings/norms to which one is obligated" (*al-ʿilm bi-aḥkām at-taklīf*), or the knowledge of "the legal rulings" (*bi-aḥkām šarīʿa*).[15] Faḫr ad-dīn's definition has adopted aspects

12 'Religion' (*dīn*) is meant here in the original and broadest sense of the word and refers to obligatory practices, especially those fundamental ones that belong to the pillars of Islam, see Faḫr ad-dīn ar-Rāzī, *al-Maḥṣūl*, vol. 1, p. 303, line 11–p. 304, line 6; cf. Tilman Nagel, *Das islamische Recht: Eine Einführung* (Westhoven: WVA-Verlag Skulima, 2001), pp. 4 f. and p. 15; see also Patrice C. Brodeur, "Religion," *Encyclopaedia of the Qurʾān*, vol. 4, p. 396 and Wilfred C. Smith, *The Meaning and End of Religion* (Minneapolis: Fortress Press, 1963) [reprint 1991], pp. 90–100 and pp. 287–290.

13 Faḫr ad-dīn ar-Rāzī, *al-Maḥṣūl*, vol. 1, p. 78, lines 3–10.

14 Al-Baṣrī, *Kitāb al-Muʿtamad*, vol. 1, p. 8, lines 9–10; cf. Faḫr ad-dīn ar-Rāzī, *at-Tafsīr al-kabīr aw Mafātīḥ al-ġayb*, ed. by Ibrāhīm Šams ad-dīn and Aḥmad Šams ad-dīn (Beirut: Dār al-Kutub al-ʿilmiyya, 2013), vol. 10, p. 151, lines 27–28; on the fact that the term *faqīh* still referred to legal scholars and theologians in the middle of the 2nd cent. H, see Josef van Ess, *Theologie und Gesellschaft im 2. und 3. Jahrhundert Hidschrah. Eine Geschichte des religiösen Denkens im frühen Islam* (Berlin [et al.]: Walter de Gruyter, 1991–1997), vol. 1, p. 51 and on the early, broader meaning of the term *fiqh*, see van Ess, *Die Erkenntnislehre*, p. 114; al-Ġazālī emphasizes that in his time this term only referred to legal scholars, see al-Ġazālī, *al-Mustaṣfā*, vol. 1, p. 8, lines 9–11; on the narrowing of the meaning of the semantic field of *fiqh*, see also Nagel, *Das islamische Recht*, pp. 6–8; for an introduction to the discipline of *fiqh*, see Baber Johansen, *Contingency in a Sacred Law: Legal and Ethical Norms in the Muslim Fiqh* (Leiden [et al.]: Brill, 1999), pp. 1–76.

15 Al-Ǧuwaynī, *al-Burhān*, vol. 1, p. 8, line 2; al-Baṣrī, *Kitāb al-Muʿtamad*, vol. 1, p. 8, line 12;

of the one given by al-Bāqillānī, who defined *fiqh* as "the knowledge of the legal rulings on the actions of those obligated [*to follow legal norms*], at which one arrives through reflection (*naẓar*)—not [*the knowledge of the*] rational [*judgements*]" (*al-ʿilmu bi-aḥkāmi afʿāli l-mukallafīna š-šarʿiyyati llatī yutawaṣṣalu ilayhā bi-n-naẓari dūna l-ʿaqliyya*).[16] Reflection (*naẓar*), which is defined by Faḫr ad-dīn according to the philosophical tradition as the "ordering/arrangement (*tartīb*) of judgements/propositions that are held to be true (*taṣdīqāt*) in the mind (*fī ḏ-ḏihn*),"[17] provides the jurist with legal rulings in accordance with divine transmission by means of the interpretation and combination of various indicators—the result is therefore legal rulings (*al-aḥkām aš-šarʿiyya*) based on revelation, whereas rational judgements are the result of the sort of reflection that does not take place on this basis. According to Faḫr ad-dīn [*ad* 2.2.1], the term 'legal [*ruling*]' (*aš-šarʿiyya*) by definition excludes 'rational judgements' (*al-aḥkām al-ʿaqliyya*), by which is meant, for example, individual perception of good and bad.[18]

---

al-Ġazālī, *al-Mustaṣfā*, vol. 1, p. 8, lines 7–8. The term *taklīf* "denotes the fact that God imposed obligations on his creatures," (see Daniel Gimaret, "Taklīf," *EI*²) or "that man is subject to divine law" (Nagel, *Das islamische Recht*, p. 11). The term is rendered as 'burden' (*Belastung*, cf. Nagel, *Das islamische Recht*, p. 10 ff.) or 'obligation' (*Verpflichtung*, cf. van Ess, *Theologie und Gesellschaft*, vol. 1, p. 207). The one on whom these obligations have been imposed is a *mukallaf*; such a person possesses the highest degree of legal capacity, cf. Joseph Schacht, *An Introduction to Islamic Law* (Oxford: Clarendon Press, 1982) [1st edition 1964], p. 124; cf. Nagel's detailed exposition of the aspects of legal capacity, Nagel, *Das islamische Recht*, pp. 32–34; cf. Faḫr ad-dīn ar-Rāzī, *al-Maḥṣūl*, vol. 1, p. 105 and p. 108, on the question of the extent to which children, sleeping persons, and the mentally ill have legal capacity in this sense. As Nagel explains, "the fact that the observance of divine law was imposed on man is certainly understood as an onerous burden" (Nagel, *Das islamische Recht*, p. 11). A comprehensive study on the concept of obligation was recently presented by Norbert Oberauer, see Nobert Oberauer, *Religiöse Verpflichtung im Islam. Ein ethischer Grundbegriff und seine theologische, rechtliche und sozialgeschichtliche Dimension* (Würzburg: Ergon, 2004).

16 Al-Bāqillānī, *at-Taqrīb*, vol. 1, p. 171, lines 10–11, cf. Vishanoff, *The Formation of Islamic Hermeneutics*, pp. 182 f.; on the term *naẓar* 'speculation,' i.e. "all consideration and deduction (*istidlāl*)," see van Ess, *Die Erkenntnislehre*, p. 10 and pp. 237 ff.

17 Faḫr ad-dīn ar-Rāzī, *al-Maḥṣūl*, vol. 1, p. 87, line 3; on the term *taṣdīq* 'belief,' see in particular Joep Lameer, *Conception and Belief in Ṣadr al-Dīn Shīrāzī (ca. 1571–1635)*: Al-Risāla fī l-taṣawwur wa-l-taṣdīq (Tehran: Iranian Institute of Philosophy, 2006), pp. 14 ff. and van Ess, *Die Erkenntnislehre*, pp. 95–113.

18 Faḫr ad-dīn ar-Rāzī, *al-Maḥṣūl*, vol. 1, p. 79, line 5 and p. 96, line 5; Faḫr ad-dīn devotes to this topic a separate, highly detailed chapter, in which he compares the opposing positions of the Muʿtazila and Ašʿariyya schools on this issue, cf. Faḫr ad-dīn ar-Rāzī, *al-Maḥṣūl*, vol. 1, pp. 123–146; cf. Nagel, *Das islamische Recht*, pp. 27–29; Weiss, *The Search*, pp. 82 ff.

The term 'applied [*legal rulings*]' (*ʿamaliyya*), on the other hand, is intended to exclude the discussion of methodological foundations and sources.[19] And [*ad* 2.2.2] the addition that 'the concrete [*legal rulings*] are deduced' (*al-mustadallu ʿalā aʿyānihā*), which the Muftī sets out in a concrete legal opinion, excludes those other areas of knowledge which could otherwise be invoked to arrive at "applied legal rulings" or which represent the prerequisites—especially theological—of the discipline of *fiqh*.[20]

The last aspect [*ad* 2.2.3] excludes, according to Faḫr ad-dīn, all those legal rulings that do not have to be deduced but are instead considered obvious, "because that [*knowledge*] is not called *fiqh*" (*fa-inna ḏālika lā yusammā fiqhan*), as it does not require any further insight. As an example of this, Faḫr ad-dīn mentions prayer and fasting, whose legal classification as obligatory is clearly stated in the Qurʾan as well as in the *aḥādīṯ*. It is the more detailed specifics that are, however, sometimes very controversial and vary between different interpretations within Islamic theology.[21]

After having thus given the definitions of the individual components of the compound, Faḫr ad-dīn goes on to define the discipline of *uṣūl al-fiqh*, which is the focus of his work:

> Consequently, we say: [3.] *Uṣūl al-fiqh* is an expression [a] for the totality (*maǧmūʿ*) [b] of the methods (*ṭuruq*) of *fiqh* [c] in a general way (*ʿalā sabīli l-iǧmāl*); [d] for the way of drawing conclusions through them [*i.e. by means of these methods*] (*wa-kayfiyyatu l-istidlāl bihā*); and [e] for the particulars of the status of the one drawing the conclusions from them (*ʿinda hāḏā naqūlu uṣūlu l-fiqhi ʿibāratun ʿan maǧmūʿi ṭuruqi l-fiqhi ʿalā sabīli l-iǧmāli wa-kayfiyyati l-istidlāli bihā wa-kayfiyyati ḥāli l-mustadilli bihā*).[22]

19 Faḫr ad-dīn ar-Rāzī, *al-Maḥṣūl*, vol. 1, p. 79, lines 7–9.

20 Cf. Faḫr ad-dīn ar-Rāzī, *al-Maḥṣūl*, vol. 1, p. 79, lines 10–14; see also al-Qarāfī, *Nafāʾis al-uṣūl*, vol. 1, p. 32, lines 7–8, according to whom *aʿyānihā* is to be understood as "individual/concrete legal rulings" (*ašḫāṣ al-aḥkām*).

21 Faḫr ad-dīn ar-Rāzī, *al-Maḥṣūl*, vol. 1, p. 80, lines 1–3; see, for example, Faḫr ad-dīn ar-Rāzī, *at-Tafsīr al-kabīr*, vol. 6, p. 124, line 25 (first main argument; Sura 2:238); cf. Nagel, *Das islamische Recht*, pp. 47–51; for a detailed study of prayer in Islamic legal thought, see Marion Holmes Katz, *Prayer in Islamic Thought and Practice* (New York [et al.]: Cambridge University Press, 2013).

22 Faḫr ad-dīn ar-Rāzī, *al-Maḥṣūl*, vol. 1, p. 80, lines 8–9.

Components [b-e] of the definition are already found in the *Kitāb al-Muʿtamad* of Abū l-Ḥusayn al-Baṣrī.[23] Component [a] is an addition used to ensure that no segment of *uṣūl al-fiqh* is considered in isolation and taken to be the entire science, "for even if it belongs to *uṣūl al-fiqh*, it is not *uṣūl al-fiqh*, because a part of something is not the thing itself" (*li-anna baʿḍa š-šayʾi lā yakūnu nafsa ḏālika š-šayʾ*).[24] This addition is directed against those works that had been considered by later scholars to belong to the genre of *uṣūl al-fiqh* despite only treating a portion of it.[25]

A method [*ad* b] is defined as that "which, with correct reflection" (*an-naẓar aṣ-ṣaḥīḥ*) "leads either to knowledge (*ʿilm*) [...] or to presumption (*ẓann*) [...]."[26] When applied correctly, it results in a legal ruling (*ḥukm šarʿī*), which is called [that which is] signified (*madlūl*)—by indicators (*al-adilla*; sg. *ad-dalīl*) and signs (*al-amārāt*, sg. *al-amāra*).[27] Elsewhere, Faḫr ad-dīn mentions, again in line with al-Baṣrī, that indicators and signs each lead to different degrees of knowledge: while it is possible to arrive at knowledge (*ʿilm*) by means of indicators, signs lead at best to presumption (*ẓann*).[28] These methods are divided between those based on the revealed texts (*samʿī*) and those based on reason-

23 Al-Baṣrī, *Kitāb al-Muʿtamad*, vol. 1, p. 9, lines 16 ff. "[...] '*uṣūl al-fiqh*' [...] in the parlance of the jurists (*ʿurf al-fuqahāʾ*) indicates 'reflection (*naẓar*) on [b] the methods (*ṭuruq*) of *fiqh* [c] in a general way (*ʿalā sabīli l-iǧmāl*),' as well as '[d] the way by which [*i.e. by means of these methods*] to draw conclusions' (*wa-kayfiyyata l-istidlāli bihā*) as well as '[e] that which pertains to the way of drawing conclusions through them' (*wa-mā yatbaʿu kayfiyyata l-istidlāli bihā*) [*i.e. 'reflecting on those who make the rulings'* (an-naẓar fī l-mustadillīna ʿalā l-aḥkām), p. 12, line 16]."

24 Faḫr ad-dīn ar-Rāzī, *al-Maḥṣūl*, vol. 1, p. 80, lines 11–12.

25 Cf. Makdisi, "The Juridical Theology of Shāfiʿī," p. 8. Aš-Šāfiʿī's *Risāla* is certainly the best example of such a work that does not belong to the genre of *uṣūl al-fiqh*, cf. Schwarb, "Capturing the Meaning of God's Speech," p. 116, fn. 23 and the research literature cited therein.

26 Faḫr ad-dīn ar-Rāzī, *al-Maḥṣūl*, vol. 1, p. 82, lines 3–4; cf. van Ess, *Die Erkenntnislehre*, pp. 364 f.

27 Faḫr ad-dīn ar-Rāzī, *al-Maḥṣūl*, vol. 1, p. 80, last line and p. 82, lines 3–5; the same wording is found in al-Baṣrī's *Kitāb al-Muʿtamad*, vol. 1, p. 9, lines 25–26.

28 Faḫr ad-dīn ar-Rāzī, *al-Maḥṣūl*, vol. 1, p. 88; al-Baṣrī, *Kitāb al-Muʿtamad*, vol. 1, p. 9, last line–p. 10, line 2. Cf. Nagel, *Das islamische Recht*, p. 15. Faḫr ad-dīn also devotes attention in his introduction to the epistemological and scientific-theoretical definitions of terms, in particular the definitions of knowledge (*ʿilm*), presumption (*ẓann*), conceptualization (*taṣawwur*) and belief (*taṣdīq*), indicator (*dalīl*), and sign (*amāra*), see Faḫr ad-dīn ar-Rāzī, *al-Maḥṣūl*, vol. 1, pp. 83–88; see for example van Ess, *Die Erkenntnislehre*, pp. 13 ff. and (on the distinction between *dalīl* and *amāra*—the latter is translated by van Ess as 'pointer' [*Fingerzeig*]) van Ess, *Die Erkenntnislehre*, pp. 364 ff. The earlier distinction between different degrees of knowledge was already adapted by al-Ǧuwaynī to the Aristotelian concept of knowledge, according to which knowledge is *per se* necessary, cf. Eichner, *The Post-Avicennian Philosophical Tradition and Islamic Orthodoxy*, pp. 181–184.

ing (*ʿaqlī*).[29] In several places, Faḫr ad-dīn answers the question of whether the methods for making legal rulings can be based primarily on reasoning emphatically in the negative:

> As concerns the rational [*methods*], in our opinion, there is no leeway (*lā maǧāl*) for them with regard to legal rulings (*aḥkām*), since we have made clear that they [*i.e. the rulings*] are established only by means of revelation/revealed law (*annahā lā tuṯbatu illā bi-š-šaʿrʿ*). But according to the Muʿtazila, there is a place for them because a judgement based on reasoning (*ḥukm al-ʿaql*) is useful with regard to the [*category*] of permission (*ibāḥa*), while it is detrimental (*fī maḍārr*) with regard to prohibition (*ḥaẓr*).[30]

In Faḫr ad-dīn's view, the five categories of legal rulings cannot be deduced and justified purely rationally—not even the category of permission (*ibāḥa*), wherein the option to perform an action exists and is neither required nor prohibited. This position is in contrast to that of the Muʿtazilite school, according to which legal rulings can be reached both by means of tradition and reasoning.[31]

Then Faḫr ad-dīn—together with Abū l-Ḥusayn al-Baṣrī, al-Ġazālī, and others—emphasizes [c] that in *uṣūl al-fiqh* one deals with the methods of deriving legal rulings "in a general way," without focusing on concrete actions and their judgement:

> When we say 'in a general way' (*ʿalā sabīli l-iǧmāl*), we mean the demonstration (*bayān*) of the fact that those indicators are indicators.—Do you not see that in *uṣūl al-fiqh* we say that consensus is an indicator merely for the purpose of demonstration? Whether there was a consensus on this [*or that*] argument is not mentioned in *uṣūl al-fiqh*.[32]

This passage also builds on Abū l-Ḥusayn al-Baṣrī's remarks: "Do you not see that when we speak of something as being obligatory, we are not addressing any specific commandment (*amr muʿayyan*)? So it is also with prohibition (*nahy*), consensus (*iǧmāʿ*), and analogy (*qiyās*). In contrast, it is different with the indic-

29 Faḫr ad-dīn ar-Rāzī, *al-Maḥṣūl*, vol. 1, p. 167, line 5.
30 Ibid., lines 6–9.
31 For more details, see Nagel, *Das islamische Recht*, pp. 25ff.
32 Faḫr ad-dīn ar-Rāzī, *al-Maḥṣūl*, vol. 1, p. 81, lines 1–3.

ators of *fiqh*, because they are specific,"[33] i.e. they articulated with regard to concrete examples.

Component [d] of the definition—"the way by which [*i.e. by means of these methods*] to draw conclusions (*kayfiyyatu l-istidlāl*)"—refers to "the conditions (*šarāʾiṭ*) under which the drawing of conclusions (*istidlāl*) on the basis of those methods is permissible."[34] Component [e], on the other hand, refers to the distinction between laypersons and scholars and their requirements when seeking legal rulings:

> [*ad* e] When we say 'the way in which one draws conclusions from them,' we mean the one who seeks God's judgement: If it is a layman (*ʿāmmī*), then it is necessary that he request a legal opinion (*waǧaba an yastaftiya*); if it is a scholar (*ʿālim*), it is necessary that he take upon himself the endeavor/that he interpret the sources himself (*waǧaba an yaǧtahida*).[35]

From his definition of *uṣūl al-fiqh*, Faḫr ad-dīn then derives the overall structure of the work.

1.3 *The Overall Structure of the Work Based on Faḫr ad-dīn's Definition of* uṣūl al-fiqh

Faḫr ad-dīn—paralleling the template provided by the *Kitāb al-Muʿtamad*[36]—derives the overall structure of his work and the topics to be dealt with in it from the definition of *uṣūl al-fiqh* at the end of his extensive introduction. Under component [b] "on the methods (*ṭuruq*) of *fiqh*" fall the textually established (*manṣūṣ*), i.e. primary, and the derived (*mustanbaṭ*), i.e. secondary, indicators and sources along with aspects related to them, set out in eight chapters: on commandments and prohibitions (*al-kalām fī l-awāmir wa-n-nawāhī*); on generality and particularity (*al-kalām fī l-ʿumūm wa-l-ḫuṣūṣ*); on that which requires explanation and that which has been made clear/explained (*al-muǧmal wa-l-mubayyan*); on the actions of the Prophet (*al-kalām fī l-afʿāl*), abrogation (*al-kalām fī n-nāsiḫ wa-l-mansūḫ*), and consensus (*al-kalām fī l-iǧmāʿ*). The text-based methods include the investigation of transmitted tradition (*al-kalām fī l-aḫbār*) while the derived (*mustanbaṭ*), secondary indicators refer mainly to conclusion by analogy and inference (*al-kalām fī l-qiyās*).

---

33 Al-Baṣrī, *Kitāb al-Muʿtamad*, vol. 1, p. 9.
34 Faḫr ad-dīn ar-Rāzī, *al-Maḥṣūl*, vol. 1, p. 81, lines 4–5.
35 Ibid., lines 6–8.
36 Al-Baṣrī, *Kitāb al-Muʿtamad*, vol. 1, pp. 11–12.

Because all of this can only be dealt with using language, it is inevitable, according to Faḫr ad-dīn, to precede these hermeneutic-methodological treatises with a chapter on language.[37]

The "way by which [*i.e. by means of these methods*] to draw conclusions" (*kayfiyyatu l-istidlāl*) mentioned in component [d] of the definition consists of a process of weighing probabilities (*tarǧīḥ*), whereby contradictory indicators are weighed against each other and, if possible, reconciled.[38] Under component [e] on the other hand, "the particulars of the status of the one drawing the conclusions from them," falls the chapter on "the conditions of independent interpretation of the sources (*šarāʾiṭ al-iǧtihād*)" as well as the chapter on the one who prepares a legal opinion and the one who requests it (*mustaftī*).[39]

Here we find the "canonical set of questions" that Robert Gleave has identified in the classical *uṣūl al-fiqh* works, namely [1.] the "[f]undamental elements of understanding the discpline," i.e. the definition of *uṣūl al-fiqh* as well as discussions of theology and linguistic theory; [2.] a discussion of the status accorded to the individual sources in the determination of a ruling; [3.] a presentation of the hermeneutical tools and [4.] the examination of all that is included under *qiyās*; and finally [5.] questions about the abilities and requirements of the jurist—chapters in which a "theory of hermeneutic authority around the notion of *ijtihād*" is developed.[40]

In the following overview, the letters A–C (in small capitals) correspond to Faḫr ad-dīn ar-Rāzī's systematization, while Gleave's schematization is given in square brackets:

FIGURE 1 *Outline of the Structure of the* Maḥṣūl[41]

A. METHODS

[*"Fundamental elements of understanding the discipline"*]

1. Introduction to the science of *uṣūl al-fiqh* (*al-kalām fī l-muqaddimāt*)
2. Chapter on language (*al-kalām fī l-luġāt*)

---

37 Faḫr ad-dīn ar-Rāzī, *al-Maḥṣūl*, vol. 1, p. 168, lines 18–19; a more detailed treatment can be found in Chapter 1, Section 2.

38 Cf. Bauer, *Die Kultur der Ambiguität*, pp. 182–183, whose term 'weighing of probabilities' (*Wahrscheinlichkeitsabwägung*) I have adopted as a translation for *tarǧīḥ*; for a detailed discussion of this topic, see Weiss, *The Search*, pp. 721 ff.

39 Faḫr ad-dīn ar-Rāzī, *al-Maḥṣūl*, vol. 1, p. 169, lines 4–7.

40 Gleave, *Islam and Literalism*, pp. 28–29.

41 As for Faḫr ad-dīn's short *uṣūl al-fiqh* work *al-Maʿālim fī uṣūl al-fiqh*, it is essentially an outline of chapters 1–11, cf. Faḫr ad-dīn ar-Rāzī, *al-Maʿālim fī uṣūl al-fiqh*, ed. by Muḥammad Ḥasan Ismaʿīl (Beirut: Dār al-Kutub al-ʿilmiyya, 2007).

[*Hermeneutical tools*]
3. Commandments and prohibitions (*al-kalām fī l-awāmir wa-n-nawāhī*)
4. Generality and restriction/particularity (*al-kalām fī l-ʿumūm wa-l-ḫuṣūṣ*)
5. That which requires explaination and that which has been made clear/ explained (*al-muǧmal wa-l-mubayyan*)

[*Use of the sources*]
6. The actions of the Prophet (*al-kalām fī l-afʿāl*)
7. Abrogation (*al-kalām fī n-nāsiḫ wa-l-mansūḫ*)
8. Consensus (*al-kalām fī l-iǧmāʿ*)
9. Traditions (*al-kalām fī l-aḫbār*)

[*Analogy and other and kinds of inference*]
10. Conclusion by analogy and inference (*al-kalām fī l-qiyās*)

B. WEIGHING CONTRADICTORY INDICATORS
11. On stalemate and the weighing of probabilities (*al-kalām fī t-taʿādul wa-t-tarǧīḥ*)

C. THE QUALIFICATIONS OF JURISTS
[*Qualification of jurists and the development of a "theory of hermeneutical authority"*]
12. On the independent interpretation of the sources (*al-kalām fī l-iǧtihād*)
13. On the muftī and the one who requests a legal opinion (*al-kalām fī l-muftī wa-l-mustaftī*)
14. On controversial methods: e.g. *istiṣḥāb/istiḥsān*

This structure largely corresponds to that of Abū l-Ḥusayn's *Kitāb al-Muʿtamad*[42]—apart from a few small differences. For example, the content of Abū l-Ḥusayn's chapter treating the acquisition of legal rulings (*fī ḥuẓr wa-l-ibāḥa*; Engl. 'On Prohibition and Permission') is already dealt with by Faḫr ad-dīn in his introduction. Additionally, Abū l-Ḥusayn, between his introduction and the beginning of his chapter on commandments, makes only a few linguistic comments that are furthermore limited to the topic of literal (*ḥaqīqa*) vs. figurative (*maǧāz*) speech and the investigation of the functions of various particles (*ḥurūf*).[43] The structure of the *Maḥṣūl* is obviously not influenced by that of the *Mustaṣfā*, whose structure is instead systematized according to the four parts of the fruit metaphor: [1.] the fruit (*ṯamara*) of the tree, i.e. the legal rul-

42 See Table 1, p. 28.
43 See Chapter 1, Section 2.

ings; [2.] the tree producing the fruit (*muṯmir*; lit. 'the fruit-bearing one'), i.e. the evidence upon which rulings are made (*adillat al-aḥkām*); [3.] the "harvesting method" or method of utilization (*ṭarīq al-istiṯmār*), under which al-Ġazālī, among others, places linguistic considerations, the study of commandments and prohibitions, and explanations of analogical conlcusions; and [4.] the harvester (*mustaṯmir*; lit. 'beneficiary').[44] Faḫr ad-dīn, on the other hand, treats the topics of the second and third parts together under the aspect of "[b] the methods (*ṭuruq*) of *fiqh*."

A few comments on the structure of the *Mustaṣfā* are warranted here. For, in addition to the aforementioned four parts of the fruit metaphor according to which the work is organized, it exhibits another special feature: an introduction following the preface, which is designed as a propaedeutic treatise on logic.[45] According to al-Ġazālī, this does not represent a specific introduction to the science of *uṣūl al-fiqh*; rather, it is "an introduction for all sciences" (*bal hiya muqaddimatu l-ʿulūm kullihā*),[46] which the teacher or copyist who may not be inclined to logic could also skip: "Whoever does not want to write down this introduction should begin the writing with the first pole [*i.e. with the first chapter pertaining to* uṣūl al-fiqh, *see Table 1*]" (*fa-man šāʾa an lā yaktuba hāḏihī l-muqaddimatu fa-l-yabdaʾ bi-l-kitābi mina l-quṭbi l-awwal*).[47]

The following table is intended to provide a structural overview of the *Maḥṣūl* in direct comparison to the *Kitāb al-Muʿtamad* on which it is modelled, as well as to the *Mustaṣfā*, whose chapter on logic is the first of its kind in this genre.

---

44 Al-Ġazālī, *al-Mustaṣfā*, vol. 1, p. 18, lines 10–11. 10–11: "Every fruit (*ṯamara*) has its own attribute (*ṣifa*) and its own essence (*ḥaqīqa*); it has something from which it is borne (*muṯmir*), a beneficiary (*mustaṯmir*), and a means of utilization (*ṭarīq al-istiṯmār*)." On the structure of the *Mustaṣfā*, see Eichner, *The Post-Avicennian Philosophical Tradition and Islamic Orthodoxy*, pp. 213 ff.

45 Al-Ġazālī, *al-Mustaṣfā*, vol. 1, pp. 30–175.

46 Ibid., line 8.

47 Ibid., lines 10–11.

TABLE 1 Structural overview of the *Maḥṣūl*[48]

Faḫr ad-dīn ar-Rāzī (606/1210): ***al-Maḥṣūl***	**Abū l-Ḥusayn al-Baṣrī (436/1044):** ***Kitāb al-Muʿtamad***	**Abū Ḥāmid Muḥammad al-Ġazālī (505/1111):** ***al-Mustaṣfā***
I. INTRODUCTION	I. INTRODUCTION	I. FOREWORD I AND FOREWORD II II. GENERAL INTRODUCTION: LOGICAL FOUNDATIONS
II. METHODS (*ṬURUQ*) OF *FIQH* 1. Chapter on language[49] 2. Commandments and prohibitions (*al-awāmir wa-n-nawāhī*) 3. Generality and particularity (*al-ʿumūm wa-l-ḫuṣūṣ*) 4. That which requires explaination and that which has been made clear/explained (*al-muǧmal wa-l-mubayyan*) 5. The actions of the Prophet (*al-afʿāl*) 6. Abrogation (*an-nāsiḫ wa-l-mansūḫ*) 7. Consensus (*al-iǧmāʿ*) 8. Traditions (*al-aḫbār*) 9. Conclusion by analogy (*al-qiyās*)	II. METHODS (*ṬURUQ*) OF *FIQH* 1. Chapter on language 2. Commandments and prohibitions 3. Generality and particularity 4. That which requires explaination and that which has been made clear/explained 5. The actions of the Prophet 6. Abrogation 7. Consensus 8. Traditions 9. Conclusion by analogy	III. FRUIT (*ṮAMARA*) (1ST POLE) Categorizations, essence, etc. of legal rulings (*aḥkām*) ——— IV. THAT WHICH BEARS THE FRUIT (*MUṮMIR*) (2ND POLE) FIRST SOURCE: Qurʾan 1. The Qurʾan as a source of law 2. Abrogation SECOND SOURCE: Sunnah 1. The Sunnah as a source of law 2. Traditions THIRD SOURCE: Consensus FOURTH SOURCE: Reasoning (*ʿaql*) and presumption of continuity (*istiṣḥāb*)

48 In this overview, the chapter headings of the *Maḥṣūl* and the *Kitāb al-Muʿtamad* have largely been retained, while the *Mustaṣfā* has been reduced to its essential structural features.

49 For a detailed discussion of this chapter, see Chapter 1, Section 2.

TABLE 1 Structure overview of the *Maḥṣūl* (*cont.*)

Faḫr ad-dīn ar-Rāzī (606/1210): ***al-Maḥṣūl***	**Abū l-Ḥusayn al-Baṣrī (436/1044):** ***Kitāb al-Muʿtamad***	**Abū Ḥāmid Muḥammad al-Ġazālī (505/1111):** ***al-Mustaṣfā***
III. WAY TO DRAW CONCLUSIONS ON THE BASIS OF THESE METHODS (*kayfiyyat al-istidlāl bi-hāḏihī ṭ-ṭuruq*) 10. Stalemate and the weighing of probabilities (*at-taʿādul wa-t-tarǧīḥ*)	III. WAY TO DERIVE THE RULINGS (*kayfiyyat al-istidlāl ʿalā l-aḥkām*) 11. Methodological and epistemological questions (e.g. rulings in the eyes of the revealed law; derivation of the categories of rulings, method of *istiṣḥāb al-ḥāl*)	V. METHOD OF UTILIZATION (*ṬARĪQ AL-ISTIṮMĀR*) (3RD POLE) 1. The external form (*ṣīġa*) and arrangement (*manẓūm*) of the linguistic expression 2. The import (*faḥwā*) of the linguistic expression and what it implies in terms of further meanings[50] 3. The meaning (*maʿnā*) and what is deduced from it by means of reasoning (conclusion by anaolgy)
IV. THE NATURE OF THE SITUATION OF THE ONE WHO DRAWS CONCLUSIONS BASED ON THEM (*kayfiyyat ḥāli l-mustadilli bi-hāḏihī ṭ-ṭuruq*) 11. The independent interpretation of the sources (*al-iǧtihād*) 12. The muftī and the one who requests a legal opinion (*al-muftī wa-l-mustaftī*) 13. On contentious issues	IV. ON THOSE WHO DERIVE THE RULINGS (*fī l-mustadillīna ʿalā l-aḥkām*) 12. The muftī and the one who requests a legal opinion (*al-muftī wa-l-mustaftī*)	VI. 'BENEFICIARIES' (*MUSTAṮMIR*) On the Muǧtahid and the Muqallid

50 These types of implication are the subject of Chapter 4.

2 Topics and Structure of the Chapter on Language

The following is a brief overview of the chapter of the *Maḥṣūl* devoted to linguistic topics,[51] the second sub-chapter of which is the focus of this work. Faḫr ad-dīn justifies the necessity of such a chapter as follows: "Since a grasp (*tamassuk*) of the textually attested (*manṣūṣāt*) [*indicators*] is only possible by means of language, it is inevitable to precede the whole discussion with a chapter on language (*bāb al-luġāt*)."[52] 'Language' here means the totality of the connections between linguistic expressions and meanings; Faḫr ad-dīn's use of the plural *al-luġāt* here is not intended to refer to different dialects or language systems, but rather to the sum of the lexical units of the Arabic language.[53]

2.1 *Word, Speech, Language, Signification: Topics, Questions, and Structure of the Chapter on Language*

The first sub-chapter "Universal Rules of Language" (*al-aḥkām al-kulliya li-luġāt*) presents a definition of "speech" (*kalām*) according to which *kalām*, in its *uṣūl al-fiqh*-related technical sense, refers to "the audible articulated sounds" (*al-aṣwātu l-mutaqaṭṭiʿatu l-masmūʿa*).[54] Faḫr ad-dīn's definition is based on

51 Faḫr ad-dīn ar-Rāzī, *al-Maḥṣūl*, vol. 1, pp. 175–418.

52 Ibid., p. 168, lines 18–19.

53 The term *luġa* is complex in its usage, cf. Tamás Iványi, "Luġa," *EALL*, vol. 3, pp. 88–95; cf. Weiss, *The Search*, pp. 113 ff.; Cornelis Versteegh, *The Explanation of Linguistic Causes. Az-Zaǧǧāǧī's Theory of Grammar* (Amsterdam: John Benjamins, 1995), p. 155, note 8; in this context, the Arabic language is meant: "[…] since Muslim scholars were preoccupied solely with Arabic, *al-lugha*, unless otherwise qualified, was understood to refer to the primordial language of the Arabs, the pristine Arabic that informed the speech of the Prophet Mohammad and his contemporaries," Weiss, *The Search*, p. 122. Faḫr ad-dīn generally uses it to refer to the totality of the connections of linguistic expressions and meanings in a spoken language—usually Arabic—for the purpose of communication, cf. for example Faḫr ad-dīn ar-Rāzī, *al-Maḥṣūl*, vol. 1, pp. 181 ff.: Here he speaks of the correlation between linguistic expressions and meanings (p. 181, line 3) and subsequently summarizes this system (e.g. p. 182, line 3) as *luġāt*. Since Faḫr ad-dīn espouses a comprehensive concept of *luġa* that is not limited to 'lexicography,' 'dialect,' or 'word,' the term 'language' is chosen here. Additionally, this is intended to avoid unnecessary exoticization, which in my opinion is evoked when the word is left untranslated—"The Lugha was …," "they spoke of the Lugha" (cf. Weiss, *The Search*, p. 113).

54 Faḫr ad-dīn ar-Rāzī, *al-Maḥṣūl*, Vol. 1, p. 177, line 4; Faḫr ad-dīn also cites another definition which, according to him, is not relevant to *uṣūl al-fiqh*—in it he defines *kalām* as *al-maʿnā l-qāʾimu bi-n-nafsi*. With these two definitions he splits al-Bāqillānī's Ašʿarite definition of *kalām* into two parts and differentiates between a theological and a philological-phonological aspect: *al-kalām* […] *huwa maʿnan qāʾimun bi-n-nafsi yuʿabbaru ʿanhū bi-hāḏihī l-aṣwāti l-masmūʿa*, al-Bāqillānī, *Kitāb at-Tamhīd*, ed. by Richard J. McCarthy (Beirut: Libraire Orientale, 1957), p. 251, lines 5–6; see also al-Bāqillānī, *at-Taqrīb*, vol. 1, p. 316;

that of Abū l-Ḥusayn al-Baṣrī, who writes: "*kalām* is that which is arranged out of differentiated, audible phonemes" (*al-kalām huwa mā ntaẓara mina l-ḥurūfi l-masmūʿati l-mutamayyizati*).[55] According to Faḫr ad-dīn, this definition is intended, among other things, to prevent single phonemes from being considered speech (*kalām*).[56]

In connection with this, Faḫr ad-dīn deals with the question of whether a single, individual word (*kalima*) can be regarded as speech (*kalām*), and explains the differences in viewpoint between "the grammarians" (*an-nuḥāt*; sg. *nāḥin*), who answer this question in the negative, and "the legal theorists" (*al-uṣūliyyūn*), who answer it in the affirmative. Faḫr ad-dīn supports the position of the grammarians: following Zamaḫšarī, he understands *kalima* as "any utterance that denotes a meaning on the basis of convention" (*kullu manṭūqin bihī dalla bi-l-iṣṭilāḥ ʿalā maʿnan*);[57] and following Ibn Ǧinnī he summarizes speech (*kalām*) as a "meaningful sentence" (*al-ǧumlatu l-mufīda*)—be it a nominal sentence (*al-ǧumlatu l-ismiyyatu*), a verbal sentence (*al-ǧumlatu l-fiʿliyyatu*), or a conditional sentence (*al-ǧumlatu š-šarṭiyyatu*).[58] The question

---

cf. Gardet, "kalam," *EI*². On the philological levels of meaning, see for example Rafael Talmon, "'Al-kalām mā kāna muktafiyan bi-nafsihī wa-huwa l-ǧumla': A Study in the history of sentence-concept and the Sībawaihian legacy in Arabic grammar," *Zeitschrift der Deutschen Morgenländischen Gesellschaft*, vol. 138 (1988): pp. 74–98; Cornelis Versteegh, *Arabic Grammar and Qurʾānic Exegesis in Early Islam* (Leiden [et al.]: Brill, 1993), pp. 99 ff. as well as Tamás Iványi, "kalam," *EALL*, vol. 2, pp. 541–545 and Richard Frank, "Meanings are Spoken of in Many Ways: The Earlier Arab Grammarians," *Le Muséon*, vol. 94 (1981): p. 263.

55 Al-Baṣrī, *Kitāb al-Muʿtamad*, vol. 1, p. 14, last line; Faḫr ad-dīn ar-Rāzī, *al-Maḥṣūl*, vol. 1, p. 177, lines 7–8.

56 Faḫr ad-dīn ar-Rāzī, *al-Maḥṣūl*, vol. 1, pp. 177–178.

57 Ibid., p. 179, lines 13–14; cf. Faḫr ad-dīn ar-Rāzī, *at-Tafsīr al-kabīr*, vol. 1, p. 29, lines 15–18 (24th main argument); cf. Abū l-Qāsim az-Zamaḫšarī, *al-Mufaṣṣal*, ed. by J.P. Broch, 1859, p. 4, line 14, see also Jean-Patrick Guillaume, "Defining the Word within the Arabic Grammatical Tradition: ʾAstarābāḏī's Predicament," in *The Word in Arabic*, ed. by Giuliano Lancioni and Lidia Bettini (Leiden [et al.]: Brill, 2011), p. 49. Zamaḫšarī, whose writings were often engaged with by Faḫr ad-dīn, subsumed *kalima* under the conceptual category of *lafẓ*. As with Ibn Sīnā—and in contrast to al-Fārābī—the "linguistic expression" no longer had to carry meaning in order to be considered *lafẓ*.

58 Faḫr ad-dīn ar-Rāzī, *al-Maḥṣūl*, vol. 1, p. 180, lines 3–5; Faḫr ad-dīn summarizes this discussion with somewhat more detail afforded to the argumentation in his *Tafsīr* (10th main argument), see Faḫr ad-dīn ar-Rāzī, *at-Tafsīr al-kabīr*, vol. 1, p. 26, lines 7–17; cf. Abū l-Fatḥ ʿUṯmān Ibn Ǧinnī, *al-Ḫaṣāʾiṣ*, ed. by Muḥammad ʿAlī an-Naǧǧār (Beirut: Dār al-Kitāb al-ʿArabī [2nd edition; reprint of the Cairo edition, 1952–1957]), vol. 1, p. 26, lines 12 f. On the development of the terms *kalām* and *ǧumla* into the grammatical technical terms for "sentence," see Talmon, "'Al-kalām mā kāna muktafiyan bi-nafsihī wa-huwa l-ǧumla'" and Georges Bohas, Jean-Patrick Guillaume, and Djamel Eddine Kouloughli, *The Arabic lin-*

of whether a word alone can be classified as speech or whether speech must be comprised of a complete sentence is of considerable legal relevance—the legal validity of a speech act, for example, could depend on it.[59]

This first sub-chapter goes on to provide an overview of the various theories regarding the origin of language that have been put forward throughout Muslim intellectual history. These are mainly limited to the question of who can be regarded as the initiator (*wāḍiʿ*, lit. 'imposer') of language(s)—whether God, or humans, or both together.[60] Faḫr ad-dīn also gives a description here of the function of language in human communities as well as a discussion of the advantages that spoken language has over communication based on other kinds of signs.[61]

Besides the investigation of the creator of language and the question of the function of spoken language, the investigation of the relationship between linguistic expressions and meanings occupies a large portion of this sub-chapter. Some questions of chief importance, in addition to the question of how language (i.e. the correlation between linguistic expressions and meanings) is

---

guistic tradition (London: Routledge, 1990), pp. 56; see also Versteegh, *Arabic Grammar and Qur'ānic Exegesis*, pp. 99ff. and id., *The Explanation of Linguistic Causes*, pp. 41–42 and p. 214.

59 This is discussed, for example, in the context of conditional divorce, see Faḫr ad-dīn ar-Rāzī, *at-Tafsīr al-kabīr*, vol. 1, p. 26, lines 18–32.

60 On the question of the origin of language, see Faḫr ad-dīn ar-Rāzī, *al-Maḥṣūl*, vol. 1, pp. 181–192; this topic will not be treated in depth here as it has been dealt with quite extensively in various monographs and essays: Bernard G. Weiss, *Language in Orthodox Muslim Thought: A Study of* Waḍʿ al-Lugha *and its Development* (Princeton: Princeton University, 1966); Henri Loucel, "L'origine du langage d'après les grammairiens arabes I–IV," *Arabica*, vol. 10 (1963): pp. 188–208, pp. 253–281 and vol. 11 (1964): pp. 57–72, pp. 151–187; Bernard G. Weiss, "Medieval Muslim Discussions of the Origin of Language," *ZDMG*, vol. 124 (1974): pp. 33–41; Andrzej Czapkiewicz, *The Views of the Medieval Arab Philologists on Language and its Origin in the Light of as-Suyūṭī's "al-Muzhir"* (Krakow: Nakł. Uniwersytetu Jagiellońskiego, 1988); Cornelis H.M. Versteegh, "Linguistic Attitudes and the Origin of Speech in the Arab World," in *Understanding Arabic: Essays in Contemporary Arabic Linguistics in Honor of El-Said Badawi*, ed. by Alaa Elgibali (Cairo: The American University in Cairo Press, 1996), pp. 15–31; id., *Landmarks in Linguistic Thought III: The Arabic Linguistic Tradition* (London [et al.]: Routledge, 1997), pp. 101–114; Mustafa Shah, "Classical Islamic Discourse on the Origins of Language: Cultural Memory and the Defense of Orthodoxy," *Numen*, vol. 58 (2011): pp. 314–343; see also Gleave, *Islam and Literalism*, pp. 30ff.; Endreß, "'This is Clear Arabic Speech,'" pp. 34–36.

61 Faḫr ad-dīn ar-Rāzī, *al-Maḥṣūl*, vol. 1, pp. 193–195; for a translation of an excerpt from this sub-chapter of the *Maḥṣūl*, see Versteegh: *Landmarks in Linguistic Thought III*, pp. 127–129.

transmitted,[62] include: [i] Does each meaning have its own discrete linguistic expression? Faḫr ad-dīn's answer is in accord with what had been argued previously: since there is an infinite number of meanings for which only a limited number of linguistic expressions is conceivable, he makes arguments for the possibility and permissibility of homonyms and figures of speech in the Arabic language, including the revealed texts—e.g. in connection with the form of the imperative (*ṣīġat al-amr*). If one accepts that there can only be a limited number of linguistic expressions that are assigned to an infinite number of meanings, then there must inevitably be expressions that signify more than one meaning in one way or another.[63] On this basis, it can then be argued that the imperative need not always indicate the obligation to perform an action. [ii] Another question at the center of the discussion of the relationship between linguistic expressions and meanings is whether linguistic expressions are primarily used for "the signification of extramentally existing things" (*li-d-dalālati ʿalā l-mawǧūdāti l-ḫāriǧiyya*) or "the signification of mental meanings" (*wuḍiʿat li-d-dalālati ʿalā l-maʿānī d-dihniyya*). According to Faḫr ad-dīn, the latter is the case:

> Whenever we see a body from afar (*idā raʾaynā ǧisman min baʿīd*) and we think it is a boulder (*wa-ẓanannāhu ṣaḫratan*), we call it by that name (*sammaynāhu bi-hādā l-ism*); then when we approach it (*fa-idā danawnā minhū*), we realize that it is a living being (*ʿarafnā annahū ḥayawān*), but we think it is a bird and thus call it that [*i.e. by the name 'bird'*] (*lākinnā ẓanannāhu ṭayran sammaynāhu bihī*). But with increasing proximity (*fa-idā izdāda l-qurb*), we recognize that it is a human being and thus call it that [*i.e. by the name 'human being'*]. Thus, the difference in names for the difference in mental forms (*aṣ-ṣuwar ad-dihniyya*) indicates that the linguistic expression signifies only them [*i.e. the mental forms*] (*fa-ḫtilāfu*

62 Faḫr ad-dīn ar-Rāzī, *al-Maḥṣūl*, vol. 1, pp. 203–217; see also Weiss, "Language and Tradition."

63 Cf. Faḫr ad-dīn ar-Rāzī, *al-Maḥṣūl*, vol. 1, pp. 262 ff.; in the *Tafsīr*, Faḫr ad-dīn speaks of infinite quiddities (*māhiyyāt*), cf. Faḫr ad-dīn ar-Rāzī, *at-Tafsīr al-kabīr*, vol. 1, p. 31, lines 12–13 (36th main argument); cf. on this question Weiss, *The Search*, pp. 143 ff. and pp. 197–198 and Zysow, *The Economy of Certainty*, p. 58. This question becomes relevant, for example, in the context of the question as to whether the imperative denotes the obligation to perform an action. The Ḥanafite scholar as-Saraḫsī argues in favor of this by saying that there exist a sufficient number of linguistic expressions such that a different linguistic expression could be selected if a certain meaning were intended; thus homonymy need not be inevitable, see Šams ad-dīn as-Saraḫsī, *Uṣūl*, ed. by Abū l-Wafāʾ al-Afġānī (Beirut: Dār al-Kutub al-ʿilmiyya, 1993 [1414]), vol. 1, p. 16, cf. Zysow, *The Economy of Certainty*, p. 58 and pp. 62–63; cf. Weiss, *The Search*, pp. 336 ff., which goes into this in detail.

l-asāmī ʿinda ḫtilāfi ṣ-ṣuwari ḏ-ḏihniyyati yadullu ʿalā anna l-lafẓa lā dalālata lahū illā ʿalayhā).[64]

These considerations, which can also be found in Faḫr ad-dīn's other deliberations on language philosophy, fall within the tradition of a passage by Aristotle on the theory of signification from his *De Interpretatione* 16a3–8:[65] According to Aristotle, [3] (spoken) sounds or linguistic expressions (φωναί) are symbols (σύμβολα) for [2] our psychological impressions, "affections in the soul"[66]—or for "things in the mind (ἐν τῇ διανοίᾳ)";[67] on the other hand, [4] written (γραφόμενα) expressions are symbols for spoken linguistic utterances. The [3] spoken and [4] written linguistic expressions vary from country to country and are signs (σημεῖα) for [2] the impressions of the soul, which are "the same for all people." The [2] impressions of the soul, in turn, are depictions (ὁμοιώματα) [1] of extramental things (πράγματα). The Greek commentary tradition understood the relationship between these planes to be that linguistic expressions directly, i.e. "firstly" (πρώτων), signify that which is in the soul, namely thoughts (νοημάτα)—and only secondarily the extramental things or facts.[68]

While the distinction between 'symbols' and 'signs' on the one hand and 'depictions' on the other, and thus different types of referential relationships—namely the distinction between [3]/[4]–[2] and [2]–[1]—is emphasized in

64 Faḫr ad-dīn ar-Rāzī, *al-Maḥṣūl*, vol. 1, p. 200, line 11–p. 201, line 2, the parallel passages can be found in Faḫr ad-dīn ar-Rāzī, *Šarḥ al-Išārāt wa-t-tanbīhāt, al-Manṭiq*, ed. by ʿAlī Reżā Nağafzādeh (Tehran: Anğomān-e Āṯār va-Mofāḫer Farhangī, 2005 [1426 h.q./1384 h.š.]), p. 21, lines 10–13; Faḫr ad-dīn ar-Rāzī, *at-Tafsīr al-kabīr*, vol. 1, p. 31, lines 6–8 (excerpt from the 35th main argument).

65 Aristotle (*De Int.* 16a3–8), *Aristotelis Categoriae et Liber de Interpretatione*, ed. by Lorenzo Minio-Paluello (Oxford: Clarendon Press, 1949): "Εστι μὲν οὖν τὰ ἐν τῇ φωνῇ τῶν ἐν τῇ ψυχῇ παθημάτων σύμβολα, καὶ τὰ γραφόμενα τῶν ἐν τῇ φωνῇ. Καὶ ὥσπερ οὐδὲ γράμματα πᾶσι τὰ αὐτά, οὐδὲ φωναὶ αἱ αὐταί· ὧν μέντοι ταῦτα σημεῖα πρώτων, ταὐτὰ πᾶσι παθήματα τῆς ψυχῆς, καὶ ὧν ταῦτα ὁμοιώματα πράγματα ἤδη ταὐτά. The English translation of this passage is taken from J.L. Ackrill's *De Int.* translation: "Now spoken sounds are symbols of affections in the soul, and written marks symbols of spoken sounds. And just as written marks are not the same for all men, neither are spoken sounds. But what these are in the first place signs of—affections of the soul—are the same for all; and what these affections are likenesses of—actual things—are also the same," J.L. Ackrill, *Aristotle. Categories and De Interpretatione* (Oxford: Clarendon Press, 1963 [reprinted 2002]), p. 43; Weidemann gives a detailed commentary on this passage, see Hermann Weidemann, "Anmerkungen," in *Aristoteles. Werke in deutscher Übersetzung vol. 1, part II: Peri Hermeneias* (Berlin: Akademie-Verlag, 2002 [1st edition 1994]), pp. 133–158.

66 The English translation is based on Ackrill, see fn. 65.

67 Aristotle, *De Int.* 23a 32 f., cf. Weidemann, "Anmerkungen," p. 135 and p. 458.

68 Cf. Weidemann, "Anmerkungen," pp. 141–142.

the Greek commentary tradition, this dichotomization became blurred in the Arabic tradition. One of the reasons for this is that Isḥāq ibn Ḥunayn's Arabic translation does not mention σύμβολα, and instead only speaks of 'signifying/referring to' and of 'depictions' (*amṯila*): "That which is uttered with the voice signifies the impressions that are in the soul (*inna mā yuḫrağu bi-ṣ-ṣawti dāllun ʿalā l-āṯāri allatī fī n-nafsi*); and that which is written (*mā yuktabu*) signifies that which is uttered with the voice."[69] Eventually, Ibn Sīnā removed the word 'depictions' (*amṯila*), writing only of 'signifying,' so that the [2]–[1] relationship became harmonized with the others. Thus through Ibn Sīnā's use of the verb *dalla* in his Arabic translation, the relationships between the planes of reference were "constructed in an even more strongly parallel way,"[70] i.e. the relationship between [2] the impressions of the soul and [1] the extramental things is not distinguished—at least linguistically—from that between [3] the linguistic expressions and [2] the impressions of the soul. Instead all reference planes are linked by the verb *dalla* in a continuous chain of signification. This formed the basis for these planes being understood in the post-Avicennian tradition as "four different possibilities for how 'a thing' (*šay*ʾ) can be."[71] Such a structure is already suggested by the heading of the chapter *al-ʿIbāra* I,1 of the *Kitāb aš-Šifā*ʾ: "On the knowledge (*maʿrifa*) of the mutual correspondence (*tanāsub*) between things (*umūr*) and concepts (*taṣawwurāt*) and linguistic expressions (*alfāẓ*) and written [*linguistic expressions*] (*kitābāt*)."[72]

This is the background of what led to the passage from the *Maḥṣūl* quoted above becoming inserted into another work by Faḫr ad-dīn, namely his commentary on Ibn Sīnā's *Išārāt wa-t-tanbīhāt*:

> [§1] Things have four levels of existence (*marātib fī l-wuğūd*): [1] The external existence (*al-wuğūd al-ḫāriğī*), [2] the mental (*aḏ-ḏihnī*), [3] that which is related to the linguistic expression (*al-lafẓī*), and [4] that which is related to writing (*al-kitāba*).

69 *An-Naṣṣ al-kāmil li-Manṭiq Arisṭū*, ed. by Farīd Ğabr (Beirut: Dār al-Fikr al-Lubnānī, 1999), vol. 1, p. 104, lines 1–2; on this passage in the Arabic tradition, see Heidrun Eichner, "Das avicennische *Corpus Aristotelicum*: Zur Virtualisierung des Aristotelestextes in der postavicennischen Tradition," in *Entre Orient et Occident: La philosophie et la science gréco-romaines dans le monde arabe*, ed. by Richard Goulet (Geneva: Droz, 2010), pp. 206ff.; see also Versteegh, "The Arabic Tradition," pp. 266ff.

70 Eichner, "Das avicennische *Corpus Aristotelicum*," p. 215.

71 Ibid., p. 226.

72 Ibn Sīnā, *Kitāb aš-Šifā*ʾ*, al-Manṭiq, al-ʿIbāra*, ed. by Maḥmūd al-Ḫuḍayrī (Cairo: Dār al-kātib al-ʿarabī li-ṭ-ṭibāʿa wa-n-našr, 1970), p. 1; cf. Eichner, "Das avicennische *Corpus Aristotelicum*," p. 213.

> [§2] [4] The [*level of*] writing signifies/refers to [3] [*the level of*] the linguistic expression, [...]. As far as [3] [*the level of*] the linguistic expression is concerned, it does not signify [1] [*the level of*] external [*existence*]—namely on the basis of the [*following*] proof:
> [§3] When you see a person from afar and think he is a boulder, then you call him that [*i.e. by the name 'boulder'*]; then, as you approach him, you recognize that he is a living being, but you think he is a bird and call him by [*the name*] 'bird'; then, with increasing proximity, you recognize his humanness and call him by [*the name*] 'man.'
> [§4] Thus, the difference in names (*iḫtilāf at-tasmiyāt*) for the difference in concepts (*ḫayālāt*) indicates that the names signify the mental forms (*aṣ-ṣuwar aḏ-ḏihniyya*), and not the external things (*al-umūr al-ḫāriǧiyya*).
> It is in the nature of people to call the mental forms (*aṣ-ṣuwar aḏ-ḏihniyya*) meanings/concepts (*maʿānī*). Thus the correctness of his [*i.e. Ibn Sīnā's*] words has become clear in that "there is a certain connection (*ʿalāqatun mā*) between the linguistic expression and the meaning," i.e. that the linguistic expression *per se* and in a primary way (*bi-l-qaṣdi l-awwali*) only signifies the mental meanings.[73]

In contrast to his treatment of the same topic in the *Maḥṣūl*, these relatively detailed explanations illustrate the tradition in which parts of Faḫr ad-dīn's work on legal theory are to be contextualized.

This tradition is illustrated in particularly striking fashion by the second, extremely complex sub-chapter, which deals with "the classification of linguistic expressions" (*taqsīm al-alfāẓ*). This sub-chapter, which is the focus of the present work, will be presented and translated below. As will be shown in detail, it represents a synthesis between logical propaedeutics and concepts of grammatical and legal theory.

Sub-chapters three to six of the *Maḥṣūl*'s chapter on language treat several of these classifications in depth, discussing various aspects of the paronymous name (*ism muštaqq*), the polyonymous name (*ism mutarādif*) (i.e. several different linguistic expressions signifying one and the same meaning), the homonymous name (*ism muštarak*), and the question of literal (*lafẓ ḥaqīqī*) and figurative linguistic expressions (*lafẓ maǧāzī*).[74]

---

73 Faḫr ad-dīn ar-Rāzī, *Šarḥ al-Išārāt wa-t-tanbīhāt, al-Manṭiq*, ed. by ʿAlī Reżā Naǧafzādeh (Tehran: Anǧomān-e Āṯār va-Mofāḫer Farhangī, 2005 [1426 h.q./1384 h.š.]), p. 21, lines 5–15.

74 See Chapter 3.

The seventh linguistic sub-chapter indicates possible sources of error in interpretation due to linguistic features such as homonymy, changes in language usage including the evolution of technical terms, figurative expressions, ellipses, and semantic narrowing. It provides the scholar with ten guidelines for resolving these sorts of discrepancies, which arise during "the attainment of what the speaker intends": If, for example, the homonymous meaning of a word conflicts with a meaning that has become established, whether in lay or technical usage, it is this established meaning that is to be considered more appropriate. If, however, this then results in a conflict with the figurative meaning, then the figurative meaning is to be considered more appropriate.[75]

The eighth sub-chapter deals with the meanings and functions of the particles *wāw*, *fāʾ*, and *innamā* as well as the prepositions *fī*, *bi-*, and *min*, discussing different problems in detail.[76] In the way of a cursory overview, I will mention a few of these problems. At the center of the issue concerning the *wāw*, Faḫr ad-dīn discusses the question, particularly important for legal hermeneutics, of whether the *wāw* in its function as a conjunction (*al-wāw al-ʿāṭifa*) should be understood simultaneously or consecutively when in the context of a temporal sequence (*tartīb*). For example, does the sentence *raʾaytu Zaydan wa-ʿAmran* mean that I saw Zayd *and* ʿAmr at the same time (*maʿan*) or that I first saw Zayd *and then* ʿAmr?[77] Faḫr ad-dīn cites the grammarian Abū ʿAlī al-Fārisī (d. 377/987), according to whom the majority of grammarians from the Baṣra and Kūfa schools are of the opinion that connection (*ǧamʿ*), not succession, is denoted by this *wāw*. This view, which Faḫr ad-dīn eloquently endorses, had already been held by Sībawayhi.[78] The *fāʾ*, on the other hand, has the function of sequence (*taʿqīb*), while *innamā* is employed for the limitation (*ḥaṣr*) of a statement.[79] With regard to the preposition *bi-*, the question is whether

---

75 Faḫr ad-dīn ar-Rāzī, *al-Maḥṣūl*, vol. 1, p. 351 ff.

76 The *Maʿālim*, on the other hand, only outlines Faḫr ad-dīn's positions on *wāw*, *innamā*, and *bi-*, cf. Faḫr ad-dīn ar-Rāzī, *al-Maʿālim fī uṣūl al-fiqh*, pp. 18–19.

77 Faḫr ad-dīn ar-Rāzī, *al-Maḥṣūl*, vol. 1, p. 364 and p. 366; his remarks are based on those of Abū l-Ḥusayn, see al-Baṣrī, *Kitāb al-Muʿtamad*, vol. 1, pp. 41–42, al-Bāqillānī, *at-Taqrīb*, vol. 1, p. 414, line 10–p. 416, line 1.

78 Faḫr ad-dīn ar-Rāzī, *al-Maḥṣūl*, vol. 1, p. 363; cf. Abū Bišr ʿAmr b. Uṯmān Sībawayhi, *al-Kitāb*, ed. by ʿAbd as-Salām Muḥammad Hārūn (Cairo: Dār al-Qalam, 1966–1977), vol. 2, pp. 41–42, see also Ulrike Mosel, *Die syntaktische Terminologie bei Sibawaih* (Munich, 1975), vol. 1, p. 57; cf. Ibn Ḫaldūn, *al-Muqaddima*, vol. 3, p. 20, line 5.

79 Faḫr ad-dīn ar-Rāzī, *al-Maḥṣūl*, vol. 1, pp. 373 ff. and pp. 381 ff. as well as Faḫr ad-dīn ar-Rāzī, *al-Maʿālim fī uṣūl al-fiqh*, p. 18, lines 13–17; this question is discussed, *inter alia*, in the context of the *argumentum e contrario*. Al-Qarāfī gives an overview of the views on *innamā* in the various schools of law and among various scholars; he attributes the position that *innamā* is only used for the 'affirmation of the statement' (*li-taʾkīdi l-iṯbāt*) to the Ḥanafite

it denotes a partitive meaning (partitivity: *tabʿīḍiyya*) in the context of transitive verbs (transitivity: *taʿaddin*)—a controversial view for which Faḫr ad-dīn argues in favor:[80] According to this partitive understanding of *bi-*, Sura 5:6 *wa-msaḥū bi-ruʾusikum* is interpreted to mean that it is sufficient, during ritual ablution, to go with one's hand over "a part of the head" (*bi-ǧuzʾin min aǧzāʾi l-raʾsi*) rather than the whole head.[81]

The ninth sub-chapter discusses fundamental theological premises that are important for the hermeneutical process—for example, it is "inconceivable that God would say something without meaning something by it" (*lā yaǧūzu an yatakallama Llāhu taʿālā bi-šayʾin wa-lā yaʿnī bihī šayʾan*).[82] After all, speech that conveys no meaning, according to Faḫr ad-dīn, is idle chatter (*haḏayān*), which is in turn a deficiency (*naqṣ*). And a deficiency in God is unthinkable (*muḥāl*)[83]—just as He does not "intend the opposite of the apparent [*meaning of His speech*] without indicating it in some way" (*lā yaǧūzu an yaʿniya bi-kalāmihī ḫilāfa ẓāhirihī wa-lā yadullu ʿalayhi al-battata*).[84] This sub-chapter furthermore includes a discussion of the degree of knowledge that one can reasonably expect to gain from linguistic analysis.[85]

FIGURE 2 *Outline of the Chapter "Speech About Language" (al-kalām fī-l-luġāt)*[86]

1. Universal rules of language (*al-aḥkām al-kulliya li-luġāt*)
2. The classification of linguistic expressions (*taqsīm al-alfāẓ*)
3. Paronymous names (*al-asmāʾ al-muštaqqa*)

---

school of law, see al-Qarāfī, *Nafāʾis al-uṣūl*, vol. 2, p. 26, see also Weiss, *The Search*, pp. 491 f.

80 Faḫr ad-dīn ar-Rāzī, *al-Maḥṣūl*, vol. 1, p. 379; id., *al-Maʿālim fī uṣūl al-fiqh*, p. 19; cf. Al-Baṣrī, *Kitāb al-Muʿtamad*, vol. 1, p. 39, line 21–p. 40, line 5; on transitivity in general, see Jonathan Owens, *The Foundations of Grammar: An Introduction to Medieval Arabic Grammatical Theory* (Amsterdam [et al.]: John Benjamins Publishing Company, 1988), pp. 167–185.

81 Faḫr ad-dīn ar-Rāzī, *at-Tafsīr al-kabīr*, vol. 11, p. 126, lines 29–30 (36th main argument) and id., *al-Maḥṣūl*, vol. 3, pp. 164–165. On the question of the function of the preposition *bi-* in this verse, see in particular ʿAbd al-ʿAzīẓ Mūsā Darwīš ʿAlī and Muḥammad ʿAlī Salīm al-Hawwārī, "Qirāʾatun luġawiyyatun fiqhiyyatun fī āyati l-wuḍūʾ," *Journal of Qurʾanic Studies*, vol. 12 (2010): pp. 307 ff.; it is mentioned in John Burton, "The Qurʾān and the Islamic Practice of wuḍūʾ," *Bulletin of the School of Oriental and African Studies*, vol. 51, no. 1 (1988): p. 48.

82 Faḫr ad-dīn ar-Rāzī, *al-Maḥṣūl*, vol. 1, p. 385.

83 Ibid., p. 386.

84 Ibid., p. 388, lines 11–14.

85 Ibid., pp. 390 ff.

86 ... According to the systematization and the wording of Faḫr ad-dīn; cf. Versteegh, *Landmarks in Linguistic Thought III*, p. 130. On the considerations surrounding the translation of *luġa*, see fn. 53.

4. Rules of polyonymy and emphasis (*aḥkām at-tarāduf wa-t-tawkīd*)
5. Homonymy (*ištirāk*)
6. Literal and figurative [*linguistic expressions*] (*ḥaqīqa wa-l-maǧāz*)
7. The discrepancy that can occur between [*the different hermeneutical*] states of linguistic expressions (*at-taʿāruḍu l-ḥāṣilu bayna aḥwāli l-alfāẓ*)
8. The explanation of those particles for which the need to recognize their meanings is increased in *fiqh* (*tafsīru ḥurūfin taštaddu l-ḥāǧatu fī l-fiqhi ilā maʿrifati maʿanīhā*)
9. The way of deriving rulings from the speech of the Mighty and Exalted God and from the speech of the Prophet (*kayfiyyatu l-istidlāli bi-ḫiṭābi Llāhi ʿazza wa-ǧalla wa-ḫiṭābi rasūlihī ʿalā l-aḥkām*)

This chapter on language in the *Maḥṣūl* is much more detailed than the comparable treatise in Abū l-Ḥusayn al-Baṣrī's *Kitāb al-Muʿtamad*. The latter, besides a few general introductory words on "speech" (*kalām*), essentially focuses on the topics of *ḥaqīqa* and *maǧāz*, in this case regarding semantic change in language use as well as the functions of various particles.[87]

Meanwhile, a further comparison of the *Maḥṣūl*'s linguistic chapter to al-Ġazālī's *Mustaṣfā* shows that the corresponding chapter in the latter is much more extensive and covers a large part of what Faḫr ad-dīn has arranged as separate treatises within the *Maḥṣūl*.

Abū Ḥāmid al-Ġazālī deals with the linguistic expression (*lafẓ*), especially the way in which a linguistic expression indicates a legal ruling, in his treatise on the "Method of Utilization" (*ṭarīq al-istiṯmār*). There he develops the methodological foundations for formulating legal rulings. This treatise consists of three parts, as follows:

> The linguistic expression (*lafẓ*) signifies the ruling (*ḥukm*) either [1.] by means of its external form (*ṣīġa*) and its (formal) arrangement (*manẓūm*), or [2.] by means of its import (*faḥwā*) and what it implies (*mafhūm*, lit. 'that which is understood'; what is meant here is the legal-theoretical concept of implication), or [3.] by means of its meaning (*maʿnā*) and that which is based on reasoning (*maʿqūl*)—and this is the means of derivation called analogy (*qiyās*).
>
> These are the three areas: [1.] The formal arrangement (*manẓūm*), [2.] the implication (*mafhūm*), [3.] and the [*derivation*] based on reasoning (*maʿqūl*).[88]

87 Cf. al-Baṣrī, *Kitāb al-Muʿtamad*, vol. 1, pp. 14–42.
88 Al-Ġazālī, *al-Mustaṣfā*, vol. 3, p. 3, lines 11–16.

The three parts thus occupy three different levels: the level of the word form, the level of meaning and context, and the level on which different meanings are brought together for the purpose of reaching conclusions through analogy.

Thus his first part is organized as follows:

FIGURE 3 *Outline of the Chapter on Language Theory in al-Ġazālī's Mustaṣfā*

V. METHOD OF UTILIZATION (ṬARĪQ AL-ISTIṮMĀR) (3RD POLE)[89]

V.1 The external form (*ṣīġa*) and arrangement (*manẓūm*) of the linguistic expression

1. Introduction:
    1. On the origin of languages
    2. On the question of whether names can be established by analogy
    3. On names that belong to the convention of a particular community of speakers
    4. On names that relate to the law: Is there a specific legal terminology?
    5. On useful speech (*al-kalām al-mufīd*) and its components
    6. On how to understand what is intended by divine speech (*ḫiṭāb*)
    7. On literal and figurative linguistic expressions
2. On that which requires explanation (*muǧmal*) and that which has been made clear/explained (*mubayyan*)
3. On the apparent (*ẓāhir*) and that which must be justified (*mu'awwal*)
4. On commandment (*amr*) and prohibition (*nahy*)
5. On the general (*ʿāmm*) and the limited/particular (*ḫāṣṣ*)

Chapters 2, 4, and 5, here included under the treatment of the linguistic expression, constitute independent chapters in the *Maḥṣūl* and the *Kitāb al-Muʿtamad*. Only the introductory sub-chapters are to some extent comparable between the *Mustaṣfā*'s and the latter two works' chapters on language.

2.2 Al-Maḥṣūl *vs.* at-Tafsīr al-kabīr*: A Comparison of the Introductory Chapters on Language*

I will now conclude the general overview of the chapter of the *Maḥṣūl* that Faḫr ad-dīn intended specifically to be about language with a brief comparison between it (and other chapters of the *Maḥṣūl* that contain linguistic insights)

89 This overview is based on al-Ġazālī's own chapter titles, given at the beginning of each unit, as well as partly on the subheadings and the content itself.

and the linguistic introduction of his Qurʾanic commentary *at-Tafsīr al-kabīr*.[90] By "linguistic introduction," I refer to a portion of his commentary on the first sura. He uses the words "I seek refuge in God" (*aʿūḏu bi-Llāh*) to systematically expound upon a number of principles of linguistic theory—followed by legal and rational points related to these words—upon which he builds over the course of the rest of his commentary.

Faḫr ad-dīn begins what could be called the preface to this introduction by describing an approach that is particularly characteristic of him—namely that one "can derive many points of discussion from but a few linguistic expressions."[91] Faḫr ad-dīn demonstrates this fact using the words "I seek refuge in God" (*aʿūḏu bi-Llāh*)—and in doing so also presents the systematization of his introduction:

> *Aʿūḏu* is one of the types of the imperfect (*al-fiʿl al-muḍāriʿ*) and the imperfect is one of the types of the verb. As for the *bi-* in *bi-Llāh*, it is a *bāʾ ilṣāq* (a *b* of affixation/agglutination), and thus belongs to the types of prepositions (*ḥurūf al-ǧarr*); the preposition belongs to the types of particles. As far as our speech 'God' is concerned, this is a specific name (*ism muʿayyan*); it belongs either to the proper names or the derived names—there are different views on this.[92] The proper name and the derived name both belong to the types of absolute names.

90 Important preliminary work on the linguistic introduction and its relationship to the *Maḥṣūl* had already been undertaken by Cornelis Versteegh; his findings are drawn upon here, cf. Cornelis Versteegh, "The Linguistic Introduction to Rāzī's *Tafsīr*," in *Studies in Near Eastern Languages and Literatures. Memorial Volume of Karel Petráček*, ed. by Petr Zemánek (Prague: Academy of Sciences of the Czech Republic, Oriental Institute, 1996), pp. 589–603. An important contribution to the study of the linguistic content is made by Muḥassab (*ʿIlm ad-dalāla ʿinda l-ʿarab*) and Michel Lagarde (*Les Secrets de l'invisible. Essai sur le Grand Commentaire de Faḫr al-Dīn al-Rāzī* [Beirut: Dar al-Bouraq, 2008], pp. 175 ff.). On this Qurʾanic commentary itself, see in particular the works of Michel Lagarde (*Index du Grand commentaire de Faḫr al-Dīn al-Rāzī* [Leiden (et al.): Brill, 1996] and *Les Secrets de l'invisible*) and Jacques Jomier, "Les Mafātiḥ al-ghayb de l'Imām Fakhr al-din al-Rāzī: quelques dates, lieux, manuscrits," *Mélanges de l'Institut Dominicain d'Études Orientales du Caire* (MIDEO), vol. 13 (1977): pp. 253–290; id., "The Qu'ranic Commentary of Imām Fakhr al-din al-Rāzī: Its Sources and its Originality," in *International Congress for the Study of the Qurʾan* (Canberra: Australian National University, 1980), pp. 93–111; id., "L'autorité de la révélation et la raison dans le commentaire du Coran de Faḫr al-Dīn al-Rāzī," in *La notion d'autorité au Moyen Age: Islam, Byzance, Occident*, ed. by George Makdisi and Dominique Sourdel (Paris: Presses Universitaires de France, 1982), pp. 245–261; id., "Fakhr al-dīn al-Rāzī (m. 606 H./1210) et les Commentaires du Coran plus anciens," *MIDEO*, vol. 15 (1982): pp. 145–172; see also Arnaldez, *Fakhr al-Dîn al-Râzî*, pp. 75 ff.

91 Faḫr ad-dīn ar-Rāzī, *at-Tafsīr al-kabīr*, vol. 1, p. 21, line 4.

92 On the question of whether *Allāh* is a proper name or a derived name, see Richard

> It has already been proven in the rational sciences (*ʿulūm ʿaqliyya*) that it is only possible to gain knowledge of the species if one has recognized the genus. For the genus is a part of the quiddity of the species. [...] The name, the verb, and the particle are three species of the genus 'word' (*kalima*)—so the investigation must also concern itself with the essence, definition, and particularities of the word. In addition, there are other linguistic expressions similar to 'word,' namely *kalām*, *qawl*, *lafẓ*, *luġa*, and *ʿibāra*.[93]

In his subsequent discussion of these terms, it is clear that Faḫr ad-dīn is citing the definitions and positions primarily from three different areas: that of the philologists in the broadest sense, that of the jurists, and that of the logicians—the *Kitāb al-Awṣat* of Ibn Sīnā is mentioned by name.[94] Throughout this chapter are a few points of thematic contact with the *Maḥṣūl*'s chapter on language—for example, in the question of how *kalām* is to be defined, in the discussion of the fact that linguistic expressions signify mental rather than extramental things, and in the question of why humans need spoken language. There are also occasional overlaps in wording between the respective passages of the two books. Overall however, one gets the impression that the length and depth of this chapter are intended to be complementary to the *Maḥṣūl*, seen for example in the discussion on the definition of "speech" (*kalām*). This applies all the more to the subsequent chapters within the linguistic-theoretical introduction of the *Tafsīr*, as it treats topics that are given little to no attention in the *Maḥṣūl*:

In the *Tafsīr*, following the discussion of the various linguistic expressions related to the "word," Faḫr ad-dīn argues that an examination of (non-distinctive) sounds (*ṣawt*) and (distinctive) phonemes (*ḥurūf*) is necessary, as words can only come about through the latter. He draws upon, among other things,

---

M. Frank, *Beings and Their Attributes: The Teaching of the Basrian School of the Muʿtazila in the Classical Period* (Albany: State University of New York Press, 1978), pp. 55–56.

93 Faḫr ad-dīn ar-Rāzī, *at-Tafsīr al-kabīr*, vol. 1, p. 21, lines 5–22.

94 Ibid., p. 29, lines 19–29. The passage is found in the *Kitāb aš-Šifāʾ* (cf. Ibn Sīnā, *Kitāb aš-Šifāʾ*, *al-Manṭiq*, *al-ʿIbāra*, p. 8, line 8, lines 15 ff.), but to my knowledge not in the *Madḫal* of the *Muḫtaṣar al-awṣat fī l-manṭiq* (cf. Ibn Sīnā, *al-Muḫtaṣar al-awṣat fī l-manṭiq*, *al-Madḫal*, Ms. Istanbul Nuruosmaniye 2763); on the fact that the two titles *al-Awṣat* and *Muḫtaṣar al-awṣat* refer to the same work, see Dimitri Gutas, *Avicenna and the Aristotelian Tradition: Introduction to Reading Avicenna's Philosophical Works. Second, Revised and Enlarged Edition, Including an Inventory of Avicenna's Authentic Works* (Leiden [et al.]: Brill, 2014 [1st edition: 1988]), p. 433.

Ibn Sīnā's findings in his treatment of this topic.[95] Such detailed phonetic and phonological discussions have no equivalent in the *Maḥṣūl*.[96] This portion is followed by a detailed discussion and classification of the three-part categorization of linguistic expressions into *ism*, *fiʿl*, and *ḥarf*. While the *Maḥṣūl* mentions these only in a short passage, in which—as will be shown in Chapter 3, Section 1—the verb and particle receive no further discussion and only a few semantic description criteria are given in relation to the name, their treatment in the *Tafsīr* is much more comprehensive. There the name and the verb as well as—somewhat less extensively—the particle are defined and discussed along with the subtypes and declension of the name and some basics of the verb.[97] In the very detailed discussion of the name, which covers several chapters, it is clear that Faḫr ad-dīn is critically engaging with Zamaḫšarī's *Mufaṣṣal*. Faḫr ad-dīn ar-Rāzī's reception of Zamaḫšarī is a topic in and of itself and certainly requires its own study.[98]

The presentation of linguistic principles in the *Tafsīr* shows—by and large—hardly any overlap with that of the *Maḥṣūl*; the two treatises instead complement one another. A thorough examination of this chapter in the *Tafsīr* on linguistic theory and the reconstruction of the numerous references to discussions and works on grammatical theory—especially to Ibn Ǧinnī's *Ḫaṣāʾiṣ* and Zamaḫšarī's *Mufaṣṣal*—is still a desideratum. Only on the basis of such an investigation would it possible to judge through which linguistic-theoretical lenses Faḫr ad-dīn was looking here. I do not consider judgements of the kind that this introduction was written primarily "from an uṣūlī point of view"[99]—a remark that applies, if at all, only to the first chapter—to be convincing for the following reasons: Firstly, as has already been pointed out, there is hardly any thematic overlap. As Versteegh also notes, Faḫr ad-dīn does not even mention aspects of classical *uṣūl al-fiqh* linguistic theory, such as "the problem of ʿāmm/ḫāṣṣ, the structure of the imperative, the use of metaphors in speech,"[100] in his linguistic introduction to the *Tafsīr*. Secondly, the proportion of investig-

95 On phonetics and phonology in the Arabic tradition, see Bohas, Guillaume, and Kouloughli, *The Arabic linguistic tradition*, pp. 76 ff.

96 Faḫr ad-dīn ar-Rāzī, *at-Tafsīr al-kabīr*, vol. 1, p. 21, lines 25 ff. and in detail pp. 35–37.

97 Ibid., pp. 37–57. On the various criteria of the description, see Owens, *The Foundations of Grammar*, pp. 125 ff. and id., "The Syntactic Basis of Arabic Word Classification," *Arabica*, vol. 36, no. 2 (July 1989): pp. 211–234. On the contents of grammatical theory treatises in general, see for example Bohas et al., *The Arabic linguistic tradition*, pp. 49–72.

98 See also the comments in Chapter 3, Section 1.

99 Versteegh, "The Linguistic Introduction to Rāzī's *Tafsīr*," p. 591.

100 Ibid.

ated topics dealing with grammatical theory and linguistics in this introduction is quite high, namely about 2/3—and this is taking into account that Faḫr ad-dīn does actually make frequent recourse to the positions of jurists in the first chapter. Thirdly, the places where Faḫr ad-dīn adopts the perspective of grammarians over that of legal theorists must also be considered: "When in grammar we say (*naḥw*) *fiʿl* and *fāʿil*, we do not mean what the scholars of legal theory mean by this."[101]—All of this leads to the conclusion that, in my opinion, the influence of legal theory on this linguistic-theoretical introduction to the *Tafsīr* should not be overestimated.

TABLE 2 Comparison of the topics related to linguistic theory in the *Maḥṣūl* and the *Tafsīr*

	Faḫr ad-dīn ar-Rāzī: *al-Maḥṣūl* **I: Vol. 1, pp. 173–418** **II–IV: vol. 2, p. 7–vol. 3, p. 223**	**Faḫr ad-dīn ar-Rāzī: *at-Tafsīr al-kabīr*,** **vol. 1, pp. 21–57**
I. CHAPTERS ON LANGUAGE	1. UNIVERSAL RULES OF LANGUAGE (*al-aḥkām al-kulliya li-luġāt*) a. Examination of the essence of speech (*kalām*) b. Examination of the imposer (*wāḍiʿ*) of language c. On the uses of spoken language[102] d. On meanings[103] e. On how one recognizes that a linguistic expression has been imposed for its meaning	1. Examination of what is connected with the "word" (*kalima*) a. A method of recognizing what linguistic expressions denote: The derivation (*ištiqāq*) b. "Word" (*kalima*) c. "Utterance" (*qawl*) d. "Language" (*luġa*) e. "Linguistic expression" (*lafẓ*) f. "Expression" (*ʿibāra*) g. Relationship between linguistic expression and meaning
		2. Analyses resulting from the (non-distinctive) sounds (*ṣawt*) and the (distinctive) phonemes (*ḥurūf*) and their rules

101 Faḫr ad-dīn ar-Rāzī, *at-Tafsīr al-kabīr*, vol. 1, p. 54.

102 This is a rendering of the content; the actual heading is: "The investigation of that which has been imposed (*mawḍūʿ*) [*in the process of the imposition of language*]," i.e. linguistic expressions, cf. Faḫr ad-dīn ar-Rāzī, *al-Maḥṣūl*, vol. 1, p. 193.

103 Literally "The study of that for which [*the linguistic expressions*] have been imposed," i.e. for the meanings, cf. Faḫr ad-dīn ar-Rāzī, *al-Maḥṣūl*, vol. 1, p. 197.

TABLE 2 Comparison of language theory topics in the *Maḥṣūl* and the *Tafsīr* (*cont.*)

Faḫr ad-dīn ar-Rāzī: *al-Maḥṣūl* **I: Vol. 1, pp. 173–418** **II–IV: vol. 2, p. 7–vol. 3, p. 223**	**Faḫr ad-dīn ar-Rāzī: *at-Tafsīr al-kabīr*,** **vol. 1, pp. 21–57**
2. THE CLASSIFICATION OF LINGUISTIC EXPRESSIONS (*taqsīm al-alfāẓ*) CLASSIFICATION I a. Presentation of the Tripartition of Signification: Introduction and notes[104] b. Logical sub-classification c. Grammatical-theoretical sub-classification d. Logical and legal-theoretical sub-classification e. Classification of the speech act and sentence f. Legal-theoretical sub-classification, i.e. overview of the types of implication CLASSIFICATION II Meta-linguistic classification of linguistic expressions	3. Investigations in connection with the name (*ism*), verb (*fiʿl*), and particle (*ḥarf*) 4. The categories of the name (*ism*)
3. Paronymous names (*al-asmāʾ al-muštaqqa*)	5. On the rules of the generic name (*asmāʾ al-aǧnās*) and the paronymous name (*asmāʾ al-muštaqqa*)
	6. On the classification of the name into declinable (*muʿrab*) and indeclinable (*mabnī*)
	7. The exact presentation of the verb (*fiʿl*)

104 The subdivisions shown here correspond to the systematization of the chapter and not to any subheadings.

TABLE 2 Comparison of language theory topics in the *Maḥṣūl* and the *Tafsīr* (*cont.*)

Faḫr ad-dīn ar-Rāzī: *al-Maḥṣūl* **I: Vol. 1, pp. 173–418** **II–IV: vol. 2, p. 7–vol. 3, p. 223**	**Faḫr ad-dīn ar-Rāzī: *at-Tafsīr al-kabīr*, vol. 1, pp. 21–57**
4. Rules of polyonymy and emphasis (*aḥkām at-tarāduf wa-t-tawkīd*)	
5. Homonymy (*ištirāk*)	
6. Literal and figurative [*linguistic expressions*] (*ḥaqīqa wa-l-maǧāz*)	
7. The discrepancy that can occur between [*the different hermeneutical*] states of linguistic expressions (*at-taʿāruḍu l-ḥāṣilu bayna aḥwāli l-alfāẓ*)	
8. The explanation of those particles for which the need to recognize their meanings is increased in *fiqh* (*tafsīru hurūfin taštaddu l-ḥāǧatu fī l-fiqhi ilā maʿrifati maʿānīhā*)	
9. The way of deriving rulings from the speech of the Mighty and Exalted God and from the speech of the Prophet (*kayfiyyatu l-istidlāli bi-ḫiṭābi llāhi ʿazza wa-ǧalla wa-ḫiṭābi rasūlihī ʿalā l-aḥkām*)	
II. Commandments and prohibitions (*al-awāmir wa-n-nawāhī*)	
III. Generality and particularity (*al-ʿumūm wa-l-ḫuṣūṣ*)	

TABLE 2 Comparison of language theory topics in the *Maḥṣūl* and the *Tafsīr* (*cont.*)

Faḫr ad-dīn ar-Rāzī: *al-Maḥṣūl* I: Vol. 1, pp. 173–418 II–IV: vol. 2, p. 7–vol. 3, p. 223	Faḫr ad-dīn ar-Rāzī: *at-Tafsīr al-kabīr*, vol. 1, pp. 21–57
IV. That which requires explanation and that which has been made clear/explained (*al-muǧmal wa-l-mubayyan*)	

3 The Chapter "The Classification of Linguistic Expressions"

3.1 *Structure*

Following the first sub-chapter's treatment of, *inter alia*, the fundamentals of the history of language, the second sub-chapter of the *Maḥṣūl*'s linguistic portion—"The Classification of Linguistic Expressions" (*fī taqsīm al-alfāẓ*)—provides a concise introduction to linguistic theory and the philosophy of language. In it, Faḫr ad-dīn presents several principles, in two parts, for categorizing different aspects of the linguistic expression or word. The first part (§§1–25), which comprises several subdivisions, makes up the majority of the chapter, while the smaller second part (§§26–28)—not the focus of the present work—discusses and classifies basic meta-linguistic principles but is more akin to an appendix in terms of length.

What follows is a brief overview of this sub-chapter's structure and principles of categorization, followed by a translation of the text. In subsequent parts of this study, I will use this groundwork to carry out a systematic and detailed examination of the individual classifications.

The first part of this sub-chapter of the *Maḥṣūl* begins with a brief presentation of three ways in which a linguistic expression can signify something [§1]: a linguistic expression signifies meaning either [1.] completely or [2.] partially, or it signifies something [3.] that does not belong to that meaning. This brief introduction is then accompanied by several notes (*tanbīhāt*) [§§2–4].[105]

Starting with the first manner of signification, namely signification by congruence (*muṭābaqa*), the linguistic expression is divided into simple (*mufrad*)

105 See Faḫr ad-dīn ar-Rāzī, *al-Maḥṣūl*, vol. 1, pp. 219–220.

and compound (*murakkab*) types [§ 5]. The first of these—the simple congruent linguistic expression—is the starting point for three further sub-classifications. The first sub-classification [§§ 6–11] overviews the basic terminology and concepts of logic and thus equates—as will be shown in detail[106]—to an introduction to the Organon or an outline of its first book, namely the *Madḫal*. The structural principle underlying this logical sub-classification is then used for the next part, as Faḫr ad-dīn himself writes: "Even if this classification (*taqsīm*) actually concerns meanings (*maʿānī*), it is nevertheless of great use (*ʿaẓīmu n-nafʿ*) for linguistic expressions (*alfāẓ*)."[107] Analytical concepts from the field of logic are thus used to structure a grammatical subject area, i.e. linguistic expressions. The second sub-classification [§§ 12–14] examines the simple congruent linguistic expression from the perspective of grammatical theory, introducing fundamental terminology from this discipline such as the three-part classification of the linguistic expression into name (*ism*), verb (*fiʿl*), and particle (*ḥarf*).[108] The third sub-classification [§§ 15–22] outlines the relationships between linguistic expression and meaning in terms of ambiguity and unambiguity, taking into account terms and concepts that primarily originate in the fields of logic and legal methodology.[109]

FIGURE 4 Rough structure of the first categorisation [I]

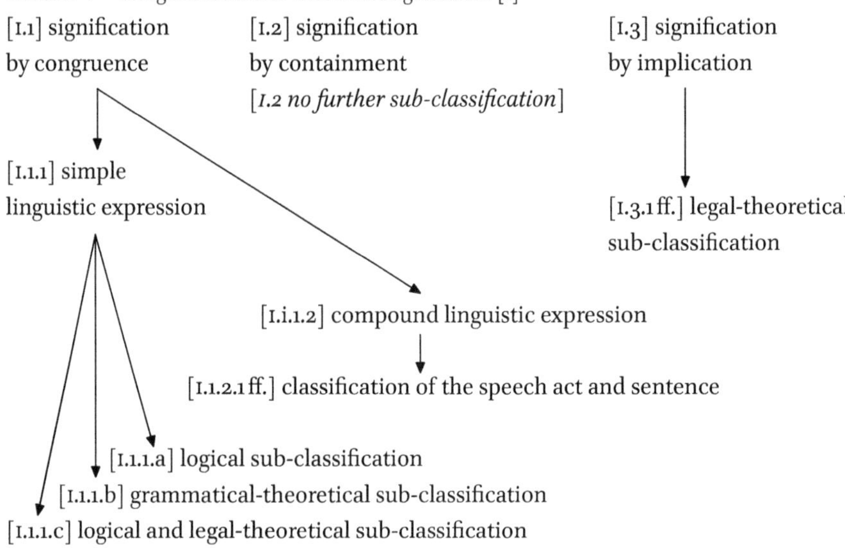

106 See Chapter 2, Section 1.
107 Faḫr ad-dīn ar-Rāzī, *al-Maḥṣūl*, vol. 1, p. 224, lines 7–8.
108 See Chapter 3.
109 See Chapter 4.

Following the subdivision of the simple linguistic expression is an overview of the considerations on compound linguistic expressions [§ 23]; this includes a classification of speech acts and sentence types, of which the declarative sentence is particularly relevant with respect to logic; the concept of the imperative or commandment (*amr*) in legal methodology is also examined in detail.[110]

While no further subdivision is made for the second manner of signification—signification by containment (*taḍammun*)—the categorization of the third manner, i.e. signification by implication (*iltizām*), is particularly complex and relevant to issues of legal methodology. For here are given the various types of implication that can have legal bearing, such as "signification by requirement" (*dalālat al-iqtiḍā'*) and "congruent implication" (*mafhūm al-muwāfaqa*). Some of these are no longer distinguished by name in Faḫr ad-dīn's concept of implication, but instead by how they fit into his new schema.[111]

3.2 *Translation*

TEXT 1: Faḫr ad-dīn ar-Rāzī: *al-Maḥṣūl fī ʿilm uṣūl al-fiqh*. Ed. by Ṭaha Ǧābir Fayāḍ al-ʿAlwānī. Riyāḍ: Ǧāmiʿat al-Imām Muḥammad b. Suʿūd al-Islāmiyya, 1979, vol. 1, pp. 219–236

"[p. 219] On the classification (*taqsīm*) of linguistic expressions (*alfāẓ*). It consists of two parts.

[*i.e. the classification is divided into main parts: Part I (§§ 1–25) with its three subdivisions and the smaller Part II (§§ 26–28)*]

[§ 1]

[I] THE FIRST PART:

The linguistic expression is either such that its signification

[I.1] is considered (*tuʿtabaru*) in relation to the entirety (*tamām*) of that which is named by it (*musammāhu*) [*the linguistic expression*];

[I.2] or in relation to that which intrinsically (*dāḫil*) [*belongs*] to what is named (*musammā*)—insofar as it is like that;

[*i.e. insofar as a (constituent) part of the meaning or quiddity is not signified in a homonymous way, see Chapter 2, Section 3.2.2*]

[I.3] or in relation to that which is extrinsic (*ḫāriǧ*) to what is named—insofar as it is like that

[*i.e. insofar as it is not actually an intrinsic part of the meaning or quiddity, and insofar as it is not signified in a homonymous way*].

110 See Chapter 3.

111 See Chapter 4.

The first [*ad* I.1] is 'congruence' (*al-muṭābaqa*),
the second [*ad* I.2] is 'containment' (*at-taḍammun*),
the third [*ad* I.3] is 'implication' (*al-iltizām*) [*iltizām, literally: becoming adherent*].

[§ 2]

[*ad* I] Notes (*tanbīhāt*):
The first [*note*]: Signification based on imposition (*dalāla waḍʿiyya*) is [*ad* I.1] signification by congruence (*dalālatu l-muṭābaqa*).
[*ad* I.2 and I.3] But as for the remaining two [*significations*], they are based on reasoning (*ʿaqliyya*)—for when a linguistic expression has been imposed for something that has been named, then the mind (*ḏihn*) turns from what is named to that which adheres (*lāzim*) to it [*the named thing*].
And that which adheres (*lāzim*) to it is,
– [*ad* 2] if it intrinsically (*dāḫil*) [*belongs*] to what is named (*musammā*) [*i.e. if it belongs to the meaning or quiddity*], [*signification by*] containment (*taḍammun*)
– [*ad* 3] if it is extrinsic (*ḫāriǧ*) to what is named [*i.e. if it does not belong to the meaning or quiddity*], [*signification by*] implication (*iltizām*).

[§ 3]

[p. 220] The second [*note*]: [*ad* 2] We only said about containment that it is the signification of a part (*ǧuzʾ*) of what is signified by the linguistic expression [*with the qualification*] 'insofar as it is like that' because we want to guard against (*iḥtirāzan*) the linguistic expression signifying by congruence a part of what is named in a homonymous way. [*ad* 3] The same applies to what was said about implication.

[§ 4]

The third [*note*] [→ *restriction of the relationship through implication*]: [*ad* 3] With regard to signification by implication (*iltizām*), external implication (*al-luzūm al-ḫāriǧī*) is not considered because substance (*ǧawhar*) and accident (*ʿaraḍ*) [*indeed*] mutually condition/implicate each other (*mutalāzimān*), but the linguistic expression that signifies one of them is not applied to the other.—However, in the case of two mutually exclusive opposites (*ḍiddāni mutanāfiyāni*), the linguistic expression signifying one of them is sometimes applied to the other, such as the speech of God, the Exalted: [*Qurʾan 42:40*] 'The recompense for an evil deed is an equally evil deed' (*wa-ǧazāʾu sayyiʾatin sayyiʾatun miṯluhā*).
That which is considered [*in terms of signification by implication*] is obviously (*ẓāhiran*) the mental implication (*al-luzūm aḏ-ḏihnī*).
Furthermore, this implication (*luzūm*) [*i.e. the mental implication*] is a condition (*šarṭ*) [*for this manner of signification*], not that which makes [*this manner of signification*] necessary (*lā mūǧib*).

[§ 5]

[p. 221] Now, let us return to part [I.1]—then we say that either

[I.1.1] none of the parts of the linguistic expression signifying by congruence signifies something while it is a part of it—and that is the simple [*linguistic expression*] (*mufrad*), such as *al-abkam* ["the mute"];

[I.1.2] or that each of its parts signifies something while being a part of it—and that is the compound [*linguistic expression*] (*murakkab*);

[I.1.3] or that one part signifies while another does not, but this does not occur (*ġayr wāqiʿ*) because it represents the combination (*ḍamm*) of something unusual (*muhmal*) with something common (*mustaʿmal*)—and this is not useful (*ġayr mufīd*).

[§ 6]

[*The first sub-classification, I.1.1.A*]

But as far as the [*ad* I.1.1] simple [*linguistic expression signifying by congruence*] is concerned, it can be subdivided according to three aspects [*Here begins the first sub-classification of the simple linguistic expression; the second begins at § 12, the third at § 15*]:

[I.1.1.A] The first [*aspect, i.e. the first sub-classification of the simple linguistic expression*] is that the simple [*linguistic expression*] is either [I.1.1.A.1] such that the conceptualization (*taṣawwur*) of its meaning itself prevents sharing in it (*šarika*), and that is the particular (*ǧuzʾī*) [*linguistic expression*]; [I.1.1.A.2] or [*the conceptualization of its meaning*] does not prevent [*sharing in it*], and that is the universal (*kullī*) [*linguistic expression*].

[§ 7]

Furthermore, the universal quiddity is either [I.1.1.A.2.1] the entire quiddity, or [I.1.1.A.2.2] a part (*ǧuzʾ*) of it, or [I.1.1.A.2.3] external to it (*ḫāriǧan ʿanhā*) [*i.e. 'that which is considered in relation to the universal quiddity is either the entire quiddity, a part of it, or external to it'*]. The first [*ad* I.1.1.A.2.1] is that which is said in answer [*to the question*] 'what is it?'; the second [*ad* I.1.1.A.2.2] is the essential (*ḏātī*), and the third [*ad* I.1.1.A.2.3] is the accidental (*ʿaraḍī*).

[*ad* I.1.1.A.2.1] As for a quiddity, it is either [I.1.1.A.2.1.1] a quiddity of a single [*thing*] or [I.1.1.A.2.1.2] a quiddity of [*several*] things. The first [*ad* I.1.1.A.2.1.1] is the quiddity according to specificity [*i.e. the entire, particularizing specification of a thing*] (*bi-ḥasabi l-ḫuṣūṣiyya*). [p. 222] As for the second [*ad* I.1.1.A.2.1.2], those things must be such that each one of them differs from every other one in individuality (*fī t-taʿayyun*).

[I.1.1.A.2.1.2.1] Furthermore, that aspect in which they differ from each other either occurs in something that belongs to their essential qualities (*muḫālafatu baʿḍihā baʿḍan fī šayʾin mina ḏ-ḏātiyāyāt*), or [I.1.1.A.2.1.2.2] it does not occur.

[*ad* I.1.1.A.2.1.2.1] If it is the first, then the complete extent (*qadr*) of that which they have in common (*muštarak baynahā*) with regard to the things (*umūr dāḫila fīhā*) that they comprise is the entire common quiddity (*tamām al-māhiyya al-muštaraka*)—for that which is more general (*aʿamm*) than it is not the complete common [*quiddity*]; and that which is more specific (*aḫaṣṣ*) than it is not the common [*quiddity*].

As for that which resembles it (*yusāwīhi*),

[I.1.1.A.2.1.2.1.1] if it resembles it in terms of quiddity, then it is that [*i.e. it pertains to the entire common quiddity*], and nothing else.

[I.1.1.A.2.1.2.1.2] if it resembles it in terms of implication (*luzūm*), but not in terms of what is understood by it (*mafhūm*) [*i.e. not the entire common quiddity*], then it is not the full extent of the common.

[*ad* I.1.1.A.2.1.2.1.2] If it is the second, then the full extent of what they have in common is each individual's (*bi-ʿaynihī*) full quiddity—since if each one of them would have a different essential aspect beyond the common extent, the difference (*muḫālafa*) between them would not only be due to individuality (*bi-taʿayyun*), but [*also*] due to essential qualities (*bi-ḏ-ḏātiyyāt*).

It has [*however*] already been assumed (*wa-qad furiḍa*) that there is no difference in the essential qualities—that is a contradiction (*ḫulf*).

[§ 8]

[*ad* I.1.1.A.2.2] As for the essential (*ḏātī*), it is either

[I.1.1.A.2.2.1] the entire common part (*tamām al-ǧuzʾ al-muštarak*), and this is the genus (*ǧins*); [p. 223] or

[I.1.1.A.2.2.2] it is the entire part that distinguishes components of the genus, and this is the specific difference (*faṣl*) or

[I.1.1.A.2.2.3] the totality resulting from the two (*al-maǧmūʿ al-ḥāṣil*) [*i.e. of the genus and specific difference*], and that is the species (*nawʿ*);

[I.1.1.A.2.2.4] or it does not act in the way [*that it has to do with the entire part*]; then it is the part of the part (*ǧuzʾu l-ǧuzʾu*): that is either the genus of the genus (*ǧinsu l-ǧins*), or the genus of the specific difference (*ǧinsu l-faṣl*), or the specific difference of the genus (*faṣlu l-ǧins*), or the specific difference of the specific difference (*faṣlu l-faṣl*).

[§ 9]

Then the genera are arranged in ascending order (*mutaṣāʿidatan*) and they end with their ascent (*irtiqāʾ*) at the genus that has no genus above it—and that is the genus of the genera (*ǧinsu l-aǧnās*).

The species (*anwāʿ*) are arranged in descending order down to the species that has no more species under it—and that is the species of the species (*nawʿu l-anwāʿ*).

[§ 10]

[*ad* I.1.1.A.2.3 (see § 7)] As for the attribute (*waṣf*), which is outside the quiddity, it is categorized according to two aspects:

[I.1.1.A.2.3.1] The first [*aspect*] is when that external [*attribute*] adheres either [I.1.1.A.2.3.1.1] to the quiddity (*māhiyya*) or [I.1.1.A.2.3.1.2] to existence (*wuǧūd*), or [I.1.1.A.2.3.1.3] it adheres to neither.

[*ad* I.1.1.A.2.3.1.1–2] Furthermore, the adhering [*attribute*] can [*adhere*] to each of the two classes [*quiddity or existence*] through an intermediate or [*adhere*] without [p. 224] an intermediate. That which adheres through an intermediate ends with the [*adhering attribute*] that has no intermediate—otherwise a circular argument (*ad-dawr aw at-tasalsul*) would follow.

[*ad* I.1.1.A.2.3.1.3] The non-adhering can disappear quickly (*sarīʿu z-zawāl*) and it can disappear slowly (*baṭīʾ*).

[I.1.1.A.2.3.2] The second [*aspect*] is when the external attribute is considered either [I.1.1.A.2.3.2.1] to be peculiar to a single species (*muḫtaṣṣun bi-nawʿin wāḥidin*), not occurring in another—and this is the proprium (*ḫāṣṣa*); or [I.1.1.A.2.3.2.2] to exist (*mawǧūd*) in it and another [*species*]—and that is the general accident (*ʿaraḍ ʿāmm*).

[§ 11]

[*Conclusion of the first sub-classification of the simple linguistic expression—transition to the second sub-classification*]

Even if this classification (*taqsīm*) actually concerns meanings (*maʿānī*), it is nevertheless of great use (*ʿaẓīmu n-nafʿ*) for linguistic expressions (*alfāẓ*).

[§ 12]

[*The second sub-classification, I.1.1.B*]

[I.1.1.B] [p. 225] The second category of the simple linguistic expression [*i.e. the second aspect, the second sub-classification of the simple linguistic expression; the first sub-classification begins at § 6, the third at § 15*]

It [*i.e. the simple linguistic expression*] is either such [I.1.1.B.1] that its meaning (*maʿnāhu*) possesses what can be known/the knowable (*maʿlūmiyya*) independently (*mustaqill*); or [I.1.1.B.2] it is not so—the second is the particle (*ḥarf*).

[*ad* I.1.1.B.1] The first is either [I.1.1.B.1.1] such that the linguistic expression signifying it denotes a particular time for its meaning—and that is the verb (*fiʿl*); or [I.1.1.B.1.2] it does not denote [*a particular time*]—and that is the name (*ism*).

[§ 13]

[*ad* I.1.1.B.1.2] The name is categorized according to two aspects:

[I.1.1.B.1.2.1] The first [*aspect*] is when the name,

[I.1.1.B.1.2.1.1] if it is a name for the particular (*li-l-ǧuzʾī*), [I.1.1.B.1.2.1.1.1] then if it is concealed (*muḍmar*), it belongs to the pronouns (*muḍmarāt*); [I.1.1.B.1.2.1.1.2] and if it is manifest (*muẓhar*), it is a proper name (*ʿalam*).

[I.1.1.B.1.2.1.2] [p. 226] If it is a name for the universal (*li-l-kullī*), then it is either a name for the quiddity itself (*li-nafsi l-māhiyya*), like the linguistic expression 'blackness' (*ka-lafẓi s-sawād*)—that is what is called the 'generic name' (*ismu l-ǧins*) according to the convention of grammarians; or [*a name*] for the fact that some thing is described (*li-mawṣūfiyyati amrin mā*) by an attribute (*bi-ṣifatin*)—and that is the derived name (*ism muštaqq*), like the linguistic expression 'beater' (*ḍārib*). For that which is understood from it is that something is unknown (*maǧhūl*) with respect to the signification of this linguistic expression, but that one knows that it is described (*mawṣūf*) by the attribute (*ṣifa*) of beating (*ḍarb*).

[§ 14]

[I.1.1.B.1.2.2] The second [*aspect*] is when the name signifies a meaning and does not denote a specific time—this occurs according to three parts:

[I.1.1.B.1.2.2.1] What is named can be a time itself (*nafsu z-zamān*)—like the linguistic expression 'time' (*zamān*), 'today' (*al-yawm*), or 'tomorrow' (*al-ġad*);

[I.1.1.B.1.2.2.2] one of the parts [*of what is named*] can be time, like 'morning drink' (*iṣṭibāḥ*)—this [*defines*] the derivation (*taṣrīf*);

[I.1.1.B.1.2.2.3] or it is neither time nor composed of time, like blackness vel sim.

[§ 15]

[*The third sub-classification, I.1.1.C*]

[I.1.1.C] [p. 227] The third category of the simple linguistic expression [*see § 6 and § 12*] is either such

[I.1.1.C.1] that the linguistic expression and the meaning are [*each*] one [*i.e. each linguistic expression has one meaning*];

[I.1.1.C.2] or that they are both multiple (*yatakaṯṯarāni*);

[I.1.1.C.3] or that the linguistic expression is multiple, while the meaning is one;

[I.1.1.C.4] or vice versa [*i.e. there is one linguistic expression with several meanings*].

[§ 16]

[*ad* I.1.1.C.1] As far as the first part is concerned,

– [I.1.1.C.1.1] it [*i.e. the combination of one linguistic expression and one meaning*] is called a proper name (*ʿalam*) if its conceptualization (*taṣawwur*) itself prevents sharing in it (*šarika*), and it is manifest (*muẓhar*) [*in contrast to the personal pronoun*];

– [I.1.1.C.1.2] if [*the conceptualization*] does not prevent [*sharing in it*], then there appears in these places, if it [*i.e. the naming*] occurs in an equivalent way, what is called a synonym (*mutawāṭiʾ*; synonymy: *tawāṭuʾ*) [*what is meant here is Aristotelian synonymy*].

– [.1.1.C.1.3] or [*if it occurs*] not (*aw lā*) in an equivalent way, then [*it is called*] ambiguous (*mušakkak*; ambiguity: *taškīk*), just like [*the linguistic expression*] 'existence' (*wuǧūd*), where that which it [*i.e. the linguistic expression 'existence'*] signifies is more suitable for the necessary [*i.e. for the necessarily existing*] than for the contingent (*mumkin*) [*what is meant here is focal homonymy/pros hen homonymy*].

[§ 17]

[*ad* I.1.1.C.2] [p. 228] As for [*the case*] in which the linguistic expressions and meanings are multiple, these are heteronyms (*mutabāyina*; heteronymy: *tabāyun*), whether those things that are named differ in terms of their essences (*bi-ḏawātihā*), or whether one [*linguistic expression*] is an attribute (*ṣifa*) of the other, such as *sayf* ('sword') and *ṣārim* ('sharp'), or an attribute of the attribute, such as *nāṭiq* ('rational') and *faṣīḥ* ('eloquent'/'correct' in terms of language use).

[§ 18]

[*ad* I.1.1.C.3] As for [*the case*] in which the linguistic expressions are multiple while the meaning is one, these are polyonymous linguistic expressions (*alfāẓ mutarādifa*; lit. 'linguistic expressions corresponding to each other'), whether they come from one language or from many languages.

[§ 19]

[*ad* I.1.1.C.4] As for [*the case*] in which the linguistic expression is single while the meanings are multiple, this linguistic expression is either such

[I.1.1.C.4.1] that it was first imposed for one meaning, then transferred from this to another meaning;

[I.1.1.C.4.2] or it was imposed for both [*meanings*] at the same time.

[*ad* I.1.1.C.4.1] As regards the first [*case*],

it is [I.1.1.C.4.1.1] either such that this transfer does not [*result*] from a relationship (*munāsaba*) between the [*second meaning to which the linguistic expression was*] transferred (*manqūl ilayhi*) and the [*meaning*] from which [*it*] was transferred (*manqūl ʿanhū*)—and this is called improvised (*murtaǧal*).

[I.1.1.C.4.1.2] or [*the transfer results*] from a relationship, and this case is either such

[I.1.1.C.4.1.2.1] that—after the transfer—the signification of the [*second meaning to which the linguistic expression was*] transferred (*manqūl ilayhi*) is stronger (*aqwā*) for the linguistic expression than the signification of the [*meaning*] from which [*it*] was transferred;

[I.1.1.C.4.1.2.2] or this is not so.

[*ad* I.1.1.C.4.1.2.1] If it is the first, the linguistic expression, in relation to the [*second meaning to which it was*] transferred (*manqūl ilayhi*), is called a 'transferred linguistic expression' (*lafẓ manqūl*).

[I.1.1.C.4.1.2.1.1] [p. 229] Furthermore, if the transferrer (*nāqil*) [*of the meaning*] is a legislator (*šāriʿ*), it [*the transferred linguistic expression*] is called a 'legal/law-related linguistic expression' (*lafẓ šarʿī*);

[I.1.1.C.4.1.2.1.2] or [*the transferrer of the meaning*] is a representative of a [*kind of*] linguistic usage (*ahl al-ʿurf*) [*i.e. a speech community with specific/different terminology*]. The linguistic usage (*ʿurf*) is either

[I.1.1.C.4.1.2.1.2.1] general (*ʿāmm*), like the linguistic expression *dābba* [*with the meanings 'crawling animal' and 'quadruped'/'beast of burden'*];

[I.1.1.C.4.1.2.1.2.2] or specific (*ḫāṣṣa*), such as the linguistic conventions/technical terms (*iṣṭilāḥāt*) that each group (*ṭāʾifa*) of scholars (*ahl al-ʿilm*) has.

[*ad* I.1.1.C.4.1.2.2] Or if it is not the case that the signification with regard to the [*second meaning to which the linguistic expression was*] transferred (*manqūl ilayhi*) is stronger (*aqwā*) than the signification with regard to the [*meaning*] from which [*it*] was transferred, then that linguistic expression

[I.1.1.C.4.1.2.2.1] in relation to the first imposure is called a 'literal [*linguistic expression*]' (*ḥaqīqī*);

[I.1.1.C.4.1.2.2.2] and in relation to the second [imposure] a 'figurative [*linguistic expression*]' (*maǧāz*).

[*ad* I.1.1.C.4.1] Furthermore, the types (*ǧihāt*) of transfer are many. Their number includes similarity (*mušābaha*); that is that which is called 'borrowed' (*mustaʿār*) in a specific way.

[§ 20]

[*ad* I.1.1.C.4.2] Or if the linguistic expression was imposed for two meanings at the same time, then [p. 230] in the intention (*irāda*) of that linguistic expression either

[I.1.1.C.4.2.1] there are both [*meanings*] in the same way (*ʿalā s-sawīya*) [*i.e. neither meaning predominates over the other, but both are equally probable*]

[I.1.1.C.4.2.2] or not in the same way.

[*ad* I.1.1.C.4.2.1] If [*both meanings*] are [*intended*] in the same way, then the single linguistic expression (*lafẓa*) is called

[I.1.1.C.4.2.1.1] a 'homonym' (*muštarak*; homonymy: *ištirāk*) with regard to both [*meanings*] at the same time (*maʿan*);

[I.1.1.C.4.2.1.2] and 'requiring explanation' (*muǧmal; lit. "that which is gathered together without distinction"*) with regard to either of the two [*meanings*].

[*ad* I.1.1.C.4.2.1.1] Due to the fact that it is known that the linguistic expression was imposed for this [*meaning*] alone and for that [*meaning*] alone, it is homonymous (*muštarak*) in this respect;

[*ad* I.1.1.C.4.2.1.2] or, if it is not known whether what is intended by it is this or that, it is certainly in need of explanation (*muǧmal*).

[*ad* I.1.1.C.4.2.2] As regards [*the case*] in which the signification of one of the two meanings by the linguistic expression is stronger, the linguistic expression

[I.1.1.C.4.2.2.1] is called 'obvious' (*ẓāhir*) as regards the predominant (*rāǧiḥ*) [*meaning*]

[I.1.1.C.4.2.2.2] and *muʾawwal* (*that which is to be explained; i.e. in need of justification*) in relation to the inferior (*marǧūḥ*) meaning [*i.e. should the interpreter decide against the* ẓāhir *meaning and in favor of the less obvious meaning when analyzing the text, this requires a justification*].

[§ 21]

Note (*tanbīh*):

[*ad* I.1.1.C.1–3; *see §15*] The first three sub-items have in common the absence of homonymy (*ištirāk*); they are thus 'unambiguous' (*nuṣūṣ*) [*as concerns their meanings*].

[*ad* I.1.1.C.4] But as far as the fourth [*point*] is concerned, it is categorized

[a] [corresponds to I.1.1.C.4.2.2.1] into the circumstance where the denotation (*ifāda*) of one of the two meanings [*by the linguistic expression*] prevails over the denotation of the second meaning—and this is the 'obvious' (*ẓāhir*) [*meaning*];

[b] [corresponds to I.1.1.C.4.2.1.2] [p. 231] and into the circumstance where it does not act in this way; that is the [*linguistic expression*] that [*denotes two meanings*] in equal measure—and that is the [*meaning*] that requires explanation (*muǧmal*); [corresponds to I.1.1.C.4.2.2.2] or [*one of the mean-*

ings] is inferior, and that is the *mu'awwal* [*meaning*] (*that which is to be explained; i.e. in need of justification*).

[§ 22]

Thus, the *naṣṣ* and *ẓāhir* [*meanings*] have in common superiority [*over an inferior meaning*]. However, the *naṣṣ* [*meaning*] is a predominant [*meaning*] that prevents conflict (*naqīḍ*) [*with another meaning*], while the *ẓāhir* [*meaning*] is a predominant [*meaning*] that does not prevent conflict [*i.e. the* ẓāhir *meaning exists alongside the* mu'awwal *meaning, while the* naṣṣ *meaning is not opposed by any other meaning for a particular linguistic expression*].

This aspect, shared by them [naṣṣ *and* ẓāhir], is what is called 'fixed/unambiguous' (*muḥkam*), and so this is the genus of the two species *naṣṣ* and *ẓāhir*. That which does not claim superiority is that which is unclear (*mutašābih*), and so this is the genus of the two species *muǧmal* and *mu'awwal*.

[§ 23]

[*ad* I.1.2; *see* §5] As for the compound [*linguistic expression*], we say that the compound linguistic expression (*lafẓ murakkab*)—as stated above—comes about from the need to get [*others*] to understand (*ifhām*).

Speech (*qawl*), that lets [*one*] understand (*mufhim*), is either such

[I.1.2.1] that it indicates (*an yufīda*) in a primary way (*awwaliyyatan*) the striving for something (*ṭalab aš-šay'*)

[I.1.2.2] or does not indicate it [*in a primary way*].

[*ad* I.1.2.1] If it is the former, it is either such

[I.1.2.1.1] that it [*i.e. speech*] indicates the striving to name the quiddity of a thing (*māhiyyatu š-šay'*), and that is inquiry (*istifhām*); or

[I.1.2.1.2: *Consideration of the hierarchy between the interlocutors*] the endeavour to achieve (*taḥṣīl*) [*something*], and that is

[I.1.2.1.2.1] from a position of superiority (*isti'lā'*)—the commandment/imperative (*amr*);

[I.1.2.1.2.2] and—from a position of obedience/submissiveness (*ḫuḍū'*)—the question (*su'āl*);

[I.1.2.1.2.3] [p. 232] and—from a position of mutual equality—the request (*iltimās*).

[*ad* I.1.2.1.2.1–3] In this way [*according to these three types of hierarchy*] also functions speech that [*aims to*] effect cessation (*ṭalab al-imtinā'*).

[*ad* I.1.2.2] As for the speech that lets [*one*] understand (*al-qawl al-mufhim*) that does not in a primary way (*awwaliyyatan*) indicate striving (*ṭalab*) for something,

[I.1.2.2.1] it carries with it either belief (*taṣdīq*) and disbelief (*takḏīb*), and that is the declarative sentence (*ḫabar*);

[I.1.2.2.2] or it does not act in this way, like the wish (*tamannin*), the hope/expectation (*tarağğin*), the oath (*qasam*), the address/exclamation (*nidāʾ*). This category (*qism*) [*ad* I.1.2.2.2] is called 'notification' (*tanbīh*) to distinguish it from another [*category*]. The species of the genus of notification are identified through induction (*istiqrāʾ*), not through limitation (*ḥaṣr*).

[§ 24]

This has all been the categorization of signification by congruence [*ad* I.1].

[§ 25]

[*ad* I.3] [*The categorization of signification by implication*]

[p. 232] With regard to the categorization of signification by implication, we say:

The meaning is obtained from signification by implication [*as follows*]:

[I.3.1] either it is obtained from the meanings of simple linguistic expressions (*min maʿānī l-alfāẓi l-mufradati*) or

[I.3.2] from the state of their composition (*min ḥāli tarkībihā*).

[*ad* I.3.] The first has two categories (*qismāni*) because the meaning signified by implication is either

[*ad* I.3.1] a condition (*šarṭ*) for the meaning signified by congruence, or

[*ad* I.3.2] follows (*tābiʿ*) from it [*i.e. the meaning signified by congruence*].

[*ad* I.3.1] If it is the first, then it is called 'signification by requirement' (*dalālat al-iqtiḍāʾ*).

[p. 233] Furthermore, the nature of that condition can [*be such that it*]

[I.3.1.1] is based on reasoning (*ʿaqliyyatan*) [*i.e. this implication occurs by rational deduction*], as in [*Muḥammad's*] words "Error (*ḫaṭaʾ*) and forgetfulness (*nisyān*) have been removed from my *umma*": for reasoning shows us that the meaning can only be correct if we find the legal ruling (*al-ḥukm aš-šarʿī*) concealed within it.

[I.3.1.2] It can also occur based on legal (*šarʿiyyatan*) considerations, as when one says "By God, I will certainly manumit this slave"; for this implies having acquired possession (*taḥṣīl al-milk*), because the fulfilment (*wafāʾ*) of this speech [*i.e. this promise*] in a legal manner is only possible afterwards [*i.e. after the acquisition of the slave by the speaker*].

[*ad* I.3.2] As for [*the case*] in which [*the implied meaning*] follows from the composition [*of linguistic expressions*], it belongs either

[I.3.2.1] to that which completes this meaning or

[I.3.2.2] to that which does not [*complete*] it.

[*ad* I.3.2.1] [p. 234] The first is like how the prohibition against saying "Fie!" [*i.e. verbally abusing*] (*taḥrīm at-taʾfīf*) indicates the prohibition against beating (*taḥrīm aḍ-ḍarb*) for the one who does not establish this by means of *qiyās* (*ʿinda man lā yaṯbutuhū bi-l-qiyās*).

[*ad* I.3.2.2] In the second case, what is signified by implication is either

[I.3.2.2.1] affirmative (*ṯubūtiyyan*) or

[I.3.2.2.2] negative (*ʿadamiyyan*).

[*ad* I.3.2.2.1] The first corresponds to the words of God [Qurʾan 2:187] "Now have relations with them" (*fa-l-āna bāširūhunna*). This extends to the moment at which the white thread (*al-ḫayṭ al-abyaḍ*) can be discerned; so it follows with regard to one who enters the state of great ritual impurity (*aṣbaḥa ǧunuban*) that his fasting is not impaired. Otherwise, it would necessarily follow that coitus (*waṭʾ*) would be forbidden in another part of the night to the extent that ablution could take place.

[*ad* I.3.2.2.2] As for the second, it is [*the question of*] whether something being explicitly mentioned allows one to assume the negation [*of the legal ruling that is*] omitted [*from the statement*] (*anna taḫṣīṣa š-šayʾi bi-ḏ-ḏikri hal yadullu ʿalā nafīhi ʿammā ʿadāhu*)—God knows …

[§ 26]

[II] [p. 235] The second part of the categorization of linguistic expressions

The signifying linguistic expression is [II.1] either such that what it signifies is a linguistic expression, or [II.2] it is not such. The second case is not taken into account in our study.

[*ad* II.1] [*In the case where*] what it signifies (*madlūluhū*) is a linguistic expression, [*the signified linguistic expression*] is either [II.1.1] a simple linguistic expression or [II.1.2] a compound linguistic expression. Both are either such [II.1.1.1]/[II.1.2.1] that they signify a meaning, or such [II.1.1.2]/[II.1.2.2] that they do not signify a meaning—this produces four [*types*].

[§ 27]

[*ad* II.1.1.1] One is when the linguistic expression constitutes a simple linguistic expression that signifies a simple meaning. This is the linguistic expression *kalima* and its types (*anwāʿ*) and classes (*aṣnāf*), because the linguistic expression *kalima* encompasses (*yatanāwalu*) the linguistic expression *ism*, which is a simple linguistic expression; and it encompasses the linguistic expression 'man' (*raǧul*), which is a simple linguistic expression that signfies a simple meaning. This applies to all (*ǧamīʿ*) names of linguistic expressions (*asmāʾ al-alfāẓ*), such as speech/utterance (*qawl*), speech (*kalām*), commandment/imperative (*amr*) and prohibition (*nahy*), general and specific (*ʿāmm wa-ḫāṣṣ*) [*name*], and the like (*wa-amṯālihā*).

[*ad* II.1.2.1] [p. 236] A second of these is when the linguistic expression constitutes a compound linguistic expression that is based on a compound meaning (*mawḍūʿ*); this linguistic expression is a 'declarative sentence' (*ḫabar*), because

it includes your utterance 'Zayd is [a] standing [one]' (*Zaydun qāʾimun*). This is a compound linguistic expression that signifies a compound meaning.
[*ad* II.1.1.2] A third of these is when the linguistic expression constitutes a simple linguistic expression that is not the basis of a meaning; this is a 'letter of the alphabet' (*ḥarf al-muʿǧam*), for it encompasses every single letter, and those letters do not signify anything (*lā yufīdu šayʾan*).—If you should say: Is it not as they said, that the linguistic expression 'alif' is a name for (temporal) expansion (*mudda*)? I say: By my words 'the letter does not signify anything' I refer to nothing other than that (temporal) expansion (*mudda*) itself, and this is how it is with the other letters.
[*ad* II.1.2.2] A fourth of these is when the linguistic expression constitutes a compound linguistic expression that is not the basis of a meaning. It is most likely (*ašbahū annahū*) that [*this kind*] does not exist (*ġayru mawǧūdin*), because composition occurs only for the sake of communicating/producing meaning (*ifāda*); so where there is no communication/production of meaning, there is no composition.

[§ 28]

Know that there are obscure details (*daqāʾiq ġāmiḍa*) in the study of the quiddity of the name, the verb, and the particle, which we have already mentioned in the book *al-Muḥarrar fī daqāʾiqi n-naḥw* ('Precise Exposition Concerning the Details of Grammar')."

CHAPTER 2

Analysis of the Introduction of the First Part [ad §§1–5] and the Logical Sub-Classification [§§6–11]

In this section, we will situate the first sub-classification [I.1.1.A; §§6–11] of the *Maḥṣūl*'s linguistic chapter within its logical context and examine it in order to understand the manifold references that the *Maḥṣūl* makes to Avicennian and Peripatetic logic. Then we will perform a detailed analysis of the introductory portion [§§1–5], with its outline of and cursory comments on the Tripartition of Signification, looking into the history of its development.

1 An Introduction to the Logic of the Avicennian *Madḫal* Genre in the *Maḥṣūl*

As mentioned previously, Faḫr ad-dīn divides the congruent linguistic expression into simple (*mufrad*) and compound (*murakkab*) types [§5], taking the simple congruent linguistic expression as the starting point for three further sub-classifications which, on closer inspection, originate in different disciplines.

The description that Faḫr ad-dīn gives for the *lafẓ mufrad* and the *lafẓ murakkab*—that the simple is such that "none of the parts of the linguistic expression signifying by congruence signifies something while it is a part of it" (*ḥīna huwa ǧuzʾuhū*), and that the compound is such that "each of its parts signifies something while being a part of it"[1]—arises from a long debate that has its origins in the definition of the name (ὄνομα/*ism*) in *De Interpretatione* 16a20–21, the second book of the Aristotelian Organon. There it says that the name is such that "none of its parts signifies on its own" (*wa-laysa wāḥidan min aǧzāʾihā dāllan ʿalā infirādihī* / ἧς μηδὲν ἐστὶ σημαντικὸν κεχωρισμένον).[2]

1 Faḫr ad-dīn ar-Rāzī, *al-Maḥṣūl*, vol. 1, p. 221, lines 2–4.

2 Aristotle (*De Int.* 16a19–21), *Aristotelis Categoriae et Liber de Interpretatione*, ed. by Minio-Paluello; *an-Naṣṣ al-kāmil li-Manṭiq Arisṭū*, ed. by Ǧabr, vol. 1, p. 107; *Manṭiq Arisṭū*, ed. by ʿAbd ar-Raḥmān Badawī (al-Kuwayt: Wikālat al-Maṭbūʿāt, 1980), vol. 1, p. 100. "The name (*ism*) is [§1] a linguistic expression (*lafẓa*), [§2] which, by convention (*bi-tawāṭuʾ*), [§3] signifies [§4] and is detached from time (*muǧarradatun mina z-zamān*). [§5] None of its parts signifies on its own (*ʿalā infirādihī*)." Arabic: *fa-l-ismu huwa lafẓatun dāllatun bi-tawāṭuʾin muǧarradatun*

 | DOI:10.1163/9789004736016_004

Like Faḫr ad-dīn, Ibn Sīnā had previously emphasized that the part as a part does not signify:[3] "Its part (*ǧuzʾuhū*) does not actually signify (*bi-l-fiʿl*) anything at all while it is its part (*ḥīna huwa ǧuzʾuhū*)."[4] In the word *insān* (person), for example, the parts *in* and *sān* do not signify "two parts of the meaning 'person' (*al-insān*)"[5] in such a way that the overall meaning comes about as a result of the compounding of these two parts of the linguistic expression; rather, something only signifies when it is "a linguistic expression standing for itself (*qāʾiman bi-nafsihī*)."[6] The compounding of such linguistic expressions that 'stand for themselves' into word and sentence structures is then ultimately what is understood to be the 'compound linguistic expression.'[7]

---

mina z-zamāni wa-laysa wāḥidan min aǧzāʾihā dāllan ʿalā infirādihī. Greek: ὄνομα μὲν οὖν ἐστὶ φωνὴ σηεμαντκὴ κατὰ συνθήκην ἄνευ χρόνου, ἧς μηδὲν μέρος ἐστὶ σημαντικὸν κεχωρισμένον. For an interpretation of ἧς μηδὲν μέρος ἐστὶ σημαντικὸν κεχωρισμένον, see Hermann Weidemann, "Anmerkungen," pp. 160–166; on simple linguistic expressions in Ibn Sīnā, see also Shams C. Inati, "Ibn Sina on Single Expressions," pp. 148 ff.

3 The addition "as a part" or "as long as it is a part" did not originate with Ibn Sīnā, but is found in even earlier scholars, see e.g. Abū Naṣr al-Fārābī, "Šarḥ al-ʿIbāra," in *al-Manṭiqiyyāt li-l-Fārābī*, ed. by Moḥammad Taqī Dānešpažūh (Qom: Maktabat-e Āyatollāh al-ʿAẓmī al-Marʿašī an-Naǧafī, 1988–1989/90 [1408–1410 h.š.]), vol. 2, p. 16, line 18.

4 Ibn Sīnā, *Kitāb aš-Šifāʾ, al-Manṭiq, al-Madḫal* 1.5, p. 26, line 5.

5 Ibid., p. 25, line 6; Faḫr ad-dīn's example of this is *abkam* ('mute'). Al-Fārābī also uses *abkam* to illustrate the simple linguistic expression, see "Šarḥ al-ʿIbāra," p. 17 and p. 41.

6 Ibn Sīnā, *Kitāb aš-Šifāʾ, al-Manṭiq, al-Madḫal* 1.5, p. 26, line 8. Due to a different understanding of what a *lafẓ* is, Ibn Sīnā is critical of expressions such as "the linguistic expression signifies this or that *per se*"; the expression *qāʾiman bi-nafsihī* replaces this formulation (Ibn Sīnā, *Kitāb aš-Šifāʾ, al-Manṭiq, al-Madḫal* 1.5, p. 25, line 15; cf. al-Fārābī, "Šarḥ al-ʿIbāra," p. 16, line 18). In contrast to al-Fārābī, according to whom a *lafẓ* is always a signifying word (al-Fārābī, "Šarḥ al-ʿIbāra," p. 15, line 13), a *lafẓ* according to Ibn Sīnā can also be a non-signifying sequence of letters (cf. Ibn Sīnā, *Kitāb aš-Šifāʾ, al-Manṭiq, al-ʿIbāra*, p. 9, lines 6–8).

These differing views manifest themselves in the question of the translation of φωνή in the Aristotelian definition of the name, see al-Fārābī, "Šarḥ al-ʿIbāra," p. 15, line 7–p. 16, line 7; Ibn Sīnā, *Kitāb aš-Šifāʾ, al-Manṭiq, al-ʿIbāra*, p. 8, line 13–p. 10, line 5, see also F.W. Zimmermann, introduction to id., *Al-Farabi's Commentary and Short Treatise on Aristotle's* De Interpretatione, translation with introduction and commentaries by F.W. Zimmermann (New York: Oxford University Press, 1981), p. lxxiv. For the same reason, Ibn Sīnā rejects the qualification that some have added to the definition of the simple linguistic expression—namely, that the part of the expression signifies "nothing of the total meaning" (*maʿnā l-kulli*); see Ibn Sīnā, *Kitāb aš-Šifāʾ, al-Manṭiq, al-Madḫal* 1.5, p. 25, line 11–p. 26, line 2.

7 Ibid., p. 24, lines 13–17: "[…] just as when we say [*the two linguistic expressions*] 'the person' (*al-insān*) and 'a scribe' (*kātib*) in our statement 'the person is a scribe' (*al-insanu kātibun*). For the linguistic expression (*lafẓa*) 'person' in it [*i.e. in the statement 'the person is a scribe'*] signifies a meaning; and the expression 'scribe' also signifies a meaning; and each of the two [*linguistic expressions*] is a part of our statement 'the person is a scribe'; and its meaning [*i.e. the meaning of one of the two parts*] is a part of the meaning we intend when we say 'the per-

The first sub-classification [§6] begins at this point. I have called it the "logical sub-classification" in accordance with its content. In it we find a schema familiar to us from Avicennian introductions to logic that mark the climax of and provisional conclusion to the commentaries and debates on Porphyrius's *Eisagoge*. This schema represents an introduction to the *arbor porphyriana* and to the study of predicables. Such an introduction—whether as part of the texts on legal methodology or as a small primer in its own right—would come to be considered a basic component of the curriculum of legal scholars just a few generations later.[8] In contrast to al-Ġazālī, who felt the need to justify his inclusion of an introduction to logic at the beginning of his *uṣūl al-fiqh* work and emphasized that it was not a genuine part of this discipline but rather an introduction to all sciences that the jurist could feel free to skip,[9] it is striking that the *Maḥṣūl* not only lacks such a justification and explanation for its logical content, but that it even completely refrains from mentioning that this content originates from the discipline of logic. Faḫr ad-dīn evidently did not feel the need to explain his intentions, and instead—as we shall see—presents his interwoven outlines and sketches to the listener or reader as a matter of course.

According to this logical introduction, the simple linguistic expression is differentiated according to whether [i] "the conceptualization (*taṣawwur*) of its meaning itself prevents sharing in it (*šarika*)" or [ii] does not prevent it, i.e. whether there are several things that [ii] share this linguistic expression and this meaning—as is the case with the universal linguistic expression (*lafẓ kullī*) 'human being'—or [i] do not share it. Into this latter case fall particular linguistic expressions (*lafẓ ǧuzʾī*), which include any proper name signifying a concrete individual and shared by no other thing.[10]

---

son is a scribe'—namely as a signification intended by the linguistic expression (*dalālatan maqṣūḍatan fī l-lafẓ*)."

8 Cf. Gerhard Endreß, "Grammatik und Logik. Arabische Philologie und griechische Philosophie im Widerstreit," in *Sprachphilosophie in Antike und Mittelalter*, ed. by Burkhard Mojsisch (Amsterdam: Gründer, 1986), pp. 163–299, esp. p. 233; see also John Walbridge, "Logic in the Islamic Intellectual Tradition: The Recent Centuries," *Islamic Studies*, vol. 39, no. 1 (2000): p. 55; as well as Street, "Arabic and Islamic Philosophy of Language and Logic," pp. 9ff. and on the development of the Avicennian 'rational sciences' in general in the *madrasa*, see Endreß, "Reading Avicenna in the Madrasa," esp. from p. 392.

9 At the same time, al-Ġazālī is convinced of the necessity of logic and writes on the same page: "He who has no comprehensive knowledge of it cannot be certain of his knowledge at all," al-Ġazālī, *al-Mustaṣfā*, vol. 1, p. 30, lines 8–9; on al-Ġazālī's appreciation of logic, see also Rudolph, "Die Neubewertung der Logik durch al-Ġazālī"; cf. Chapter 2, Section 2.3.2.

10 The wording Faḫr ad-dīn chooses here—*immā an yamnaʿa nafsu taṣawwuri maʿnāhu mina š-šarikati* [...] *aw lā yamnaʿa*—is similar to a passage from Ibn Sīnā's *Išārāt wa-t-*

Next [§§7–10], Faḫr ad-dīn distinguishes between the essential linguistic expression (*lafẓ ḏātī*), which signifies the quiddity (*māhiyya*)—the essential nature—of something in whole or in part, and the accidental linguistic expression (*lafẓ ʿaraḍī*), which signifies something extrinsic. With the subsequent categorization of these types of simple universal linguistic expressions, Faḫr ad-dīn quite matter-of-factly adopts into his work on legal methodology the result of a discussion in which Ibn Sīnā had first had to establish this concept of the essential linguistic expression.[11]

---

tanbīhāt; there it says: *wa-l-ǧuzʾī huwa llaḏī nafsu taṣawwuri maʿnāhu yamnaʿu wuqūʿa š-šarikati fīhi*, Ibn Sīnā, *al-Išārāt wa-t-tanbīhāt*, ed. by Moǧtabā az-Zāriʿī (Qom: Būstān-e Ketāb, 2008), p. 45, lines 3–4. A detailed parallel passage can be found in the *Madḫal* of the *Kitāb aš-Šifāʾ*: [1] "Either its meaning [*i.e. that of the simple linguistic expression*] is a meaning that it [*i.e. the linguistic expression*] signifies (*maʿnāhu al-wāḥid allaḏī yadullu ʿalayhī*) in such a way that it is possible in the mind (*lā yamtaniʿu fī ḏ-ḏihn*) that, with regard to its conceptualization (*min ḥayṯu taṣawwurihī*) [*i.e. with regard to the conceptualization of the meaning*], several things share it [*i.e. the meaning*] in the same way (*ištirāku l-kaṯrati fīhi ʿalā s-sawiyati*), in that about each one of them it is said *that it is this* (*innahū huwa*)—namely according to a sharing that takes place on one and the same level [*and not subordinately*] (*ištirākan ʿalā daraǧatin wāḥidatin*), just as for example how we say 'human being.' For it [*i.e. the linguistic expression 'human being'*] has a meaning in the mind; and this meaning corresponds (*muṭābiq*) in one and the same way (*ʿalā waǧhin wāḥidin*) to Zayd, ʿAmr, and Ḫālid, because each one of them is a human being. [...] [2] Or its meaning [*i.e. the meaning of the linguistic expression*] is such that in the mind the coming about of the sharing of it [*by several things*] is impossible (*bi-ḥayṯu yamtaniʿu fī ḏ-ḏihni īqāʿu š-šarikati fīhi*), i.e. that [*the sharing*] of the one specific/realized thing that is intended (*fī l-muḥaṣṣal al-wāḥid al-maqṣūd bihī*), as when we say 'Zayd' [*is impossible*]. For although it may be that many share it [*i.e. the expression 'Zayd'*], they only share it with regard to what is heard [*i.e. on a purely acoustic level*]; as however concerns its one meaning (*maʿnāhu al-wāḥid*), it is impossible to accept one of them as something that shares it [*i.e. the meaning 'Zayd,' which must refer to a specific Zayd*]. For its only meaning (*al-wāḥid min maʿānīhā*) is the essence of one specific Zayd (*ḏāt al-mušār ilayhī*, lit. 'the essence of a specific him'); and the essence of this specific Zayd prevents it from being taken for anything else in the mind." Ibn Sīnā, *Kitāb aš-Šifāʾ, al-Manṭiq, al-Madḫal* I.5, p. 26, line 10–p. 27, line 4.

On Ibn Sīnā's theory of universals in general, see, for example, Michael E. Marmura, "Quiddity and Universality in Avicenna," in *Neoplatonism and Islamic Thought*, ed. by Parviz Morewedge (Albany, NY: State University of New York Press, 1992), pp. 77–87 and id., "Avicenna's Chapter on Universals in the Isagoge of his Shifāʾ," in *Islam, Past Influence and Present Challenge*, ed. by Alford T. Welch and Pierre Cachia (Edinburgh: Edinburgh University Press, 1979), pp. 34–56; see Jon McGinnis, "Logic and Science: The Role of Genus and Difference in Avicenna's Logic, Science and Natural Philosophy," *Documenti e Studi sulla Tradizione filosofica medievale*, vol. 18 (2007): pp. 165–187.

11 Ibn Sīnā's view, according to which the essential linguistic expression encompasses genus, species, and specific difference, opposes the doctrine that equates 'essential' with 'constituent' (cf. Ibn Sīnā, *Kitāb aš-Šifāʾ, al-Manṭiq, al-Madḫal* I.6, p. 33) and as a consequence does not consider the species name as an essential linguistic expression: "For our saying

Faḫr ad-dīn specifies [§7] whether the signified quiddity is [i] the "quiddity of a single" thing—an example of this "is the linguistic expression 'sun' (*šams*), if it applies to this particular [*sun*]"[12]—or [ii] the quiddity of several things. In this latter case, a distinction must be made as to whether these things are a single species or several species, i.e. whether there is a distinction only at the level of the individuals or whether there is also a difference of an essential kind. The linguistic expression 'human being,' for example, specifies the quiddity of several things that are such "that each one of them differs from the other in individuality (*fī t-taʿayyun*)"; this is a single species, and as such there is no difference with regard to "essential properties" (*ḏātiyyāt*). Different are the more general linguistic expressions that signify the quiddity of several things that represent different species, such as in the case of

> the signification of the linguistic expression 'animal' when it applies to the ox (*ṯawr*), donkey, and horse at the same time. For example, one asks: 'What are these things?'—And one says [*in reply*]: 'animals'; for the linguistic expression 'animals' signifies the completeness (*kamāl*) of their essential qualities (*ḥaqīqatihā*), inasmuch as, regarding to these [*three*], one asks about their totality and one seeks the core of the essential nature that is common to them (*kunhu l-ḥaqīqati llatī lahā bi-š-šarika*).[13]

Even if these species have in common that they are animals, they differ with regard to other essential characteristics that make them what they are in the

'essential linguistic expression' signifies an expression whose meaning stands in relation to the essence of the thing (*fa-inna qawlanā lafẓun ḏātiyyun yadullu ʿalā lafẓin li-maʿnāhi nisbatun ilā ḏāti š-šayʾ*), whereby the meaning of the essence of the thing is not connected to the essence of the thing [*i.e. not to the thing itself*] (*wa-maʿnā ḏāti š-šayʾi lā yakūnu mansūban ilā ḏāti š-šayʾ*); rather, one connects to a thing something that it is not [*i.e. something that is not completely identical with it—be it a part of it or something completely different*] (*innamā yunsabu ilā š-šayʾi mā laysa huwa*). Therefore [*i.e. since one does not connect the whole of the quiddity as the whole of the quiddity to itself*], it is understandable that the opinion is held (*fa-bi-l-ḥarā an yuẓanna*) that it is most appropriate for the linguistic expression 'essential' to mean [*only*] the 'concepts that constitute the quiddity' (*anna lafẓa ḏ-ḏātiyyi innamā l-awlā bihī an yaštamila ʿalā l-maʿānī llatī tuqawwimu l-māhiyyata*), and that 'the linguistic expression signifying [the entire] quiddity' is not essential. Thus, 'human being' [*i.e. an expression signifying the whole of the quiddity*] would not be essential to human beings; rather, [*only*] 'living being' and 'rational' would be essential to human beings." Ibn Sīnā, *Kitāb aš-Šifāʾ, al-Manṭiq, al-Madḫal* I.5, p. 31, lines 1–5; see also Strobino, "Per Se, Inseparability, Containment and Implication", pp. 243f.

12 Ibn Sīnā, *Kitāb aš-Šifāʾ, al-Manṭiq, al-Madḫal* I.8, p. 41, lines 16–17.

13 Ibn Sīnā, *Kitāb aš-Šifāʾ, al-Manṭiq, al-Madḫal* I.8, p. 41, line 18–p. 42, line 1.

first place, because “the condition of being an animal (*ḥayawāniyya*) alone does not signify the quiddity of human and horse alone”;[14] instead, this requires an essential, species-forming difference, i.e. the specific difference (*faṣl*). The essential linguistic expressions [§ 8] make up three of the five predicables (*al-alfāẓ al-ḫamsa/quinque voces*): the genus (*ǧins*), such as ‘animal,’ which is characterized by specific differences (*fuṣūl*, sg. *faṣl*), such as ‘rational’ or ‘whinnying,’ into different species (*anwāʿ*, sing. *nawʿ*), such as that of the human being and that of the horse. The *arbor porphyriana* is constructed in the following way [§ 9]: “Then the genera are arranged in ascending order (*mutaṣāʿidatan*) and they end with their ascent (*irtiqāʾ*) at the genus that has no genus above it—and that is the genus of the genera (*ǧinsu l-aǧnās*),” i.e. the *summum genus*. “The species (*anwāʿ*) are arranged in descending order down to the species that has no more species under it, and that is the species of species (*nawʿu l-anwāʿ*),”[15] i.e. the *infima species*.

In describing those linguistic expressions that signify extrinsic attributes, Faḫr ad-dīn builds—again, quite matter-of-factly—upon the Avicennian distinction between essence and existence, whereby an absolute essence on the one hand is distinguished from its existence in thought or in extramental reality on the other. In this passage of the *Maḥṣūl* [§ 10], extrinsic properties that adhere to the quiddity as a quiddity are distinguished from those that adhere to the realized quiddity. In the brevity of his presentation, Faḫr ad-dīn refrains from giving examples. But in a parallel passage in his *Manṭiq al-Mulaḫḫaṣ*, he gives ‘the evenness/the fact of being even’ that is attached to the number ‘four’ as an example of the first case[16] and the blackness of the dark-skinned person (*zanǧī*) for the second case.[17] These extrinsic properties are attached subsequently and are not constitutive of the quiddity itself:

> Rather, they are subsequent followers and adherents (*tawābiʿ wa-lawāzim*) that do not belong among those things that help the quiddity to be realized (*laysat mimmā yuḥaqqiqu l-māhiyya*), but rather among those

14 Ibid., p. 42, lines 6–7.

15 Faḫr ad-dīn ar-Rāzī, *al-Maḥṣūl*, vol. 1, p. 223, lines 5–7.

16 Ibn Sīnā gives the following as examples of attributes that adhere to the quiddity as a quiddity: “Thus evenness (*zawǧiyya*) is attached to duality (*iṯnayniyya*); and the triangle has attached to it the fact that its three angles correspond to two right angles [*i.e. that the sum of its angles is 180°*]—not because of one of the two modes of existence (*lā li-aḥadi l-wuǧūdayn*), but because it is a triangle.” Ibn Sīnā, *Kitāb aš-Šifāʾ, al-Manṭiq, al-Madḫal* 1.6, p. 34, lines 11–13.

17 Faḫr ad-dīn ar-Rāzī, *Manṭiq al-Mulaḫḫaṣ*, ed. by Aḥad Farāmarz Qarāmalekī and Ādīne Aṣġarīnežād (Tehran: Dānešgāh-e Emām Ṣādeq, 2002/3), p. 17, lines 13–14.

> that are assigned to the quiddity subsequently. The quiddity is thus consolidated without them (*fa-l-māhiyyatu tuṯbatu dūnahā*).[18]

After Faḫr ad-dīn mentions the difference between direct, primary extrinsic attributes and indirect, secondary ones, he comes to discuss the naming of two types of attribute: Extrinsic attributes that are unique to only one species are called propria (*ḫawāṣṣ*; sg. proprium, Arabic *ḫāṣṣa*), while those that can be assigned to several species are called general accidents (*aʿrāḍ ʿāmma*; sg. *ʿaraḍ āmm*).[19]

FIGURE 5 *Outline of the Introduction and the Logical Sub-Classification*

[I] The first part is divided into:
- [I.1] the linguistic expression that signifies by congruence (*muṭābaqa*)
  - [I.2] the linguistic expression that signifies by containment (*taḍammun*)
  - [I.3] the linguistic expression that signifies by implication (*iltizām*)
    - [I.1.1] the simple linguistic expression signifying by congruence has three sub-classifications
      - [I.1.1.A]: The first sub-classification of the simple linguistic expression [= *logical sub-classification*] consists of the following categories
        - [I.1.1.A.1] simple particular linguistic expression
        - [I.1.1.A.2] simple universal linguistic expression
          - [I.1.1.A.2.1] signifies the complete quiddity = that which is said in answer [*to the question*] "what is it?"
          - [I.1.1.A.2.2] a part of it = the essential (*ḏātī*)
          - [I.1.1.A.2.3] or something external (*ḫāriǧ*) = the accidental (*ʿaraḍī*)
            - [I.1.1.A.2.1.1] = the quiddity of a single thing or
            - [I.1.1.A.2.1.2] = the quiddity of several things
          - [*ad* I.1.1.A.2.2] As for the essential (*ḏātī*), it is either
            - [I.1.1.A.2.2.1] the genus (*ǧins*)
            - [I.1.1.A.2.2.2] the specific difference (*faṣl*)
            - [I.1.1.A.2.2.3] the species (*nawʿ*)
            - [I.1.1.A.2.2.4] the genus of the genus (*ǧinsu l-ǧins*); the genus of the specific difference (*ǧinsu l-faṣl*); the specific difference of the genus (*faṣlu l-ǧins*); the specific difference of the specific difference (*faṣlu l-faṣl*)

18 Ibn Sīnā, *Kitāb aš-Šifāʾ, al-Manṭiq, al-Madḫal* I.6, p. 35, lines 7–8.
19 Cf. Ibn Sīnā, *Kitāb aš-Šifāʾ, al-Manṭiq, al-Madḫal* I.14, p. 84, line 18–p. 85, line 10.

[*ad* I.1.1.A.2.3] As for the attribute (*waṣf*), which is external to the quiddity:

[I.1.1.A.2.3.1] The first aspect is:

[I.1.1.A.2.3.1.1] The attribute (*waṣf*) adheres to the quiddity (*māhiyya*) or

[I.1.1.A.2.3.1.2] to the existence (*wuǧūd*) or

[I.1.1.A.2.3.1.3] it adheres to neither of them

[*ad* I.1.1.A.2.3.1.1–2] Adhering through an intermediate or without an intermediate

[*ad* I.1.1.A.2.3.1.3] The non-adherent can disappear quickly (*sarīʿu z-zawāl*) and it can disappear slowly (*baṭīʾ*).

[*ad* I.1.1.A.2.3.2] The second aspect of the attribute:

[I.1.1.A.2.3.2.1] the proprium

[I.1.1.A.2.3.2.2] the general accident

In his commentary on Ibn Sīnā's *Išārāt wa-t-tanbīhāt*, Faḫr ad-dīn gives the following summary at the end of the first treatise:

> Let us end this treatise with the explanation (*bayān*) of the arrangement (*tartīb*) of its chapters and say: The linguistic expression (*lafẓ*) signifies either by congruence (*bi-l-muṭābaqa*), containment (*taḍammun*), or implication (*iltizām*). All of these are either simple (*mufrad*) or compound (*murakkab*). The simple is either universal (*kullī*) or particular (*ǧuzʾī*); the universal is either essential (*ḏātī*) or accidental (*ʿaraḍī*); the essential is either such that it signifies the quiddity (*māhiyya*) or it does not; it signifies the quiddity either according to pure specificity (*bi-l-ḫuṣūṣiyyati l-maḥḍa*) or according to pure commonality (*aš-šarikati l-maḥḍa*) or according to specificity and sharedness together; the accidental (*al-ʿaraḍī*) is either an adherent (*lāzim*) or a non-adherent (*ġayr lāzim*). It adheres either to the quiddity or to the existence. That which is [*adherent*] to the quiddity [*is*] either [*adherent*] through an intermediary (*bi-wasaṭ*) or without an intermediary; if it is that which is separable (*mufāriq*) [*i.e. that which is non-adherent*], then it is either [*such that it*] disappears slowly (*baṭīʾu z-zawāl*) or quickly. This is the totality of the nodes of this *nahǧ* (*fa-hāḏihī ǧumlatu maʿāqidi hāḏā n-nahǧ*).[20]

20 Faḫr ad-dīn ar-Rāzī, *Šarḥ al-Išārāt*, p. 92, lines 10–16 (or id., *Šarḥ al-Išārāt wa-t-tanbīhāt*, Ms. Berlin or. oct. 1802, fol. 35ʳ, lines 9–15, *oriental count*).

This rough summary, which ignores many aspects and reduces the first treatise to is basic framework of sub-classifications—the predicables are only discussed in the second treatise—provides both the structuring principle of the logical sub-classification of the *Maḥṣūl* and the beginning of the logical section of the *Mulaḫḫaṣ*[21] as well as the template for the other sub-classifications of the linguistic expression. This sub-classification of the simple linguistic expression in the *Maḥṣūl* is, on the one hand, an introduction to logic in the tradition of the Porphyrian Eisagoge and is based on the structure of the Avicennian *Madḫal* treatises. On the other hand, Faḫr ad-dīn's own emphasis is conspicuous here—as will be examined in detail. It should above all be noted that in all these cases, Faḫr ad-dīn makes the Tripartition of Signification, which will be analyzed in detail, the starting point of his outlines and treatises.

2 The Historical Background of the Tripartition of Signification

2.1 *The Introduction of the Tripartition in Ibn Sīnā's* Kitāb aš-Šifāʾ, al-Manṭiq, al-Madḫal *1.8*

The introduction [§§1–5] of the sub-chapter "The Classification of Linguistic Expressions" is rich in presuppositions and contains cursory remarks on the three manners of signification (*muṭābaqa*, *taḍammun*, and *iltizām*) along with their conditions and limitations. But before considering it in detail, I will first reconstruct a layer of the original context[22] of these manners of signification in order to establish a basis upon which to examine and categorize the relevant passages of the text. My focus in this chapter is on Ibn Sīnā's text—for it is Ibn Sīnā who established this classification of linguistic expressions as a three-part division within the *Madḫal* genre. It had been preceded by a two-part division not only in Ibn Sīnā's writings, but also in al-Fārābī's, as will be shown later;[23] and it is Ibn Sīnā who comments most extensively on this tripartition and its historical background, namely in the chapter "On the Classification of the Uni-

21 See Faḫr ad-dīn ar-Rāzī, *Manṭiq al-Mulaḫḫaṣ*, pp. 15–21.

22 As already mentioned in the introduction, Strobino treats this topic in detail and embeds it within the *burhān* complex, cf. Strobino, "Per Se, Inseparability, Containment and Implication," pp. 255–262; my remarks focus on the linguistic-philosophical and hermeneutical development of this tripartite division.

23 See Chapter 2, Section 2.2.1; following this, the development in Ibn Sīnā's *Madḫal* treatises is traced: from rather casual remarks concerning two manners of signification to a systematic derivation and outline of the three manners of signification, see Chapter 2, Section 2.3.

versal Simple Linguistic Expression (*al-lafẓ al-mufrad al-kullī*) into its Five Subdivisions" in the *Madḫal* of the *Kitāb aš-Šifāʾ*.[24] This chapter, *Madḫal* I.8, stands in the context of the question of the correct way of determining the quiddity in order to obtain knowledge that can be considered certain and it serves as an introduction to the study of predicables. Ibn Sīnā begins the chapter *Madḫal* I.8 with a short summary, based on the preceding chapters (i.e. *Madḫal* I.5–7),[25] roughly comparable in content (with some deviations) to §7 of the *Maḥṣūl*'s logical sub-classification: The universal simple linguistic expression is "essential (*ḏātī*) or accidental (*ʿaraḍī*)"; the essential linguistic expression is either such "that it is in a certain way suitable to signify the quiddity" (*ṣāliḥun li-d-dalālati ʿalā l-māhiyyati bi-waǧhin*), or such "that it is not at all suitable to signify the quiddity" (*ġayru ṣāliḥin li-d-dalālati ʿalā l-māhiyyati aṣlan*); the former signifies either "the quiddity of a single thing or several things that do not differ in an essential way" (*lā taḫtalifu iḫtilāfan ḏātiyyan*)—the species; or it signifies the quiddity of things "whose essences differ in an essential way" (*taḫtalifu ḏawātuhā iḫtilāfan ḏātiyyan*)—the genus.[26] The genus, such as 'animal,' is that which is shared by several things, which then only become what they are through essential differences (*bi-l-fuṣūli ḏ-ḏātiyya*).[27] Ibn Sīnā then emphasizes that the specific differences, in contrast to the genus, do not indicate the entire shared essential nature:

> As for [*the linguistic expression*] 'sentient,' it signifies a part of the totality (*ǧuzʾ mina l-ǧumla*) of what the singification of the linguistic expression 'animals' encompasses, so that this [*i.e. 'sentient'*] is [*only*] a part of the completeness (*kamāl*) of the essential nature (*ḥaqīqa*) that they [*i.e. the various species*] share, but not the completeness (*tamām*) [*of this common essential nature*]; the same applies to the case of 'rational' in relation to (*bi-l-qiyās ilā*) man.[28]

The specific difference 'sentient' subdivides the genus 'animate body' and is constitutive of the species 'animal'; 'animal' itself functions as a genus for various species that share in it. The specific difference 'rational' subdivides the genus 'animal' and constitutes the *infima species* 'man.'[29] The specific differ-

24 Ibn Sīnā, *Kitāb aš-Šifāʾ, al-Manṭiq, al-Madḫal* I.8, p. 41, line 9–p. 46, last line.
25 See Chapter 2, Section 1.
26 Ibn Sīnā, *Kitāb aš-Šifāʾ, al-Manṭiq, al-Madḫal* I.8, p. 41, lines 12–16.
27 Ibid., p. 42, lines 6–9; cf. Chapter 2, Section 1.
28 Ibn Sīnā, *Kitāb aš-Šifāʾ, al-Manṭiq, al-Madḫal* I.8, p. 42, lines 9–11.
29 For Ibn Sīnā's explanation of this sub-classification, see Ibn Sīnā, *Kitāb aš-Šifāʾ, al-Manṭiq,*

ence itself has a smaller scope of signification than the species that it constitutes—an aspect that will be discussed in more detail below. Against Ibn Sīnā's view that the specific difference—in the present example 'sentient'—signifies only a part of what the species—'animal'—signifies, Ibn Sīnā cites the following objection raised by unspecified parties (in form it could be a fictitious objection, but it will be shown that this is not the case):

> But someone might say that [*the linguistic expression*] 'animal' has no signification that would not be the same as [*the linguistic expression*] 'sentient being' (*ḥassās*)—for an animal is nothing other than 'an animate body' (*illā ǧisman ḏā nafsin*) and likewise a 'sentient being' is nothing other than 'an animate body.'[30]

According to this objection, the two linguistic expressions 'animal' and 'sentient' would be equivalent in intent; both would signify an 'animate body.' In this case, they would be interchangeable, such that, as a consequence of this assumption, 'sentient' could function as a genus of 'man' without further specification:

> If it were not for what we have recognized in the investigation of what is said in answer [*to the question*] 'what is it,'[31] then there would be no difference between the genus and its specific difference and one would assume that 'sentient' is the genus of 'man,' which has [*in fact*] been assumed.[32]

The problem from which the objection—adequate: [animal: animate body], also adequate: [capable of perception: animate body]—results has at its core various layers of logic and ontology, as will be demosntrated.[33] Ibn Sīnā works through this complex of problems in various contexts.[34]

---

al-Madḫal 1.11, p. 62, line 15–p. 63, line 7. On the specific difference in Ibn Sīnā, see in detail Sylvia DiVincenzo, "Avicenna against Porphyry's Definition of Differentia Specifica," *Documenti e studi sulla tradizione filosofica medievale*, vol. 26 (2015): pp. 129–183.

30 Ibn Sīnā, *Kitāb aš-Šifāʾ, al-Manṭiq, al-Madḫal* 1.8, p. 42, lines 11–13.

31 This cross-reference refers to Ibn Sīnā, *al-Muḫtaṣar al-awṣat fī l-manṭiq, al-Madḫal*, Ms. Istanbul Nuruosmaniye 2763, fol. 4^{r}, lines 7–15; see Chapter 2, Section 2.3.

32 Ibn Sīnā, *al-Muḫtaṣar al-awṣat fī l-manṭiq, al-Madḫal*, Ms. Istanbul Nuruosmaniye 2763, fol. 5^{r}, lines 5–6.

33 See Chapter 2, Section 2.2.

34 Cf. Strobino, "Per Se, Inseparability, Containment and Implication."

At this point in the chapter *Madḫal* I.8, Ibn Sīnā answers the question about the correct determination of the quiddity with a treatise on basic rules of signification, i.e. what it means for a linguistic expression to signify a meaning:

> So we say in response: Our saying that the expression signifies a meaning (*inna qawlanā inna l-lafẓa yadullu ʿalā maʿnan*) is not to be understood in the way you have understood it, i.e. that, whenever the linguistic expression signifies, it is inevitable that this meaning is present (*lam yakun budda min wuǧūdi ḏālika l-maʿnā*).[35]

The objection cited above by Ibn Sīnā is based, among other things, on an inadequate use of the different manners of signification. One of the ways in which a linguistic expression can signify—and which is erroneously regarded in this objection as a primary form of signification—is when, for example, a word that indicates the undergoing an action implies the agent of the action, i.e. "that, whenever the linguistic expression 'moving (*mutaḥarrik*)' signifies [*something that exists*], it is inevitable that there be a mover (*muḥarrik*)";[36] and "that, whenever the expression 'roof (*saqf*)' signifies [*something that exists*], it is inevitable that there is a base (*asās*) [*that supports the roof*]."[37] Even though this is one of the manners in which a word can signify, it is by no means the primary way in which we understand meanings; that is, when we say 'word X signifies meaning X,' we exclude this manner of signification: "Yet we do not say: 'What is understood by the expression 'moving' and what it signifies is the 'mover'; and what is understood by the expression 'roof' and what it signifies is the 'base' [*that supports the roof*].'"[38] Instead, what is understood by 'word X signifies meaning X' or "the signification of the linguistic expression" (*dalālat al-lafẓ*) is the primary signification, i.e. a signification of what is intended in a primary way as the meaning without implicatures.[39]

---

35 Ibn Sīnā, *Kitāb aš-Šifāʾ, al-Manṭiq, al-Madḫal* I.8, p. 42, lines 13–15.

36 Ibid., lines 15–16; while this example uses form V, in later works Ibn Sīnā gives the passive participle and the active participle of form I as an example of this manner of signification: "Signification by implication is like when [*the linguistic expression*] 'creature' (*maḫlūq*) signifies the creator (*ḫāliq*)," Ibn Sīnā, *Manṭiq al-Mašriqiyyīn*, ed. s.n. (Cairo: al-Maktaba as-Salafiyya, 1910), p. 14, line 21. This linguistic-theoretical consideration—be it with the example pair *mutaḥarrik/muḥarrik* or *maḫlūq/ḫāliq*—is based on a variety of lines of inquiry from metaphysics and natural philosophy that are beyond the scope of this study.

37 Ibn Sīnā, *Kitāb aš-Šifāʾ, al-Manṭiq, al-Madḫal* I.8, p. 42, lines 16–17.

38 Ibid., lines 17–18.

39 Ibid., line 19–p. 43, line 1; for the translation of *al-qaṣd al-awwal* as 'primarily' in this context, see Kwame Gyekye, "The Terms *Prima Intentio* and *Secunda Intentio* in Arabic Logic,"

The signification of further, implied meanings does not fall under this primary manner of signification:

> If there is another meaning that comes to it [*only*] by means of an extrinsic connection through which the mind (*ḏihn*)—at the time it perceives it [*i.e. the other/second meaning*]—also perceives that first meaning, [*if this should be the case*] then the linguistic expression does not signify it [*i.e. the other/second meaning*] in a primary way (*bi-l-qaṣd al-awwal*).[40]

This hints at a relationship of transfer between a first and a second meaning using that sort of parlance that is employed in writings on language theory to describe figurative language. There it is said "that you understand [*first*] one meaning for the linguistic expression, and subsequently that meaning provides you with another meaning."[41] As we shall see, in his two later writings the *Manṭiq al-Mašriqiyyīn* and *al-Išārāt wa-t-tanbīhāt*, Ibn Sīnā would further concretize the terminology that he here only hints at;[42] and using this as a basis, Faḫr ad-dīn would ultimately expand and elaborate upon the relationship between the theorems of logical and linguistic theory laid out here.[43]

The aforementioned relationship of implication between a word form that indicates the undergoing of an action and the agent of the action, for example, belongs to this sort of additional meaning based on an extrinsic connection.[44] The signification of the genus by the specific difference is another example of an extrinsic manner of signification: the specific difference 'sentient' signifies the genus 'animate body' neither in a primary nor in a secondary way, whereas the species 'animal' signifies the genus 'animate body' in an intrinsic way. The linguistic expression 'sentient,' or any other specific difference at that, has its own meaning. That the specific difference does not have the same meaning as the species that is constituted by it is one of the things that Ibn Sīnā endeavors to demonstrate in this treatise on the theory of signification, but which is nonetheless deeply rooted in a larger logical framework.[45]

Speculum, vol. 46, no. 1 (Jan. 1971): pp. 32–38 and Zimmermann, *Al-Farabi's Commentary*, p. 100.

40 Ibn Sīnā, *Kitāb aš-Šifāʾ, al-Manṭiq, al-Madḫal* 1.8, p. 43, lines 1–3.

41 ʿAbd al-Qāhir al-Ǧurǧānī, *Dalāʾil al-iʿǧāz*, ed. by Muḥammad ʿAbd al-Munʿim Ḫafāǧī (Cairo: Maktabat al-Qāhira, 1969 [1389 H.]), p. 263, lines 2–3; see Chapter 2, Section 3.2.1.

42 See Chapter 2, Section 2.3.

43 See Chapter 2, Section 3.2.1.

44 See Chapter 2, Section 2.3.

45 Cf. Strobino, "Per Se, Inseparability, Containment and Implication."

The two examples of extrinsic manners of signification differ in their relationships of predication: In the latter, the extrinsic meaning 'animate body' is simultaneously "predicated of that of which the meaning of the expression" 'sentient' is predicated, whereas in the former case—the participle constructions—there is no relationship of predication.[46]

Ibn Sīnā then continues the differentiation between the primary (*awwal*), secondary (*ṯānī*), and extrinsic (*ḫāriǧ*) manners of signification:

[1.] "As far as the primary [*manner*] is concerned, it behaves like our talk of 'animals'; for it signifies [*primarily*] the totality (*ǧumla*) of 'sentient, animate bodies' (*yadullu ʿalā ǧumlati l-ǧismi ḏī n-nafsi l-ḥassās*)"[47]—i.e. the primary manner of signification exists for a species in the case of a complete definition consisting of the *genus proximum* and specific difference.

[2.] The secondary manner of signification is understood to refer to the signification of individual, intrinsic essential parts; i.e. that the species signifies either the genus or the specific difference of its definition:

> As for the secondary manner, it is like the fact that it [*i.e. the linguistic expression 'animal'*] signifies 'body' (*fa-ka-dalālatihī ʿalā l-ǧism*); for the meaning 'body' is necessarily (*ḍarūratan*) contained in the meaning 'the state of being an animal' (*muḍammanun*); for that [*linguistic expression*] which signifies the state of being an animal ecompasses (*ištamala*) the meaning 'body'—not in the manner that it would refer to it from the outside [*i.e. extrinsically*] (*lā ʿalā annahu yušīru min ḫāriǧin*).[48]

The secondary manner of signification is therefore a state of being encompassed, included, contained within:[49] Upon mention of the species 'animal,' one can infer one of the superordinate genera, in this case the genus 'body,' according to the *arbor porphyriana*, since it represents an intrinsic essential component. This manner of signification corresponds to the signification of the common quiddity (*māhiyya muštaraka*).

[3.] In the extrinsic manner of signification (*dalāla ḫāriǧiyya*) on the other hand, something is signified that is extrinsic in relation to what the expression actually signifies, whether in a primary or secondary manner.[50]

46 Cf. Ibn Sīnā, *Kitāb aš-Šifāʾ, al-Manṭiq, al-Madḫal* I.8, p. 43, lines 3–4.
47 Ibid., lines 6–7.
48 Ibid., lines 7–9.
49 Accordingly, Strobino translates *taḍammun* as "containment," see Strobino, "Per Se, Inseparability, Containment and Implication."
50 Ibn Sīnā, *Kitāb aš-Šifāʾ, al-Manṭiq, al-Madḫal* I.8, p. 43, lines 9–11.

Following this, Ibn Sīnā gives the primary, secondary, and extrinsic manners of signification their own names:

> If we [*now*] want to summarize all of this briefly and succinctly, then we assign three points of view/manners (*awǧuh*) to the signification that comes about by means of linguistic expressions:
> [*ad* 1] Signification by way of congruence (*dalālatu muṭābaqa*)—just as [*the linguistic expression*] 'animal' signifies the totality of the 'sentient, animate body.'
> [*ad* 2] Signification by way of containment (*dalālatu taḍammun*)—just as the linguistic expression 'animal' signifies the 'body.'
> [*ad* 3] Signification by way of implication (*dalālatu luzūm*)—just as the linguistic expression 'roof' signifies the 'base.'[51]

Ibn Sīnā introduced the term *muṭābaqa*[52] for the primary manner of signification—thereby using a word that had already been employed in a wide variety of contexts and disciplines[53]—in order to emphasize the congruency and

51 Ibn Sīnā, *Kitāb aš-Šifā', al-Manṭiq, al-Madḫal* I.8, p. 43, lines 12–15.

52 *Muṭābaqa* (verbal noun of form III of *ṭabaqa*) can be translated, depending on the context, as "match, conformity, correspondence, agreement," see Edward W. Lane, *An Arabic-English Lexicon*, vol. 5, pp. 1825a–b and Ibn Manẓūr, *Lisān al-ʿArab al-muḥīṭ* (Būlāq: Al-maṭbaʿa al-amīriyya, 1883–1890 [1300–1308]), vol. 12, pp. 78. The Latin version of the *Madḫal* of the *Šifā'* translates *dalālat al-muṭābaqa* with *significatio parilitatis*, Ibn Sīnā, "Logyca," in *Avicennae perhypatetici philosophi ac medicorum facili primi opera in lucem redacta ac nuper quantum ars niti potuit emendata* (Venice: Scotus 1508; reprint: Frankfurt a.M.: Minerva, 1961), fol. 5vb, lines 1–2.

53 (1.) In al-Fārābī, the term *muṭābiq*—apparently synonymous with *musāwiyan*—is found, among other things, in the context of relationships of correspondence, such as the complete and adequate definition of a species, even if not yet as a technical term, see Abū Naṣr al-Fārābī, "Kitāb Īsāġūǧī ay al-Madḫal," ed. by D.M. Dunlop, *The Islamic Quarterly*, vol. 3 (1956–1957): pp. 123–124, § 11.

(2.) In texts based on Aristotle's *Posterior Analytics*, the term is mainly used to express a relationship of correspondence, namely "the 'correspondence' (*al-muṭābaqa*) of one's belief whether affirmative or negative, with the state of affairs that obtains externally," Deborah L. Black, "Knowledge (*ʿilm*) and Certitude (*yakīn*) in al-Fārābī's Epistemology," *Arabic Sciences and Philosophy*, vol. 16 (2006): pp. 17–18. Since, in the context of the Tripartition of Signification, *muṭābaqa* is not used in the sense of this correspondence relationship, but rather serves to denote the *congruence* between word and concept, I do not translate this term—unlike Strobino, "Per Se, Inseparability, Containment and Implication"—with 'correspondence' in this context.

(3.) In grammatical theory, the term *muṭābaqa* is used for different types of syntactic congruency, see Ahyaf Sinnū and Ǧirār Ǧihāmī, *Mawsūʿat muṣṭalaḥāt al-ʿulūm an-*

convertibility of the species and its complete definition in this manner of signification. For the secondary manner of signification, Ibn Sīnā chose the term *taḍammun* (literally, *being contained, inclusion*)[54] to express the intrinsic—and

---

naḥwiyya. Silsilat mawsū'āt al-muṣṭalaḥāt al-'arabiyya wa-l-islamiyya (Beirut: Maktabat Lubnān Nāširūn, 2010), vol. 3, pp. 4675–4676; see Muhammad Abdel Haleem, "Qur'ān," *EALL*, vol. 4, p. 26.

(4.) In the *'ilm al-badī'*, on the other hand, *muṭābaqa* (alongside *ṭibāq* and *taṭbīq*) is the technical term for chiastic or antithetical word order or syntax, see Faḫr ad-dīn ar-Rāzī, *Nihāyat al-īǧāz fī dirāyat al-i'ǧāz*, ed. by Bakrī Šayḫ Amīn (Beirut: Dār al-'ilm li-l-malāyīn, 1985), p. 285, lines 10 ff., also Sīrāǧ ad-dīn as-Sakkākī, *Miftāḥ al-'ulūm*, ed. by 'Abdul Ḥamīd Hindāwī (Beirut: Dār al-Kutub al-'ilmiyya, 2011), p. 533; see Simon, *Mittelalterliche arabische Sprachbetrachtung*, p. 6; see August F.M. Mehren, *Die Rhetorik der Araber* (Copenhagen: Otto Schwartz, 1853), pp. 97 ff.

54 See Edward W. Lane, *An Arabic-English Lexicon*, vol. 5, p. 1804c and Ibn Manẓūr, *Lisān al-'Arab al-muḥīṭ*, vol. 17, p. 126. The Latin version of the *Madḫal* of the *Šifā'* translates *dalālat at-taḍammun* with *significatio continentie*, Ibn Sīnā, "Logyca," fol. 5[vb], lines 3–4.

Taḍammun too is a term with a variety of uses in Arabic philology:

(1.) In grammatical theory, *taḍammun* can refer, when discussing the relationship between the possibility of declension (*i'rāb*) and the impossibility of declension (*binā'*), to certain names which, due to their basic structure, have characteristics of particles (*ḥurūf*). This can explain why certain names are indeclinable (*mabnī*), although it is actually part of their basic structure to be declinable (*mu'rab*). *Taḍammun* thus means the containment of certain properties, which are actually characteristic of particles and not of names, in the function of certain names; *taḍmīn* is also sometimes used instead of *taḍammun* for this; see Ahyaf Sinnū and Ǧirār Ǧihāmī, *Mawsū'at muṣṭalaḥāt al-'ulūm an-naḥwiyya*, vol. 1, pp. 1813–1814; see also Adrian Gully, "Taḍmīn: 'Implication of Meaning' in Medieval Arabic," *Journal of the American Oriental Society*, vol. 117, no. 3 (1997): p. 468.

(2.) On the other hand, *taḍmīn* (less often *taḍammun*) refers to the phenomenon whereby a verb is used in the meaning of another verb due to a certain preposition, see Gully, "Taḍmīn," pp. 466–468.

(3.) In poetry, *taḍmīn* is used to mean, among other things, enjambment—a structural dependency on a rhyme scheme. Until around the 11th century, this was regarded as a fundamental poetic error that was to be avoided; later it developed into an accepted poetic device, see Amidu Sanni, "On *Taḍmīn* (Enjambment) and Structural Coherence in Classical Arabic Poetry," *Bulletin of the School of Oriental and African Studies, University of London*, vol. 52, no. 3 (1989): pp. 463–466; id., "Again on *taḍmīn* in Arabic Theoretical Discourse," *Bulletin of the School of Oriental and African Studies, University of London*, vol. 61, no. 1 (1998): pp. 1–7; see also Wolfhart Heinrichs, *Arabische Dichtung und griechische Poetik: Ḥāzim al-Qarṭāǧannīs Grundlegung der Poetik mit Hilfe aristotelischer Begriffe* (Beirut: Orient-Institut, 1969), p. 13. The term has other functions as well, see Sanni, "Again on *taḍmīn*," pp. 7 ff. and Gully, "Taḍmīn," pp. 473 ff. Ibn Sīnā's use of the extrinsic manner of signification comes very close to one of the ways in which the term *taḍmīn* is used by ar-Rummānī (d. 384/994), see Bruce Fudge, "Taḍmīn: The Notion of 'Implication' according to al-Rummānī," in *Classical Arabic Humanities in Their Own Terms: Festschrift for Wolfhart Heinrichs on His 65th Birthday Presented by His Students and Colleagues*, ed. by Beatrice Gruendler (Leiden [et al.]: Brill, 2008), p. 479.

one-sided—relationship between the species and its genus or the specific difference that constitutes it.

Ibn Sīnā expresses the reverse relationship of signification—that of the specific difference to the species constituted by it or to the genus divided by it—with the term *luzūm*, which had already been used in writings on logic as a technical term for various forms of implication.[55] Ibn Sīnā would ultimately go on to give the third manner of signification its own name, the one with which was subsequently identified, namely *iltizām* (literally, *becoming attached*).[56]

The following diagram is intended to illustrate the Tripartition of Signification:[57]

55 *Luzūm*, *maṣdar* of *lazima* (to attach oneself to someone, to cling to someone), "necessary consequence, necessity," *WKAS*, vol. II, part 1, p. 566a; on *lazima*, see Ibn Manẓūr, *Lisān al-ʿArab*, vol. 16, pp. 14–15.

The Latin version of the *Madḫal* of the *Šifāʾ* translates the term as *significatio comitantie*, Ibn Sīnā, "Logyca," fol. 5vb, lines 4–5.

(1.) In the terminology of Arabic logic, *luzūm* refers to various types of implication relationships, especially in hypothetical propositions and syllogisms, see Farīd Ǧabr and Rafīq al-ʿAǧam [eds.], *Mawsūʿat muṣṭalaḥāt ʿilm al-manṭiq ʿinda l-ʿarab* (Beirut: Maktabat Lubnān Nāširūn, 1996), pp. 773–774; see in detail on this, i.e. on al-Fārābī's and Ibn Sīnā's conceptions of *luzūm*, the dissertation by Kamran I. Karimullah, *Avicenna (d. 1037), Logical Theory, and the Aristotelian Tradition* (Montreal: McGill University 2014), [http://digitool.library.mcgill.ca/R/?func=dbin-jump-full&object_id=123019&local_base=GEN01-MCG02, retrieved October 2015], especially pp. 106 ff.; p. 310, fn. 301; and pp. 326 ff.; cf. id., "Unusual Syllogisms: Avicenna and Najm al-Dīn al-Kātibī on *per impossibile* Syllogisms and Implication (*luzūm*)," *Oriens*, vol. 43, no. 1–2 (2015): pp. 223–271, esp. pp. 250 ff.; cf. Cornelia Schöck, "Discussions on Conditional Sentences from the Year AH 17/ AD 638 to Avicenna," in *Classical Arabic Philosophy: Sources and Reception*, ed. by Peter Adamson (London [et al.]: The Warburg Institute, 2007), pp. 67–68; Tony Street, "Ṭūsī on Avicenna's Logical Connectives," *History and Philosophy of Logic*, vol. 16 (1995): pp. 257–268; Schöck, *Koranexegese, Grammatik and Logik*, p. 83.

(2.) On the multiple meanings of *luzūm* in grammatical theory, see Ahyaf Sinnū and Ǧirār Ǧihāmī, *Mawsūʿat muṣṭalaḥāt al-ʿulūm an-naḥwiyya*, vol. 3, pp. 4116–4119.

(3.) In addition, *luzūm/iltizām* is a technical term in rhyme theory, see Simon, *Mittelalterliche arabische Sprachbetrachtung*, p. 7 and Seeger A. Bonebakker, "Luzūm mā lā yalzam," *EI*².

56 Ibn Sīnā only uses the term *iltizām* as part of the Tripartition of Signification in his later writings, see Chapter 2, Section 2.3.

57 This is a simple and incomplete outline, but sufficient for our purposes. For the logical notation, see Strobino, "Per Se, Inseparability, Containment and Implication," p. 258.

FIGURE 6 The three manners of signification in the context of the study of predicables

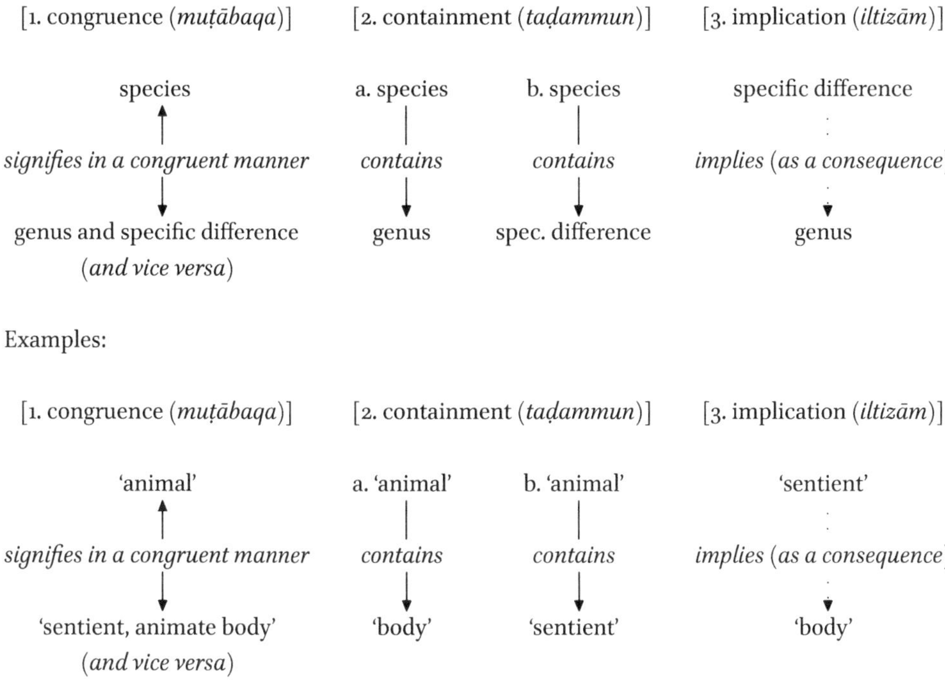

On the basis of this excursus into the theory of signification, Ibn Sīnā finally refutes the argument that both the species and the specific difference signify 'animate body' in a congruent manner:

In a congruent way, the specific difference 'sentient' only signifies "something that has sensory perception" (*šay'un lahū ḥissun*); but because we know, according to Ibn Sīnā, that that which has sensory perception must be a 'body' and 'animate,' 'sentient' signifies 'body' by means of implication.[58] The congruent manner of signification extends only to the intensional level, implication to the extensional level. The sentence "Every sentient being is an animal" is false from an intensional point of view, while it is true from an extensional point of view: "[…] so the fact that every sentient being is an animal (*kullu ḥassāsin ḥayawānun*) is evident not according to secure, certain proof/observation (*bayān yaqīnī*), but according to a fact of existence (*bayān wuǧūdī*)."[59] No certain knowledge results from implication; this extrinsic manner of signification

58 Ibn Sīnā, *Kitāb aš-Šifā', al-Manṭiq, al-Madḫal* I.8, p. 43, lines 16–17.

59 Ibn Sīnā, *Kitāb aš-Šifā', al-Manṭiq, Kitāb al-Burhān*, ed. by Abū l-ʿAlā ʿAfīfī (Cairo: al-Hay'a al-ʿĀmma li-Šu'ūn al-Maṭābiʿ al-Amīriyya, 1956), p. 104, line 19.

is not the manner of signification meant when "we speak here of the 'signifying expression (*lafẓ dāll*).'"[60]

On the basis of this tripartition, Ibn Sīnā can argue that the specific difference 'sentient' signifies only a part of what 'animal' signifies; for while 'animal' congruently signifies 'sentient animate body,' 'sentient' signifies only the aspect that it has 'sensory perception'; i.e., 'sentient' says nothing about *what* the thing that has sensory perception is, but only specifies *how* it is:

> By 'that [*linguistic expression*] which signifies howness (*ayyiyya*),' we mean precisely 'that [*linguistic expression*] whose suitability is only for [*signifying the*] howness and not for [*signifying the*] quiddity (*mā innamā ṣulūḥuhū li-l-ayyiyyati faqaṭ dūna l-māhiyya*),' so that it does not signify a 'constituting term that completes a common or specific quiddity (*maʿnā muqawwimun yutimmu māhiyyatan muštarakatan aw ḫāṣṣatan*),' but rather a 'constituting term that is specific to/specifies [*something*] (*maʿnā muqawwim yaḫuṣṣu*).' So when we say 'that [*linguistic expression*] which signifies howness (*ad-dāll ʿalā l-ayyiyya*),' we [*thereby*] intend this meaning [*i.e. 'constituting and specific'*].[61]

The disregard for the distinction between the indication of what a thing is and how a thing is, i.e. between whatness (*māhiyya*) and howness (*ayyiyya*),[62] and the concomitant equation of the scope of signification of the genus and the specific difference lead, among other things, to the specific difference ultimately being taken for a genus, such that the genus of 'man' would be 'sentient.'[63]

---

60 Ibn Sīnā, *Kitāb aš-Šifāʾ, al-Manṭiq, al-Madḫal* 1.8, p. 44, line 3.

61 Ibid., p. 45, lines 10–13.

62 This term was erroneously read as *anniyya/inniyya* in some places in the Avicennian oeuvre, cf. for example Michael E. Marmura, "Avicenna on the Division of the Sciences in the *Isagoge* of his *Shifāʾ*," *Journal of the History of the Arabic Science*, vol. 4, no. 2 (1980): p. 240. In this specific context in the *Madḫal* of the *Kitāb aš-Šifāʾ* it must be read as *ayyiyya*, see in detail Amos Bertolacci, "A Hidden *Hapax Legomenon* in Avicenna's Metaphysics: Considerations on the Use of *Anniyya* and *Ayyiyya* in the *Ilāhiyyāt of* the *Kitāb al-Šifāʾ*," in *The Letter before the Spirit. The Importance of Text Editions for the Study of the Reception of Aristotle*, ed. by Aafke M.I. van Oppenraay and Resianne Fontaine-van-Gelder (Leiden [et al.]: Brill, 2012), pp. 289–310, and in relation to the *Kitāb al-Maqūlāt* of the *Kitāb aš-Šifāʾ*, see Alexander Kalbarczyk, *Predication and Ontology: Studies and Texts on Avicennian and Post-Avicennian Readings of Aristotle's* Categories (Berlin: De Gruyter, 2018), pp. 281–282.

63 Ibn Sīnā, *al-Muḫtaṣar al-awṣat fī l-manṭiq, al-Madḫal*, Ms. Istanbul Nuruosmaniye 2763, fol. 5ʳ, lines 5–6.

In order to avoid this problem when providing a definition, Ibn Sīnā prescribes the secondary and extrinsic manners of signification as criteria for checking the genus in a kind of guide to determining the genus of a thing.[64]

With this classification of signification, Ibn Sīnā further expands upon a distinction made by al-Fārābī, as will be shown below.

2.2 *Two Problems Underlying the Tripartition of Signification*

2.2.1 *De Int.* 11 and the Problem of Redundancy in the Definition

Before Ibn Sīnā, al-Fārābī had also made a distinction between the secondary and extrinsic manners of signification; however, his distinction did not yet go hand in hand with a terminological differentiation: both fell under *luzūm*. Al-Fārābī demonstrates in the chapter "The Enumeration of the Circumstances that Lead to Errors Concerning the Meanings/Concepts" (*iḥṣā'u l-amkinati l-muġliṭati mina l-ma'ānī*) of his guide the *"Book of Circumstances that Lead to Errors"* (*Kitāb al-Amkina al-Muġliṭa*)[65] how to avoid "either falsehood (*kiḏb*) or redundancy (*faḍl*), meaningless chatter (*haḏayān*), and repetition (*takrīr*)"[66] arising trough the incorrect combination of linguistic expressions. In the style of *De Int.* 11, al-Fārābī here discusses the question of whether and how predicates that apply to a thing independently of each other—the term for these predicates in al-Fārābī is *al-muṭlaqāt*—can also be stated in conjunction with each other.[67] Al-Fārābī therefore tests whether the argument 'S is P_1; S is P_2; therefore S is P_1P_2' is correct for various sentences:[68] The argument "Zayd is a man, Zayd is an animal, therefore Zayd is a man-animal" (*Zaydun insānun wa-Zaydun ḥayawānun fa-iḏan Zaydun insānun ḥayawānun*) is redundant,[69] while the argument "Zayd is skillful; Zayd is a doctor; therefore Zayd is a skilful doctor" is false.[70] Especially in relationships of predication that are

---

64 Cf. Ibn Sīnā, *Manṭiq al-Mašriqiyyīn*, p. 52, lines 5 ff.

65 Abū Naṣr al-Fārābī, "Kitāb al-Amkina al-Muġliṭa," in *al-Manṭiq 'inda l-Fārābī*, ed. by Rafīq al-'Ağam (Beirut: Dār al-Mašriq, 1985–1986), vol. 2, pp. 131–164; or in *al-Manṭiqiyyāt li-l-Fārābī*, ed. by Moḥammad Taqī Dānešpažūh (Qom: Maktabat-e Āyatollāh al-'Aẓmī al-Mar'ašī an-Nağafī, 1988–1989/90 [1408–1410 h.š.]), vol. 1: *an-Nuṣūṣ al-manṭiqiyya*, pp. 195–228.

66 Al-Fārābī, "Kitāb al-Amkina al-Muġliṭa," ed. by 'Ağam, p. 145, line 9 or ed. by Dānešpažūh, p. 209, line 19.

67 Al-Fārābī, "Kitāb al-Amkina al-Muġliṭa," ed. by 'Ağam, p. 145, lines 8–9 or ed. by Dānešpažūh, p. 209, lines 18–19; al-Fārābī, "Šarḥ al-'Ibāra," p. 163, lines 7 ff.; Weidemann, "Anmerkungen," p. 370.

68 Cf. Weidemann, "Anmerkungen," p. 373.

69 Al-Fārābī, "Kitāb al-Amkina al-Muġliṭa," ed. by 'Ağam, p. 145, line 12 or ed. by Dānešpažūh, p. 209, line 22.

70 This is my formulation of *De Int.* 20b35–36 of the Arabic Aristotle. Al-Fārābī quotes the

meant to be considered true in all circumstances, such as definitions, "repetition and redundancy" must be excluded; to this end, two conditions must be met:

> Namely, [1.] that they [*i.e. the linguistic expressions in question*] are not predicated of each other in an accidental manner (*lā bi-l-ʿaraḍ*) and [2.] that one of the two [*i.e. one of the two meanings of the linguistic expressions*] is not contained in the other (*wa-an lā yanhaṣira aḥaduhumā fī l-āḫar*). This is like our saying 'Zayd is an animal (*Zaydun ḥayyun*); Zayd is one who walks bipedally (*Zaydun maššāʾun ḏū riğlayni*); so Zayd is a bipedal animal (*fa-iḏan Zaydun ḥayyun maššāʾun ḏū riğlayni*).'[71]

The aforementioned false conclusion 'skillful doctor' is to be avoided due to the first condition; for both skillfulness and being a doctor are accidentally predicated of Zayd.[72] On the other hand, the second condition, according to which one of the two predicates must not be contained (*yanḥaṣiru*; Greek. ἐνυπάρχει)[73] in the other—as "when 'animal' or 'bipedal' is contained in 'man' […] as a component of its meaning"[74]—aims to avoid redundancy; for "if we say about Zayd that he is a man, it follows necessarily (*ḍarūratan*) that he is an animal;

text as follows: "If it is correct to say of him [*i.e. a certain person*] that he is seeing/skillful (*baṣīr*), and if it is correct to say of him that he is a physician (*ṭabīb*), it is not the case that he is a skillful physician (*ṭabīban baṣīran*)," al-Fārābī, "Šarḥ al-ʿIbāra," p. 165, lines 6–8; the Greek text in the Minio-Paluellos edition reads: ἀλλ' οὐχί, εἰ σκυτεὺς καὶ ἀγαθός, καὶ σκυτεὺς ἀγαθός ("But if someone is good and a cobbler it does not follow that he is a good cobbler," Aristotle, "De Interpretatione," in *The Complete Works of Aristotle: The Revised Oxford Translation*, ed. by Jonathan Barnes [Princeton, NJ: University Press, 1984], vol. 1, p. 33).

71 Al-Fārābī, "Kitāb al-Amkina al-Muġliṭa," ed. by ʿAğam, p. 146, lines 11–13 or ed. by Dānešpažūh, p. 210, line 23–p. 211, line 2; based on *De Int.* 21a5–18 (translation by Ackrill): "Clearly, then, one is led into many absurdities if one lays down without restriction that the compounds [*of several predicates into one*] come about. How the matter should be put we will now explain. Of things predicated, and things they get predicated of, those which are said accidentally, either of the same thing or of one another, will not be one. […] Nor, consequently, will the cobbler who is (without qualification) good, though an animal which is two-footed will (since this is not accidental). Further, where one of the things is contained in the other, they will not be one. This is why 'white' is not repeated [*i.e. when something is white*] and why a man is not an animal man or a two-footed man; for two-footed and animal are contained in man."

72 Cf. Weidemann, "Anmerkungen," pp. 379–380.

73 Al-Fārābī: *yanḥaṣiru*; Aristotle, *De Int.* 21a16 and *De Int.* 21a17–18: ἐνυπάρχει; Arist. Arab, *De Int.* 21a16: *maḥṣūran*; *De Int.* 21a17–18: *ḥaṣarnā*.

74 Weidemann, "Anmerkungen," pp. 374–375.

and if we say about Zayd that he is a man, it follows that he is bipedal. If these implicatures/attachments (*lawāzim*) are linked to the things by which they are implied, then this is […] meaningless chatter (*hadayān*)"[75]—i.e. the phrases "bipedal man," "man-animal," and "sentient animal" would be pointless formulations.

However, the state of being contained or implied is obviously subject to misunderstanding: thus, even the correct form of the predication could be accused of redundancy, "due to the fact that whenever we assume 'a man who walks' (*al-insānu māšiyan*), it follows that it is an animal (*lazima an yakūna ḥayawānan*), such that one could think that animal is contained within [*the meaning of the linguistic expression*] 'one who walks.'"[76]—Such an identification of two different relationships of implication can be found, for example, in Stephanus's commentary on *De Int.* 11: "'Two-footed' is contained within 'man' (ἐν γὰρ τῷ ἀνθρώπῳ μὲν ἐμπεριέχεται τὸ δίπουν) and 'animal' in 'two-footed' (ἐν δὲ τῷ δίπουν τὸ ζῷον). And within 'rational,' 'animal' is again contained (καὶ ἐν τῷ λογικῷ δὲ πάλιν ἐμπεριέχεται τὸ ζῷον) […]"[77] In his commentary on *De Int.* 21a17–18, Al-Fārābī quotes a train of thought in which this aspect of identification mentioned by Stephanus appears as an argument against a supposed case of redundancy. This is allegedly "the old aporia (*aš-šakk al-qadīm*), which was brought forth by Aṭaranṭiyās":[78]

75 Al-Fārābī, "Šarḥ al-ʿIbāra," p. 168, lines 2–5.

76 Al-Fārābī, "Kitāb al-Amkina al-Muġliṭa," ed. by ʿAǧam, p. 146, lines 13–14 or ed. by Dānešpažūh, p. 211, lines 3–4.

77 Stephanus, *In Aristotelis librum de interpretatione commentarium*, in English translation in *'Philoponus': On Aristotle On the Soul 3.9–13, with Stephanus: On Aristotle On Interpretation*, translated by William Charlton (London: Duckworth, 2000), p. 171. An Arabic version of Stephanus's commentary has not survived; the *Fihrist* lists him as a commentator, but gives no indication of the language of the commentary, see Ibn an-Nadīm, *Kitāb al-Fihrist*, ed. by Gustav Flügel (Leipzig: F.C.W. Vogel, 1871–1872), vol. 1, p. 249.

78 'Aṭaranṭiyās' possibly stands—as Dānešpažūh also surmises (al-Fārābī, "Šarḥ al-ʿIbāra," p. 175, fn. 1)—for Archytas of Tarentum (d. c. 355–350 BC) or for Pseudo-Archytas: The *Pseudo-Archytea* include writings that were apparently written by various thinkers in antiquity and late antiquity and then attributed to Archytas of Tarentum, cf. Thomas A. Szlezák, *Pseudo-Archytas über die Kategorien* (Berlin [et al.]: De Gruyter, 1972), esp. p. 1, p. 13, and p. 19; Zimmermann, on the other hand, surmises that it could be Antisthenes (d. c. 365 BC), cf. id., *Al-Farabi's Commentary and Short Treatise on Aristotle's* De Interpretatione, p. 152, fn. 1. Al-Fārābī also thought he was quoting a pre-Aristotelian thinker here ("That which Aristotle mentioned is very useful in forming a definition (*taḥdīd*) and solves the old aporia (*šakk*) brought forth by Aṭaranṭiyās," al-Fārābī, "Šarḥ al-ʿIbāra," p. 175, lines 14–15); in my opinion, however, the terminology and examples in this quotation speak in favor of a post-Aristotelian or even post-Porphyrian origin.

> "Why is it not the case that [*mentioning the linguistic expression*] 'rational' when defining man (*fī taḥdīdi l-insān*) makes [*mentioning the linguistic expression*] 'animal' superfluous? Just as [*the linguistic expression*] 'animal' (*ḥayawān*) makes it superfluous for [*the linguistic expression*] 'sentient' (*ḥassās*) to be made a condition.—If it were not so, then it would not suffice to say 'animal' without adding 'sentient.'[79]
>
> If 'rational' is set as a predicate (*maḥmūl*) of something, then it follows necessarily (*ḍarūratan*) that it is an animal. Since 'rational' is nothing other than 'animal,' 'rational' is nothing other than 'sentient.' Furthermore, 'animal' makes 'sentient' superfluous—thus if we were to make 'sentient' a condition, this would be redundant; likewise, it is redundant if we make 'animal' a condition together with 'sentient.'"[80]

This argument cited by al-Fārābī aims to demosntrate the supposed redundancy of the phrase "sentient animal" on the basis of the redundancy of the phrase "rational animal." The terms 'rational,' 'animal,' and 'sentient' are equated; and from the fact that 'animal' makes 'sentient' "superfluous," it is concluded that 'rational' also makes 'animal' superfluous. In other words, an identical relationship is assumed on the basis of two specific differences, even though the predicables fulfill different functions: The specific difference 'sentient' divides the genus 'animate body' and constitutes the species 'animal.' The compound 'sentient animal' is just as redundant as 'rational man'; for both cases consist of a juxtaposition of the species and the specific difference that constitutes it. The compound 'sentient animate body' corresponds to the formulation 'rational animal' in terms of the juxtaposition of its predicables; both cases consist of naming the genus and the specific difference that divides it.—The difference between genus and species, between dividing and constituting specific differences, is blurred in the quoted argument. Moreover, the genus can make the specification of a specific difference superfluous because the one signifies the quiddity common to the different species, while the other merely signifies the more specific howness;[81] conversely, the specific difference cannot make the specification of the genus superfluous. This is due to the different relationships of implication that are present in the two relationships of predication, and which are explained by al-Fārābī as follows:

---

79 My understanding of this sentence is based on Zimmermann's complementary negation, see id., *Al-Farabi's Commentary*, p. 152, fn. 2.

80 Al-Fārābī, "Šarḥ al-ʿIbāra," p. 175, lines 15–21; see also Zimmermann's translation, *Al-Farabi's Commentary*, p. 152.

81 See Chapter 2, Section 2.1.

> [1.] One of the two is like how the existence of the wall implies 'brick' (*luzūm al-labini ʿan wuǧūdi l-ḥāʾiṭ*; lit. 'the adherence of the bricks to the existence of the wall'); that is, by imposing the totality [*of a thing*], the part of the thing is implied (*luzūmu ǧuzʾi š-šayʾi ʿan waḍʿi ǧumlatihī*). For the bricks are contained in [*the meaning of*] 'wall' (*fa-inna l-labina munḥaṣiratun fī l-ḥāʾiṭ*).[82]
> [2.] The second is that the existence of the roof implies 'wall' (*luzūmu l-ḥāʾiṭi ʿan wuǧūdi s-saqf*; lit. 'the adherence of the wall to the existence of the roof'); that is, a thing is implied by a thing that is extrinsic to its totality [*i.e. the totality of the implied thing*] (*luzūmu šayʾin ʿan šayʾin ḫāriǧin ʿan ǧumlatihī*).[83]

In the first type of implication, the meaning of a linguistic expression implies an intrinsic part of what is signified. This is—in Ibn Sīnā's usage—the signification of containment (*taḍammun*), just as the species implies the genus in which it shares and the specific difference by which it is constituted (just as, for example, 'animal' implies 'sentient' and 'body'[84]). Al-Fārābī gives the example of the wall: 'wall' is described (not defined) as a "solid/unyielding, thick body (*ǧism mutaṣallib ḏū sumk*), which is composed of stones (*ḥiǧāra*) or bricks (*labin*) or clay (*ṭīn*) and is made to carry a roof (*uʿidda li-yaḥmila s-saqf*) and to protect against the winds (*yaṣūna mina l-riyāḥ*)."[85] Here, al-Fārābī combines the material cause with the final cause into a series of attributes that differentiate the genus 'body' into the species 'wall';[86] according to the first type of implication, the species 'wall' thus contains, for example, 'brick' or the genus 'body.'

82 In his *De Int.* commentary, al-Fārābī attributes this type of implication to Aristotle as a solution to the problem: "This [*aporia*] was solved by Aristotle saying, in reference to the fact that 'animal' implies 'sentient,' that the existence of the totality [*of a thing*] implies the existence of the part of the thing (literally, 'the adherence of the existence of the part of the thing to the existence of its totality'). This is because 'sentient' is a part of 'animal' or a part of its definition," al-Fārābī, "Šarḥ al-ʿIbāra," p. 176, lines 1–3.

83 Al-Fārābī, "Kitāb al-Amkina al-Muġliṭa," ed. by ʿAǧam, p. 146, lines 16–18 or ed. by Dānešpažūh, p. 211, lines 7–10.

84 Al-Fārābī, "Kitāb al-Amkina al-Muġliṭa," ed. by ʿAǧam, p. 146, lines 20–21 or ed. by Dānešpažūh, p. 211, lines 14–15.

85 Al-Fārābī, *Kitāb al-Ḥurūf*, ed. by Muḥsin Mahdī (Beirut: Dār al-Mašriq, 1970), p. 167.

86 Aristotle gives the following example in *Metaphysics* vol. 2, 1043a15 ff.: "stones, bricks, and timbers" as "the potential house" are the *causa materialis* of the house; "covering for bodies and chattels" as "actuality" are its *causa finalis*. The statement of the final cause answers the question of 'why' and is at the center of Aristotelian epistemology, see Aristotle, *Metaphysics* [English] in *The Complete Work of Aristotle: The Revised Oxford Translation*, ed. by Jonathan Barnes (Princeton, NJ: University Press, 1984), vol. 2, p. 1646.

The second type of implication, in which no intrinsic part but rather something extrinsic is implied, is based either—according to the schema of the previous example ['wall' = 'body created to support a roof']—on the fact that the specific difference ('roof') implies the species ('wall'), or—according to the understanding of later generations—on the fact that 'wall' does not function as a species here, but rather as a equivalent of the genus: If 'house' signifies 'the totality of wall and roof' (*maǧmūʿi l-ǧidāri wa-s-saqf*), 'roof' would, according to the second type of implication, signify the genus 'wall.'[87] This is the type of implication to which Ibn Sīnā refers with the term *luzūm* (and later *iltizām*).[88]

Abū l-Ḥasan Bahmanyār b. al-Marzubān (d. 458/1066), a disciple of Ibn Sīnā, later summarized this as follows: The one type of implication is when the linguistic expression "'house' signifies the wall alone (*waḥdahū*) and the species signifies the genus," while the other type of implication is when the linguistic expression "'roof' signifies the wall and the specific difference signifies the genus."[89]

According to the first type of implication, formulations such as 'Zayd is a man-animal' (*Zaydun insānun ḥayawānun*) or 'a sentient animal' are redundant[90] because 'man' already implies/contains 'animal' and 'animal' implies/contains 'sentient.' Meanwhile in the formulation 'Zayd is a bipedal, walking

According to al-Fārābī, it is a description (*rasm*), not a definition (*ḥadd*), since carrying the roof does not constitute the essence of the wall, see al-Fārābī, "Fuṣūl," in *al-Manṭiqiyyāt li-l-Fārābī*, ed. by Moḥammad Taqī Dānešpažūh (Qom: Maktabat-e Āyatollāh al-ʿAẓmī al-Marʿašī an-Naǧafī, 1988–1989/90 [1408–1410 h.š.]), vol. 1: an-Nuṣūṣ al-manṭiqiyya, p. 27; id., "Kitāb al-Burhān," in *al-Manṭiq ʿinda l-Fārābī*, ed. by Māǧid Faḫrī (Beirut: Dār al-Mašriq, 1987), p. 48; or in *al-Manṭiqiyyāt li-l-Fārābī*, vol. 1, p. 296; see also Strobino, "Per Se, Inseparability, Containment and Implication," p. 260.

87 ʿUmar b. Sahlān as-Sāwī (fl. 540/1145), *al-Baṣāʾir an-naṣīriyya fī ʿilm al-manṭiq*, ed. by Rafīq al-ʿAǧam, (Beirut: Dār al-fikr al-lubnānī, 1993), p. 33; cf. al-Fārābī, *Kitāb al-alfāẓ al-mustaʿmala fī l-manṭiq*, ed. by Muḥsin Mahdī (Beirut: Dār al-Mašriq, 1986), p. 103, lines 4–7.

88 See Chapter 2, Section 2.3.

89 Abū l-Ḥasan Bahmanyār b. al-Marzubān, *Kitāb at-Taḥṣīl*, ed. by Mortaḍā Moṭahharī (Tehran: Entešārāt-e dānešgāh, 1997 [1375]), p. 13, lines 3–6; on Bahmanyār, see for example David C. Reisman, "Bahmanyār b. al-Marzubān," *EI*[3]; id., *The Making of the Avicennan Tradition. The Transmission, Contents, and Structure of Ibn Sīnā's* al-Mubāḥāṯāt (*The Discussions*) (Leiden: Brill, 2002), pp. 185–195; Ahmed H. al-Rahim, "Avicenna's Immediate Disciples: Their Lives and Works," in *Avicenna and his Legacy. A Golden Age of Science and Philosophy*, ed. by Tzvi Y. Langermann (Turnhout: Brepols, 2009), pp. 9–14 as well as Eichner, *The Post-Avicennian Philosophical Tradition and Islamic Orthodoxy*, pp. 9–11 and id., "Dissolving the Unity of Metaphysics: From Fakhr al-Dīn al-Rāzī to Mullā Ṣadra al-Shirāzī," *Medioevo*, vol. 32 (2007): pp. 155–157.

90 Al-Fārābī, "Kitāb al-Amkina al-Muġliṭa," ed. by ʿAǧam, p. 145, line 12 or ed. by Dānešpažūh, p. 209, lines 22–23.

animal' there is no redundancy, because 'one who walks' does not contain 'animal,' but instead only implies it—namely in the second manner, which does not create redundancy.[91]

The differentiation between the two types of implication is also important in another respect, namely in connection with the ontological determination of the specific difference.

2.2.2 The Infinite Regress of the Specific Difference

A further problem for which the classification of signification represented a solution or explanation is closely linked to the ontological determination of the specific difference. This problem involves the question of whether the specific difference itself belongs to a genus,[92] i.e. either to the genus it divides or to another genus. Ammonius and the commentators who followed him held the view that the specific differences belong to the *summum genus* of the substance, "since they are completers of substances and part of them and the parts of substances are themselves substance."[93] However, this results in the aporia whereby the specific difference assumes, in relation to the genus to which it belongs, the function of a species, which in turn requires a specific difference for the purpose of delimitation: "Consequently, every specific difference would have a specific difference, and this would continue *ad infinitum*."[94] Ibn Sīnā proposes the following solution to the aporia:

---

91 Al-Fārābī, "Kitāb al-Amkina al-Muġliṭa," ed. by ʿAǧam, p. 146, line 20 or ed. by Dānešpažūh, p. 211, line 14.

92 On the question of when the *summum genus* should be regarded as a category, see Ibn Sīnā, *Kitāb aš-Šifāʾ, al-Ilāhiyyāt*, ed. Ǧurǧ Qanawātī and Saʿīd Zāyid (Cairo: al-Hayʾa al-ʿĀmma li-Šuʾūn al-Maṭābiʿ al-Amīriyya, 1960), p. 234, lines 12–15.

93 John Ellis, "Alexander's Defense of Aristotle's Categories," *Phronesis*, vol. 39, no. 1 (1994): pp. 70–71, fn. 5; on this argument, see Alexander of Aphrodisias, "Risāla fī l-faṣli ḫāṣṣatan wa-mā huwa," in *Die arabische Version einer unbekannten Schrift des Alexander von Aphrodisias über die Differentia specifica*, ed. by Albert Dietrich (Göttingen: Vandenhoeck und Ruprecht, 1964), pp. 124, §5–6.

94 Ibn Sīnā cites this aporia: "'It is apparent that each species is distinguished (*munfaṣil*) from those that share with it the [*same*] genus [*i.e. from the other species*] by the specific difference (*faṣl*). Furthermore, this specific difference is also a specific meaning (*maʿnā ayḍan mina l-maʿānī*) [*with which it should behave in one of the following two ways*]:

[1.] Either it is [*a meaning that is*] the most general of predicates (*aʿamm al-maḥmūlāt*); or [2.] it is a meaning (*maʿnā*) that falls under the most general of predicates (*taḥta aʿamm al-maḥmūlāt*).

[*ad* 1] It is inconceivable to say that every specific difference is the most general of predicates, for 'rational' (*nāṭiq*) and many such things are neither [*themselves*] a category (*maqūla*) nor in the determination of a category (*fī ḥukmi maqūlatin*).

> What one must know in order to solve this aporia (*šakk*) is:
> [1.] There is that [*kind of*] predication (*ḥaml*) in which the predicate (*maḥmūl*) is constitutive (*muqawwim*) of the quiddity of the subject (*mawḍūʿ*).
> [2.] And [*there is that kind of predication*] in which something adheres (*lāzim*) to it [*i.e. the subject*] that is not constitutive of its quiddity, such as existence (*wuǧūd*).[95]

Ibn Sīnā presents two general types of predication that can be used to explain how the genus can be predicated of a subject. In the first type, the genus is predicated of the species; for "the genus is predicated of the species in such a way that it is part of its quiddity."[96] This is the secondary manner of signification, i.e. that of containment (*taḍammun*).[97] In contrast, in the second type, the genus is "predicated of the specific difference in such a way that it is something that adheres to it (*lāzim lahū*), not in such a way that it is part of its quiddity."[98] 'Animal' is thus predicated of the specific difference 'rational' in such a way

> that it adheres to it (*lāzim lahū*), not in such a way that it is part of its quiddity. For by 'rational' one means only 'a thing endowed with reason' (*šayʾ lahū nuṭq*) as well as 'a thing that has a soul endowed with reason,' without our saying 'rational/endowed with reason' itself containing a clear indication (*bayān*) as to whether this thing is a substance or not a substance; however, adhering [*to it*] (*illā annahū yalzamu*) is the fact that this thing cannot be anything other than a substance, a body, and sentient.[99]

[*ad* 2] Thus it would remain that it [*i.e. the specific difference*] falls under the most general of predicates; and every [*meaning*] that falls under a meaning more general than it [*itself*] is distinguished (*munfaṣil*) from those that [*together with it*] share it [*i.e. the more general meaning*] by means of a specific difference (*faṣl*) by which it is specified. Consequently, every specific difference would have a specific difference, and this would continue *ad infinitum*.'" Ibn Sīnā, *Kitāb aš-Šifāʾ, al-Ilāhiyyāt*, p. 231, lines 6–13.

95 Ibn Sīnā, *Kitāb aš-Šifāʾ, al-Ilāhiyyāt*, v,6, p. 231, lines 14–16.

96 Ibid., p. 232, line 16.

97 See Chapter 2, Section 2.1.

98 Ibn Sīnā, *Kitāb aš-Šifāʾ, al-Ilāhiyyāt*, v,6, p. 232, line 17.

99 Ibid., p. 233, lines 1–4. Ibn Sīnā expresses the same view in the part on categories in the *Kitāb aš-Šifāʾ*: "As to the differences that are logical differences in the proper sense (*fuṣūl manṭiqiyya ḥaqīqiyya*), such as 'rational' (*nāṭiq*) [→ *in contrast to the previously mentioned form* nuṭq], in such a difference—even if it can be nothing other than a substance—the

The way in which the genus is predicated of the specific difference corresponds to the extrinsic implicative type, i.e. implication (*luzūm/iltizām*): 'rational' implies 'animal,' 'body,' and ultimately also 'substance.' But the specific difference itself has no part in this genus, as there is no commonality in the quiddity and therefore there is no need for further differentiation by a further specific difference.[100] "Rational/that which is endowed with reason" (*nāṭiq*) itself falls under the genus 'that which perceives' (*al-mudrik*)—just as 'sentient/that which is endowded with senses' (*ḥassās*) does, namely in such a way that the genus is intrinsically predicated of it. *Al-mudrik*, on the other hand, which "falls under the substance" (*yaqaʿu taḥta l-ǧawhar*), does not relate to substance as it does to a genus, but rather as it does to something that adheres (*lāzim*).[101]

2.3 *The Generalization of the Tripartition of Signification*

Proceeding from the various logical and ontological problems outlined above, Ibn Sīnā summarizes the discussion of the manners of signification in the *Madḫal*. His treatment of this topic in his *Madḫal* books and *Madḫal*-equivalent passages demonstrates a development, the knowledge of which is useful for understanding the classification of signification as it would later be conceived of in all its aspects by Faḫr ad-dīn. This is due not least to a continuous process of generalization that occurred in Ibn Sīnā's Tripartition Signification, continued, as we will see, by Faḫr ad-dīn ar-Rāzī.

I will therefore now trace this development textually in order to show that where the treatment of the manners of signification is placed within the structure of the text in each *Madḫal* book changes in connection with the terminology.

---

meaning of substantiality (*ǧawhariyya*) is not contained (*ġayr muḍammanin*), as you have already learned." Ibn Sīnā, *Kitāb aš-Šifāʾ, al-Manṭiq, al-Maqūlāt*, ed. by Ibrāhīm Madkūr (Cairo: al-Hayʾa al-ʿāmma li-šuʾūn al-maṭābiʿ al-amīriyya, 1959), *al-Maqūlāt* III,2, p. 101, lines 19–20.

100 Ibn Sīnā, *Kitāb aš-Šifāʾ, al-Ilāhiyyāt*, V,6, p. 233, line 7.

101 Ibid., lines 6–8. Although implication can amount to a *per se* 2 predication and although the present connection between genus and specific difference is a necessary implication (*iltizām*), according to Strobino the genus/difference problem should not be linked to the *per se* predication ("Per Se, Inseparability, Containment and Implication", p. 242, fn. 105): "For the genus to be a per se 2 of a differentia that divides the genus (in the way rational divides animal), the differentia would have to be in the definition of the genus, which is evidently not (possibly) the case."

2.3.1 The Development of the Tripartition into a Structural Feature in Ibn Sīnā's Oeuvre

2.3.1.1 *Differentiation in the Spirit of* De Int. *11:* al-Muḫtaṣar al-awṣat fī l-manṭiq *and the* Kitāb an-Naǧāt

In the earliest *Madḫal* treatise available to us, which can be dated to the "Transition Period" (403–404/1013–1014)[102] of the Avicennian oeuvre, Ibn Sīnā emphazises the distinction between two types of implication in the context of discussing the correct determination of the quiddity and in connection with the study of predicables. Here however, we do not find a tripartite division nor is the distinction between the manners of signification characterized as being of general relevance to languistic theory. The relevant passage from the as yet unedited *Madḫal* of the *Muḫtaṣar al-awṣat fī l-manṭiq*[103] is quoted below:

> [§1] You must know that there is a difference between 'that which contains' (*al-mutaḍammin*) and 'that which implies' (*al-multazim*).
> [§2] For 'man' contains 'animal' (*al-ḥayawān*), whereas 'rational' (*nāṭiq*) does not contain 'animal,' but [*merely*] implies 'the state of being an animal' (*al-ḥayawāniyya*); for 'rational' (*nāṭiq*) exists only as an animal, even if 'the state of being an animal' is a meaning that is extrinsic with relation to it [*i.e. 'rational'*] (*maʿnā ḫāriǧī minhū*) and which is [*only*] attached to it (*mulāzim lahū*).
> [§3] As for 'man,' however, 'the state of being an animal' is intrinsic with relation to it (*dāḫilan fīhi*); for by 'man' we mean 'rational animal,' whereas by 'rational' (*nāṭiq*) we do not mean 'animal' and by 'animal' we do not mean 'rational.' An example of this is our talk of 'house' and 'roof'; for neither of them can replace 'wall' (*badalahū min ḥāʾiṭ*), but 'house' contains the meaning of wall, and 'roof' implies it [*i.e. the meaning of wall*].
> [§4] The one who seeks the linguistic expression that signifies the 'what it is' of something must not ignore this difference such that instead of taking that which contains the totality of the essential attributes, he takes that which [*only*] implies the totality [*of the essential attributes*] as that which

---

102 For an overview of the chronology of Ibn Sīnā's most important works, see Gutas, *Avicenna and the Aristotelian Tradition*, p. 165.

103 On the placement of the work within the chronology of the Avicennian oeuvre, on the description of the manuscripts, and on the edition of the part of this work treating categories, see Alexander Kalbarczyk, "*The Kitāb al-Maqūlāt of the Muḫtaṣar al-awṣaṭ fī l-manṭiq*: A Hitherto Unknown Source for Studying Ibn Sīnā's Reception of Aristotle's *Categories*," *Oriens*, vol. 40, no. 2 (2012): pp. 305–354; see also Gutas, *Avicenna and the Aristotelian Tradition*, p. 433.

> is said [*in answer to the question*] 'what is it?'—It is that which contains (*al-mutaḍammin*) that is required.[104]

Building on al-Fārābī, who removes the problem from the context of *De Int.* 11 and discusses it in his general guide to avoiding errors, Ibn Sīnā already points out in the *Madḫal* of the *Muḫtaṣar* that predicables perform different functions with regard to implication and that these differences must be taken into account when stating definitions. In contrast to al-Fārābī, Ibn Sīnā's differentiation also manifests itself terminologically: he distinguishes between 'that which contains' (*al-mutaḍammin*) and 'that which implies' (*al-multazim*).

Although the *Muḫtaṣar* is—in keeping with its genre—a short textbook that mainly provides summaries of concepts and in which problems are not dealt with in depth, Ibn Sīnā devotes a relatively large amount of space to this difference, linked to the distinction between the indication of *whatness* by the genus and *howness* by the specific difference:

> About the essential, which is said in answer to the question 'how is the thing?' (*fī ḏ-ḏātī l-maqūli fī ǧawābi ayyumā š-šay'*):
> [§1] This is the essential, simple linguistic expression (*al-lafẓ al-mufrad aḏ-ḏātī*), which is not such that it in any way signifies the quiddity for which it is an attribute (*waṣf*)—neither in the way of commonality nor specificity. Rather, it is only suitable for distinguishing essentially (*ḏātiy-yan*) those things that share in a quiddity, such as 'sentient' and 'rational.'
> [§2] For 'sentient' is not a specific quiddity of man or the ox or the horse, because each of them requires something additional to make it what it is. Nor is it a common quiddity of man, the ox, or the horse. This is because they—beside the fact that they are sentient—have other meanings (*maʿānī*), such as that they move of their own volition, that they ingest food, etc.
> [§3] Even though these meanings (*maʿānī*) adhere to 'sentience' (*ḥas-sāsiyya*) [*i.e. they are implied by the meaning 'sentience'*], they are not contained within it [*i.e. by the meaning 'sentience'*] (*fa-in kānat talzamu l-ḥassāsiyyata fa-laysat mutaḍamminatan lahū*). 'Sentient' is not the common quiddity of the meaning (*maʿnā*) that is more general than 'animal,' because 'sentience' only exists in animals. So 'sentient' is in no sense a quiddity for these things.

104 Ibn Sīnā, *al-Muḫtaṣar al-awṣat fī l-manṭiq, al-Madḫal*, Ms. Istanbul Nuruosmaniye 2763, fol. 4^{r}, lines 7–15.

> [§ 4] It is the same with 'rational' (*nāṭiq*); for the state of being 'rational' (*nāṭiq*) corresponds to the state of being 'sentient' in this respect, since only 'sentient' is capable of distinguishing 'animal' from 'plant', and 'rational' [*is capable*] of distinguisching 'man' from 'incapable of speech' (*ʿuǧm*).[105]

In this passage, Ibn Sīnā takes up this distinction again and emphasizes that the specific difference can only signify the howness, and not the whatness of a thing; in the discussion of the specific difference two chapters later, Ibn Sīnā again refers to the fact that the specific difference 'sentient' should not be taken for the genus of 'man,' as "has indeed been assumed" (*qad ẓunna*).[106]

In the *Madḫal* of the *Kitāb an-Naǧāt*, we can recognize the same approach to the discussion and placement of the two types of implication as in the *Madḫal* of the *Muḫtaṣar*: In the two chapters on the genus and on the specific difference, there is a condensed summary of the two previously quoted passages of the *Muḫtaṣar*—with the difference that here the verbal nouns *iltizām* and *taḍammun* are used as technical terms:

> There is a difference between implication (*iltizām*) and containment (*taḍammun*); for [*the linguistic expression*] 'roof' implies 'wall' (*as-saqf yaltazimu l-ḥāʾiṭ*) and does not contain it (*wa-lā yataḍammanuhū*), while [*the linguistic expression*] 'house' implies and contains 'wall.'[107]

The similarity to the approach of the Transition Period can be explained by the fact that the *Kitāb an-Naǧāt* consists to such a large extent of excerpts

105 Ibid., fol. 4r, lines 16–14v, line 8.

106 Ibid., fol. 5r, lines 5–6.

107 Ibn Sīnā, *Kitāb an-Naǧāt min al-ġaraq fī baḥr aḍ-ḍalālāt*, ed. by Moḥammad Taqī Dānešpažūh (Tehran: Entešārāt-e Dānešgāh-e Tehran, 1985–1986 [1364]), p. 15, lines 1–2. The entire passage in question reads: "For 'sentient' does not signify the complete (*kamāl*) common quiddity for man and horse—even if it signifies some essential meaning, namely the fact that something possesses sensory perception (*ḥiss*), whereas it [*i.e. the linguistic expression 'sentient'*] does not possess the [*maʿānī*] of 'moving voluntarily,' 'developing,' and 'feeding itself,' etc.—[*and it*] only [*signifies*] by way of implication (*iltizām*), not by way of containment (*taḍammun*). There is a difference between implication and containment, for [*the linguistic expression*] 'roof' implies 'wall' and does not contain it, while [*the linguistic expression*] 'house' implies and contains 'wall.'" Ibn Sīnā, *Kitāb an-Naǧāt*, p. 14, line 13–p. 15, line 2. The passage from the chapter on the specific difference reads: "There is a difference between 'rational' and 'man'; for 'man' is an 'animal being that has rationality (*nuṭq*),' while 'rational' is 'some thing'—but one does not know what thing it is—which has rationality (*nuṭq*)." Ibn Sīnā, *Kitāb an-Naǧāt*, p. 16, lines 5–6.

from earlier works that it was written "practically without composing a single line anew."[108] According to the bio-bibliographical tradition, the logic of this work is based on the *Muḫtaṣar al-aṣġar fī l-manṭiq*, which, like the *Muḫtaṣar al-awṣat*, was written in the year 404 (1013/4).[109] The use of the two terms as technical terms can in turn be traced back to the actual date of composition of the *Kitāb an-Naǧāt* (between 417/1026 and 418/1027) in the Middle Period (ca. 411–418/1020–1027).[110]

2.3.1.2 *The* Madḫal *of the* Kitāb aš-Šifāʾ

In contrast to the two aforementioned *Madḫal* treatises (those of the *Muḫtaṣar al-awṣat* and the *Kitāb an-Naǧāt* or the *Muḫtaṣar al-aṣġar*), the *Madḫal* of the *Kitāb aš-Šifāʾ*[111]—also belonging within the framework of the study of predicables and the correct determination of the quiddity—presents a three-part classification of signification for the first time[112] and also gives a detailed introduction to one of its main points of discussion, as described above.[113] The introduction of the manners of signification takes place with reference to general aspects of language theory that claim validity beyond the semantics of predicables. Although this is a more complex problem, Ibn Sīnā limits himself to the aspect of equating two predicables. His answer to this problem is an excursus on what is generally understood by signification. In his illustration of signification by implication, Ibn Sīnā hints at linguistic-theoretical connections that would be fully developed in later works, namely implication on the basis of word form and the indication of a relationship of transfer.[114] With his excursus on these theorems, Ibn Sīnā illustrates the relevant relationship of signification between specific difference and species/genus and thus lays the foundation for the detailed discussion of predicables,[115] though at the same time also goes well beyond this.

---

108 Gutas, *Avicenna and the Aristotelian Tradition*, p. 116.

109 Alexander Kalbarczyk, "The *Kitāb al-Maqūlāt* of the *Muḫtaṣar al-awṣaṭ fī l-manṭiq*," pp. 311–312; Gutas, *Avicenna and the Aristotelian Tradition*, p. 116.

110 Gutas, *Avicenna and the Aristotelian Tradition*, p. 165; p. 115: "[…] *The Salvation* was thus written in 417/1026 or 418/1027."

111 On the purpose and genesis of this work and the dating of the treatises it contains, see Gutas, *Avicenna and the Aristotelian Tradition*, pp. 103–115; Gutas, p. 107, gives the dates for the composition of this *Madḫal* as 412–414/1022–1024.

112 That is, for the first time in the writings available to us—there may have been a similar version in writings that have been lost, for example in the *Madḫal* of the work *al-Ḥāṣil wa-l-maḥṣūl*, see Gutas, *Avicenna and the Aristotelian Tradition*, pp. 94–100.

113 For a detailed discussion of the relevant chapter *Madḫal* I.8, see Chapter 2, Section 2.1.

114 See Chapter 2, Section 2.1 pp. 73f.

115 In the following chapters of the *Madḫal*, the different manners of signification are referred

2.3.1.3 *The* Manṭiq al-Mašriqiyyīn

In the *Madḫal*-equivalent treatise of the work the *Manṭiq al-Mašriqiyyīn*, whose genesis Gutas attributes to the so-called "Period of Eastern Philosophy" (ca. 418–420/1027–1029),[116] there is a separate chapter in which the Tripartition of Signification is enumerated schematically and without any further indication as to points of discussion:

> About the number [*of ways*] in which the linguistic expression signifies a meaning (*fī ʿadadi dalālati l-lafẓi ʿalā l-maʿnā*)
> [§1] There are three ways in which the linguistic expression signifies a meaning (*aṣnāfu dalālati l-lafẓi ʿalā l-maʿnā ṯalāṯatun*): [1.] signification by congruence (*dalālatu l-muṭābaqa*), [2.] signification by containment (*dalālatu t-taḍammun*), and [3.] signification by implication (*dalālatu l-iltizām*)—and that is transfer (*naql*) by means of the meaning (*min ṭarīqi l-maʿnā*).
> [*ad* 1] As for signification by congruence, this is like the fact that the linguistic term 'man' signifies 'rational animal' (*ḥayawān nāṭiq*).
> [*ad* 2] As for signification by containment, this is like how [*the linguistic expression*] 'man' signifies [*the meanings*] 'animal' and 'rational'; for each of the two is a part of what 'man' signifies by congruence.
> [*ad* 3] Signification by implication is like how [*the linguistic expression*] 'creature' (*maḫlūq*) signifies the 'creator' (*ḫāliq*), just as [*the linguistic expression*] 'father' (*ab*) [*signifies*] the 'son' (*ibn*), just as [*the linguistic expression*] 'roof' [*signifies*] the 'wall,' and just as [*the linguistic expression*] 'man' [*signifies*] 'possessing the faculty of laughter.'[117]

Several aspects of this enumeration are noteworthy: firstly, this is the first time in the Avicennian oeuvre as we know it that an enumeration of all three manners of signification, albeit brief and schematic, is given in its own separate section, which is also located before and not in the chapter on the correct

---

to repeatedly, for example in the chapter on the genus, Ibn Sīnā, *Kitāb aš-Šifāʾ, al-Manṭiq, al-Madḫal* I.9, p. 49, lines 3–5 and in the second part of the *Madḫal*, Ibn Sīnā, *Kitāb aš-Šifāʾ, al-Manṭiq, al-Madḫal* II.1, p. 95, lines 2ff. and II,4, p. 110, lines 5ff.

116 Gutas, *Avicenna and the Aristotelian Tradition*, p. 145 and p. 132; on the genesis, naming, transmission, and structure of this work, see Gutas, *Avicenna and the Aristotelian Tradition*, pp. 119–144, as well as id., "Avicenna's Eastern ('Oriental') Philosophy: Nature, Contents, Transmission," *Arabic Sciences and Philosophy*, vol. 10 (2000): pp. 159–180; see also Yaḥyā Mahdavī, *Fehrest-e nosḫehā-ye moṣannafāt-e Ebn-e Sīnā/Bibliographie d'Ibn Sina* (Tehran: Entešārāt-e Dānešgāh-e Tehrān, 1954 [1333 h.š.]), pp. 80ff.

117 Ibn Sīnā, *Manṭiq al-Mašriqiyyīn*, p. 14, lines 15–22.

determination of the quiddity and before the study of predicables. This observation is consistent with Gutas's comments on Ibn Sīnā's approach in this work. He writes that Ibn Sīnā's objective when writing this work was to systematically present rather controversial content while avoiding "references to views of other philosophers."[118]

Secondly, it is noteworthy in this passage that the focus of the significtion of implication is expanded: while in the *Madḫal* of the *Kitāb aš-Šifāʾ* Ibn Sīnā used implication primarily to solve the question of how the genus is predicated of the specific difference, here he adds an additional type of implication to this difference–genus signification (which is represented here by the example of 'roof' and 'wall'):[119] The species signifies the proprium according to the extrinsic manner of signification. Thus 'man' implies 'possessing the faculty of laughter.' This form of implication results on the one hand from the inclusion of inseparable attributes in general[120] and on the other hand, formulated in a somewhat simplified fashion, from a consistent application of the aforementioned schema[121] with the same subject:

FIGURE 7 Modified: the three manners of signification in the context of the study of predicables

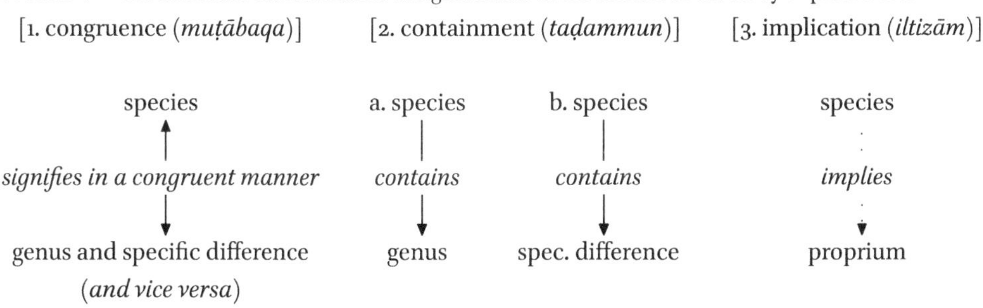

Furthermore, Ibn Sīnā incorporates relational implication ('father' implies 'son') into the extrinsic manner of signification and now explains the type of implication by word form, already present in the *Kitāb aš-Šifāʾ*, with the example of a passive participle that implies its unmentioned agent: The passive participle *maḫlūq* ('creature') implies the meaning of the agent *ḫāliq* ('creator'), even if it does not signify it in a primary or secondary way.[122] In this way, Ibn

118 Gutas, "Avicenna's Eastern ('Oriental') Philosophy," p. 159.
119 See Chapter 2, Section 2.2.1.
120 See in more detail Strobino, "Per Se, Inseparability, Containment and Implication."
121 See Chapter 2, Section 2.1, p. 79.
122 See Chapter 2, Section 2.1 and Ibn Sīnā, *Kitāb aš-Šifāʾ, al-Manṭiq, al-Madḫal* 1.8, p. 42,

Sīnā also draws on the theorems of Arabic stylistics/linguistics, as this type of implication had been described by Abū l-Ḥasan ar-Rummānī (d. 384/994) with the technical term *taḍmīn*. By this he meant "the presence of a meaning (*ḥuṣūl maʿnan*) in it [*i.e. in the speech* (kalām)] without a name (*ism*) or an attribute (*ṣifa*) being mentioned for it [*i.e. for the meaning contained in the speech*] (*ʿibāratun ʿanhū*)."[123] The word form implication that we find in Ibn Sīnā is called by ar-Rummānī "implication made necessary by the structure" (*taḍmīn tūǧibuhū l-bunya*),[124]—a type of implication that ar-Rummānī, according to Bruce Fudge, does not regard as a "rhetorical device" but as a "property of language."[125] Accordingly, 'knowing/known' (*maʿlūm*) implies a 'knower' (*ʿālim*)[126] and 'caused/produced' (*muḥdaṯ*) implies a 'causer/producer' (*muḥdiṯ*).[127]

Another aspect that had already been introduced in the parallel passage of the *Kitāb aš-Šifāʾ*[128] and which is developed here is the transfer relationship that underlies signification by implication: "[3.] signification by implication (*dalālatu l-iltizām*) [...] is the transfer (*naql*) by means of the meaning (*min ṭarīqi l-maʿnā*)."[129] It is in this passage that *naql* is found in this context for the first time. This idea is explained in the second paragraph of the passage in question:

> [§2.1]—This [*i.e. signification by implication*] is so because it [*i.e. the linguistic expression signifying by implication*] first signifies by congruence the meaning that it signifies first; this meaning is accompanied by

---

lines 15–16. The theological and ontological depths that this type of implication has are ignored in the passages in question.

123 Abū l-Ḥasan ar-Rummānī, "an-Nukat fī iʿǧāz al-Qurʾān," in *Ṯalāṯ rasāʾil fī iʿǧāz al-Qurʾān*, ed. by M. Ḫalaf Allāh and M. Zaġlūl Sallām (Cairo: Dār al-Maʿārif, 2012), 1968, p. 102, lines 16–17; see also Fudge, "Taḍmīn," p. 469. Fudge renders this term in this context as 'implication,' see Fudge, "Taḍmīn," p. 478, pp. 468–469.

124 Ar-Rummānī, "an-Nukat fī iʿǧāz al-Qurʾān," p. 103, line 2.

125 Fudge, "Taḍmīn," p. 478.

126 Ar-Rummānī, "an-Nukat fī iʿǧāz al-Qurʾān," p. 103, line 4.

127 Ibid., p. 102, line 19; see also Fudge, "Taḍmīn," p. 479 and Sanni, "Again on *taḍmīn*," pp. 17 f. I do not intend to argue in favor of Ibn Sīnā being directly influenced by ar-Rummānī; rather, my aim is to show how the distinction between two types of implication limited to the field of the study of predicables developed into a classification of signification whose roots must also be located in Arabic philology and rhetoric. Incidentally, ar-Rummānī himself was accused of "mixing grammar and logic in a way that could not be taken seriously by either grammarians or logicians," Endreß, "Grammatik und Logik," pp. 202–203.

128 See Ibn Sīnā, *Kitāb aš-Šifāʾ, al-Manṭiq, al-Madḫal* 1.8, p. 43, lines 1–3; cf. Chapter 2, Section 2.1.

129 Ibn Sīnā, *Manṭiq al-Mašriqiyyīn*, p. 14, line 17.

> another meaning (*wa-yakūnu ḏālika l-maʿnā yaṣḥabuhū maʿnan āḫar*), so that the mind also turns to this second meaning (*fa-yantaqilu ḏ-ḏihnu ayḍan ilā ḏālika l-maʿnā ṯ-ṯānī*), which corresponds to the first meaning (*yuwāfiqu*)[130] and accompanies it (*yaṣḥabuhū*).[131]

Thus, a linguistic expression first signifies its primary meaning, whereupon, building on the first meaning, a subsequent meaning comes into focus and

---

130 Several indications suggest that *yurāfiqu* should be read instead of *yuwāfiqu*: "so that the mind also turns to this second meaning, WHICH GUIDES (*YURĀFIQU*) THE FIRST MEANING and accompanies it" instead of "so that the mind also turns to this second meaning (*fa-yantaqilu ḏ-ḏihnu ayḍan ilā ḏālika l-maʿnā ṯ-ṯānī*), WHICH CORRESPONDS TO THE FIRST MEANING (*YUWĀFIQU*) and accompanies it (*yaṣḥabuhū*)."

[1.] One indication is that, in the parallel passages, Ibn Sīnā speaks of the second meaning only adhering to the first and not corresponding to it, see for example Ibn Sīnā, *al-Išārāt wa-t-tanbīhāt*, p. 42, line 15–p. 43, line 1: "[*The linguistic expression signifies a meaning*] [3.] by way of following (*istitbāʿ*) and implication (*iltizām*), in the sense that the linguistic expression signifies a meaning by congruence, whereby a meaning adheres to that meaning THAT IS DIFFERENT FROM IT (*wa-yakūnu ḏalika l-maʿnā yalzamuhū maʿnan ġayruhū*), like an EXTERNAL COMPANION (*ar-rafīq al-ḫāriǧī*)." [2.] Another indication is provided by Abū l-ʿAbbās al-Faḍl b. Muḥammad al-Lawkarī (d. after 503/1109) in the *Bayān al-ḥaqq bi-ḍimān aṣ-ṣidq, al-Manṭiq, al-Madḫal*, ed. by Ibrāhīm Dibāǧī (Tehran: Mo'assase-ye entešārāt-e Amīr Kabīr 1986 [1364]). The parallel passage is identical to the relevant passage in Ibn Sīnā's *Manṭiq al-Mašriqiyyīn* except for this previously cited formulation:

Lawkarī, *Bayān al-ḥaqq*, p. 131, line 12–p. 132, line 4	**Ibn Sīnā, *Manṭiq al-Mašriqiyyīn*, p. 14, line 21–p. 15, line 2**
[ad 3] *As for* signification by implication, it is like how [*the linguistic expression*] 'creature' (*maḫlūq*) signifies the creator (*ḫāliq*), just as [*the linguistic expression*] 'father' (*ab*) [*signifies*] the 'son' (*ibn*), just as [*the linguistic expression*] 'roof' [*signifies*] the 'wall,' and just as [*the linguistic expression*] 'man' [*signifies*] 'possessing the faculty of laughter,' *and the like.*	[ad 3] Signification by implication is like how [*the linguistic expression*] 'creature' (*maḫlūq*) signifies the creator (*ḫāliq*), just as [*the linguistic expression*] 'father' (*ab*) [*signifies*] the 'son' (*ibn*), just as [*the linguistic expression*] 'roof' [*signifies*] the 'wall,' and just as [*the linguistic expression*] 'man' [*signifies*] 'possessing the faculty of laughter.'
[§ 2]—This is because it [*the linguistic expression signifying by implication*] first signifies by congruence that meaning which it signifies first; this meaning is accompanied by another (*wa-yakūnu ḏālika l-maʿnā yaṣḥabuhū maʿnā āḫar*), so that the mind also turns to this second meaning, WHICH GUIDES (*YURĀFIQU*) THE FIRST MEANING and accompanies it.	[§ 2]—This is because it [*the linguistic expression signifying by implication*] first signifies by congruence that meaning which it signifies first; this meaning is accompanied by another (*wa-yakūnu ḏālika l-maʿnā yaṣḥabuhū maʿnā āḫar*), so that the mind also turns to this second meaning, WHICH CORRESPONDS TO THE FIRST MEANING (*YUWĀFIQU*) and accompanies it.

131 Ibn Sīnā, *Manṭiq al-Mašriqiyyīn*, p. 14, line 22–p. 15, line 2.

is linked to the actual meaning of the linguistic expression. This presentation of the signification relationship, in which a first, original meaning and a second, extended meaning participate, reveals implication in the context of linguistic theory. The implication relationship suddenly appears as a relationship of transfer, similar to that underlying the "new metaphor" as we find it described since the writings of ar-Rummānī, where a linguistic expression is also linked to an external meaning.[132]

Ibn Sīnā then provdes a schematic hierarchy of the three manners of signification:

> [2.2] Signification by congruence and signification by containment have in common that neither of them is a signification of something outside the [*signified*] thing.
> [2.3] Signification by containment and signification by implication have in common that each of them requires the first signification [*i.e. signification by congruence*].[133]

Both types of implication require the signification of congruence, which Ibn Sīnā in the *Kitāb aš-Šifāʾ* therefore calls the 'primary manner of signification'; i.e. in both manners of signification, the primary meaning signified by congruence is evoked first. Only then does the contained or adhering thing come into focus. Both the meaning signified by congruence and the meaning signified by containment remain within this meaning; only implication goes beyond it. The hierarchization of a primary, secondary, and extrinsic meaning in the *Kitāb aš-Šifāʾ* forms the basis of this explanation.[134]

In addition to the new and systematic overview of the three manners of signification, the implication relationship between specific difference and genus is also discussed in this work in its usual place and context:

> […] for 'sentient' is understood by way of congruence only to be something 'that has sensory perception,' and 'rational' is understood only to be something 'that has the faculty of reason.' So if that also signifies other

132 See Wolfhart Heinrichs, *The Hand of the Northwind. Opinions on Metaphor and the Early Meaning of Istiʿāra in Arabic Poetics* (Wiesbaden: Franz Steiner, 1977), p. 40; Fudge, "Taḍmīn," p. 468; ar-Rummānī, "an-Nukat fī iʿǧāz al-Qurʾān," pp. 85–86. However, this connection between implication and metaphor is only explicitly established later by Faḫr ad-dīn; see Chapter 3, Section 2.2.

133 Ibn Sīnā, *Manṭiq al-Mašriqiyyīn*, p. 15, lines 3–6.

134 See Chapter 2, Section 2.1.

> meanings (*maʿānī*)—such as that one knows (*min ḥayṯu yuʿalamu*) that 'sentient' can only be a body that has a soul, and it is the same with 'rational'—then that signification [*i.e. the signification of these other, additional meanings*] comes about by way of implication, not by way of containment.[135]

2.3.1.4 *The Classification of Signification as a Propaedeutic for Logic:* al-Išārāt wa-t-tanbīhāt

Ibn Sīnā's *al-Išārāt wa-t-tanbīhāt*, written roughly between 421/1030 and 425/1034, is considered his "last philosophical summa."[136] As in the *Manṭiq al-Mašriqiyyīn*, Ibn Sīnā devotes a separate section to the enumeration of the classification of signification. However, the placement of this part within the section on logic differs: Whereas the enumeration of the Tripartition in the *Manṭiq al-Mašriqiyyīn* was preceded by the introduction to simple and compound linguistic expressions, to particular and universal linguistic expressions, as well as to the foundations of predication, here the Tripartition is introduced just after the introductory considerations on the purpose of logic. It functions as the actual beginning of the logical treatise, followed by the sections on predication, on simple and compound linguistic expressions—here one finds aspects that previously used to only be discussed later in the work, in the passages about the *De Int.*[137]—and on particular and universal linguistic expressions. Because the logician must know "the principles of explanatory speech (*mabādiʾu l-qawli š-šāriḥ*) and the manner (*kayfiyya*) of its composition,"[138] the basics of language are bundled together at the beginning of the treatise on logic, starting with the kinds of signification:

> So let us begin by determining the way in which the linguistic expression signifies meaning.

---

135 Ibn Sīnā, *Manṭiq al-Mašriqiyyīn*, p. 15, lines 18–21; in this work too, this aspect is repeated in several places, see Table 3, p. 103 f.

136 Gutas, *Avicenna and the Aristotelian Tradition*, p. 155. Street considers this work to be the most important of all Ibn Sīnā's works, Street, "Arabic Logic," p. 539. On the history of this work's reception, see Endreß, "Reading Avicenna in the Madrasa," pp. 410–415 and Wisnovsky, "Avicenna's Islamic Reception," pp. 193–199; on the editorial history, see Joep Lameer, "Towards a New Edition of Avicenna's *Kitāb al-Ishārāt wa-l-tanbīhāt*," *Journal of Islamic Manuscripts* vol. 4 (2013): pp. 199–248.

137 Like, for example, the remarks on *ism* and *fiʿl* as components of the sentence, cf. Ibn Sīnā, *al-Išārāt wa-t-tanbīhāt*, p. 44.

138 Ibn Sīnā, *al-Išārāt wa-t-tanbīhāt*, p. 42, lines 1–2.

> 'Reference to (*išāra ilā*) the signification of meaning by the linguistic expression':
> The linguistic expression signifies a meaning
> [1.] either by way of congruence (*muṭābaqa*), in the sense that this linguistic expression (*lafẓ*) has been taken as a basis (*mawḍūʿ*) for that meaning (*maʿnā*) and in relation to it (*wa-bi-izāʾihī*)—just as 'triangle' signifies 'the form enclosed by three sides' (*aš-šaklu l-muḥīṭu bihi ṯalāṯatu aḍluʿ*);
> [2.] or by way of containment (*taḍammun*), in the sense that the meaning is a part of that meaning which corresponds to it [*i.e. the linguistic expression*] in a congruent manner—just as 'triangle' signifies form (*šakl*); for it [*i.e. the word 'triangle'*] does not signify form in the way that it is a name for form (*lā ʿalā annahu ismun li-š-šakli*), but rather [*the word 'triangle' signifies form*] in the way that it is a name for the meaning of which 'form' is a part [*i.e. 'form' shares in the meaning of the name 'triangle'*];
> [3.] or by way of having as a consequence (*istitbāʿ*) and implication (*iltizām*), in the sense that the linguistic expression signifies a meaning by congruence, whereby a meaning is attached to that meaning that is different from it, just like an external companion (*ar-rafīq al-ḫāriǧī*); not like a part of it but like a companion that is an implication of/adherent to it [*i.e. of/to that first meaning*], just like how the linguistic expression 'roof' (*saqf*) signifies the 'wall' (*ḥāʾiṭ*), and just as 'man' signifies 'receptive to the art of writing' (*qābil ṣanʿat al-kitāba*).[139]

Here, for the first time in this context, Ibn Sīnā uses the phrase "that this linguistic expression has been taken as a basis for that meaning (*yakūna ḏālika l-lafẓu mawḍūʿan li—ḏālika l-maʿnā*)." In doing so, he gives an explanation for congruent signification that goes beyond the description of being "primary" or signifying "in a primary way"—as in the *Madḫal* of the *Kitāb aš-Šifāʾ*—as well as beyond illustration by means of an example ("As for signification by congruence, this is like the fact that the linguistic expression 'man' signifies 'rational animal' [*ḥayawān nāṭiq*]")—as in the work the *Manṭiq al-Mašriqiyyīn*. This explanation thus breaks away from predicable semantics, which is one reason, among other factors, why the classification of signification leaves the framework of logic over the course of its reception history and finds use in other disciplines as if it had never belonged to logic to begin with. Moreover, in this passage the term implication is supplemented by a further term: 'having as a consequence' (*istitbāʿ*).[140]

---

139 Ibn Sīnā, *al-Išārāt wa-t-tanbīhāt*, p. 42, line 5–p. 43, line 3.

140 Ibn Sīnā prefers to use this term to express sequential relationships in syllogisms, see, for

Due to the change in the Tripartition's placement in the text as well as to the method of allusion that characterizes this work[141] and the concise, cursory style associated with it, the Tripartition of Signification appears as a classification of fundamental, topic-independent, propaedeutic relevance.

This approach in the *Išārāt* encouraged subsequent scholars, especially commentators of this work, to not only restore the context and discussion of the Tripartition by referring to other works of Ibn Sīnā, but also to transfer the Tripartition to other contexts and areas of inquiry. The introduction of the classification of signification into *uṣūl al-fiqh* is just one example of this.[142]

But in this work, too, implication is also discussed outside of this enumeration, in the context, as we have seen before, of the correct determination of the quiddity:

> [§1.1] When we say: 'this and that linguistic expression signifies this and that,' we mean only the manner [*of signification*] of congruence and containment, not the manner [*of signification*] of implication.—How could it be otherwise? After all, what is signified by implication is unlimited (*ġayr maḥdūd*).
> [§1.2] Furthermore, if what is signified by implication were to be considered [*legitimate*] [*i.e. if 'this and that linguistic expression signifies this and that' were not understood to mean only the first two manners of signification*], then that which is not constitutive [*of quiddity/meaning*] would be suitable for signifying 'what it is'—such as 'possessing the faculty of laughter'; for it signifies 'rational animal' by way of implication.
> [§1.3] However, all [*logicians*] have already agreed that something like this is not suitable as an answer [*to the question of*] 'what it is.'[143]

---

example, Ibn Sīnā, *Kitāb an-Naǧāt*, pp. 95–96 or id., *Kitāb aš-Šifāʾ*, *al-Manṭiq*, *Kitāb al-Qiyās*, ed. by Saʿīd Zāyid (Cairo: al-Hayʾa al-ʿĀmma li-Šuʾūn al-Maṭābiʿ al-Amīriyya, 1964), p. 498.

141 See Gutas, *Avicenna and the Aristotelian Tradition*, pp. 157–158 and pp. 346–350.

142 With regard to the Tripartition as a propaedeutic and topic-independent item of curriculum in the field of logic, see, for example, the treatment of the topic in as-Sāwī, *al-Baṣāʾir an-naṣīriyya*, pp. 33 and Abū l-Barakāt al-Baġdādī (d. ca. 560/1165), *Kitāb al-Muʿtabar fī l-ḥikma*, ed. by Zayn al-ʿAbidīn al-Musāwī (Haydarābād 1938–1939; reprint Ǧubayl: Dār wa-maktabat bībliyūn, 2012), vol. 1, p. 56, lines 2–18. To a certain extent, this also applies to al-Ġazālī's treatment of the Tripartition in his *Miʿyār al-ʿilm*, whose first treatise—albeit as a propaedeutic for syllogism—also begins with a description of the Tripartition; Abū Ḥazālīmid Muḥammad al-Ġazālī, *Miʿyār al-ʿilm*, ed. by Sulaymān Dunyā (Cairo: Dār al-Maʿārif, 1961), p. 72. As Janssens (cf. Janssens, "Al-Ghazzālī's *Miʿyār al-ʿilm fī fann al-manṭiq*," pp. 42–43) correctly notes, this description goes back to the *Išārāt*—terminologically and partly in terms of content; there are, however, deviations.

143 Ibn Sīnā, *al-Išārāt wa-t-tanbīhāt*, p. 53, lines 5–10.

What is particularly striking about this account is the introduction of a new type of implication, namely the signification of the species by the proprium ('possessing the faculty of laughter' signifies 'rational animal' by way of implication). The type of implication in which the proprium is signified by the species had already been introduced in the *Manṭiq al-Mašriqiyyīn*; in the *Išārāt*, the question of the scope of signification of the specific difference is finally extended to the scope of signification of the proprium.

2.3.1.5 *Summarizing Overview*

The examination of the relevant passages in Ibn Sīnā's *Madḫalāt* has shown that the development of the three-part classification of signification out of the two types of implication ultimately resulted in a change in its placement and contextualization within the works on logic. We see a progressive generalization of the classification of signification accompanied by a systematization: in the early *Madḫal* treatises and *Madḫal*-equivalent passages, a distinction is only made between 'that which contains' (*al-mutaḍammin*) and 'that which implies' (*al-multazim*). This distinction, which was intended to draw attention to the two different implicative functions of the predicables, built upon al-Fārābī's treatment of this topic in his guide on the avoidance of errors (following *De Int.* 11). But it represents a terminological development, since al-Fārābī had labelled both types of implication as *luzūm*. The *Madḫal* of Ibn Sīnā's *Kitāb aš-Šifāʾ* introduces three types of signification. This was intended—with recourse to connections to general linguistic theory (implication based on the word form/indication of a relationship of transfer)—amongst other things to provide clarity about the signification relationships of the predicables, in particular with regard to the question of how the genus is predicated of the specific difference. Finally, his *Manṭiq al-Mašriqiyyīn* listed all three modes of signification in a separate section largely detached from the rest of the content, and expanded the relationship of implication: it added the 'species/proprium' relationship to the 'specific difference/genus' relationship. This passage also contained allusions and explanations (including various hierarchization models of the types of signification, implication based on the word form, and elaboration of the transfer relationship on the basis of ar-Rummānī's "new metaphor"), which were taken up and further developed by later scholars such as Faḫr ad-dīn ar-Rāzī. In Ibn Sīnā's influential work *al-Išārāt wa-t-tanbīhāt*, the general presentation of the classification of signification as seen in the *Manṭiq al-Mašriqiyyīn* reached its climax. For it is firstly found in a different place in the text: Here it forms the actual beginning of the treatise on logic, just after the remarks on the purpose of logic. Secondly, it is discussed at this prominent point together with the parts of the *De Int.* that treat languistic theory. And thirdly, in his explanation of congruence, Ibn Sīnā draws on general linguistic-philosophical wording that breaks away from predicable semantics and proved to be formative for the work's subsequent reception. Combined with the method of allusion that characterizes the *Išārāt*, the Tripartition of Signification appears as a classification of fundamental and propaedeutic relevance.

Thus throughout the course of the classification becoming generalized and systematized, we see among other things a change in the presentation, placement, and definition of the manners of signification. This progressive, systematic method of presentation increased the relevance of the classification, turning it into one of the basics that logicians were expected to learn at the beginning of their training.

In the following, the placement of the discussion of the manners of signification in the respective *Madḫal* and *Madḫal*-equivalent sections is illustrated in the form of a table, since it is not only the content but also the aspects of structure that bears importance for the assessment of the development of the manners of signification and for their further reception.

TABLE 3 Simplified structure of the *Madḫal* treatises and *Madḫal*-equivalents of Ibn Sīnā's various works[144]

1. Writings of the Transition Period (403–404/1013–1014):	**2. Middle Period (ca. 411–418/1020–1027):**	**3. Period of Eastern Philosophy (ca. 418–421/1027–1030):**	**4. Late Period (ca. 418–428/ca. 1027–1037):**
Muḫtaṣar al-awṣat and *Kitāb an-Naǧāt* (or *Muḫtaṣar al-aṣġar*)	*Kitāb aš-Šifā'* (Origin of the *Madḫal*: 412–414/1022–1024)	*Manṭiq al-Mašriqiyyīn* (ca. 418–420/1027–1029)	*al-Išārāt wa-t-tanbīhāt* (ca. 421–425/1030–1034)
(Mention of the two types of implication)	(Detailed introduction and discussion of the Triparition)	(Schematic enumeration of the Tripartition; expansion of implication)	(Schematic enumeration of the Tripartition; expansion of implication)

144 In the table, # indicates the topic area in which the discussion of the two types of implication or the Tripartition of Signification occurs. The table provides a simplified structure of the thematic complexes; these are not chapter headings. For the creative periods, see Gutas, *Avicenna and the Aristotelian Tradition*, p. 165. The logical treatises of other works are not included in the table because they do not discuss the problems associated with the manners of signification or the classification itself.

TABLE 3 Simplified structure of the *Madḫal* treatises and *Madḫal*-equivalents (*cont.*)

1. Writings of the Transition Period (403–404/1013–1014):	**2. Middle Period (ca. 411–418/1020–1027):**	**3. Period of Eastern Philosophy (ca. 418–421/1027–1030):**	**4. Late Period (ca. 418–428/ca. 1027–1037):**
introduction	introduction	introduction	introduction
simple/compound linguistic expression	simple/compound linguistic expression	simple/compound linguistic expression	The signification of the meaning by the linguistic expression#
universal/particular	universal/particular	universal/particular	predication
essential/accidental	essential/accidental	–	simple/compound linguistic expression
correct determination of the quiddity (*#Muḫtaṣar*)	correct determination of the quiddity	predication	universal/particular
genus (*#Naǧāt*)	introduction to the doctrine of predicables#	classes of the signification of the meaning by the linguistic expression#	essential/accidental/that which adheres/the separable […]
species	genus#	classes of the signification of the subject by the predicate#	correct determination of the quiddity#
specific difference (*#Muḫtaṣar/#Naǧāt*)	species	classes of the determination of the quiddity	genus and species
proprium	[…] specific difference	constitutives/adherents/accidents	specific difference#
general accident	proprium	classes of different meanings#	proprium and general accident
	general accident	[…] investigation of the genus#	definition#

2.3.2 The Tripartition of Signification in the Writings of al-Ġazālī

Subsequent scholars adopted Ibn Sīnā's prioritization of the Tripartition of Signification and gave it a prominent place in their respective works on logic. This can be seen, for example, in Abū l-Ḥasan Bahmanyār b. al-Marzubān's (d. 458/1066) *Kitāb at-Taḥṣīl*, in the *Madḫal* of the *Bayān al-ḥaqq bi-ḍimān aṣ-ṣidq* by Abū l-ʿAbbās al-Faḍl b. Muḥammad al-Lawkarī (d. after 503/1109), in ʿUmar b. Sahlān as-Sāwī's (fl. 540/1145) *al-Baṣā'ir an-naṣīriyya fī ʿilm al-manṭiq*, and in Abū l-Barakāt al-Baġdādī's (ca. 560/1165) *Kitāb al-Muʿtabar fī l-ḥikma*. In the latter two, we see the approach used in the *Išārāt*, where the Tripartition of Signification is understood and presented as a propaedeutic and topic-independent item of curriculum in the field of logic.[145] This finding also applies to al-Ġazālī's treatment of the Tripartition in his *Miʿyār al-ʿilm*, whose first treatise—albeit as a propaedeutic to syllogism—also begins with a presentation of the Tripartition. As Janssens correctly notes, this presentation bases its terminology on that used in the *Išārāt*, but there are significant deviations.[146] In al-Ġazālī's case, his engagement with the Tripartition of Signification is not limited to his works on logic. He also introduces it into his work on legal theory, even though there it is placed within a separate chapter on logic and is not connected to the rest of the content. This is because the content of the work forms two different categories of indicators: those in the logic section correspond to indicators based on reason (*al-adilla al-ʿaqliyya*) while those in the section on legal theory correspond to indicators based on imposition (*waḍʿiyya*).[147]

The introduction to logic in al-Ġazālī's *Mustaṣfā*—which he writes is not a part of the discipline of *uṣūl al-fiqh*, but rather an introduction to all sciences—

145 Cf. Ibn al-Marzubān, *Kitāb at-Taḥṣīl*, p. 13, lines 3–6; Lawkarī, *Bayān al-ḥaqq*, p. 1312; as-Sāwī, *al-Baṣā'ir an-naṣīriyya*, p. 33; and al-Baġdādī, *Kitāb al-Muʿtabar*, vol. 1, p. 56, lines 5–18.

146 Cf. al-Ġazālī, *Miʿyār al-ʿilm*, p. 72 as well as Janssens, "Al-Ghazzālī's *Miʿyār al-ʿilm fī fann al-manṭiq*," pp. 42–43 and Ibn Sīnā, *al-Išārāt wa-t-tanbīhāt*, p. 42, line 5–p. 43, line 3.

147 Cf. al-Ġazālī, *al-Mustaṣfā*, vol. 3, p. 23; the chapter on logic is found in al-Ġazālī, *al-Mustaṣfā*, vol. 1, pp. 30–175. On al-Ġazālī's discussion of Avicennian logic, see esp. Rudolph, "Die Neubewertung der Logik durch al-Ġazālī" and Jules Janssens, "Al-Ghazālī: The Introduction of Peripatetic Syllogistic in Islamic Law (and Kalām)," *MIDEO*, vol. 28 (2010): pp. 219–233; Wael B. Hallaq, "Logic, Formal Arguments and Formalization of Arguments in Sunnī Jurisprudence," *Arabica*, vol. 37 (1990): pp. 315–322; Robert Brunschvig, "Valeur et fondement du raisonnement juridique par analogie d'après al-Ġazālī," *Studia Islamica*, no. 34 (1971): pp. 57–88; on the influence of Avicennian philosophy in general on al-Ġazālī's theology, see Richard Frank, "Al-Ghazâlî's Use of Avicenna's Philosophy," *Revue des Études Islamiques*, no. 55–57 (1987–1989): pp. 271–285. On the evaluation of al-Ġazālī's logic as too watered down "to be recognizably Farabian or Avicennian," see Street, "Arabic and Islamic Philosophy of Language and Logic," p. 11.

corresponds in large part, as Janssens has already worked out, to his logical work, also aimed at jurists, the *Kitāb Miḥakk an-naẓar*. This correspondence extends to the passage that is of interest to us, as the following table shows:[148]

TABLE 4 The correspondence between the passage on the tripartition of signification from al-Ġazālī's *Mustaṣfā* and that of his *Miḥakk an-naẓar*

Al-Ġazālī: *al-Mustaṣfā*, Vol. 1, p. 92, line 8–p. 93, line 6 [or, in the edition by Muḥammad Yūsuf Naǧm. Beirut: Dār Ṣādir, 2010, vol. 1, p. 40, line 22–p. 41, line 6]	**Al-Ġazālī: *Kitāb Miḥakk an-naẓar*, p. 73, line 6–p. 74, line 1**
[§ 1] The signification of meaning by the linguistic expression is limited to three ways, namely [1.] congruence (*muṭābaqa*), [2.] containment (*taḍammun*), and [3.] implication (*iltizām*).	[§ 1] The signification of meaning by the linguistic expression is limited to three ways, namely [1.] congruence (*muṭābaqa*), [2.] containment (*taḍammun*), and [3.] implication (*iltizām*).
[§ 2] For the linguistic expression 'house' [*ad* 1] signifies the meaning 'house' by way of congruence and [*ad* 2] signifies 'roof' only by way of containment; for [*the linguistic expression*] 'house' contains 'roof' because 'house' is an expression (*'ibāra*) for 'roof' and 'walls' (*ḤĪṬĀN*, SG. *ḤĀʾIṬ*). This is just like how the linguistic expression 'horse' signifies 'body,' since a horse is nothing other than a body.	[§ 2] For the linguistic expression 'house' [*ad* 1] signifies the meaning 'house' by way of congruence and [*ad* 2] signifies 'roof' only by way of containment; for [*the linguistic expression*] 'house' contains 'roof' because 'house' is an expression (*'ibāra*) for 'roof' and 'walls' (*ĞUDRĀN*, SG. *ĞIDĀR*). This is just like how the linguistic expression 'horse' signifies 'body,' since a horse is nothing other than a body, since every time we say 'horse,' we find the corporeality in the equineness.—So let us use the term (*tasmiya*) 'containment' for this manner [*of signification*] and [*the term*] 'congruence' for the first manner.

148 Cf. Janssens, "Al-Ghazzālī's *Mi'yār al-'ilm fī fann al-manṭiq*," pp. 39–66 and id., "Review: Frank Griffel: Apostasie und Toleranz im Islam," *Journal of Islamic Studies*, vol. 14, no. 1 (2003): p. 71. On the fact that the *Miḥakk* is a textbook for legal scholars, see Rudolph, "Die Neubewertung der Logik durch al-Ġazālī," p. 86, fn. 48.

TABLE 4 The conformity of the passage of the tripartite division of the designation (*cont.*)

Al-Ġazālī: *al-Mustaṣfā*, Vol. 1, p. 92, line 8–p. 93, line 6 [or, in the edition by Muḥammad Yūsuf Naǧm. Beirut: Dār Ṣādir, 2010, vol. 1, p. 40, line 22–p. 41, line 6]	**Al-Ġazālī: *Kitāb Miḥakk an-naẓar*, p. 73, line 6–p. 74, line 1**
[§ 3] [*ad* 3] As for the way of implication, this is like how the linguistic term 'roof' signifies the wall (*ḥā'iṭ*); for it [*i.e. the linguistic expression 'roof'*] was not imposed for the [*meaning*] 'wall' in the way that the linguistic expression 'wall' was imposed for it—namely, in such a way that it is congruent in relation to it. It [*i.e. the meaning 'wall'*] IS NOT CONTAINED (*MUTAḌAMMAN*), since 'wall' is not a part [*of the meaning*] 'roof' in the way that 'roof' is a part [*of the meaning*] of 'house' itself, and in the way that 'wall' is a part [*of the meaning*] of 'house' itself. Rather, it [*i.e. the signification by implication*] is like a companion (*rafīq*) and that which externally adheres (*lāzim ḫāriǧ*) to the essence of the roof, and from which 'roof' cannot be detached.	[§ 3] [*ad* 3] As for the way of implication, this is like how the linguistic expression 'roof' signifies the wall (*ḥā'iṭ*); for it [*i.e. the linguistic expression 'roof'*] was not imposed for the [*meaning*] 'wall' in the way that the linguistic expression 'wall' was imposed for it—namely, in such a way that it is congruent in relation to it. It [*i.e. the linguistic expression 'roof' signifies 'wall'*] not BY CONTAINMENT (*BI-TAḌAMMUN*), since 'wall' is not a part [*of the meaning*] 'roof' in the way that 'roof' is a part [*of the meaning*] of 'house' itself, and in the way that 'wall' is a part [*of the meaning*] of 'house' itself. Rather, it [*i.e. the signification by implication*] is like a companion (*rafīq*) and that which externally adheres (*lāzim ḫāriǧ*) to the essence of the roof, and from which 'roof' cannot be detached, so that its signification is of a different kind (*namaṭ*). Let us then create another linguistic expression for it, namely 'implication' (*iltizām*) and 'having as a consequence' (*istitbāʿ*).
[§ 4] Beware, in investigations based on reasoning (*naẓar al-ʿaql*), of using linguistic expressions that signify by way of implication. Limit yourself instead to [*the linguistic expressions*] that signify by way of congruence or containment.	[§ 4] Beware, in investigations based on reasoning (*naẓar al-ʿaql*), of using linguistic expressions that signify by way of implication; otherwise you will strengthen your opponent (*aw tumakkinu ḫaṣmaka*). Limit yourself instead to [*the linguistic expressions*] that signify by way of congruence or containment.

This passage from the *Mustaṣfā* is also partly (§ 3 and § 4) based on Ibn Sīnā's *Išārāt wa-t-tanbīhāt*, as the following table shows:

TABLE 5 Comparison between the passage on the tripartition of signification from al-Ġazālī's *Mustaṣfā* and that from Ibn Sīnā's *Išārāt wa-t-tanbīhāt*

Al-Ġazālī: *al-Mustaṣfā*, vol. 1, p. 93, lines 3–8 [or, in the edition by Muḥammad Yūsuf Naǧm. Beirut: Dār Ṣādir, 2010, vol. 1, p. 41, lines 4–7]	**Ibn Sīnā: *al-Išārāt wa-t-tanbīhāt*, p. 43, lines 1–3 and p. 53, lines 5–6**
[§ 3] […] Rather, it [*i.e. the signification by implication*] is like a companion (*rafīq*) and that which externally adheres (*lāzim ḫāriǧ*) to the essence of the roof, and from which 'roof' cannot be detached.	[3.] […], like an external companion (*ar-rafīq al-ḫāriǧī*), not like a part of it, but like a companion that is adherent to it [*i.e. to that first meaning*], just like how the linguistic expression 'roof' (*saqf*) signifies the 'wall' (*ḥā'iṭ*) […].
[§ 4] Beware, in investigations based on reasoning (*naẓar al-ʿaql*), of using linguistic expressions that signify by way of implication. Limit yourself instead to [*the linguistic expressions*] that signify by way of congruence or containment. For the signification by implication cannot be traced back to the definition (*ḥadd*), since [*the linguistic expression*] 'roof' implies 'wall' and 'wall' implies 'base' and 'base' implies 'earth.'	[§ 1.1] When we say: 'this and that linguistic expression signifies this and that,' we mean only the manner [*of signification*] of congruence and containment, not the manner [*of signification*] of implication. —How could it be otherwise? After all, what is signified by implication is unlimited (*ġayr maḥdūd*).

The references to the *Išārāt* concern the description of implication and the indication that implication is not permitted in the determination of the quiddity. I discuss the debate about the evaluation of implication elsewhere in this book.[149]

Al-Ġazālī places the classification of signification, as the first categorization of the relationship between word and meaning, at the beginning of the chapter on demonstrative proof (*burhān*), which follows the chapter on defini-

149 Cf. Chapter 2, Section 3.2.4, p. 144 ff.

tion (*ḥadd*). Unlike other post-Avicennian scholars, however, in this integrated work of logic he does not place the classification of signification at the very beginning or in a *Madḫal*-equivalent passage in the context of the definition of predicables. But this approach is not surprising in view of the work's focus on syllogistics, which also observable in his *Miḥakk* and *Miʿyār* and which, according to Rudolph, can be explained by al-Ġazālī's central concern with the "connection between philosophical logic and traditional Islamic argumentation."[150]

The second categorization, which follows the classification of signification, concerns universality/particularity, while the third distinguishes between polyonymy, heteronymy, Aristotelian synonymy, and homonymy.[151] Despite Faḫr ad-dīn ar-Rāzī's disdain for the *Mustaṣfā*,[152] this chapter, organized in this way, functions as a precursor and pioneer for Faḫr ad-dīn's large-scale synthesis, which combines different components from different traditions together.[153]

It remains to be noted that al-Ġazālī introduced the classification of signification into his work on legal theory, that the way it is presented also testifies to an engagement with Ibn Sīnā's *Išārāt*, and that the structure of the chapter in question is reflected to a certain extent in the corresponding chapter of Faḫr ad-dīn's *Maḥṣūl*, which will be discussed in Chapter 3, Section 2.

3 The Tripartition of Signification in Faḫr ad-dīn ar-Rāzī [*ad* §§1–4]

3.1 *The Continued Generalization of the Tripartition*

Having traced the genesis of the classification of signification—from the two-part division in al-Fārābī and in Ibn Sīnā's early writings to a three-part division in the writings of Ibn Sīnā's middle and later periods—and having worked out the systematization of this classification in Ibn Sīnā's writings, we can now use this basis to return to our source text, the *Maḥṣūl* as presented in Chapter 1, to take a closer look at Faḫr ad-dīn's treatment of this classification. The focus will

150 Rudolph, "Die Neubewertung der Logik durch al-Ġazālī," p. 86.

151 Al-Ġazālī, *al-Mustaṣfā*, vol. 1, p. 95, line 9–p. 96; cf. Janssens, "Al-Ghazzālī's *Miʿyār al-ʿilm fī fann al-manṭiq*," pp. 44 and Muḥassab, *ʿIlm ad-dalāla ʿinda l-ʿarab*, p. 103; for an explanation of the parallel passage in the *Maḥṣūl*, see Chapter 3, Section 2.1.

152 Cf. Faḫr ad-dīn ar-Rāzī, *Munāẓarāt Faḫr ad-dīn ar-Rāzī*, ed. by Fathalla Kholeif (Beirut: Dār al-Mašriq, 1966), pp. 45 f. of the Arabic text and pp. 67 ff.; see Frank Griffel, *Al-Ghazālī's Philosophical Theology* (New York: Oxford University Press, 2009), p. 117.

153 See in particular Chapter 3 of this study, in which the efforts towards the synthesis of grammar and logic as well as of legal theory and logic are shown by means of Faḫr ad-dīn's subsequent classifications.

first be on the function of the classification in Faḫr ad-dīn's outline concept. Then we will deal in detail with paragraphs one to four, in which the classification is described and explained.

As we have already established, our source text is divided into two main parts, the first of which is the focus of our interest and consists of several sub-classifications. The first of these, which we have called the logical sub-classification, has already been examined and contextualized in detail; the others will form the subject of later chapters and sections of this book.[154] The passage made up of paragraphs one to four is an introduction to the sub-classifications that follow it, with the first paragraph outlining the classification of signification briefly and concisely—without examples to illustrate what is meant—and then with the three following paragraphs providing comments, qualifications, and explanations. Subsequently [§ 5], as has already been shown,[155] the linguistic expression signifying by congruence is subdivided into the simple and the compound. And finally, the simple linguistic expression signifying by congruence is subdivided into several further categories.

The following outline illustrates the introduction in the context of the sub-classifications:

FIGURE 8 *The Tripartition in Faḫr ad-dīn ar-Rāzī*

[I] The first part is categorized into:
- [I.1] the linguistic expression signifying by congruence (*muṭābaqa*)
- [I.2] the linguistic expression signifying by containment (*taḍammun*)
- [I.3] the linguistic expression signifying by implication (*iltizām*)
  - [I.1.1] the simple linguistic expression signifying by congruence (has three sub-classifications)
    - [I.1.1.A]: The first category of simple linguistic expression [*Logical sub-classification*] is categorized into the
      - [I.1.1.A.1] simple particular linguistic expression
      - [I.1.1.A.2] simple universal linguistic expression
      - [...]
        - [I.1.1.A.2.2.1] the genus (*ǧins*)
        - [I.1.1.A.2.2.2] the specific difference (*faṣl*)
        - [I.1.1.A.2.2.3] the species (*nawʿ*)

154 See Chapter 2, Section 1.

155 See Chapter 2, Section 1.

[…]
[I.1.1.A.2.3.2.1] the proprium
[I.1.1.A.2.3.2.2] the general accident

[I.1.1.B] The second category of the simple linguistic expression [*Grammatical-theoretical sub-classification*]

[I.1.1.B.1] name (*ism*)/ verb (*fiʿl*)
[I.1.1.B.2] particle (*ḥarf*)

[*ad* I.1.1.B.1]

[I.1.1.B.1.1] signifies a specific time for its meaning: verb (*fiʿl*) or
[I.1.1.B.1.2] it does not signify the specific time: name (*ism*)

[*ad* I.1.1.B.1.2] The name is categorized according to two aspects:

[I.1.1.B.1.2.1] The first aspect:

[I.1.1.B.1.2.1.1] a name for the particular (*li-l-ǧuzʾī*):

[I.1.1.B.1.2.1.1.1] pronouns
[I.1.1.B.1.2.1.1.2] proper names

[I.1.1.B.1.2.1.2] a name for the universal (*li-l-kullī*): 'generic name' (*ism al-ǧins*) and derived name (*ism muštaqq*), like e.g. *ḍārib*

[…]

[I.1.1.C] The third category of the simple linguistic expression [*Logical and legal-theoretical sub-classification*]

[I.1.1.C.1] one meaning exists for one linguistic expression
[I.1.1.C.2] or both are multiple
[I.1.1.C.3] multiple linguistic expressions for one meaning;
[I.1.1.C.4] or vice versa [*i.e. there is a linguistic expression with several meanings*]
[…]

[*ad* I.1.2] The compound linguistic expression signified by congruence: Making one understand (*ifhām*) [*Sub-classification of the speech act and sentence*]:

[I.1.2.1] Speech intended to make one understand something indicates in a primary way (*awwaliyyatan*) the striving for a thing (*ṭalab aš-šayʾ*)
[I.1.2.2] or it does not;

[*ad* I.1.2.1] either in the way

[I.1.2.1.1] that the speech indicates the striving to name the quiddity of a thing (*māhiyyat aš-šayʾ*), and that is inquiry (*istifhām*); or

[I.1.2.1.2] [*taking into account the hierarchy between the interlocutors*] the endeavor to achieve (*taḥṣīl*) something, and that is

[I.1.2.1.2.1] in the case of superiority (*isti'lā'*): command/imperative (*amr*);
[I.1.2.1.2.2] in the case of obedience/submissiveness (*ḫuḍū'*): question (*su'āl*);
[I.1.2.1.2.3] in case of equality: request (*iltimās*).
[*ad* I.1.2.1.2.1–3] Also according to the three types of hierarchy respectively: speech that aims to effect cessation (*ṭalab al-imtinā'*);
[*ad* I.1.2.2] speech intended to make one understand something does not indicate in a primary way striving (*ṭalab*) for a thing:
[I.1.2.2.1] declarative sentence (*ḫabar*): either belief (*taṣdīq*) and disbelief (*takḏīb*);
[I.1.2.2.2] or it does not act in this way, like the wish, hope/expectation, oath, exclamation.
[This has all been the categorization of signification by congruence [*ad* I.1]]

[*ad* I.3] The categorization of signification by implication [*Legal-theoretical implication*]
[I.3.1] Meaning is obtained either from simple linguistic expressions or
[I.3.2] from compound linguistic expressions
[*ad* I.3.1] Implied meaning represents a condition (*šarṭ*) for the meaning signified by congruence
[*ad* I.3.2] Implied meaning follows (*tābi'*) from the meaning signified by congruence
[*ad* I.3.1] If it is the first, it is called 'signification by requirement' (*dalālat al-iqtiḍā'*). Furthermore, this condition can be
[I.3.1.1] by deduction based on reasoning, or
[I.3.1.2] by legal derivation
[*ad* I.3.2] *implied meaning* that follows from compound linguistic expressions:
[I.3.2.1] completes the meaning
[I.3.2.2] or does not.
[*ad* I.3.2.1] e.g. *a fortiori qiyās* [= *mafhūm al-muwāfaqa*].
[*ad* I.3.2.2] In the second, the [*legal judgement*] signified by implication is either
[I.3.2.2.1] affirmed [corresponds to *mafhūm al-muwāfaqa*; but this is not Rāzī's terminology] or
[I.3.2.2.2] negated [corresponds to *mafhūm al-muḫālafa*].

The tripartite classification serves as a structuring principle for the entire categorization, with the first and third manners of signification each acting as the starting point for further classification systems.[156] This structuring principle represents a reversal of the order established by Ibn Sīnā. He had divided the linguistic expression into the simple and compound, the simple into the universal and particular, and finally the universal into the essential and accidental. These in turn were then assigned to the five predicables. Thus the Tripartition of Signification here served, as we have already established, to specify the mutual relationships of signification between the predicables.[157]

FIGURE 9 The Tripartition in Ibn Sīnā

[1.] linguistic expression:
 [1.1] simple linguistic expression:
  [1.1.1] universal:
   [1.1.1.1/2] essential/accidental:
    [*ad* 1.1.1.1] genus; spec. difference; species
     [*ad* 1.1.1.2] proprium; general accident

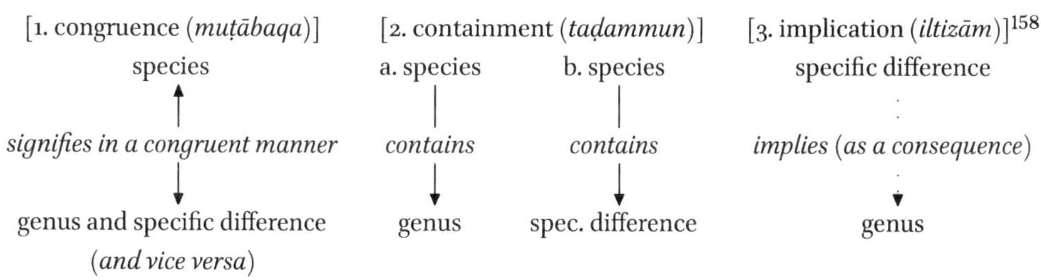

In Ibn Sīnā, the classification of signification falls under the simple universal essential linguistic expression.

Faẖr ad-dīn, however, begins his categorization with the three manners of signification. In the following illustration we see the sub-classification of the linguistic expression that signifies in a congruent way:

156 For the "[I.1.1.A] logical sub-classification," see Chapter 2, Sections 1–2; for the "[I.1.1.B] grammatical-theoretical sub-classification," see Chapter 3, Section 1; for the "[I.1.1.C] logical and legal-theoretical sub-classification" as well as for the "[I.1.2.1 ff.] sub-classification of the speech act and sentence," see Chapter 3, Section 2, and for "[I.3] legal-theoretical implication," see Chapter 4.

157 See Chapter 2, Section 2.1.

158 For the extension of the *iltizām* concept to the implication relationships of species–proprium and proprium–species, see Chapter 2, Section 2.3, especially p. 101 f.

FIGURE 10 Rough Structure of the Logical Sub-Classification [I.1.1.A]

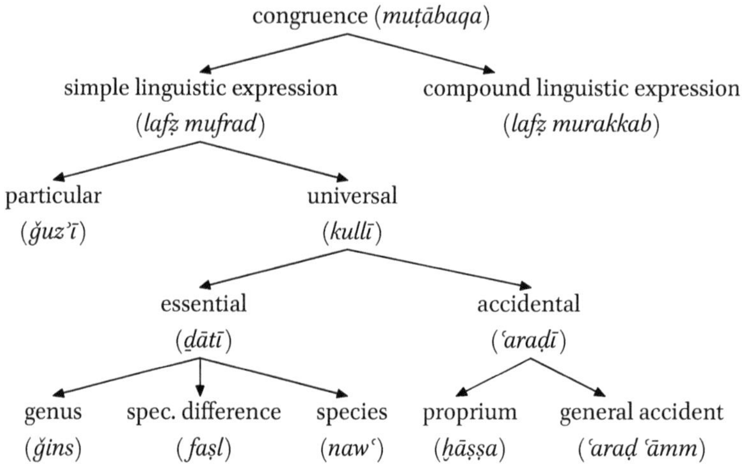

The linguistic expression that signifies by congruence is either simple or compound, with the simple being either universal or particular. The universal linguistic expression signifying by congruence is either essential or accidental, with the former subdivided into the predicables of genus, species, and specific difference and the latter into the predicables of accident and proprium.

In contrast to Ibn Sīnā's conception of these manners of signification, the range of applications of congruence is expanded: It no longer only describes the simple universal essential linguistic expression in the context of the study of predicables and predication theory, but all linguistic expressions, be they particular or universal. It is not only the manner of signification of congruence that is generalized—rather, this generalization also encompasses the other two manners of signification, as will be explained in detail.[159] In Faḫr ad-dīn's summary of the first treatise of the *Išārāt wa-t-tanbīhāt*, this principle of generalization is clear: "The linguistic expression (*lafẓ*) signifies either by congruence (*muṭābaqa*), containment (*taḍammun*), or implication (*iltizām*). All of these are either simple (*mufrad*) or compound (*murakkab*). The simple is either universal (*kullī*) or particular (*ǧuzʾī*) […]."[160] The relevance that this classification in its generalized form has for Faḫr ad-dīn is illustrated by other parallel passages. For example, Faḫr ad-dīn's outline of the *Maḥṣūl*, the *Maʿālim fī uṣūl al-fiqh*, begins with the following passage:

159 See in particular Chapter 4.
160 Faḫr ad-dīn ar-Rāzī, *Šarḥ al-Išārāt wa-t-tanbīhāt, al-Manṭiq*, p. 92, lines 10–11.

The first treatise. On the rules of language. The first main argument. On the categorization of linguistic expressions.
[1] Thus we say: the linguistic expression is considered either in relation to the completeness (*tamām*) of what is named (*musammāhu*) by it [*i.e. by the linguistic expression*]—that is 'the congruence' (*al-muṭābaqa*);
[2] or [*in relation*] to a part of what is named, insofar as it is [*actually*] its part—that is 'the containment' (*at-taḍammun*);
[3] or [*in relation*] to what is extrinsic (*ḫāriǧ*) to what is named and what is attached to it in the mind, insofar as it [*actually*] behaves in this way—the third is 'the implication' (*al-iltizām*).
[*ad* 1] The [*linguistic expression*] signifying by congruence is either [1.1] such that its part signifies something of the meaning—that is the compound (*murakkab*) [*linguistic expression*], or [1.2] it is not [*such that its part signifies a part of the meaning*]—and that is the simple (*mufrad*) [*linguistic expression*].
[*ad* 1.2] Furthermore, the simple [*linguistic expression*] can be subdivided according to three aspects:
[1.2.1] [see Text 1, § 6, I.1.1.A] First, the simple [*linguistic expression signifying by congruence*] is either such [1.2.1.1] that the conceptualization (*taṣawwur*) of its meaning itself prevents the occurrence of sharing in it (*šarika*)—and this is the particular (*ǧuzʾī*) [*linguistic expression*]; [1.2.1.2] or [*the conceptualization of its meaning*] does not prevent [*sharing in it*]—that is the universal (*kullī*) [*linguistic expression*].
[1.2.2] [see Text 1, § 12, I.1.1.B] Secondly, the simple [*linguistic expression signifying by congruence*] is either such [1.2.2.1] that what it names does not possess the knowable (*maʿlūmiyya*) independently (*lā yastaqillu*) [see Text 1, § 12: *here* musammā *instead of* maʿnā]—and this is the particle (*ḥarf*), or [1.2.2.2] it possesses it independently; then it is either such [1.2.2.2.1] that it does not signify a particular time—and that is the name (*ism*), or [1.2.2.2.2] it signifies [*a particular time*]—that is the verb (*fiʿl*).
[1.2.3] [see Text 1, § 15, I.1.1.C] Thirdly, [*it can be the case with a simple linguistic expression that*] either [1.2.3.1] there is one linguistic expression and one meaning; or that [1.2.3.2] the linguistic expression is multiple and the meaning is multiple; or that [1.2.3.3] the linguistic expression is multiple and the meaning is single; or that [1.2.3.4] the linguistic expression is single and the meaning is multiple.[161]

161 Faḫr ad-dīn ar-Rāzī, *al-Maʿālim fī uṣūl al-fiqh*, p. 11.

In this passage too, the classification of signification is used as a structuring principle—the three subdivisions are assigned to the simple congruent linguistic expression as in the *Maḥṣūl* (Text 1); in this outline, however, the other two types of signification are not further subdivided.

The logical section of Faḫr ad-dīn's *Mulaḫḫaṣ* also begins—after an introduction discussing the subject of logic—with the classification as the highest organizing principle:

> [§1] [p. 15] The meaningful linguistic expression (*al-lafẓ al-mufīd*) is
> [1] considered either in relation to the entirety (*tamām*) of what is understood by it (*mafhūmihī*);
> [2] or [*in relation*] to what is categorized under it (*aw mā indarağa fīhi*), insofar as it behaves in this way (*min ḥaytu huwa ka-ḏālika*) [*see Text 1, §1 and §3*]
> [3] or [*in relation to that*] which is extrinsic to it (*ḫāriğ ʿanhū*) and adheres to it in the mind (*al-lāzim lahū fī ḏ-ḏihn*).
> [§2] [*Signification by*] congruence [*is categorized*] into two parts, because the part of the linguistic expression either [1.1] signifies a part of the meaning—that is the compound (*muʾallaf*) [*linguistic expression*], or [1.2] it is not [*such that its part signifies a part of the meaning*], and that is the simple (*mufrad*) [*linguistic expression*]. [*ad* 1.2] [*The simple linguistic expression*] is either such [1.2.1] that the conceptualization (*taṣawwur*) of its meaning itself prevents sharing (*šarika*) in it—and that is the particular (*ğuzʾī*) [*linguistic expression*];
> [1.2.2] or [*the conceptualization of its meaning*] does not prevent [*sharing in it*], that is the universal (*kullī*) [*linguistic expression*]. [...]
> [§8] [*ad* 1.1] As for the compound [*linguistic expression*], we say that the need for speech (*qawl*)[162] is to get someone to understand something (*ifhām*). Speech (*qawl*), which is that which effects understanding (*mufhim*), is either such [1.1.1] that it indicates (*an yufīda*) in a primary way (*awwaliyyatan*) the striving for a thing (*ṭalab aš-šayʾ*) or [1.1.2] does not indicate it.[163]

In the *Mulaḫḫaṣ*—unlike in the *Maʿālim* or the *Maḥṣūl*—the classification is only used as the starting point for the logical classification and the classification of speech acts and sentences, as is in accordance with its genre.[164]

---

162 The *Maḥṣūl* reads *lafẓ murakkab* instead of *qawl*, Faḫr ad-dīn ar-Rāzī, *al-Maḥṣūl*, vol. 1, p. 231, line 10.

163 Faḫr ad-dīn ar-Rāzī, *Manṭiq al-Mulaḫḫaṣ*, p. 15, first–last line and p. 18, lines 4–5.

164 For the classification of speech acts and sentences, see Chapter 3 of this study.

TABLE 6 The classification of signification as the starting point for various sub-classifications in the *Maḥṣūl*, *Maʿālim*, and *Mulaḫḫaṣ*

Maḥṣūl **Tripartition of Signification as the starting point for the following sub-classifications:**	***Maʿālim*** **Tripartition of Signification as the starting point for the following sub-classifications:**	***Mulaḫḫaṣ*** **Tripartition of Signification as the starting point for the following sub-classifications:**
[I.1.1.A] logical sub-classification	[I.1.1.A] logical sub-classification	[I.1.1.A] logical sub-classification
[I.1.1.B] grammatical-theoretical sub-classification	[I.1.1.B] grammatical-theoretical sub-classification	–
[I.1.1.C] logical and legal-theoretical sub-classification	[I.1.1.C] logical and legal-theoretical sub-classification	–
[I.1.2.1 ff.] sub-classification of the speech act and sentence	–	[I.1.2.1 ff.] sub-classification of the speech act and sentence
[I.3.1 ff.] legal-theoretical sub-classification	–	–

All of these passages go to show that Faḫr ad-dīn attached a high degree of relevance to the classification, namely in two respects. Firstly, he considered it so important that he opened his chapters and even entire works with it; and secondly, he made this classification the starting point for the organization of linguistic expressions. In doing so, he continued a development that had started with Ibn Sīnā, throughout the course of which the propaedeutic benefits of the classification were continusously expanded upon.[165]

A further passage in Faḫr ad-dīn's *Išārāt* commentary shows the context in which he places this classification, thereby reveling the general and fundamental level he actually considers it to occupy:

165 See in particular Chapter 2, Section 2.3.

> [Ibn Sīnā] said: "[Since there is a certain connection (*ʿalāqatun-mā*) between the linguistic expression and the meaning, and since the states (*aḥwāl*) in the linguistic expressions can have an influence on the states in the meanings, it is also incumbent upon the logician to consider the aspect of the absolute linguistic expression (*ǧānib al-lafẓ al-muṭlaq*),] insofar as that [*linguistic expression*] is not limited to the language of a particular group of people (*min ḥayṯu ḏālika ġayru muqayyadin bi-luġati qawmin*)—except in rare cases."
>
> I say: This means that the investigation of languages [a] can be based on reasoning (*qad yakūnu ʿaqliyyan*); just like when we say that the signifying linguistic expressions are either name (*ism*), verb (*fiʿl*), or particle (*ḥarf*) and their significations are either by congruence (*muṭābaqa*), containment (*taḍammun*), or implication (*iltizām*)—these are examples of those general investigations (*abḥāṯ ʿāmma*) of all languages. [b] Or there may be a specific study of the language of one group of people that ignores other [*groups*]. [*ad* a] The first belongs to what the logician must deal with, [*ad* b] the second lies outside the field of logic.[166]

The question of the extent to which linguistic expressions belong to the domain of logic has been much debated. Whereas previously the view had been held that "'the subject matter of logic [is] the reflection on linguistic expressions insofar as they signify meanings,'"[167] in the end, Ibn Sīnā designated the second intelligibles as the actual subject matter of logic.[168] However, even if linguistic expressions do not formally belong to the subject matter, they still have a bearing upon it due to the relationship, according to *De Int.* 16a3–8, that exists between linguistic expressions and meanings. This can be seen in the examples of grammatically correct but contextually incorrect word combinations in *De Int.* 11.[169] And thus the logician must deal with them in a certain way, "inso-

166 Faḫr ad-dīn ar-Rāzī, *Šarḥ al-Išārāt*, p. 22, lines 8–12 (or Ms. Berlin or. oct. 1802, fol. 9v, lines 8–13).

167 Ibn Sīnā, *Kitāb aš-Šifāʾ, al-Manṭiq, al-Madḫal* 1.4, p. 23, lines 5–6—here Ibn Sīnā paraphrases al-Fārābī, cf. Abū Naṣr al-Fārābī, *Iḥṣāʾ al-ʿulūm*, ed. by ʿAlī Abū Mulḥim (Beirut: Dār wa-maktabat al-hilāl, 1996), pp. 33 ff.

168 For a discussion of the actual subject matter of logic in the Arabic tradition, see A.I. Sabra, "Avicenna on the Subject Matter of Logic," *The Journal of Philosophy*, vol. 77, no. 11 (Nov. 1980): pp. 746–764; Street, "Arabic and Islamic Philosophy of Language and Logic," pp. 19–28; Endreß, "Grammatik und Logik," pp. 205 ff.; Khaled el-Rouayheb, "Post-Avicennan Logicians on the Subject Matter of Logic: Some Thirteenth- and Fourteenth-Century Discussions," *Arabic Sciences and Philosophy*, vol. 22 (2012): pp. 69–90; Gyekye, "The Terms *Prima Intentio* and *Secunda Intentio* in Arabic Logic," pp. 36–38.

169 See Chapter 2, Section 2.2.1.

far as that [*linguistic expression*] is not limited to the language of a certain group of people (*min ḥayṯu ḏālika ġayru muqayyadin bi-luġati qawmin*)." Faḫr ad-dīn interprets this qualification as follows: There are two ways of studying languages, namely [1] on the one hand, the general, rational studies that do not focus on any particular language but instead deal with structures that are found in all languages, and [2] on the other hand, special studies that deal with a particular language in an empirical way. [*ad* 1] As an example of one such general study, Faḫr ad-dīn gives the classification of linguistic expressions into name (*ism*), verb (*fiʿl*), and particle (*ḥarf*) and that of the manners of signification into congruence (*muṭābaqa*), containment (*taḍammun*), and implication (*iltizām*). Faḫr ad-dīn sets the most basic classification of Arabic grammar, namely the *aqsām al-kalām*, up next to the Tripartition of Signification and at the same time transfers a set of justifications that have been put forward in grammatical theory to the latter. The justification that the *aqsām al-kalām* do not have to be derived inductively, but are instead arrived at purely through reasoning, can be found in the grammarian az-Zaǧǧāǧī (d. either 337/948 or 339–340/949–950).[170] In response to the accusation that the followers of Sībawayhi had adopted the *aqsām al-kalām* through unquestioning faith in authority (*taqlīd*), without proof (*burhān*) or argument (*ḥuǧǧa*), az-Zaǧǧāǧī responds that "among things there are those things that are known axiomatically, without proof and without evidence (*bi-badīhati l-ʿaql bi-ġayri burhānin wa-lā dalīlin*)":[171]

> [...] just as we know axiomatically, without evidence, that it is inconceivable for a body in one and the same situation [1.] to be still and moving [*at the same time*] or [2.] to be not still and not moving [*at the same time*] (*kamā annā naʿlamu badīhatan bi-ġayri dalīlin anna wuǧūda ǧismin fī ḥālin wāḥidatin sākinan mutaḥarrikan aw lā sākinan wa-lā mutaḥarrikan muḥālun*). [...] And just as we know that it is inconceivable for a body [3.] to be in two places in one and the same situation and at the same time (*kamā annā naʿlamu anna wuǧūda ǧismin wāḥidin fī makānayni fī ḥālin wāḥidatin wa-waqtin wāhidin muḥālun*), and [4.] just as it is inconceivable that it is in no place at all (*kamā anna wuǧūdahū lā fī makānin muḥālun*).[172]

170 Versteegh, *The Explanation of Linguistic Causes*, p. 3.

171 Abū l-Qāsim az-Zaǧǧāǧī, *al-Īḍāḥ fī ʿilal an-naḥw*, ed. by Māzin al-Mubārak (Beirut: Dār an-Nafāʾis, 1979 [1399]), p. 42, lines 4–5.

172 Az-Zaǧǧāǧī, *al-Īḍāḥ*, p. 42, lines 5–9.

These purely rationally accessible axioms include—in quite Aristotelian fashion—[1./3.] the principle of contradiction and [2./4.] the principle of excluded middle. According to az-Zağğāğī, with regard to their degree of recognition and certain knowledge, axioms of this kind are similar to what can be recognized "through clear indicators/evidence" (*bi-d-dalāʾil al-wāḍiḥa*),[173] that which is agreed upon and not doubted. This includes the classification into *ism*, *fiʿl*, and *ḥarf*. Furthermore, on a purely rational level, it can be deduced, az-Zağğāğī says, that this classification is valid for all languages. And according to az-Zağğāğī, this can even be proven empirically.[174]

This is the background to Faḫr ad-dīn's statement about the study of general linguistic structures. The equivalent of this classification of linguistic expressions is, at the level of signification, the categorization into the three manners of signification. Both classifications are principles that the logician must deal with, while specific investigations of particular languages can be disregarded.

The reorientation resulted, it can be provisionally stated, in three functions for the classification of signification. Firstly, as has just been explained, the classification of signification is contrasted with the classification of linguistic expressions on a general linguistic level. These two classifications thus represent two fundamental principles of language: all linguistic expressions can be categorized as either name (*ism*), verb (*fiʿl*), or particle (*ḥarf*), and their manners of signification as either congruence (*muṭābaqa*), containment (*taḍammun*), or implication (*iltizām*).

Secondly, the classification of signification is used as a fundamental organizing principle under which the classification of linguistic expressions is subordinated. For it is the simple linguistic expression signifying by congruence that is divided—purely at the classificatory level of technical terms—into *ism*, *fiʿl*, and *ḥarf*.[175]

Thirdly, in Faḫr ad-dīn also lives on the distinction in the old discussions, predating Ibn Sīnā, that revolve around the correct determination of the quiddity and the problem of redundancy in the definition, in which Ibn Sīnā's terminology was authoritative:[176]

> [§ 7] It is thus perfectly clear that the linguistic expression that signifies the essential nature (*ḥaqīqa*) signifies the genus and the specific differ-

173 Ibid., line 9.

174 Ibid., p. 50, lines 6–7.

175 See Chapter 3, Section 1.

176 For a detailed discussion of this topic, see Chapter 2, Section 2.2.1.

> ence [*of the respective thing*] by containment. As for the linguistic expression that signifies the specific difference [*of the thing*], it signifies the genus only by implication. […][177]

Consequently, Faḫr ad-dīn also uses this old distinction in his commentary on the *Išārāt*.

3.2 *Notes and Limitations on the Classification of Signification* [*ad §§ 2–4*]

Now that we have worked out the three functions that Faḫr ad-dīn's types of signification fulfill, the following chapter will examine the notes [§§ 2–4] that Faḫr ad-dīn makes about the classification of signification, which are partly based on Ibn Sīnā's own suggestions. We will see that Faḫr ad-dīn's remarks form the basis for further discussion in post-Rāzian logic. By "post-Rāzian" logic compendia, I mean works that engage with Faḫr ad-dīn's logic or can be shown to have been influenced by it. These include, for example, the logical treatises of the *Išārāt* commentaries of Naṣīr ad-dīn aṭ-Ṭūsī (d. 672/1274) and Sayf ad-dīn al-Āmidī (d. 631/1233) as well as Quṭb ad-dīn ar-Rāzī at-Taḥtānī's (d. 766/1365) meta-commentary on the *Išārāt*. All three not only work off of Faḫr ad-dīn's own commentary, but also build to a considerable extent upon his elaborations and explanations. The same can be said—at least for the passages relevant for our purposes—of the logic compendium the *Kašf al-asrār ʿan ġawāmiḍ al-afkār* by Afḍal ad-dīn al-Ḫūnaǧī (d. 646/1248) and the influential introduction to logic *ar-Risāla aš-šamsiyya* by Naǧm ad-dīn al-Kātibī as well as the commentaries that the latter work generated (for example Ǧamāl ad-dīn al-Ḥillī's *al-Qawāʿid al-ǧaliyya fī šarḥ ar-Risāla aš-šamsiyya*). A multi-layered network of debates emerged with scholars like Ǧamāl ad-dīn al-Ḥillī, Quṭb ad-dīn ar-Rāzī at-Taḥtānī (d. 766/1365), ʿAḍud ad-dīn al-Īǧī (d. 756/1355), and Šarīf al-Ǧurǧānī (d. 816/1413), who provided commentaries and meta-commentaries on various works of logic and who were also active in other fields, not least in the field of legal theory.

3.2.1 [ad § 2] [Note 1] The Hierarchization of the Manners of Signification: *dalāla waḍʿiyya* and *dalāla ʿaqliyya*

3.2.1.1 *The Link with ʿAbd al-Qāhir al-Ǧurǧānī's* maʿnā *and* maʿnā l-maʿnā

In the first note, Faḫr ad-dīn re-categorizes the tripartite classification of signification:

177 Faḫr ad-dīn ar-Rāzī, *Šarḥ al-Išārāt*, p. 88, lines 14–16.

> [§ 2] [*ad* I] Notes (*tanbīhāt*):
> The first [*note*]: Signification based on imposition (*dalāla waḍʿiyya*) is [*ad* I.1] signification by congruence (*dalālatu l-muṭābaqa*).
> [*ad* I.2 and I.3] But as for the remaining two [*significations*], they are [*significations*] based on reasoning (*ʿaqliyya*)—for when a linguistic expression has been imposed for something that has been named, then the mind (*ḏihn*) turns from what is named to that which adheres (*lāzim*) to it [*i.e. the named thing*].[178]

Faḫr ad-dīn distinguishes here between [i] a signification based on the imposition of the linguistic expression for a meaning, the *dalāla waḍʿiyya*, to which signification by congruence is assigned, and [ii] an inferred signification based on reasoning, the *dalāla ʿaqliyya*. This type of signification is comprised of containment and implication.

FIGURE 11 *dalāla waḍʿiyya/dalāla ʿaqliyya* [Text 1, § 2]

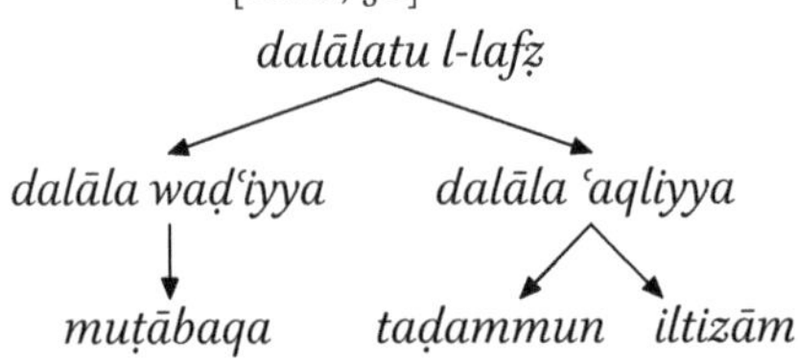

The term *dalāla waḍʿiyya* and its identification with congruent signification is based on Ibn Sīnā's *Išārāt wa-t-tanbīhāt*. There it is stated, for the first time in this context, that the linguistic expression signifying by congruence signifies a meaning "in the sense that this linguistic expression (*lafẓ*) has been taken as the basis/imposed (*mawḍūʿ*) for that meaning/concept (*maʿnā*) and in relation to it (*wa-bi-izāʾihī*)."[179] The description of *dalāla ʿaqliyya* as an activity in which a mental transfer is carried out from one meaning to another goes back terminologically to Ibn Sīnā's *Manṭiq al-Mašriqiyyīn*:

178 Faḫr ad-dīn ar-Rāzī, *al-Maḥṣūl*, vol. 1, p. 219, lines 11–14.

179 Ibn Sīnā, *al-Išārāt wa-t-tanbīhāt*, p. 42, lines 9–10; on the classification of this passage in the Avicennian oeuvre, see Chapter 2, Section 2.3.1.

Faḫr ad-dīn ar-Rāzī: *al-Maḥṣūl*, vol. 1, p. 219, lines 13–14	Ibn Sīnā: *Manṭiq al-Mašriqiyyīn*, p. 15, lines 1–2
[…] for when a linguistic expression has been imposed for something that has been named (*li-anna l-lafẓa iḏā wuḍiʿa li-l-musammā*), then the mind (*ḏihn*) turns from what is named to that which adheres (*lāzim*) to it [*the named thing*] (*intaqala ḏ-ḏihnu mina l-musammā ilā l-lāzimihī*).	[…] this meaning is accompanied by another (*wa-yakūnu ḏālika l-maʿnā yaṣḥabuhū maʿnā āḫar*), so that the mind also turns to this second meaning (*fa-yantaqilu ḏ-ḏihnu ayḍan ilā ḏālika l-maʿnā ṯ-ṯānī*).

Ibn Sīnā applies this description only to implication; he then however makes the following hierarchization: "[§ 2.3] Signification by containment and signification by implication have in common that each of them requires the first signification [*i.e. signification by congruence*]."[180] In his *Šarḥ al-Išārāt*, Faḫr ad-dīn also outlines the two manners of signification of containment and implication as following the first manner of signification:

> I say that signification by congruence is a signification based on imposition (*al-waḍʿiyya*). As for signification by containment and by implication, they are two [*significations*] based on intellect (*ʿaqliyyatān*). For if a linguistic expression has been imposed with regard to a meaning, then it is not possible (*imtanaʿa*) that it does not signify its parts and adherents through a subordinate consequentiality (*tabaʿiyya*).[181]

According to Faḫr ad-dīn, the congruent manner of signification based on imposition always has something additional that it co-signifies when the meaning or quiddity has parts or adherents, i.e. when it is compound or implies something. The relationship that exists purely between the linguistic expressions that signify the quiddity and the conceptualization of this quiddity is in this case transcended in one way or another:

> [§ 14] Signification based on imposition (*dalāla waḍʿiyya*) is [*ad* 1] [*signification by*] congruence (*al-muṭābaqa*), [*ad* 2 and 3] while the remaining

180 Ibn Sīnā, *Manṭiq al-Mašriqiyyīn*, p. 15, lines 5–6.
181 Faḫr ad-dīn ar-Rāzī, *Šarḥ al-Išārāt*, p. 33, lines 10–11.

> two [*significations*] are followers (*tābiʿātān*)—not in absolute terms (*lā muṭlaqan*), but rather with regard to the first [*ad* 2] on the condition that the quiddity is compound, and with regard to the second [*ad* 3] that it [*i.e. the quiddity*] implies something (*malzūm*). [...]
> As for these two [*ad* 2 and 3], they exist only alongside congruence due to the fact that the attainment of a follower (*tābiʿ*) is impossible, when the follower lacks something to follow (*matbūʿ*).[182]

In this passage, Faḫr ad-dīn thus places the discussion back into the context of the determination of the quiddity: congruent signification corresponds to the complete determination of the quiddity, containment can only occur in the case of a compound quiddity, and implication only in the case that the quiddity has something that attaches to it. Thus containment and implication are both based on congruence. However, according to Faḫr ad-dīn, there are two ways of deriving this distinction between *dalāla waḍʿiyya* and *dalāla ʿaqliyya*: One, as already mentioned, arises from the original context of the determination of the quiddity, combined with the problem of redundancy in the definition, and can therefore be described as a logical-philosophical deduction. The other is of a linguistic-theoretical nature:

> [§15] These classes (*aqsām*) [*of hierarchization; see §14*] can also result from another classification (*bi-taqsīm āḫar*), namely from the fact that the signification of a meaning (*maʿnā*) by a linguistic expression can be based either [*ad* 1] on an imposition (*waḍʿiyya*) or [*ad* 2 and 3; *see Text 1, §2*] on reasoning (*ʿaqliyya*). The first is the type of signification in which the linguistic expression [*signifies*] the entirety of what is named, because we necessarily know that each linguistic expression must not signify the entirety of that which is named based on reasoning. The second is the fact that the linguistic expression signifies that which adheres to the named thing. If this adhering thing is intrinsic to the [*named thing*], it is [*the signification*] of containment; if not, it is [*the signification*] of implication (*iltizām*).[183]

In this passage, the distinction is not embedded in a philosophical context as before. Instead, the arguments made are based in linguistic theory: It is now not the relationship between definition and quiddity that is of interest, but

182 Faḫr ad-dīn ar-Rāzī, *Manṭiq al-Mulaḫḫaṣ*, p. 19, line 9–p. 20, line 3.
183 Ibid., p. 20, lines 4–8.

more generally that between linguistic expression and meaning. The premises on which this relationship is based include the fact that a linguistic expression must first of all signify on the basis of something having been imposed—whether this imposition goes back to God or man remains to be seen.[184] Since this pure relationship with imposition is transcended in linguistic usage, a further type of signification must be assumed in which meaning must be derived in some way, be it through the context of speech or through other factors.

Faḫr ad-dīn develops the linguistic-theoretical dimension of the distinction merely hinted at here in his rhetorical work the *Nihāyat al-īǧāz fī dirāyat al-iʿǧāz*, thereby linking it to distinctions made by the important linguistic theorist ʿAbd al-Qāhir al-Ǧurǧānī (d. 471/1078):

> First chapter: On the classes (*aqsām*) of the signification of meaning by the linguistic expression: it [*i.e. signification*] is based either [1.] on imposition (*waḍʿiyya*) or [2.] on reasoning (*ʿaqliyya*).
>
> [§1] [*ad* 1] As for [*signification*] based on imposition, it is like the significations in which the linguistic expressions [*signify*] the meanings for which they have been set/imposed—just like how the [*linguistic expressions*] 'stone' (*ḥaǧar*) and 'wall' (*ǧidār*), 'sky' (*samāʾ*) and 'earth' (*arḍ*) signify what is named by them. There is no doubt about the fact that it [*i.e. this type of signification*] is based on imposition—otherwise, a meaning would not change when a different word is used (lit. 'it would not be possible for the significations to be different from one imposition to another').
>
> [*ad* 2] As for [*signification*] based on reasoning, it occurs either [2.1] in the way that it is intrinsic (*dāḫil*) to what is understood by the linguistic expression (*mafhūm al-lafẓ*), just like how the linguistic expression 'house' signifies 'roof,' which is a part of what is understood by 'house.' There is no doubt that it [*i.e. this type of signification*] is based on reasoning due to the fact that it is impossible for the linguistic expression to be imposed for a composite essential nature (*ḥaqīqa*) without including its parts.
>
> Or, [2.2] [*signification based on reasoning*] occurs in such a way that it is extrinsic (*ḫāriǧ*) to it [*i.e. to what is understood by the linguistic expression* (mafhūm al-lafẓ)], just like how the linguistic expression 'roof' signifies 'wall.' For since the separation of the roof from the wall is ordinarily (*ʿādatan*) impossible, the linguistic expression that indicates the essential

184 See Chapter 1, Section 2.1.

nature of the roof is suitable for indicating the wall through the signification [*of the linguistic expression*] for the former [*i.e. for 'roof'*], so that this signification is based on reasoning.
[§ 2] The Šayḫ [*'Abd al-Qāhir*] commented on what we were talking about by saying:
"There is a concise expression (*'ibāra muḫtaṣara*) here, namely that one says: [*ad* 1] 'the meaning' (*al-ma'nā*) and [*ad* 2] 'the meaning of the meaning' (*ma'nā l-ma'nā*): [*ad* 1] By 'meaning' is meant that which is understood by the apparent linguistic expression (*al-mafhūm mina ẓāhiri l-lafẓ*), and this is that which is understood by it directly/without mediation (*bi-ġayr wāsiṭa*). [*ad* 2] By 'meaning of the meaning' [*is meant*] that a meaning is understood [*first*] by the linguistic expression, and then this meaning indicates another meaning."[185]
[§ 3] Know that metonymy (*kināya*)[186] and the figurative expression (*maǧāz*) and comparison (*tamṯīl*) fall only into this class. The first two significations [*i.e. congruence and containment*] are not considered in the *'ilm al-faṣāḥa*.[187]

After the preface and the introduction follows the opening of the first of two treatises. It begins with the first paragraph [§ 1] quoted above, explaining the distinction between *dalāla waḍ'iyya* and *dalāla 'aqliyya* and the further subdivision into the tripartite classification of signification, which is introduced here without technical terms. After introducing this classification in the already familiar schema—it differs only in that the two-part distinction is mentioned first and then the Tripartition—Faḫr ad-dīn quotes 'Abd al-Qāhir al-Ǧurǧānī, on whose two main works the *Dalā'il al-i'ǧāz* and *Asrār al-balāġa* Faḫr ad-dīn heavily relied when writing the *Nihāyat al-īǧāz fī dirāyat al-i'ǧāz*. In it, Faḫr ad-dīn summarizes anew the most imporant points made by 'Abd al-Qāhir.[188]

185 This quotation corresponds (with marginal differences) to 'Abd al-Qāhir al-Ǧurǧānī, *Dalā'il al-i'ǧāz*, p. 262, last line–p. 263, line 3; see Chapter 2, Section 2.1.

186 For a critique of the translation of the term *kināya* as 'metonymy,' see Joseph Dichy, "Kinâya, a Tropic Device from Medieval Arabic Rhetoric, and Its Impact on Discourse Theory," in *Proceedings of the 5th Conference of the International Society for the Study of Argumentation* (ISSA), *University of Amsterdam, 25–28 June 2002*, ed. by Frans van Eemeren, J. Anthony Blair, Charles A. Willard, and A. Francisca Snoeck Nenkemans (Amsterdam: *Sic* Sat, 2003), pp. 237–241.

187 Faḫr ad-dīn ar-Rāzī, *Nihāyat al-īǧāz*, pp. 87–88.

188 Faḫr ad-dīn ar-Rāzī, *Nihāyat al-īǧāz*, p. 75. An examination of the work and its dependence on the two above-mentioned works of 'Abd al-Qāhir—beyond Faḫr ad-dīn's remark in his introduction—remains a desideratum for the time being.

In the quotation from ʿAbd al-Qāhir's *Dalāʾil al-iʿǧāz*, his distinction between [i] 'meaning' and [ii] 'meaning of the meaning' is outlined:[189] 'meaning' (*al-maʿnā*) is the immediately comprehended, obvious meaning of a linguistic expression, while the 'meaning of the meaning' (*maʿnā l-maʿnā*) is a second meaning that can only be comprehended through the mediation of the first meaning. In the first case, the intended meaning can be taken from the linguistic expression alone (*waḥdahū*). In the second case this is not possible, according to ʿAbd al-Qāhir. Instead, the situation is as follows: "The linguistic expression signifies that meaning which necessitates its imposition in the language, and then a second signification is found in that meaning through which the goal is achieved."[190] Faḫr ad-dīn links his distinction to that of ʿAbd al-Qāhir, indicating that his distinction between *dalāla waḍʿiyya* and *dalāla ʿaqliyya* is based on ʿAbd al-Qāhir's distinction between the meaning and the meaning of the meaning.[191] The connection of the *dalāla ʿaqliyya*—Faḫr ad-dīn's term for ʿAbd al-Qāhir's category of *maʿnā l-maʿnā*—to rhetorical figures now emerges quite explicitly: According to ʿAbd al-Qāhir, it is the catch-all for "*kināya, istiʿāra,* and *tamṯīl*" and according to Faḫr ad-dīn—somewhat more generally—it is the catch-all for "*kināya, maǧāz,* and *tamṯīl*."[192]

Faḫr ad-dīn's distinction between *dalāla waḍʿiyya* and *dalāla ʿaqliyya* corresponds, simply put, essentially to the distinction between a literal meaning and those meanings that can in some way be regarded as transferred. 'Literal' here includes the fact that there is a relationship of imposition between the linguistic expression and the meaning and that this relationship is immediately clear to the listener.[193] The hierarchization between the three manners of sig-

189 See, for example, Kamal Abu Deeb, *Al-Jurjānī's Theory of Poetic Imagery* (Warminster: Aris and Phillips, 1979), pp. 75 ff. and Margaret Larkin, *The Theology of Meaning: ʿAbd al-Qāhir al-Jurjānī's Theory of Discourse* (New Haven, CT: American Oriental Society, 1995), pp. 75–76.

190 ʿAbd al-Qāhir al-Ǧurǧānī, *Dalāʾil al-iʿǧāz*, p. 262, lines 7–8.

191 Yunis Ali has already made the connection—on an associative level—between the concept of *maʿnā l-maʿnā* and *iltizām*, see Yunis Ali: *Medieval Islamic Pragmatics*, p. 76 and p. 156.

192 ʿAbd al-Qāhir al-Ǧurǧānī, *Dalāʾil al-iʿǧāz*, p. 262, line 8; Faḫr ad-dīn ar-Rāzī, *Nihāyat al-īǧāz*, p. 88, line 9. The connection between the *dalāla ʿaqliyya*, especially the signification of *iltizām*, and the theory of *maǧāz* is discussed in Chapter 3, Section 2.2 of this study. Simon sees Faḫr ad-dīn's distinction as one that was transferred from logic to rhetoric and was made productive by Faḫr ad-dīn for the further development of the theory of *maǧāz*: "Ar-Rāzī contributes to the theory of *majāz* by introducing notions from logic and advocating a methodological approach that focuses on the way things are referred to by *dalāla waḍʿiyya* or *dalāla ʿaqliyya*," Udo Gerald Simon, "Majāz," p. 119.

193 See also Gleave, *Islam and Literalism*, pp. 57–59.

nification results from the fact that the category of the transferred meaning, i.e. the meaning of the meaning, is based on the literal meaning.[194]

FIGURE 12 *Concretization:* dalāla waḍʿiyya/dalāla ʿaqliyya

linguistic expression (*lafẓ*)
↓ signifies
[process of signification: *dalāla waḍʿiyya: muṭābaqa*]

the meaning [= *al-maʿnā*]
↓ signifies
[process of signification: *dalāla ʿaqliyya*: *taḍammun* and *iltizām*]

additional meaning [= *maʿnā l-maʿnā*]

3.2.1.2 *Post-Rāzian Controversies: Three Approaches*

The terms *dalāla waḍʿiyya* and *dalāla ʿaqliyya* introduced by Faḫr ad-dīn were adopted and implemented by subsequent scholars, whether in logic, *uṣūl al-fiqh*, or rhetoric (*ʿilm al-balāġa*) and here in particular in the *ʿilm al-bayān*—albeit in some cases with considerable modifications. In addition, this distinction sparked a discussion about how exactly the tripartite classification should be assigned to correspond to it. While Faḫr ad-dīn—and after him, in a modified form, Naṣīr ad-dīn aṭ-Ṭūsī[195] and Sīrāǧ ad-dīn as-Sakkākī (d. 626/1229)[196]—[a] take the view that only the congruent manner of signification is to be called *dalāla waḍʿiyya*, subsequent literature discusses whether [b] the manners of signification of congruence and containment are to be regarded as *dalāla waḍʿiyya* while implication is based on reasoning or whether [c] all three manners of signification are based on imposition:

[*ad* a] Naṣīr ad-dīn specifies Faḫr ad-dīn's distinction as follows: "I say: Signification by congruence is a pure [*signification*], based on imposition (*waḍʿiyya ṣirfa*), while signification by containment and by implication [*come about*] both by reasoning and by imposition."[197] Thus, while the congruent mean-

194 See also Weiss, *The Search*, p. 323.

195 Naṣīr ad-dīn aṭ-Ṭūsī emphasizes that the manners of signification of containment and implication are based on both imposition and reasoning, see Naṣīr ad-dīn aṭ-Ṭūsī, *Ḥall muškilāt al-Išārāt*, in Ibn Sīnā, *Išārāt wa-t-tanbīhāt*, ed. by Sulaymān Dunyā (Cairo: Dār al-Maʿārif, 1960–1968), vol. 1, p. 139. This emphasis is based on Faḫr ad-dīn's statement that the signification of containment and implication are based on congruence.

196 As-Sakkākī, *Miftāḥ al-ʿulūm*, p. 437, lines 16–17.

197 Aṭ-Ṭūsī, *Ḥall muškilāt al-Išārāt*, vol. 1, p. 187. This position is advocated in, among others, Iṣfahānī's *Maḥṣūl* commentary, cf. al-Iṣfahānī, *al-Kāšif ʿan al-Maḥṣūl*, vol. 2, p. 7, lines 9–15.

ing "is based on the lexical establishment (*waḍʿī*) of the word, the other two are inferred by reasoning (*ʿaqlī*)."[198] Quṭb ad-dīn ar-Rāzī at-Taḥtānī explains in his meta-commentary on the *Išārāt* entitled *al-Muḥākamāt bayna l-Imām wa-n-Naṣīr fī Šarḥ al-Išārāt* why, in Naṣīr ad-dīn's view, containment and implication are to be regarded as both *dalāla waḍʿiyya* and *dalāla ʿaqliyya* as follows:

> [§1] His [*i.e. Naṣīr ad-dīn aṭ-Ṭūsī's*] saying "signification by congruence is a [pure (*ṣirfa*)] [*signification*] based on imposition": Signification by congruence occurs by means of mere imposition (*bi-muǧarradi l-waḍʿi*), while signification by containment and implication occur by means of the participation of reasoning (*ʿaql*) and imposition (*waḍʿ*):
> [§2] [1] As for the fact that they both occur due to imposition, it is as follows: If the linguistic expression had not been imposed with respect to the whole and [*with respect to*] that to which it is adhered (*malzūm*), then it would not signify the part, inasfar as it is a part [*of the whole*], and it would not signify that which is adhered (*lāzim*), inasfar as it is adhered to something.
> [2] As for the fact that they both occur according to reasoning, it is as follows: When (*iḏā*) the whole and that to which it [*i.e. the thing adhering*] adheres are understood by the linguistic expression, the mind judges/decides that the part and the mentally adhering thing (*al-lāzim aḏ-ḏihnī*) are understood by the linguistic expression.[199]

This is ultimately a specification of the hierarchization as we find it in Faḫr ad-dīn: If these two manners of signification are based on the first manner of signification, but by definition transcend it in one respect or another, then the reasoning-based signification is ultimately, albeit indirectly, based on the imposition-based signification.

[*ad* b] Sayf ad-dīn al-Āmidī (d. 631/1233), in his meta-commentary on the *Išārāt* entitled the *Kašf at-tamwīhāt fī Šarḥ at-Tanbīhāt* and in his *uṣūl al-fiqh* work *al-Iḥkām fī uṣūl al-aḥkām*, likewise does not deny that containment and implication must to a certain extent be deduced: It is correct that the significations of containment and implication can both be regarded as a form of

198 Simon, *Mittelalterliche arabische Sprachbetrachtung*, p. 63, fn. 7 and pp. 38–39.

199 Quṭb ad-dīn ar-Rāzī at-Taḥtānī (d. 766/1365), *al-Muḥākamāt bayna l-Imām wa-n-Naṣīr fī Šarḥ al-Išārāt*, Ms. Berlin Petermann I 549, fol. 22ᵛ, lines 7–13. On this scholar, see for example Stewart, *Islamic Legal Orthodoxy*, pp. 77 f.

rational/deductive reflection (*naẓar ʿaqlī*), since an inference—either to what it contains or to what is adhered to it—is in each case required by the signified meaning.[200] However, in the case of containment, the inferred meaning is a part of the congruent meaning, "therefore signification by containment—in contrast to signification by implication—is literal" (*fa-li-ḏālika kānat dalālatu t-taḍammunin lafẓiyyatan bi-ḫilāfi d-dalālati l-iltizāmin*).[201]

Al-Āmidī and later Ibn al-Ḥāǧib (d. 646/1249)[202] use the terms 'literal' (*lafẓiyya*) and 'non-literal signification' (*dalāla ġayr lafẓiyya*) instead of Faḫr ad-dīn's distinction.[203] The term *lafẓī* had already been used in this context by ʿUmar b. Sahlān as-Sāwī (fl. 540/1145), whose work *al-Baṣāʾir an-naṣīriyya fī ʿilm al-manṭiq*, after discussing the subject matter of logic, begins with the classification of signification. There it says of implication: "It is as if this is not a literal signification (*ka-anna hāḏā laysa dalālatan lafẓiyyatan*); rather, it is such that the mind turns from that meaning which the linguistic expression signifies on the grounds of imposition (*bi-l-waḍʿ*) to another meaning adhering to it, which is close to it."[204] Implication is not a literal signification, but a mental signification (*dalāla ḏihniyya*).[205]

Al-Āmidī expands on this aspect mentioned by as-Sāwī and does not adopt the distinction between *dalāla waḍʿiyya* and *dalāla ʿaqliyya*: Congruence and containment are thus literal significations, whereas implication is not literal because that which is signified is not located within what the linguistic expression signifies.[206]

200 Sayf ad-dīn al-Āmidī, *al-Iḥkām fī uṣūl al-aḥkām*, ed. by ʿAbd ar-Razzāq ʿAfīfī (Riyāḍ: Dār aṣ-Ṣumayʿī, 2003), vol. 1, p. 32, lines 13–14.

201 Ibid., line 16.

202 See Ǧamāl ad-dīn Ibn al-Ḥāǧib, *Kitāb Muntahā al-wuṣūl wa-l-amal fī ʿilmay al-uṣūl wa-l-ǧadal*, ed. s.n. (Beirut: Dār al-Kutub al-ʿilmiyya, 1985 [1405]), p. 17, lines 6–7 and id., *Muḫtaṣar al-muntahā fī s-sūl wa-l-amal fī ʿilmay al-uṣūl wa-l-ǧadal*, ed. by Naẓīr Ḥamādū (Algiers: Dār Ibn Ḥazm, 2006), p. 221; cf. Yunis Ali, *Medieval Islamic Pragmatics*, p. 144.

203 In this context, *lafẓiyya* cannot be translated as 'linguistic'; both *lafẓiyya* and *ġayr lafẓiyya* refer to linguistic significations; al-Āmidī distinguishes here between a literal and a non-literal signification. Later, as we will see, an explicit distinction is made between significations using spoken language and those using sign language.

204 As-Sāwī, *al-Baṣāʾir an-naṣīriyya*, p. 33, lines 17–18.

205 Sayf ad-dīn al-Āmidī, *Kašf at-tamwīhāt fī Šarḥ at-Tanbīhāt*, Ms. Berlin Petermann II 596, fol. 13ᵛ, lines 17–18, or in the newly published edition: al-Āmidī, *Kašf at-tamwīhāt fī Šarḥ ar-Rāzī ʿalā l-Išārāt wa-tanbīhāt*, ed. by Aḥmad Farīd al-Mazīdī (Beirut: Dār al-Kutub al-ʿilmiyya, 2013 [1434]), p. 54, line 10.

206 Al-Āmidī, *al-Iḥkām*, vol. 1, pp. 32–33.

FIGURE 13 Illustration of Sayf ad-dīn al-Amidī's differentiation

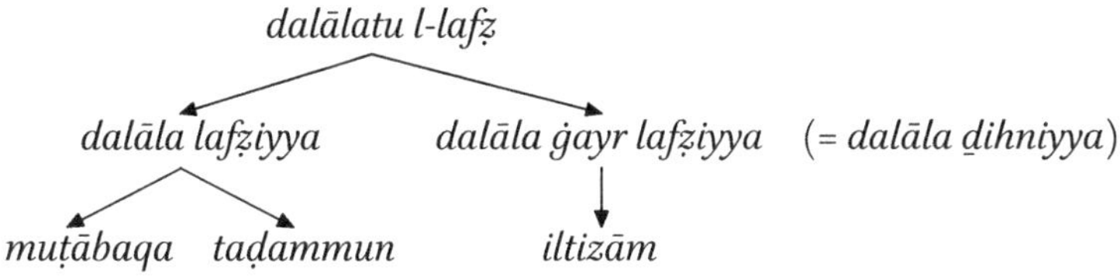

The prioritization of the first two manners of signification can—in one respect—be traced back to Ibn Sīnā: "[§ 2.2] Signification by congruence and signification by containment have in common that neither of them is a signification for something outside the [*signified*] thing."[207] While position b draws on this second note in the classification of signification in Ibn Sīnā's *Manṭiq al-Mašriqiyyīn*, position a is based on the third note in this text: "[§ 2.3] Signification by containment and signification by implication have in common that each of them requires the first signification [*i.e. signification by congruence*]."[208]

[*ad* c] The third position is ultimately a further development of Naṣīr ad-dīn aṭ-Ṭūsī's position, according to which "significations by containment and by implication [*come about*] both through reasoning and through imposition." Here it is already established that containment and implication are based on imposition in a certain way that is not yet further specified. In his work the *Kašf al-asrār ʿan ġawāmiḍ al-afkār*, Afḍal ad-dīn al-Ḫūnaǧī (d. 646/1248) opposes those who claim "that it [*i.e. signification by implication*] is not a signification based on imposition (*annahā laysat dalālatan waḍʿiyyatan*)"[209]—and thus against a position advocated by Faḫr ad-dīn. According to Afḍal ad-dīn, it is to be argued "that implication is a signification based on imposition, because the linguistic expression only signifies that which adheres to the thing named by it (*ʿalā lāzimi musammāhu*) because it has been imposed for that to which [*the adhering thing*] adheres (*malzūm*)."[210] There is therefore a relationship of imposition, since the relationship of implication is based on the congruent relationship of signification. This aspect does not differ from position a; however, contrary to position a, it is thereby concluded that all three manners of signification are to be called "based on imposition." Afḍal ad-dīn then differentiates this level as follows: "By 'signification based on imposition' is meant

207 Ibn Sīnā, *Manṭiq al-Mašriqiyyīn*, p. 15, lines 3–4.

208 Ibid., lines 5–6.

209 Afḍal ad-dīn al-Ḫūnaǧī, *Kašf al-asrār ʿan ġawāmiḍ al-afkār*, ed. by Khaled El-Rouayheb (Tehran: Iranian Institute of Philosophy and Institute of Islamic Studies, Free University of Berlin, 2010), p. 12, line 1.

210 Al-Ḫūnaǧī, *Kašf al-asrār*, p. 12, lines 13–14.

that [*signification*] by way of imposition occurs [*either*] from the beginning/a priori (*ibtidāʾan*) or through mediation (*bi-wāsiṭati*).”[211] Signification by congruence is the kind that is based from the beginning on the imposition between the linguistic expression and the meaning. The other two manners of signification build on it, so that they are only based on imposition through mediation, i.e. indirectly. The hierarchization of the last level thus corresponds again to position a and even includes the distinction with/without mediation that ʿAbd al-Qāhir al-Ǧurǧānī had already put forward and that Faḫr a-dīn had linked to the Tripartition of Signification.

FIGURE 14 Illustration of Afḍal ad-dīn al-Ḫūnaǧī's differentiation

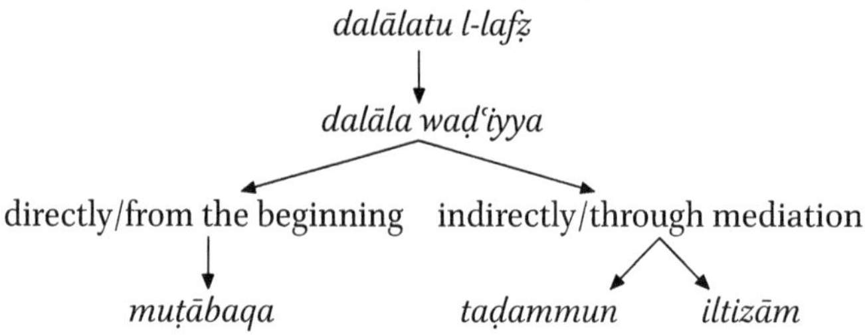

In the further development of position c, the distinction becomes even more complex: in Naǧm ad-dīn al-Kātibī's (d. 657/1276) much commentated work *ar-Risāla aš-šamsiyya*, the internal hierarchization of the three manners of signification based on imposition is eliminated:

> The first chapter on linguistic expressions:
> The signification of meaning through the linguistic expression
> [1.] by means of (*bi-tawassuṭ*) imposition for it [*i.e. for the meaning*] is signification by congruence—just as [*the linguistic expression*] ‘man’ signifies ‘rational animal’;
> [2.] by means of [*imposition*] (*bi-tawassuṭihī*) for what is contained in it [*i.e. in the congruent meaning*] (*daḫala fīhī*) is containment—just as [*the linguistic expression ‘man’*] signifies ‘animal’;
> [3.] by means of [*imposition*] for that which is extrinsic to it is implication (*iltizām*)—just as [*the linguistic expression ‘man’*] signifies ‘disposition to knowledge and the art of writing.’[212]

211 Ibid., lines 14–15.

212 Naǧm ad-dīn al-Kātibī, “ar-Risāla aš-šamsiyya,” ed. by Aloys Sprenger, in *Bibliotheca Indica: A Collection of Oriental Works. No. 88. First Appendix to the Dictionary of the Technical Terms used in the Sciences of the Mussulmans, containing the Logic of the Arabians* (Calcutta:

Since no possible hierarchization emerges from this description, commentators of the *Risāla šamsiyya* have debated the exact classification and its internal organization. Because the answering of this question serves as the basis upon which other complexes of questions—be it in logic with regard to the legitimacy or illegitimacy of implication in definitions or premises, or in *uṣūl al-fiqh* with regard to the legitimacy or illegitimacy of various types of legal implication and other forms of inference—that bear on implication in the broadest sense are ultimately treated.[213]

Ǧamāl ad-dīn al-Ḥillī (d. 726/1325) prefaces his explanation of this passage in his *al-Qawāʿid al-ǧaliyya fī šarḥ ar-Risāla aš-šamsiyya* with a quotation from Ibn Sīnā's *al-ʿIbāra* in order to explain what is meant by signification (*dalāla*) in the first place: "'When the name that is heard impresses upon the imagination (*al-ḫayāl*), its meaning is impressed upon the soul such that the soul realizes that this [*name*] that is heard belongs to this meaning. Every time that sensory perception brings it [*i.e. the name that is heard*] to the soul, the soul turns to its meaning.'"[214] He then subdivides signification as follows: According to this, a linguistic expression [a] can signify according to nature (*ṭabʿ*), "just as *aḫ* signifies injury to the breast";[215] [b] it can signify on the basis of reasoning

Carbery, 1854), p. 3 (Arabic), lines 5–6; a brief overview of this work and its textual history is provided by Street ("Arabic Logic," pp. 581–582); on the commentary tradition, see also Sabine Schmidtke, "Two Commentaries on Najm al-Dīn al-Kātibī's *al-Shamsiyya*, Copied in the Hand of David b. Joshua Maimonides (fl. ca. 1335–1410 CE)," in *Law and Tradition in Classical Islamic Thought*, ed. by Michael Cook, Najam Haider, Intinsar Rabb, and Asma Sayeed (New York: Palgrave McMillan, 2013), pp. 203–225, esp. pp. 205–206.

213 On the relevance in logic, see Chapter 2, Section 3.2.4 of this study; in *uṣūl al-fiqh*, see Chapter 4, Section 2.2.2.

214 Ǧamāl ad-dīn al-Ḥillī, *al-Qawāʿid al-ǧaliyya fī šarḥ ar-Risāla aš-šamsiyya*, ed. by Fāris Ḥassūn Tabrīziyān (Qom: Muʾassasat an-našr al-islāmī, 1992 [1412]), p. 195, lines 3–5; Ibn Sīnā, *Kitāb aš-Šifāʾ, al-Manṭiq, al-ʿIbāra*, p. 4, lines 8–10; cf. Chapter 1, Section 2 of this study; on this scholar and in particular on the chronological placement of this work, see Sabine Schmidtke, *The Theology of ʿAllāma al-Ḥillī (d. 726/1325)* (Berlin: Klaus Schwarz Verlag, 1991), p. 61; this work is still used in traditional Šīʿite legal studies, cf. Stewart, *Islamic Legal Orthodoxy*, p. 73; on his logic, see in particular Tony Street, "Al-ʿAlāma al Ḥillī (d. 1325) and the Early Reception of Kātibī's *Shamsīya*: Notes towards a Study of the Dynamics of Post-Avicennan Logical Commentary," *Oriens*, vol. 44 (2016): pp. 267–300.

215 Al-Ḥillī, *al-Qawāʿid al-ǧaliyya*, p. 195. This example is cited by Ibn Sīnā to show that a linguistic expression does not have to signify by convention (*tawāṭuʾ*), but can also signify in another way, see Ibn Sīnā, *Kitāb aš-Šifāʾ, al-Manṭiq, al-ʿIbāraq*, p. 9, line 13 (technically, Ibn Sīnā used *aḥaḥ* for injury to the breast and reserved *aḫ* for pain in general—al-Ḥillī apparently combined two examples for this type here). Ibn Sīnā does not yet call this type *ṭabʿ*; the designation *ṭabʿ* is found in post-Avicennian literature, including in grammatical writings, see for example Ibn Yaʿīš, *Šarḥ al-Mufaṣṣal li-z-Zamaḫšarī* (ed. s.n., s.l., 1876–1886), p. 21, lines 21–24.

(*ʿaql*), "just as the sound (*ṣawt*) signifies/reveals the one who utters the sound (*muṣawwit*)."[216] This example does not refer to the relationship of implication based on the word form, but rather only to the fact that a sound gives away the presence of the one who has made this sound; [c] or it can signify according to imposition (*waḍʿ*). Only the latter, according to Ǧamāl ad-dīn al-Ḥillī, is the type of signification that is relevant in this context, i.e. in the discipline of logic:

> [...] [*signification by the linguistic expression*] can occur according to imposition (*bi-ḥasabi l-waḍʿ*). What is intended (*maqṣūd*) here is the last. It [*i.e. signification according to imposition*] does not go beyond these three [*manners of signification*], as what is understood by the linguistic expression,
> [1.] is either the meaning for which the linguistic expression has been imposed/set, such that the signification is the signification of congruence, just like how 'man' signifies 'rational animal'—because the imposer of language (*wāḍiʿ*) has imposed the linguistic expression 'man' for this meaning;
> [2.] or that which is understood by the linguistic expression is one of the parts of that meaning—that is the signification of containment, just like how 'man' signifies 'animal' or 'rational,' for the understanding of the whole entails the understanding of each individual part (*fa-inna fahma l-maǧmūʿi yastalzimu fahma kulli wāḥidin min aǧzāʾihī*);
> [3.] or that which is understood by the linguistic term is the extrinsic meaning (*al-maʿnā al-ḫāriǧī*)—that is the signification of implication, just like how 'man' signifies 'receptive to the art of writing' (*qābil ṣanʿat al-kitāba*), for this meaning is not the one for which it [*i.e. the linguistic expression 'man'*] has been imposed/set (*fa-inna hāḏā l-maʿnā laysa huwa l-mawḍūʿ lahū*).[217]

All three manners of signification fall under the category of *dalāla waḍʿiyya* or—in al-Ḥillī's terminology—'signification according to imposition' (*bi-ḥasabi l-waḍʿ*). But here too an internal differentiation is made, according to which a direct relationship of imposition only exists in the first case. Consequently,

216 Al-Ḥillī, *al-Qawāʿid al-ǧaliyya*, p. 195; see also the parallel passage in his commentary on Naṣīr ad-dīn aṭ-Ṭūsī's logical compendium the *Taǧrīd fī l-manṭiq*, Ǧamāl ad-dīn al-Ḥillī, *al-Ǧawhar an-naḍīd fī manṭiq at-taǧrīd*, ed. by Muḥsin Bīdārfar (Qom: Intišārāt-i Bīdār, 1984 [1363]), p. 8.

217 Al-Ḥillī, *al-Qawāʿid al-ǧaliyya*, p. 195.

there is no substantial difference from position a, but rather 'only' a terminological difference, which can nevertheless have substantial consequences in the discussion about the permissibility of implication in certain contexts.[218]

FIGURE 15 Illustration of the Differentiation in Ǧamāl ad-dīn al-Ḥillī's *al-Qawāʿid al-ǧaliyya fī šarḥ ar-Risāla aš-šamsiyya*

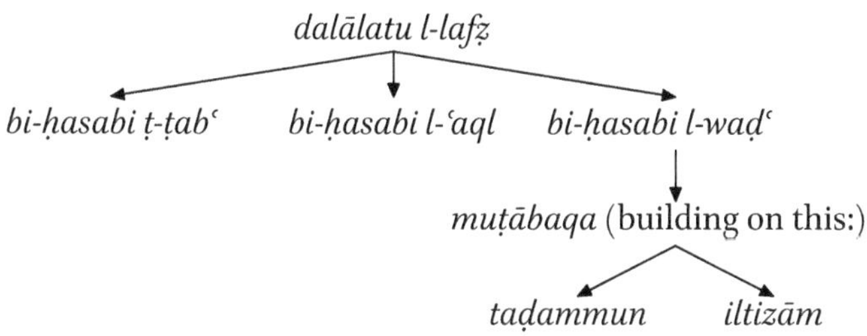

The further terminological development of this sub-classification gained momentum on this basis in the subsequent commentaries on the *Risāla šamsiyya*: Thus Quṭb ad-dīn ar-Rāzī at-Taḥtānī in his commentary the *Taḥrīr al-qawāʿid al-manṭiqiyya* connects the three different classifications together—i.e. [I] *muṭābaqa/taḍammun/iltizām*, [II] *dalāla waḍʿiyya/ṭabīʿiyya/ʿaqliyya*, and [III] *dalāla lafẓiyya/ġayr lafẓiyya*:

> [§ 1] If the signifier (*dāll*) is a linguistic expression (*lafẓ*), then the signification is linguistic (*lafẓiyya*, literally: 'verbal'), and if not, it is not linguistic (*ġayr lafẓiyya*, literally: 'not verbal')—just like signification by the line (*ḫaṭṭ*) [*i.e. the line in the sand* (al-ḫatt bi-raml), *analyzed in the field of geomancy*][219] and by the *ʿuqad* (knot), by gestures (*al-išārāt*) and by the statue/monument (*an-nuṣub*).
> [1.] The linguistic expression (*dalāla lafẓiyya*) either corresponds to what the one who establishes it (*ǧāʿil*) has established (*ǧaʿala*); this is the [1.1] imposed (*waḍʿiyya*) [*signification*], just like how 'man' signifies 'rational animal.' Imposition (*waḍʿ*) means that the linguistic expression is established for a meaning;
> – or this is not so (*aw lā*), [1.2] and [*the linguistic signification*] must be (*lā yaḫlū*) either according to the requirement of nature (*iqtiḍāʾ aṭ-ṭabīʿ*)—that is the natural [*signification*] (*ṭabīʿiyya*), just like how 'aḫ' signifies pain

218 See Chapter 4, Section 2.2.
219 Cf. Toufic Fahd, "Khaṭṭ (*bi-raml*)," *EI*^{2}.

(*waǧaʿ*); for the nature of the speaker requires the articulation (*talaffuẓ*) [*of pain*] when pain arises in him;
– or it is not so (*aw lā*); this is the [1.3] rational (*ʿaqliyya*) [*signification*], just like how the linguistic expression, [p. 29] which is heard behind the wall (*al-lafẓ al-masmūʿ min warāʾ al-ǧidār*), signifies the presence of the speaker (*wuǧūd al-lāfiẓ*).
[§ 2] What is intended (*maqṣūd*) here is the imposed linguistic signification [1.1] (*dalāla lafẓiyya waḍʿiyya*); this is the fact that by the linguistic expression, whenever it is uttered, its meaning is understood due to the knowledge of its imposition (*waḍʿ*)—and that is either [*signification*] by congruence, by containment, or implication.[220]

Quṭb ad-dīn ar-Rāzī at-Taḥtānī opens up a new level in this schematization: he considers signification in the general sense. This occurs either through linguistic or non-linguistic signs, i.e. Quṭb ad-dīn divides signification in general into that type which occurs by means of a linguistic expression (that is in some respect through a sequence of letters)[221] and that which does not occur by means of a linguistic expression but insead by means of other signs—such as gestures (*išārāt*) and traces (*aṯar*).[222] One is the *dalāla lafẓiyya*—and in this respect is to be understood as 'linguistic signification.' This term has a different meaning here than al-Āmidī's *dalāla lafẓiyya* and must therefore be translated differently.[223] Al-Āmidī really only means a 'literal signification,' that is 'literal' as opposed to 'figurative.'

Quṭb ad-dīn divides the level of linguistic signification into the aforementioned (i.e. the one by Ǧamāl ad-dīn al-Ḥillī) tripartite division of imposed, nat-

220 Quṭb ad-dīn ar-Rāzī at-Taḥtānī, *Taḥrīr al-qawāʿid al-manṭiqiyya: Šarḥ ar-Risāla aš-šamsiyya, wa-bi-asfal ṣaḥāʾifihī Ḥāšiya ʿalā Taḥrīr al-qawāʿid al-manṭiqiyya*, ed. by Aḥmad Amīn ʿUmrān (Cairo: Muṣṭafā al-Bābī l-Ḥalabī wa-awlāduhū, 1948), p. 28, line 10–p. 29, line 2.

221 I.e., if we follow Ibn Sīnā's definition of *lafẓ*, to which Quṭb ad-dīn ar-Rāzī at-Taḥtānī indirectly refers with his examples, see Ibn Sīnā, *Kitāb aš-Šifāʾ, al-Manṭiq, al-ʿIbāra*, pp. 8–9.

222 Quṭb ad-dīn gives this example in the parallel passage in his commentary on Sirāǧ ad-dīn al-Urmawī's *Maṭāliʿ al-anwār*, see Quṭb ad-dīn ar-Rāzī at-Taḥtānī, *Lawāmiʿtānī fī šarḥ Maṭāliʿ al-anwār*, ed. s.n. (Istanbul, 1885 [1303]), p. 27, lines 20–21.

223 This fact is ignored by Mohamed Yunis Ali in his presentation, resulting in the suggestion of a similarity between the classifications where none exists. In reality, the pair verbal/non-verbal means something completely different in one classification than in the other, cf. Mohamed M. Yunis Ali, *Medieval Islamic Pragmatics*, pp. 143–144, namely "literal" in the one and "oral" in the other. Moreover, this equation leads to other misunderstandings and incorrect conclusions in Yunis Ali's explanations; see, for example, the elaborations upon an alleged point of criticism, which, upon closer analysis of the technical terms, turns out not to be one after all, Yunis Ali, *Medieval Islamic Pragmatics*, p. 156.

ural, and rational signification. In this classification, too, 'rational signification' does not in any respect refer to a transferred signification, but likewise only the fact that the linguistic expression represents a trace indicating the existence of a speaker. Only that signification in which—by convention or divine imposition—there is a direct relationship between linguistic expression and meaning is relevant for this discipline, i.e. for logic. This signification is then subdivided into the Tripartition of Signification that was the starting point for Faḫr ad-dīn, namely congruence, containment, and implication. A hierarchization of the three manners of signification is carried out in this position—as in position [a]: The manners of signification of containment and implication both require congruence.[224]

FIGURE 16 Quṭb ad-dīn ar-Rāzī at-Taḥtānī's *Taḥrīr al-qawāʿid al-manṭiqiyya*

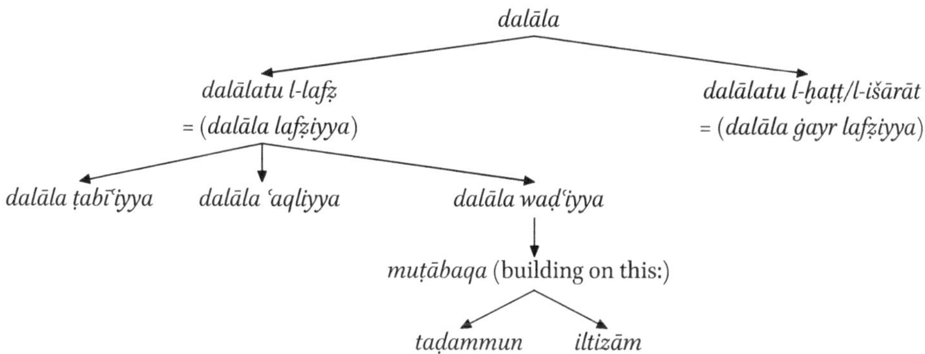

Quṭb ad-dīn's classification resulted in the entry "imposed linguistic signification" (*ad-dalāla al-lafẓiyya al-waḍʿiyya*) in Šarīf al-Ǧurǧānī's (d. 816/1413) lexicon the *Kitāb at-Taʿrīfāt*:

> The imposed linguistic signification (*ad-dalāla al-lafẓiyya al-waḍʿiyya*): This "is the fact that for the linguistic expression, whenever it is uttered" or presented, "its meaning is understood on the basis of the knowledge of its imposition." It is divided into [*signification by*] congruence, containment, and implication; for the linguistic expression signifying on the basis of imposition "signifies the entirety of that for which it has been imposed" by congruence, its part by containment, and that which adheres to it [*i.e. the entire meaning*] in the mind by implication [...].[225]

224 Quṭb ad-dīn ar-Rāzī at-Taḥtānī, *Taḥrīr al-qawāʿid al-manṭiqiyya*, p. 32, lines 14–15.
225 ʿAlī b. Muḥammad aš-Šarīf al-Ǧurǧānī, *Kitāb al-Taʿrīfāt*, ed. s.n. (Cairo: al-Maṭbaʿa al-Ḫayriyya, 1888), p. 46, last line–p. 47, line 3.

This lexicon entry, in which the references to Quṭb ad-dīn's classification are obvious, can to a certain extent be seen as the end point of the debate about the correct hierarchization and classification of signification—the consideration of all three manners of signification as "imposed linguistic signification" proves to have been authoritative and continued to be handed down over the centuries.

3.2.1.3 *Summary and Conclusion*

The distinction between *dalāla waḍʿiyya* and *dalāla ʿaqliyya*, which Faḫr ad-dīn cites in the *Maḥṣūl* as the first note on the three manners of signification is, in his logical writing, situated—just like these three manners themselves—in the logical-philosophical context of the correct determination of the quiddity. But beyond this rather narrow frame of reference, Faḫr ad-dīn establishes an additional connection: there are already references in the *Manṭiq al-Mulaḫḫaṣ* to linguistic theory, which are explicated upon in his rhetorical writing in response to ʿAbd al-Qāhir al-Ǧurǧānī's works. There, Faḫr ad-dīn derives his distinction from ʿAbd al-Qāhir's influential distinction between [i] 'meaning' (*al-maʿnā*) and [ii] 'meaning of the meaning' (*maʿnā l-maʿnā*). The category of 'meaning' corresponds to the congruent signification relationship based on imposition, while the category of 'meaning of the meaning' is equated with the signification relationship based on reasoning, which includes containment and implication. Subsequent writings would discuss the assignment of the three manners of signification to the *waḍʿiyya*/*ʿaqliyya* distinction:[226]

[a] Some scholars shared Faḫr ad-dīn's classification system, according to which only the congruent manner of signification is to be considered *dalāla waḍʿiyya*; [b] some considered both congruence and containment to be *dalāla waḍʿiyya*; and in the end [c] all three manners of signification were designated as *dalāla waḍʿiyya*. However, this last position is not as different from the initial position in terms of its evaluation and hierarchization of the individual manners of signification as it might seem at first glance. What changes here is the concept of *dalāla ʿaqliyya*, which had previously been regarded as a catch-all for transferred meanings. In position [c], the *dalāla ʿaqliyya* is a form of rational signification that is related to language and the articulation of sounds, but not to words *per se*—just as the one who is hiding can betray himself through a noise, or the one who needs help can draw attention to himself by crying out. In these cases, the issue is something other than the relationship between

226 Šihāb ad-dīn al-Qarāfī gives a concise summary of this disagreement, cf. al-Qarāfī, *Nafāʾis al-uṣūl*, vol. 1, p. 265, lines 10–22.

the word and its meaning; rather, the focus is on the relationship between the speaker and his breath or the sounds he makes as a sign of his presence. It is therefore only logical to categorize containment and implication as the type of signification that is based on the imposition between word and meaning, since this is the "meaning of the meaning of the linguistic expression," i.e. the meta-meaning of the linguistic expression. Positions [a] and [c] share the assumption that in order to understand containment and implication, a further inference, a further act of mental effort, is required.

A major difference between positions [b] and [c] is what is meant by the distinction between *dalāla lafẓiyya* and *dalāla ġayr lafẓiyya*: In [b] it refers to the difference between literal and figurative meaning, whereas in [c] it refers to the difference between linguistic signification and non-linguistic signification, with the latter meaning, for example, body language or reading tracks in the sand.[227]

The discussion about the classification of the three manners of signification holds a certain relevance for legal practice: By associating the three manners of signification with this more general distinction, Faḫr ad-dīn created a hierarchization that also simultaneously says something about the degree of certainty of knowledge that can be obtained from the respective categories of signification. Only the first manner of signification can—under certain conditions, as we will see later[228]—lead to a status of certainty of knowledge. In contrast, the other two manners of signification have little epistemological value. Position [b], on the other hand, advocated by al-Āmidī and Ibn al-Ḥāǧib, states that the first two manners of signification, i.e. congruence and containment, are to be regarded as imposed, literal relationships of signification, which consequently leads to an epistemological valorization of containment for the process of interpretation. This is because meanings can be declared as literal—and thus as epistemologically certain—that would otherwise fall into the epistemologically less certain *ʿaqlī* realm. Position [c], on the other hand, by merely designating the three manners of signification as *dalāla waḍʿiyya*, makes no statements as to their epistemological value. It does not imply an upvaluation of containment and implication because *dalāla waḍʿiyya* and *dalāla ʿaqliyya* now have a differ-

227 As already mentioned, I consider Yunis Ali's treatment of this topic to be problematic, since the differences between the concepts masked by identical terminology are not taken into account, resulting in alleged comparability (cf. Yunis Ali, *Medieval Islamic Pragmatics*, pp. 142–146). Furthermore, in his approach, different arguments of different scholars are read into each other and blended together (cf. Yunis Ali, *Medieval Islamic Pragmatics*, e.g. p. 156).

228 See part 4.

ent conceptual scope than in position [a]. What is meant is nothing other than that the manners of signification assigned to *dalāla waḍʿiyya* are all based on a relationship of imposition between word and meaning—even if they transcend this relationship of imposition.

3.2.2 [ad § 3] [Note 2] Containment vs. Homonymy

Now that the first note provided by Faḫr ad-dīn on the classification of signification has been examined, we can consider the second note:

> [§ 3] The second [*note*]: [*ad* 2] We only said about containment (*taḍammun*) that it is the signification of a part (*ǧuzʾ*) of what is signified by the linguistic expression, [*with the qualification*] 'insofar as it is like that' (*min ḥayṯu huwa ka-ḏālika*), because we want to guard against the linguistic expression signifying by congruence a part of that which is named in a homonymous way (*ʿalā sabīli l-ištirāk*). [*ad* 3] The same applies to what was said about implication (*iltizām*).[229]

This note refers to [§ 1] and the outline of containment contained therein: "The linguistic expression is either such that its signification [...] [1.2] is [*considered*] in relation to what intrinsically [*belongs*] (*dāḫil*) to what is named (*musammā*)—insofar as it is this way (*min ḥayṯu huwa ka-ḏālika*)."[230] Thus, containment is that manner of signification in which the linguistic expression signifies an intrinsic part of the meaning. The qualification 'insofar as it is this way' (*min ḥayṯu huwa ka-ḏālika*) is the subject of this second note and we can infer from it that there are manners of signification in which a part of the meaning is signified without it being through signification by containment—namely when a linguistic expression signifies this part in a homonymous way.

Since this note is—characteristically for this chapter—kept very brief, we must refer to other works by Faḫr ad-dīn for a detailed explanation. In order to understand this second note, we therefore turn to Faḫr ad-dīn's *Išārāt* commentary:

> [*Containment is not to be confused with homonymy*] [see Text 1, § 3] Know that it may seem immediately obvious (*rubbamā yasbuqu ilā l-awhām*) that whenever the linguistic expression signifies a meaning, its signification of the part of that meaning—however it [*i.e. the signification*] may

229 Faḫr ad-dīn ar-Rāzī, *al-Maḥṣūl*, vol. 1, p. 220, lines 1–3.
230 Ibid., p. 219, lines 5–6.

be—is signification by containment; but this is false (*bāṭil*), since it is conceivable that the linguistic expression signifies the meaning as well as the part [*of this meaning*] by congruence in a homonymous way (*bi-l-muṭābaqa ʿalā l-ištirāk*); just like e.g. 'the possible' (*al-mumkin*)—for it signifies 'the specifically possible' (*al-mumkin al-ḫāṣṣ*) and 'the generally possible' (*al-mumkin al-ʿāmm*), which is a part of what is understood by 'the specifically possible' (*al-mumkin al-ḫāṣṣ*). It [*i.e. the linguistic expression* mumkin] signifies both in a homonymous way (*bi-štirāki l-ism*).

Rather, it is a condition (*šarṭ*) of the signification by containment that the linguistic expression does not signify the part of the meaning in a primary way and *per se* (*awwalan wa-bi-d-ḏāt*), but in a secondary way and *per accidens* (*ṯāniyan wa-l-bi-l-ʿaraḍ*).[231]

Faḫr ad-dīn begins by stating that not every process of signification in which a part of the meaning for which the linguistic expression has been imposed is signified amounts to containment. After all, it is conceivable that the linguistic expression could signify in a congruent manner, signifying both the overall meaning and a part of it simultaneously. According to Faḫr ad-dīn in § 20 of our source text, homonymy means that two meanings are intended simultaneously by a single linguistic expression, whereby neither meaning is more probable than the other; as an example, Faḫr ad-dīn gives the linguistic expression *al-mumkin*; "for it signifies 'the specifically possible' (*al-mumkin al-ḫāṣṣ*) and 'the generally possible' (*al-mumkin al-ʿāmm*)" equally, i.e. the one-sided concept of possibility (corresponding to *al-mumkin al-ʿāmm*) and the two-sided concept of possibility (corresponding to *al-mumkin al-ḫāṣṣ*) are both signified congruently and homonymously by *mumkin*.[232]

Such a manner of signification is therefore not to be understood as containment: Containment should not be confused with homonymy. The essential difference is that the homonymous signification is a signification of equal rank (regardless of whether one of the meanings is regarded as part of another or not), whereas containment is a subordinate signification—in the sense that the linguistic expression signifies a meaning in a primary way and only in secondary way does it signify a part of it:

231 Faḫr ad-dīn ar-Rāzī, *Šarḥ al-Išārāt*, p. 32, line 12–p. 33, line 1.

232 On the distinction between the one-sided and two-sided concept of possibility, see Ibn Sīnā, *Kitāb aš-Šifāʾ*, *al-Manṭiq*, *al-Qiyās*, p. 162, lines 1–3; al-Ǧurǧānī, *Kitāb al-Taʿrīfāt*, pp. 102–103; Street, "An Outline of Avicenna's Syllogistics," pp. 135–136; Jaakko Hintikka, "Aristotle's Different Possibilities," in *Time and Necessity: Studies in Aristotle's Theory of Modality*, ed. by Jaakko Hintikka (Oxford: Clarendon Press, 1973), pp. 27–40.

> We mean [*by containment*] the fact that it [*i.e. the linguistic expression*] signifies the part as a subordinate consequence (*tābiʿan*) of the signification of the whole (*al-kull*), just like how the linguistic expression 'triangle' (*muṯallaṯ*) signifies the form (*šakl*); for 'triangle' does not signify form *per se*, but rather the signification of it [*occurs*] due to the fact that it is categorized under 'triangle' (*li-indirāǧihī taḥta l-muṯallaṯ*).
>
> Thus, the result (*ḥāṣil*) is that the signification by containment is an expression (*ʿibāra*) for the signification in which the linguistic expression [*signifies*] the meaning due to being categorized under that for which the linguistic expression was imposed (*li-indirāǧihī taḥta mā wuḍiʿa l-lafẓ bi-izāʾihī*).[233]

Like Ibn Sīnā in the *Išārāt*, Faḫr ad-dīn also cites the example of the triangle for this case, in which the species—'triangle'—in its definition—"'the form surrounded by three sides'" (*aš-šaklu l-muḥīṭu bihi ṯalāṯatu aḍluʿ*)[234]—contains the genus without signifying it in a primary way.

The subordination of signification is emphasized not only with regard to containment, but also with regard to implication. This note is also adopted in the post-Rāzian literature.[235]

3.2.3 [ad § 4] [Note 3] *luzūm ḏihnī* vs. *luzūm ḫāriǧī*

The third note focuses on the type of signification of implication that is meant by mental implication (*al-luzūm aḏ-ḏihnī*) and not external implication (*al-luzūm al-ḫāriǧī*). Faḫr ad-dīn begins this note with a more detailed description of this external implication:

> [§ 4] The third [*note*] [*restriction of the relationship of implication*]: [*ad 3*] With regard to signification by implication (*iltizām*), external implication (*al-luzūm al-ḫāriǧī*) is not considered because substance (*ǧawhar*) and accident (*ʿaraḍ*) [*indeed*] mutually adhere/implicate (*mutalāzimān*), but the linguistic expression that signifies one of them is not applied to the other.[236]

---

233 Faḫr ad-dīn ar-Rāzī, *Šarḥ al-Išārāt*, p. 33, lines 1–4.

234 Ibn Sīnā, *al-Išārāt wa-t-tanbīhāt*, p. 42, lines 10–13.

235 See, for example, Naṣīr ad-dīn aṭ-Ṭūsī, *Ḥall muškilāt al-Išārāt*, p. 187, lines 3–5 (the line count does not follow that of the original text) and (already with modified premises) Quṭb ad-dīn ar-Rāzī at-Taḥtānī, *Taḥrīr al-qawāʿid al-manṭiqiyya*, p. 29, lines 14–22.

236 Faḫr ad-dīn ar-Rāzī, *al-Maḥṣūl*, vol. 1, p. 220, lines 4–8.

This note refers to a passage from Ibn Sīnā's *Kitāb al-Burhān* II.5, where a distinction is made between two ways in which something can be necessary for a thing: "Things are necessary according to a relationship of implication (*luzūm*), without one of them being necessary for the other according to substance (*ǧawhar*) and nature (*ṭabīʿa*)—these are the externally adhering things (*lawāzim ḫāriǧiyya*)."[237] This pertains to the aforementioned distinction between extrinsic qualities that adhere to the quiddity as a quiddity or those that adhere to the realized quiddity.[238] The latter type of *luzūm* is useless "in the acquisition (*kasb*) of certain knowledge (*ʿilm yaqīnī*)."[239] According to Faḫr ad-dīn, such a relationship is not to be understood under the relationship of implication of the third manner of signification, which Faḫr ad-dīn now calls mental implication (*al-luzūm aḏ-ḏihnī*). In external implication (*al-luzūm al-ḫāriǧī*) there is no overlap in the signification, i.e. "the linguistic expression signifying one of the two [*is*] not applied to the other"; there is no kind of relationship of signification[240]—apart from, as Faḫr ad-dīn further explains in the *Maḥṣūl*, the case of "two mutually exclusive opposites (*ḍiddāni mutanāfiyāni*)," where the occurrence of one indicates the non-occurrence of the other.[241]

The term *luzūm ḏihnī*, coined by Faḫr ad-dīn, is based on Ibn Sīnā's description of implication as a type of signification in which the mind (*ḏihn*) turns from the primary, congruent meaning to the implied meaning: "This [*primary*] meaning is accompanied by another (*wa-yakūnu ḏālika l-maʿnā yaṣḥabuhū maʿnan āḫar*), such that the mind also turns to this second meaning (*fa-yantaqilu ḏ-ḏihnu ayḍan ilā ḏālika l-maʿnā ṯ-ṯānī*)."[242] The fact that the mind can perform this turning is due to the relationship between the two meanings; it is this relationship to which Faḫr ad-dīn refers with the term mental implication. Before Faḫr ad-dīn, al-Ġazālī had already specified the manner of signification of implication in this sense: "As for implication (*iltizām*), [*it is that*] which is not separable (*lā yufāriqu*) from the essence at all, yet the understand-

237 Ibn Sīnā, *Kitāb aš-Šifāʾ*, *Kitāb al-Burhān*, II.5, p. 150, lines 6–7.

238 See also the detailed explanations of Strobino, "Per Se, Inseparability, Containment and Implication," p. 262: "Properties that are necessary in essence and nature are per se 1, i.e., either the constituents of the quiddity of something or the quiddity itself. Properties that are necessary in implication are per se 2 when that of which they hold is necessary to them in essence and nature. Properties that are necessarily implied without an essential connection in either direction are merely inseparable."

239 Ibn Sīnā, *Kitāb aš-Šifāʾ*, *Kitāb al-Burhān*, II.5, p. 150, line 7.

240 Faḫr ad-dīn ar-Rāzī, *Manṭiq al-Mulaḫḫaṣ*, p. 20, lines 9–13.

241 Faḫr ad-dīn ar-Rāzī, *al-Maḥṣūl*, vol. 1, p. 220, line 6.

242 Ibn Sīnā, *Manṭiq al-Mašriqiyyīn*, p. 15, lines 1–2.

ing (*fahm*) of the essential nature (*ḥaqīqa*) and the quiddity (*māhiyya*) is not based on it (*ġayr mawqūf*)."[243] Faḫr ad-dīn in the *Maḥṣūl* indicates that the fact that such a relationship of implication exists represents neither a 'cause' for the conceptualization of the quiddity nor for its realization; rather, it follows from the conceptualization. For example, 'two' implies 'evenness' (*zawǧiyya*). One could render *luzūm ḏihnī* with 'essential implication' instead of 'mental implication.' In relation to signification by implication, the existence and comprehension of the mental relationship of implication of course represent an important condition for such a type of signification to exist at all.[244]

The distinction between *luzūm ḏihnī* and *luzūm ḫāriǧī* is also maintained in post-Rāzian literature in this context[245] and eventually also finds its way into Šarīf al-Ǧurǧānī's *Kitāb at-Taʿrīfāt*.[246] In the later *uṣūl al-fiqh* literature (based on al-Qarāfī), this distinction becomes relevant in connection with the dispute over the legitimacy of the *argumentum e contrario*.[247]

3.2.4 [Note 4] The Discussion on the Assessment of Implication

To these three notes that Faḫr ad-dīn adds to the classification of signification in the *Maḥṣūl*, he adds a further note in the *Šarḥ al-Išārāt* in order to justify the following, already quoted restriction, which Ibn Sīnā gives in the *Išārāt* with regard to the three types of signification:

> [§1.1] When we say: 'this and that linguistic expression signifies this and that,' we mean only the manner [*of signification*] of congruence and containment, but not the manner [*of signification*] of implication. How could it be otherwise? After all, what is signified by implication is unlimited (*ġayr maḥdūd*).[248]

Due to the fact that a quiddity can possess countless implicatures and due to the fact that what is signified by implication is "not constitutive" of the quiddity of a thing, implication is to be avoided when determining the quiddity—

---

243 Al-Ġazālī, *Kitāb Miḥakk an-naẓar*, p. 79, lines 4–5.

244 Faḫr ad-dīn ar-Rāzī, *al-Maḥṣūl*, vol. 1, p. 220, lines 7–8 and in more detail Faḫr ad-dīn ar-Rāzī, *Manṭiq al-Mulaḫḫaṣ*, p. 17, lines 9–13; cf. Yunis Ali, *Medieval Islamic Pragmatics*, p. 152; for the context of this argumentation, see Chapter 2, Section 2.1.

245 See, for example, al-Ḫūnaǧī, *Kašf al-asrār*, p. 11, lines 3–8 and Quṭb ad-dīn ar-Rāzī at-Taḥtānī, *Taḥrīr al-qawāʿid al-manṭiqiyya*, p. 31.

246 See Šarīf al-Ǧurǧānī, *Kitāb at-Taʿrīfāt*, p. 83.

247 See Chapter 4, Section 2.2.2.

248 Ibn Sīnā, *al-Išārāt wa-t-tanbīhāt*, p. 53, lines 5–6; see Chapter 2, Section 2.3.

otherwise "what is not constitutive [*of the quiddity*] would be suitable for the signification of 'what it is.'"[249] Faḫr ad-dīn does not quite agree with the reasoning, which we also know from al-Ġazālī's *Mustaṣfā*, among others:[250]

> Signification by implication is not to be avoided in the sciences (*ʿulūm*) because it is said to be based on reasoning (*ʿaqliyya*); otherwise (*wa-illā*) [*this speech*] would invalidate the use of containment as well. Nor [*is it to be avoided*] because the implicatures are infinite (*ġayr mutanāhiya*); for the obvious amongst them (*al-bayyina minhā*) are finite.[251]

Faḫr ad-dīn first refers to the distinction between *dalāla waḍʿiyya* and *dalāla ʿaqliyya*.[252] This is not the reason why implication should be avoided; otherwise, according to Faḫr ad-dīn's decree, the exclusion would also have to apply to containment. Nor does Faḫr ad-dīn consider Ibn Sīnā's reasoning, according to which 'implication' means that a quiddity can possess an infinite number of adherents, to be entirely convincing as a justification for the exclusion. Instead of the number, his argument is concerned with the precision of the signification: implication, i.e. mental or essential implication (*luzūm ḏihnī*), in this context only refers to the obvious implicatures (*al-lawāzim al-bayyina*)—i.e. those in which the relationship of implication to the implicant is not doubted by means of conceptualization and which do not require proof to obtain this certain knowledge.[253] And these are limited in number and, in contrast to the entirety of all possible implicatures, can be recognized, even if their signification is not precise (*ġayr maḍbūṭ*):

> Rather, the reason is that, in the signification in which the linguistic expression [*signifies*] the implicature of the thing named, [*it is as follows*:] [a] If the fact that the implication is apparent is considered for [*this type of signification*], then it belongs to that which differs from person to person (*yaḫtalifu bi-ḫtilāfi l-ašḫāṣ*), such that what is signified is not precise (*fa-lā yakūnu l-madlūlu maḍbūṭan*);
>
> [b] if the fact [*that the implication is apparent*] is not considered for [*this type of signification*], this is inconceivable, because the aim of uttering linguistic expressions is to cause meanings to be understood (*ifhām*

249 Ibn Sīnā, *al-Išārāt wa-t-tanbīhāt*, p. 53, lines 7–8.
250 Cf. al-Ġazālī, *al-Mustaṣfā*, vol. 1, p. 93, lines 7–8; see also Chapter 2, chapter 2.3.2.
251 Faḫr ad-dīn ar-Rāzī, *Manṭiq al-Mulaḫḫaṣ*, p. 20, last line–p. 21, line 1.
252 See Chapter 2, Section 3.2.1.
253 This is al-Ǧurǧānī's definition, see Šarīf al-Ǧurǧānī, *Kitāb at-Taʿrīfāt*, p. 82.

> *al-maʿānī*), and if this is not achieved, then the linguistic expression is not meaningful/not significant (*lam yakun al-lafẓ mufīdan*).[254]

In this section, Faḫr ad-dīn argues that implication is to be understood as obvious implicatures—elsewhere he had already ruled out that it is to be understood as the totality of all implicatures; because the consequence that "a single linguistic expression signifies an infinite number of meanings due to the fact that the implicatures are infinite" is inconceivable.[255] And if the obvious implication were not to be understood as 'implication,' then the linguistic expression would be meaningless and would not achieve its goal of causing meaning to be understood. It can be assumed that Faḫr ad-dīn here means that the word 'implication' itself would then be emptied of its meaning; not the linguistic expression in general, which would still signify on the basis of imposition. Consequently, the implicit conclusion of the above argumentation is: [a] is true, but due to the imprecision of the signification of meaning, the use of this manner of signification should be avoided.

But when should we refrain from using implication? In the *Mulaḫḫaṣ*, Faḫr ad-dīn speaks in general terms of the fact that this type of signification should be avoided "in the sciences (*ʿulūm*)." In the parallel passage in the *Šarḥ al-Išārāt* on the other hand, he does not make any specification—only later in this work does he say that if implication is permissible, "the propria (*ḫawāṣṣ*) and accidents would [*also*] be suitable for the signification of 'what it is,' "[256] from which it can be concluded that Faḫr ad-dīn, like Ibn Sīnā, 'only' wants to avoid implication in the definition and determination of the quiddity.

Naṣīr ad-dīn aṭ-Ṭūsī also comments on the question of the context to which this restriction applies:

> By this signification [*i.e. Ibn Sīnā's restriction above*] he means the signfication of the quiddity (*dalāla ʿalā l-māhiyya*) or the meaning of the name. [*He does*] not [*mean*] an absolute signification (*dalāla muṭlaqa*) as understood by the commentator [*i.e. ar-Rāzī*] who took this so far as to assume that signification by implication is to be avoided in all areas (*fī ǧamīʿi l-mawāḍiʿ*).[257]

254 Faḫr ad-dīn ar-Rāzī, *Manṭiq al-Mulaḫḫaṣ*, p. 21, lines 1–5.
255 Faḫr ad-dīn ar-Rāzī, *Šarḥ al-Išārāt*, p. 33, last line.
256 Ibid., p. 89, line 14.
257 Aṭ-Ṭūsī, *Ḥall muškilāt al-Išārāt*, p. 181, lines 7–9 (the line count does not follow that of the original text).

Ibn Sīnā's restriction refers only to the determination of the quiddity or to the primary meaning of a name; it may well be that this type of signification is permissible in other areas.[258]

Faḫr ad-dīn, however, was not the first to formulate this remark in this way, and it can be assumed that the term *ʿulūm* is not meant here as absolutely as Naṣīr ad-dīn understood it. While al-Ġazālī notes that one should be wary of "using linguistic expressions that signify by implication in investigations based on reasoning/deductive reflection (*naẓar al-ʿaql*),"[259] we find in ʿUmar b. Sahlān as-Sāwī (fl. 540/1145) the following remark: "That which is used in the sciences (*ʿulūm*) is signification by congruence and containment, not signfication by implication."[260] Al-Ġazālī's choice of words makes it clear that not all disciplines are meant—only those that primarily utilize reasoning (*ʿaql*), as opposed to tradition (*naql*).

Another reason for assuming that Naṣīr ad-dīn's criticism is not entirely accurate and that Faḫr ad-dīn does not understand this note in such a strict manner is that he actually considers the use of implication to be permissible in other areas or takes its use as a given, such that he examines its sub-areas in more detail—be it in rhetoric or in *uṣūl al-fiqh*. The difference between the use of implication and the understanding of implication must be taken into account: Within logical writings, attention must be paid to avoiding implication in order to produce precise definitions and correct syllogisms and to counteract redundancy and erroneous conclusions—whereas in legal theory, profound knowledge of the various types of implication is required to interpret the sacred texts and derive legal formulations. This is also the reason why Faḫr ad-dīn dispenses with this fourth note in the *Maḥṣūl* but mentions it in his logical writings. For al-Ġazālī, on the other hand, who still understood the Tripartition of Signification as a purely logical classification and who did not yet transfer it, as Faḫr ad-dīn would later do, to the hermeneutical apparatus of *uṣūl al-fiqh*, the aspect of understanding implication plays no role; this is why this note is also found in the logical introduction to his *Mustaṣfā* and not in the part on legal theory.

---

258 Naṣīr ad-dīn aṭ-Ṭūsī, *Ḥall muškilāt al-Išārāt*, p. 182, line 4.

259 Al-Ġazālī, *Kitāb Miḥakk an-naẓar*, p. 73, lines 18–19; for a comparison between this passage and the parallel passage in the *Mustaṣfā*, see Chapter 2, Section 2.3.2.

260 As-Sāwī, *al-Baṣāʾir an-naṣīriyya*, p. 33, lines 18–19.

4 Summary: The Development, Establishment, and Generalization of the Classification of Signification

This chapter has analyzed the historical background and lines of tradition of the chapter "The Classification of Linguistic Expressions" (*fī taqsīm al-alfāẓ*) of the legal-theoretical work *al-Maḥṣūl fī ʿilm uṣūl al-fiqh*. First, the logical tradition underlying §§1–11 was revealed, showing that the first examination of the simple linguistic expression [§§6–11] is a logical introduction to the study of predicables, which follows in the tradition of the Porphyrian Eisagoge and which is oriented towards the basic framework of Avicennian *Madḫal* treatises. On the one hand, it is striking how naturally Faḫr ad-dīn incorporates logical propaedeutics into this legal-theoretical text; on the other hand, the cursory nature of these propaedeutics is conspicuous, and suggests that Faḫr ad-dīn could presuppose this knowledge in his readers, needing only to hint at it but by no means fully explain it.

This logical introduction is preceded by an outline of the classification of signification. Here, a distinction is made between three different ways in which a linguistic expression can signify a meaning. This classification has a special function in this chapter. However, since Faḫr ad-dīn does not explain how this outline came about or clarify the extent of its interpretation—but makes the further sub-classifications of the chapter along with the logical introduction dependent upon it—it was first necessary (in preparation for this work) to consult writings from various other disciplines and traditions for an explanation. Finally we were able to determine that an answer to the question of the emergence and development as well as the historical background of the problem is given in the writings in the field of logic, namely primarily in the *Madḫal* and the *Burhān* of the Arabic reception of the Organon:

A derivation of the classification from the perspective of its development through time is outlined by Ibn Sīnā in *Madḫal* 1.8 of the *Kitāb aš-Šifāʾ*. This is in the context of the question of the correct determination of the quiddity for the attainment of certain knowledge. In connection with the correct determination of the quiddity, Ibn Sīnā refutes the objection that the specific difference is attributed with the same scope of signification as the species constituted by it. This he does with a fundamental treatise on what it means when we speak of a linguistic expression signifying a meaning. The possible objection is based on a misuse of the different manners of signification. In the course of this, Ibn Sīnā distinguishes between a primary, secondary, and extrinsic type of signification and ultimately assigns the terms *dalālatu muṭābaqa*, *dalālatu taḍammun*, and *dalālatu luzūm* to these types. With these manners of signification, he can finally demonstrate the difference between the signification of whatness/the quiddity (*māhiyya*) and howness (*ayyiyya*) and consequently assign different manners of signification to the various predicables.

In tracing the origins of the classification of signification, we found that it emerged from the distinction between a secondary and an extrinsic type of signification. Al-Fārābī discusses this distinction in a passage based on *De Int.* 11 of his guide "*Book of Circumstances that Lead to Errors*" (*Kitāb al-Amkina al-Muġliṭa*) in order to explain the extent to which predicates that apply to a thing independently of each other may also be stated in conjunction with each other. In order to show when a formulation in a definition or statement is redundant or meaningless and when it is not, al-Fārābī distinguishes between two types of implication, which he does not yet differentiate terminologically—both fall under *luzūm*.

These two types of implication are also applied by Ibn Sīnā in the area of the ontological specification of the specific difference: Ibn Sīnā uses the two types of signification here to answer the question of whether the specific difference in turn belongs to a genus, which would result in the aporia of the infinite regress of the specific difference.

Based on the various logical and ontological layers of problems, Ibn Sīnā bundles the discussion of the two manners of signification in the *Madḫal* treatises of his works. Here he gradually develops them into the threefold division *dalālatu muṭābaqa*, *dalālatu taḍammun*, and *dalālatu iltizām*, which is ultimately no longer offered as a solution to a specific problem, but rather, in the later writings and in particular in the *Išārāt wa-t-tanbīhāt*, gets combined with other topics at the beginning of the treatises on logic to form a bundle of principles related to langauge.

Tracing the development of the Tripartition of Signification in Ibn Sīnā's writings reveals a mode of presentation whose degree of systematization increases from one work to the next and which leads to the classification of signification being understood in increasingly general terms—until it finally becomes embedded as part of the fundamentals that logicians had to learn at the beginning of their careers.

Faḫr ad-dīn continues this approach by defining the classification of signification on several levels as the highest principle of organization: Whereas Ibn Sīnā had previously attempted to use this classification primarily to capture the manners of signification of predicables, i.e. universal linguistic expressions, Faḫr ad-dīn extends it to all linguistic expressions. At the same time, he sees the status of this classification in the language system as so fundamental that he compares it with the tripartite division of linguistic expressions into *ism*, *fiʿl*, and *ḥarf*: All linguistic expressions can be divided into either name (*ism*), verb (*fiʿl*), or particle (*ḥarf*), and their manners of signification into either congruence (*muṭābaqa*), containment (*taḍammun*), or implication (*iltizām*).

Faḫr ad-dīn develops a set of conditions and remarks on the classification of signification—like the distinction between *dalāla waḍʿiyya* and *dalāla ʿaqliyya*—which would go on form the subject of discussions, commentaries, and explanations in the writings of later thinkers.

In addition, the classification of signification in the *Maḥṣūl*, the *Maʿālim*, and the *Mulaḫḫaṣ* serves as a starting point for further classifications that characterize the linguistic expression from different points of view. In this chapter I have highlighted the fact that it can be seen as the starting point for the categorization of logic. The extent to which this logical categorization of the simple linguistic expression can be regarded as a structural principle for the other subcategorizations of the classification of signification will be examined in the next chapters,[261] as will the question of which legal-theoretical implications can be subsumed under *iltizām*.[262]

---

261 See Chapter 3.

262 See Chapter 4.

CHAPTER 3

The Grammatical-Theoretical and Logical and Legal-Theoretical Sub-Classifications [ad §§12–23]

1 The Logical Sub-Classification as a Template for the Grammatical Sub-Classification [ad §§12–14]

According to Faḫr ad-dīn, the sub-classification in the *Maḥṣūl* that I called the 'logical sub-classification' and dealt with in detail in Chapter 2 is not only useful for logic, but can also be applied to other areas such as grammar: "Even though this classification (*taqsīm*) actually concerns meanings (*maʿānī*), it is nevertheless of great use (*ʿaẓīmu n-nafʿ*) for linguistic expressions (*alfāẓ*)."[1] Thus, in the overview that follows, he presents the congruent simple linguistic expression from the perspective of grammatical theory. Here I will subject this overview to a brief examination in order to reveal its connections with the logical sub-classification.

Faḫr ad-dīn begins this sub-classification with the distinction [*ad* §12] between the simple linguistic expression that [a] can convey information independently, and that which [b] cannot, but instead must always be connected with another linguistic expression: "It [*i.e. the simple linguistic expression*] is either such that its meaning (*maʿnāhu*) independently (*mustaqill*) possesses what can be known/the knowable (*maʿlūmiyya*); or it is not so."[2] The latter [b] is the particle (*ḥarf*),[3] while the former [a] is further differentiated according to whether it indicates "a certain time," like the verb (*fiʿl*), or not, like the name (*ism*).[4]

1 Faḫr ad-dīn ar-Rāzī, *al-Maḥṣūl*, vol. 1, p. 224, lines 7–8. Here we can recognize the old dichotomy of subject areas, according to which logic has to do with meanings and grammar with linguistic expressions, see in detail Endreß, "Grammatik und Logik," e.g. p. 212, as well as Chapter 2, Section 3.1.

2 Faḫr ad-dīn ar-Rāzī, *al-Maḥṣūl*, vol. 1, p. 225, line 3.

3 The details of this differentiation will not be dealt with in depth here; Faḫr ad-dīn discusses the related debate in more detail elsewhere, cf. Faḫr ad-dīn ar-Rāzī, *at-Tafsīr al-kabīr*, vol. 1, p. 39, line 20–p. 40, line 4 and (identical in wording to the *Tafsīr* passage) id., *Sāḥirat aṭ-ṭarf*, ed. by Muḥammad Muḥammad Fahmī ʿUmar (Medīna: Dār az-Zamān, 2006 [1427]), p. 35, line 5–p. 36, line 13; see also al-Qarāfī's discussion of Faḫr ad-dīn's specification of the particles, al-Qarāfī, *Nafāʾis al-uṣūl*, vol. 1, p. 282, lines 15–26.

4 Faḫr ad-dīn ar-Rāzī, *al-Maḥṣūl*, vol. 1, p. 225, lines 5–7. On the categorization of the name

This deduction is what Faḫr ad-dīn alludes to in his commentary on the *Išārāt wa-t-tanbīhāt* when he says "that the study of languages (*al-baḥṯ ʿan al-luġāt*) can be based on reasoning (*qad yakūnu ʿaqliyyan*)."[5]

Faḫr ad-dīn continues with a categorization of the name, leaving both verb and particle out of further discussion.[6] First, he categorizes the name [*ad* §13]—in accord with the logical template—on the basis of the criterion of particularity/universality. The names that signify the particular include the pronoun (*muḍmarāt*) and the proper name (*ʿalam*).[7] To the name established "for the universal" (*li-l-kullī*), he assigns the "generic name" (*ism al-ǧins*), understood as the "name for the quiddity itself (*li-nafsi l-māhiyya*), like the linguistic expression 'blackness' (*ka-lafẓi s-sawād*)."[8] But an additional universal name is put on a level with the generic name, corresponding to the logical schema of genus and attribute/specific difference, namely the "derived name" (*ism muštaqq*). It describes the fact "that something is described by an attribute (*bi-ṣifatin*) (*li-mawṣūfiyyati amrin mā*)"; as an example, Faḫr ad-dīn gives the *ism al-fāʿil* "beater" (*ḍārib*). That which is given this name is "unknown" (*maǧhūl*)—one knows only that it is "described (*mawṣūf*) by the attribute (*ṣifa*) of beating

in Sībawayh, cf. Werner Diem, "Nomen, Substantiv und Adjektiv bei den arabischen Grammatikern," *Oriens*, vol. 23/24 (1974): pp. 317 ff.

5 Faḫr ad-dīn ar-Rāzī, *Šarḥ al-Išārāt*, p. 22, line 9; cf. Chapter 2, Section 3.1. On the reception history of this deduction, cf. Bernard G. Weiss, "A Theory of the Parts of Speech in Arabic (Noun, Verb and Particle): A study in "ilm al-waḍʿ,"" *Arabica*, vol. 23, no. 1 (Feb. 1976): pp. 23–36. A separate study could be performed examining the extent to which the grammatical-theoretical sub-classification briefly presented in this chapter functions as the template for Īǧī's *Risālat al-waḍʿ* and the commentaries that refer to it, see ʿAḍud ad-dīn al-Īǧī, *Risālat al-waḍʿ*, ed. by ʿUmar Aḥmad ar-Rāwī (together with *Šarḥ* and *Ḥāšiya*) (Beirut: Dār al-Kutub al-ʿilmiyya, 2010), pp. 9–11 and Bernard G. Weiss, "*ʿIlm al-waḍʿ*: An Introductory Account of a Later Muslim Philological Science," *Arabica*, vol. 34 (Nov. 1987): pp. 339–356.

6 On Faḫr ad-dīn's treatment and classification of the name (*ism*) in his *Tafsīr*, see Muḥassab, *ʿIlm ad-dalāla ʿinda l-ʿarab*, pp. 91–139; on *fiʿl* and *ḥarf*, see ibid., pp. 141–159. On the three-part classification of linguistic expressions into *ism*, *fiʿl*, and *ḥarf* in general, see for example Jean-Patrick Guillaume, "'Le discours tout entier est nom, verbe et particule.' Elaboration et constitution de la théorie des parties du discours dans la tradition grammaticale arabe," *Langages*, vol. 23, no. 92 (1988): pp. 25–36; Yasir Suleiman, "Sībawaihi's 'Parts of Speech' According to Zajjājī: A New Interpretation," *Journal of Semitic Studies*, vol. 35, no. 2 (Autumn 1990): pp. 245–263 as well as Versteegh, *The Explanation of Linguistic Causes*, pp. 27–40 and the overview article by Michael G. Carter, "Parts of Speech," *EALL*, vol. 3, pp. 546–552.

7 Faḫr ad-dīn ar-Rāzī, *al-Maḥṣūl*, vol. 1, p. 225, lines 9–10. On proper names in early Arabic grammatical theory, see Amal E. Marogy, "Zayd, ʿAmr and ʿAbdullāhi: Theory of Proper Names and Reference in Early Arabic Grammatical Tradition," in *The Foundations of Arabic Linguistics: Sībawayhi and Early Arabic Grammatical Theory*, ed. by Amal E. Marogy (Leiden [et al.]: Brill, 2002), pp. 119–134.

8 Faḫr ad-dīn ar-Rāzī, *al-Maḥṣūl*, vol. 1, p. 226, lines 1–2.

(*ḍarb*)."[9] This example makes it particularly clear what exactly Faḫr ad-dīn means when he says that the preceding logical classification can also be transferred to the grammatical classification: On the one hand, the generic name of the grammarians is shown to be a parallel of the genus of the logicians; on the other hand, the paronym (*ism muštaqq*) in the function of an attribute is compared to the specific difference. Thus, the logical discussion about the scope of signification of the specific difference is now transferred to the (grammatical-theoretical) discussion about the derived name.[10] On this basis, the stand-alone paronymous name—like the stand-alone specific difference and the stand-alone proprium—signifies the substance or the generic name by implication:

> It is understood from a black thing (*aswad*) that it is something that has blackness (*sawād*). But what the essential nature (*ḥaqīqa*) of this thing is lies outside of this understanding—if one knows it, then one knows it by implication (*iltizām*).—And what indicates this [*i.e. what makes it clear that it is an implication*] is the fact that you say: the black thing (*aswad*) is a body. For if by 'black thing' (*aswad*) one were to understand [*in a congruent way*] that it is a body that possesses blackness (*sawād*), then one would stoop to the position of having to say: The body that possesses blackness must be a body.[11]

The argumentation is identical to what we have already encountered in the logical texts of Ibn Sīnā and Faḫr ad-dīn ar-Rāzī: The linguistic expression has not actually been imposed for the meaning that we ultimately understand by it—i.e. "beating" (*ḍārib*) does not congruently signify "man" or "body"; it does so only implicitly.[12]

---

9 Ibid., lines 3–5. On the grammatical-theoretical and logical connections between the attribute (*ṣifa*), the active participle (*ism al-fāʿil*), and the description (*waṣf*), see Schöck, "Name (*ism*), Derived Name (*ism mushtaqq*) and Description (*waṣf*)," pp. 329–360.

10 The "identification of that which is signified by the different grammatical categories 'name/noun' and 'description' with the logical distinction between substance/essence and accidens" does not go back to Faḫr ad-dīn, but to Ibn al-Muqaffaʿ and al-Fārābī and can also be found in al-Ġazālī, see Schöck, "Name (*ism*), Derived Name (*ism mushtaqq*) and Description (*waṣf*)," p. 331, pp. 345–346, and pp. 353–354.

On the background of the logical discussion about the scope of signification of the specific difference, see Chapter 2, Section 2.

11 Faḫr ad-dīn ar-Rāzī, *al-Maḥṣūl*, vol. 1, p. 251, lines 2–6; cf. id., *Sāḥirat aṭ-ṭarf*, p. 53, lines 15–16 and id., *at-Tafsīr al-kabīr*, vol. 1, p. 46, lines 24–25.

12 Cf. also al-Ġazālī's argumentation, Schöck, "Name (*ism*), Derived Name (*ism mushtaqq*) and Description (*waṣf*)," pp. 353–354.

FIGURE 17 Rough structure of the grammatical-theoretical sub-classification [I.1.1.B]

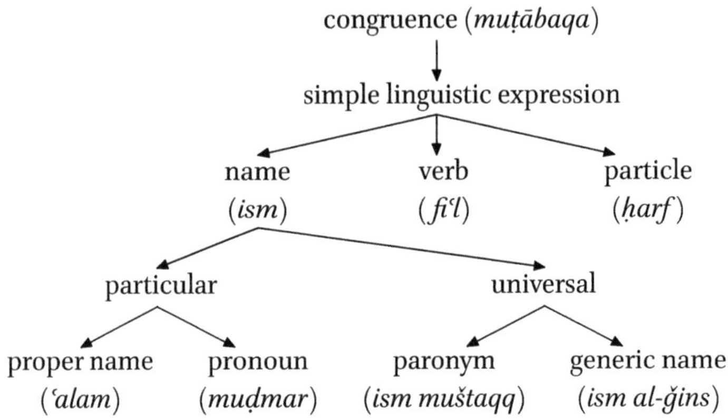

Faḫr ad-dīn [*ad* §14] then distinguishes the extent to which the name, which in contrast to the verb does not connote a specific time, takes time into account in a different way than a verb: What is signified by a name can [a] be "a time itself" (*nafsu z-zamān*), as in the time adverbs " 'today' (*al-yawm*) or 'tomorrow' (*al-ġad*)" or the noun "time" (*zamān*); [b] a part of it can express a reference to time, as in the name 'morning drink' (*iṣṭibāḥ*); [c] or it has no temporal reference at all, i.e., "it is neither time nor composed of time, like blackness."[13]

Two aspects of this grammatical-theoretical classification [*ad* §12–14] in the *Maḥṣūl* are particularly striking. Firstly is the fact that Faḫr ad-dīn disregards the particle and the verb in the further differentiation; secondly, it is noticeable that, of the diverse criteria used by Arabic grammarians to describe the name—phonological, morphological, syntactic, and semantic criteria—by mentioning the particularity/universality and the time-reference of the meaning, Faḫr ad-dīn relies here only on the semantic criteria.[14] The focus here is therefore only on the word–meaning relationship, which makes sense insofar as the semantic analytical criteria are precisely those that make up the basis for comparison between the logical and the grammatical-theoretical sub-classifications.[15]

13 Faḫr ad-dīn ar-Rāzī, *al-Maḥṣūl*, vol. 1, p. 226, lines 6–11.

14 Cf. Owens, *The Foundations of Grammar*, pp. 125 ff. and id. "The Syntactic Basis of Arabic Word Classification," pp. 211–234. In the parallel passages of this classification in the *Tafsīr al-kabīr* and in the *Sāḥirat aṭ-ṭarf*, Faḫr ad-dīn goes beyond the semantic criteria, see Faḫr ad-dīn ar-Rāzī, *at-Tafsīr al-kabīr*, vol. 1, pp. 46 ff. and id., *Sāḥirat aṭ-ṭarf*, pp. 54 ff.

15 Faḫr ad-dīn ar-Rāzī informs us that he wrote in more detail about grammatical theory in his work *al-Muḥarrar fī daqāʾiq an-naḥw* (cf. Faḫr ad-dīn ar-Rāzī, *al-Maḥṣūl*, vol. 1, p. 236,

2 Analysis of the Logical and Legal-Theoretical Sub-Classification [ad §§15–22] and the Sub-Classification of the Sentence [ad §23]

"After the philologists had categorized speech into *ism*, *fiʿl*, and *ḥarf*, the Uṣūlīs adopted a different classification for their own purposes"[16]—so writes al-Ǧuwaynī. And Faḫr ad-dīn does exactly that: After outlining the grammatical-theoretical classification, he devotes himself to another, much more extensive categorization. This will now be briefly introduced without going into the historical development of its individual concepts. Instead what will be emphasized at this point is the systematization underlying the categorization and the attempt at synthesis that is once again evident here.

As in the previous sub-classifications, Faḫr ad-dīn makes the distinction between the simple and the compound linguistic expression the starting point for his further categorization. The first will be examined here, followed by a consideration of some of the resulting questions—namely, into which manner(s) of signification the signification of figurative language is to be classified; in addition, constative and performative utterances will be examined on the basis of the classification of the compound linguistic expression.

2.1 *The Logical and Legal-Theoretical Sub-Classification as a Synthesis of Two Disciplines*

The simple linguistic expression is divided, with regard to its relationship to meaning, into four further categories, which are known from the Peripatetic-

last line); al-Qarāfī also cites this title, al-Qarāfī, *Nafāʾis al-uṣūl*, vol. 1, p. 294, lines 9–10. This might be one of his lost works, cf. al-ʿAlwānī, *al-Imām Faḫr ad-dīn ar-Rāzī*, p. 140 (no. 180: *al-Muḥarrar fī ḥaqāʾiq/daqāʾiq an-naḥw*); Anawati gives an overview of the bio-bibliographical works in which this work is mentioned, see Anawati, *Fakhr al-Dīn al-Rāzī: tamhīd li-dirāsat ḥayātihī wa-muʾallafātihī*, pp. 230–231.

Faḫr ad-dīn also wrote a commentary on az-Zamaḫšarī's *Mufaṣṣal*; unfortunately, a study of his discussion of the *Mufaṣṣal* remains a desideratum for the time being, but it can be carried out even without the *Mufaṣṣal* commentary, since in some of his writings he repeatedly deals—whether by name or not by name—with positions advocated by Zamaḫšarī. On Faḫr ad-dīn's activities involving grammatical theory, see Versteegh, "The Linguistic Introduction to Rāzī's *Tafsīr*," p. 592; for a list of the grammarians to whom Faḫr ad-dīn refers in his commentary, see Jomier, "Fakhr al-dīn al-Rāzī (m. 606 H./1210) et les Commentaires du Coran plus anciens," pp. 161–166. In addition to an investigation of Faḫr ad-dīn's reception of grammatical theory, an investigation of the reception of the *Maḥṣūl* by the grammarians is also needed; Versteegh has pointed out that there are some quotations from the *Maḥṣūl* in as-Suyūṭī's *Muzhir*, cf. Versteegh, "The Linguistic Introduction to Rāzī's *Tafsīr*," p. 599.

16 Al-Ǧuwaynī, *al-Burhān*, vol. 1, p. 59, lines 15–16.

Avicennian tradition of the *Categories*[17] and which will now be examined more closely with regard to Faḫr ad-dīn's adaptation of them:

[I.1.1.C.1] One linguistic expression has one meaning:

In this first category—as with the first two sub-classifications—the particular relationship is again dinstinguished from the universal. The former corresponds to the proper name (*ʿalam*). The latter is divided on the one hand into Aristotelian synonymy (*tawāṭuʾ*), i.e. a shared name (such as 'animal') has the same meaning, (i.e. the same definition or description) in the same way for all species that share it (be it man, horse, ox, etc.);[18] and on the other hand into the ambiguous (*mušakkak*) case, whereby the shared name has the same meaning, but not in the same way for all the species that share it, such as 'being':[19]

> [*ad* C.1] As far as the first part is concerned [*i.e. one linguistic expression corresponds to one meaning*],
> – [C.1.1] it [*i.e. the combination of one linguistic expression and one meaning*] is called a proper name (*ʿalam*) if it is such that its conceptualiza-

17 Cf. for example Ibn Sīnā's detailed engagement with this classification, Ibn Sīnā, *Kitāb aš-Šifāʾ, al-Manṭiq, al-Maqūlāt* I,2, pp. 9–17 and Faḫr ad-dīn's list in his commentary on Ibn Sīnā's *ʿUyūn al-ḥikma*, Faḫr ad-dīn ar-Rāzī, *Šarḥ ʿUyūn al-ḥikma*, ed. by Aḥmad Ḥiǧāzī Aḥmad as-Saqqā (Cairo: Maktabat al-Anǧilū al-Miṣriyya, 1986), vol. 1, pp. 53–54 as well as id., *Manṭiq al-Mulaḫḫaṣ*, pp. 22–23; also in Faḫr ad-dīn's other *uṣūl al-fiqh* work *al-Maʿālim fī uṣūl al-fiqh*, pp. 11–12. On Ibn Sīnā's reception and adaptation of this classification, see Tiana Koutzarova, *Das Transzendentale bei Ibn Sīnā* (Leiden [et al.]: Brill, 2009), pp. 211–230 and Amos Bertolacci, "The 'Ontologization' of Logic. Metaphysical Themes in Avicenna's Reworking of the Organon," in *Methods and Methodologies. Aristotelian Logic East and West 500–1500*, ed. by Margaret Cameron and John Marenbon (Leiden [et al.]: Brill, 2011), pp. 27–51, esp. pp. 41–49.

18 This explanation is based on Ibn Sīnā, *Kitāb aš-Šifāʾ, al-Manṭiq, al-Maqūlāt* I,2, p. 9, lines 6–8; cf. al-Ġazālī's adaptation in his *Mustaṣfā*, vol. 1, p. 96, lines 7 ff.

19 For this, the term focal homonymy or *pros hen* homonymy has become established in Western research literature on ancient philosophy: This refers to a "multiplicity of meanings" that "are systematically connected insofar as they are all related to one thing, namely a core meaning. […] The unity lies in the core meaning […] as the uniform point of reference for all secondary uses; the multiplicity in the different ways of referring to it," Christoph Horn and Christof Rapp (eds.), *Wörterbuch der antiken Philosophie* (Munich: C.H. Beck, 2002), p. 374. There is no space in this study to go into this ontological debate; instead, reference should be made to the existing literature on *taškīk* predication, especially Alexander Treiger, "Avicenna's Notion of Transcendental Modulation of Existence (*taškīk al-wuǧūd, analogia entis*) and its Greek and Arabic Sources," in *Islamic Philosophy, Science, Culture and Religion: Studies in Honor of Dimitri Gutas*, ed. by Felicitas Opwis and David Reisman (Leiden: Brill, 2012), pp. 327–363; Koutzarova, *Das Transzendentale bei Ibn Sīnā*, pp. 220 ff. and Bertolacci, "The 'Ontologization' of Logic," pp. 45 f.

> tion (*taṣawwur*) itself prevents sharing in it (*šarika*), and it is manifest (*muẓhar*) [*in contrast to the personal pronoun*];
> – [C.1.2] if [*the conceptualization*] does not prevent [*sharing in it*], then there appears in these places, if it [*i.e. the naming*] occurs in an equivalent way, what is called a synonym (*mutawāṭi'*; synonymy: *tawāṭu'*) [*what is meant here is Aristotelian synonymy*].
> – [C.1.3] or [*if it occurs*] not (*aw lā*) in an equivalent way, then [*it is called*] ambiguous (*mušakkak*; ambiguity: *taškīk*), just like [*the linguistic expression*] 'existence' (*wuǧūd*), where that which it [*i.e. the linguistic expression 'existence'*] signifies is more suitable for the necessary [*i.e. for the necessarily existing*] (*wāǧib*) than for the contingent (*mumkin*) [*what is meant here is focal homonymy/pros hen homonymy*].[20]

[I.1.1.C.2] Several linguistic expressions have several meanings:

In his *Mustaṣfā*, al-Ġazālī explains this by writing "different names" have been imposed "for different meanings" (*al-asāmī l-muḫtalifatu li-l-ma'ānī l-muḫtalifa*),[21] i.e. there is no connection of any sort between the word forms or the meanings. Faḫr ad-dīn in turn explains this heteronymy (Arab. *tabāyun*) in such a way that, although there does not have to be an essential connection between the meanings, there certainly can be:[22]

> [*ad* I.1.1.C.2] As for [*the case*] in which the linguistic expressions and meanings are multiple, these are heteronyms (*mutabāyina*; heteronymy: *tabāyun*, *lit.* 'difference'), whether those things that are named differ in terms of their essences (*bi-ḏawātihā*), or whether one [*linguistic expression*] is an attribute (*ṣifa*) of the other, such as *sayf* ('sword') and *ṣārim* ('sharp'), or an attribute of the attribute, such as *nāṭiq* ('rational') and *faṣīḥ* ('eloquent'/'correct' in terms of language use).[23]

With this, Faḫr ad-dīn again adopts the explanations from Ibn Sīnā's *Categories*. There Ibn Sīnā distinguishes between heteronymy concerning completely different things that have different names due to the essential difference between

---

20 Faḫr ad-dīn ar-Rāzī, *al-Maḥṣūl*, vol. 1, p. 227, lines 5–10; cf. id., *Šarḥ 'Uyūn al-ḥikma*, vol. 1, pp. 53–54.

21 Al-Ġazālī, *al-Mustaṣfā*, vol. 1, p. 96, lines 4–6.

22 Contemporary definitions, on the other hand, make a semantic connection a condition for heteronymy, cf. Sebastian Löbner, *Semantik: Eine Einführung* (Berlin [et al.]: De Gruyter, 2003), p. 128.

23 Faḫr ad-dīn ar-Rāzī, *al-Maḥṣūl*, vol. 1, p. 228, lines 1–3.

them, such as "stone and horse," and heteronymy concerning one and the same thing signified by different names because different aspects of it are emphasized: Thus *sayf* signifies "the essence of the tool" (*yadullu ʿalā ḏāti l-āla*) that represents the sword, while *ṣārim*, also a name for 'sword,' "signifies its sharpness" (*yadullu ʿalā ḥiddatihā*).[24] This manner of signification must be distinguished from synonymy in the modern sense:

[I.1.1.C.3] Several linguistic expressions have one meaning:

Polyonymy (Arab. *tarāduf*; lit. 'correspondence') is what is known in modern semantics as synonymy, namely the case in which several linguistic expressions signify the same meaning,[25] as for example how *layṯ* and *asad* both signify the meaning 'lion.'[26]

It is important, Faḫr ad-dīn emphasizes elsewhere—again following Ibn Sīnā's *Categories*—to separate heteronymy and polyonymy. For example, the words *sayf*, *muhannad*, and *ṣārim* refer to the sword—but all three emphasize different aspects, so that each word ultimately conveys different information; the first word indicates that the sword is made of iron, the second that it is made in the Indian style, and the third that it is sharp.[27] In the case of polyonymy, i.e. 'total synonymy' in modern parlance, the different words convey the same information—such as "sofa–couch" or "child–kid."[28]

[I.1.1.C.4] One linguistic expression has several meanings:

Faḫr ad-dīn provides this case with a detailed internal differentiation:

Either [4.1] the linguistic expression was "first imposed for one meaning" and then "transferred from this to another meaning" or [4.2] the linguistic expression was imposed for both meanings simultaneously. The former type is further subdivided: Either [4.1.1] the transfer is such that there is no correspondence of content (*munāsaba*) between the two meanings—"this is what is improvised (*murtağal*)"; or [4.1.2] there is a correspondence of content, which is again further subdivided—namely, according to whether the linguistic expression [4.1.2.1] preferably signifies the second, later meaning. In this case, where the linguistic expression is called a 'transferred linguistic expression' (*lafẓ manqūl*), Faḫr ad-dīn further considers the domains in which such a form of signification occurs: On the one hand, such transferred linguistic expressions

24 Ibn Sīnā, *Kitāb aš-Šifāʾ, al-Manṭiq, al-Maqūlāt* I,2, p. 16, lines 4–11.
25 Faḫr ad-dīn ar-Rāzī, *al-Maḥṣūl*, vol. 1, p. 228, lines 4–5.
26 Ibid., p. 255, line 2; al-Ġazālī, *al-Mustaṣfā*, vol. 1, p. 95, last line.
27 Al-Qarāfī, *Nafāʾis al-uṣūl*, vol. 1, p. 291, lines 22–23.
28 Cf. Faḫr ad-dīn ar-Rāzī, *al-Maḥṣūl*, vol. 1, p. 253 and Löbner, *Semantik*, p. 117.

[4.1.2.1.1] may be legal terms, i.e. a linguistic expression signifies the legal meaning more strongly than the original meaning, which may already have been forgotten.

Another domain [C.4.1.2.1.2] is represented by the transferred linguistic expression in general language usage—*dābba* is an example. It was imposed "for everything that crawls," was narrowed down to the meaning 'quadruped' in general usage, and is also used for the 'pack or riding animal.'[29] There is also the specific language usage of a certain group of speakers—"just like the linguistic conventions/technical terms (*iṣṭilāḥāt*) that each group (*ṭā'ifa*) of scholars (*ahl al-ʿilm*) has."[30]

If, on the other hand, the linguistic expression [4.1.2.2] does not signify either of the two meanings for which it has been imposed in succession to a greater degree than the other, then the linguistic expression "in relation to the first imposure is called a 'literal [*linguistic expression*]' (*ḥaqīqī*) and in relation to the second [imposure] is called a 'figurative [*linguistic expression*]' (*maǧāz*)."[31]

Thus to call a linguistic expression literal necessarily means that there exists a transferred meaning for it as well, which is not subordinate to it (i.e. the figurative meaning).

Next, Faḫr ad-dīn [4.2] subjects the linguistic expression that has been imposed for both meanings *simultaneously* to a more detailed dissection. Here, too, the question is asked whether it is equally likely for both meanings to be meant: If so [4.2.1], then "the single linguistic expression [4.2.1.1] with regard to both [*meanings*] at the same time (*maʿan*) is called 'homonymous' (*muštarak*; homonymy: *ištirāk*)" and [4.2.1.2] "with regard to either of the two [*meanings*] 'requiring explanation' (*muǧmal; lit.* 'that which is gathered together without distinction')." What is meant is that, although rough information is conveyed, a detailed elaboration is missing, for example with regard to prayer.[32]

---

29 Cf. al-Ġazālī, *al-Mustaṣfā*, vol. 3, p. 15, lines 8–9; also Faḫr ad-dīn ar-Rāzī, *al-Maḥṣūl*, vol. 1, p. 289, lines 14ff.; Sayf ad-dīn al-Āmidī, *Muntahā as-sūl fī ʿilm al uṣūl*, ed. by Aḥmad Farīd al-Mazīdī (Beirut: Dār al-Kutub al-ʿilmiyya, 2003 [1424]), p. 12; see Edward W. Lane, *An Arabic-English Lexicon*, vol. 3, p. 842b; cf. Weiss, *The Search*, p. 131.

30 Faḫr ad-dīn ar-Rāzī, *al-Maḥṣūl*, vol. 1, p. 229, lines 3–4.

31 Ibid., lines 6–7; he addresses the topic of *ḥaqīqa/maǧāz* in detail at a later point, see ibid., pp. 285–349; cf. al-Baṣrī, *Kitāb al-Muʿtamad*, vol. 1, pp. 16–38; al-Ġazālī, *al-Mustaṣfā*, vol. 3, pp. 32–35.

32 Faḫr ad-dīn ar-Rāzī, *al-Maḥṣūl*, vol. 3, p. 153, lines 2–9; see also Mohammad H. Kamali, *Principles of Islamic Jurisprudence* (Cambridge: Islamic Texts Society, 2013), pp. 135–138; on the predecessor concept (*ǧumla*) in aš-Šāfiʿī, see Vishanoff, *The Formation of Islamic Hermeneutics*, pp. 52–54.

If [4.2.2], on the other hand, one of the two meanings is more probable than the other, then the linguistic expression is called 'obvious' (*ẓāhir*) with regard [4.2.2.1] to the more probable meaning. If, however, the interpreter decides in favor of the less probable meaning when analyzing the text, this is [4.2.2.2] 'that which is to be explained/justified' (*mu'awwal; lit. 'that which is explained'*).[33] This makes it clear that the *ẓāhir* meaning, which is simply the "preponderant meaning"[34] of a word, also includes the possibility of the *mu'awwal* meaning and that both are related to each other.

In the end, Faḫr ad-dīn states in summary that the first three of the four categories "have in common the absence of homonymy (*ištirāk*)—they are therefore 'unambiguous establishments' (*nuṣūṣ*)" with regard to their meanings.[35] He finishes by distinguishing between the two genera of unambiguity vs. ambiguity: thus, "that which is fixed/unambiguous (*muḥkam*)" can function as the generic term for *naṣṣ* and *ẓāhir*, while "that which is ambiguous (*mutašābih*)" can function as the generic term for *muǧmal* and *mu'awwal*.[36]

The individual definitions can already be found in the writings of earlier scholars and, given the wealth of research and instructional literature, do not require further explanation at this point. What is striking, however, is the way in which the terms are related to each other in this schema. At first glance, it is noticeable that Faḫr ad-dīn combines a logical classification of the *Categories* with a legal-theoretical one, placing them into a new arrangement. Al-Ġazālī, for example, had separated both types of classification by discipline. In accordance with the logical tradition, he followed the distinction between polyonymy, heteronymy, synonymy, and homonymy from *Cat.* 1 in the *Mustaṣfā*'s chapter

33 See also Faḫr ad-dīn ar-Rāzī, *al-Maḥṣūl*, vol. 3, p. 153, line 11–p. 154, line 1; cf. the detailed explanations of the concept of *ta'wīl* and *mu'awwal*, Kamali, *Principles of Islamic Jurisprudence*, pp. 119–122 and Gleave, *Islam and Literalism*, pp. 51–52.

34 Gleave, *Islam and Literalism*, p. 64.

35 Faḫr ad-dīn ar-Rāzī, *al-Maḥṣūl*, vol. 1, p. 230, line 10.

36 Ibid., p. 231, lines 6–9. On the classifications of unambiguity/ambiguity, see Kamali, *Principles of Islamic Jurisprudence*, pp. 123–133 and, in the context of Qur'anic hermeneutics, Herbert Berg, "Polysemy in the Qur'ān," *Encyclopaedia of the Qur'ān*, vol. 4, pp. 155–158; for a critical analysis of the English translations of the terms *ẓāhir* and *ḥaqīqa* (with reference to Weiss, Yunis Ali, and Vishanoff), see Gleave, *Islam and Literalism*, pp. 55–60, for an examination of these terms in relation to Šāfiʿī's *Risāla*, see ibid., pp. 99 ff. and Vishanoff, *The Formation of Islamic Hermeneutics*, pp. 50–56; and in relation to Bāqillānī's *Taqrīb*, see Gleave, *Islam and Literalism*, pp. 116–120, on the dichotomy *muḥkam/mutašābih*, see Vishanoff, *The Formation of Islamic Hermeneutics*, p. 17; for a discussion of the various terms and their exegetical relevance, see Šukrija H. Ramić, *Language and the Interpretation of Islamic Law* (Cambridge: The Islamic Texts Society, 2003), pp. 92 ff.

FIGURE 18 *Overview of the logical and legal-theoretical sub-classification*

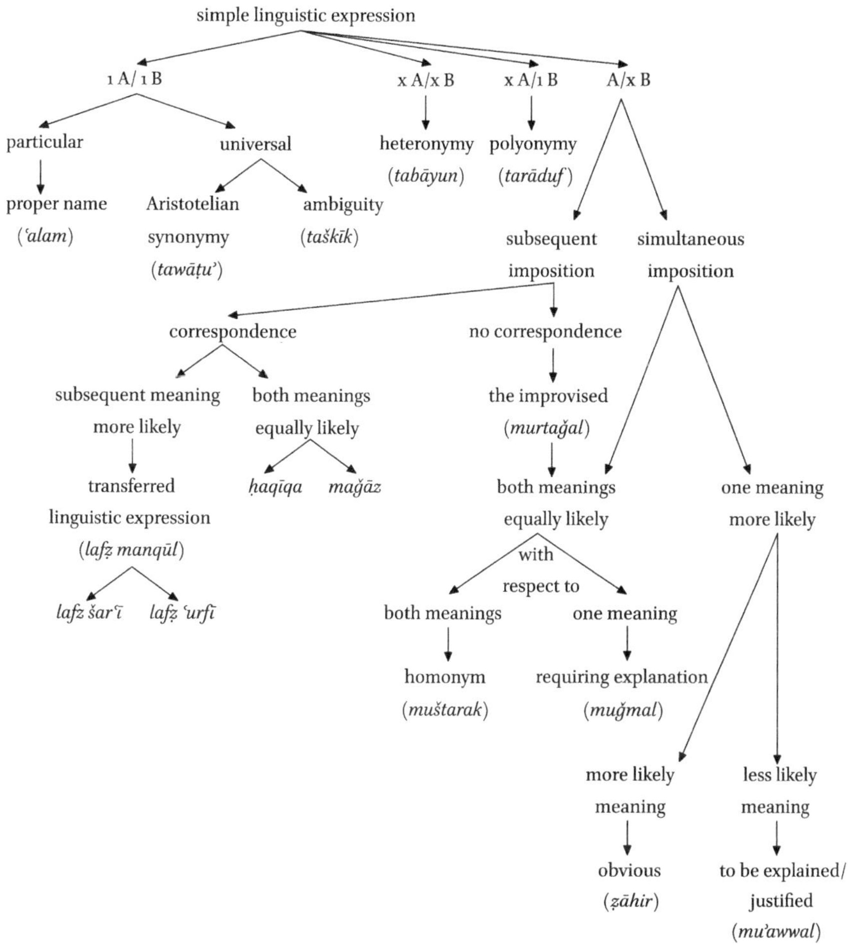

on logic[37] while he discussed the distinctions between the legal-theoretical technical terms *muǧmal*, *ẓāhir*, *muʾawwal*, etc. and between *ḥaqīqa* and *maǧāz* in the genuinely legal-theoretical chapter "On the External Form (*ṣīga*) and Arrangement (*manẓūm*) of the Linguistic Expression."[38] It is important to note,

37 Al-Ġazālī, *al-Mustaṣfā*, vol. 1, p. 95, line 9–p. 96; cf. Janssens, "Al-Ghazzālī's *Miʿyār al-ʿilm fī fann al-manṭiq*," p. 44.

38 Al-Ġazālī, *al-Mustaṣfā*, vol. 1, p. 23, lines 15 f. and vol. 3, p. 27, pp. 32–35, and pp. 37–38; for the structure of the *Mustaṣfā* and this chapter in particular, see Chapter 1, Section 2.1 of this book.

though, that al-Ġazālī had indeed already linked the classification of signification with this sub-classification from *Cat.* 1 in the *Mustaṣfā*'s chapter on logic.[39]

In his synthesis of the two categories, Faḫr ad-dīn initially applies the same dichotomous structural principles as in the two previous classifications, i.e. 'simple vs. compound' and 'particular vs. universal.' At the same time, he relates the logical classifications to the legal-theoretical ones; *muǧmal*, for example, is now the legal-theoretical equivalent of *muštarak*.

Faḫr ad-dīn offers a systematic overview of the terminological repertoire by synthesizing various classifications, all of which deal with the relationship between linguistic expression and meaning for the purposes of exegesis and the formulation of definitions or legal judgements.

2.2 *The Figurative Expression* (maǧāz) *in Relation to Congruence* (muṭābaqa) *and Implication* (iltizām)

First of all, it can be noted that, under the category of "signification by congruence," Faḫr ad-dīn includes those "exegetical pairings"[40] (e.g. *ẓāhir* and *mu'awwal* / *ḥaqīqa* and *maǧāz*) that are described as exegetical instruments with regard to "what is explicitly pronounced" (*manṭūq*). The word–meaning relationship is thus understood in such a way that the meaning arises from the "external form (*ṣīġa*) and arrangement (*manẓūm*) of the linguistic expression"[41] and is not hidden between the lines, as it is in implication (*mafhūm*, lit. "that which is understood").[42] It can also be stated that the classifications collected by Faḫr ad-dīn under *manṭūq* are subsumed under the generic term *dalālat al-muṭābaqa*, which is much more comprehensive, as the analyses of the previous sub-classifications of the *Maḥṣūl* have shown.

It has already been established that Faḫr ad-dīn ar-Rāzī classifies the *dalālat al-muṭābaqa* as a "manner of signification based on imposition" (*dalāla waḍ'iyya*), which he contrasts with the "manner of signification based on reasoning" (*dalāla 'aqliyya*)—equating to containment (*taḍammun*) and implication (*iltizām*). In the *Maḥṣūl*, the former also includes figurative signification (*maǧāz*), as Faḫr ad-dīn mentions once implicitly and once explicitly. Firstly, in relation to their meanings, Faḫr ad-dīn classifies those lingustic expressions that signify two meanings for which they have been imposed consecutively, where neither of the two is more likely to be meant, into *ḥaqīqa* and *maǧāz*; the *ḥaqīqa*

39 For al-Ġazālī's treatment of the classification of signification, see Chapter 2, Section 2.3.2.
40 Gleave, *Islam and Literalism*, p. 44.
41 Al-Ġazālī, *al-Mustaṣfā*, vol. 3, p. 402 or vol. 1, p. 23, lines 15 f.
42 The *manṭūq–mafhūm* dichotomy is discussed in more detail in Chapter 4.

expression signifies the meaning of the first imposure and the *maǧāz* expression signifies the meaning of the second imposure—both are thus based on a relationship in which the linguistic expression has been imposed for the meaning.[43] Here, *ḥaqīqa* and *maǧāz* thus appear as two relational terms that indicate two subordinate relationships of imposition, with *ḥaqīqa* already referring to the fact of the second imposure.

Thus, *maǧāz* attests to a subordinate relationship of imposition, whereas homonymy has a simultaneous relationship of imposition.[44] Assigning *magāz* to the congruent manner of signification is consistent insofar as Faḫr ad-dīn's homonymy is also assigned to this manner of signification and mistakenly regarding homonymy as containment or implication is warned against.

The assignment of *maǧāz* to *muṭābaqa* also agrees with Faḫr ad-dīn's remark, which he makes at the end of the treatment of the categories I.1.1.A-C and I.1.2: "This has all been the categorization of signification by congruence";[45] he then moves on to treat implication.

Maǧāz, or the linguistic expression classified as such, therefore belongs to the category of *manṭūq* and the manner of signification of congruence.[46] *Dalālat al-muṭābaqa* thus encompasses a conception of the "literal" manner of signification, which in the *ḥaqīqa/maǧāz* dichotomy cannot be limited to *ḥaqīqa*, and instead includes both.[47] This assignment, it must be emphasized,

---

43 Faḫr ad-dīn ar-Rāzī, *al-Maḥṣūl*, vol. 1, p. 229, lines 6–7; on the fact that in classical *uṣūl al-fiqh* literature linguistic expressions and not meanings are referred to as *maǧāz* or *ḥaqīqa*, see also Gleave, *Islam and Literalism*, p. 36. For in-depth literature on *maǧāz* in legal theory and rhetoric, see above all Wolfhart Heinrichs, "Contacts Between Scriptural Hermeneutics and Literary Theory in Islam: The Case of Majāz," *Zeitschrift für Geschichte der Arabisch-Islamischen Wissenschaften*, vol. 7 (1991–1992): pp. 253–284, as well as id., *The Hand of the Northwind. Opinions on Metaphor and the Early Meaning of Istiʿāra in Arabic Poetics* (Wiesbaden: Franz Steiner, 1977).

44 Subordination as a difference between *maǧāz* and homonymy is also indicated in Faḫr ad-dīn's rhetorical work, cf. Faḫr ad-dīn ar-Rāzī, *Nihāyat al-īǧāz*, p. 168, lines 4–5.

45 Faḫr ad-dīn ar-Rāzī, *al-Maḥṣūl*, vol. 1, p. 232, lines 7–8.

46 See also Bayḍāwī's summary: "The [*divine*] speech (*al-ḫiṭāb*) signifies the legal judgement (*ḥukm*) either [1.] in an explicit way (*bi-manṭūqihī*), so that it is traced back to the legal (*šarʿī*) [*mode of speech*], then to that of language usage (*ʿurfī*), then to the linguistic/lexicographical (*luġawī*), then to the figurative (*maǧāzī*) [*mode of speech*] […]," ʿAbdallāh b. ʿUmar al-Bayḍāwī, *Minhāǧ al-wuṣūl ilā ʿilm al-uṣūl*, ed. by Salīm Šabʿānīya (Damascus: Dār Dāniya, 1989), p. 68, lines 11–12; see also Chapter 4 of this book; cf. also Weiss, *The Search*, p. 473: "But even when expressions signify nonliteral meanings, they remain part of the ordered language, the composed lines, of the text."

47 Cf. Gleave's examination of the terms that are often translated as 'literal meaning' or understood as such in the Western research literature, Gleave, *Islam and Literalism*, pp. 55–60, esp. p. 60.

only applies to simple linguistic expressions such as the word "lion," which has the animal as its first meaning and a brave person as its second, or the word "donkey," which singifies the animal and a stupid person.[48] In the case of compound linguistic expressions, on the other hand, there is no congruent manner of signification, i.e. no relationship of imposition of any kind, but rather a "signification based on reasoning" (*dalāla ʿaqliyya*),[49] i.e. a transfer relationship from the first to the second meaning.[50] The former was called by ʿAbd al-Qāhir al-Ǧurǧānī *maǧāz luġawī*, the latter—less as a rhetorical phenomenon than as a phenomenon encountered by the Qurʾanic exegete—*maǧāz ʿaqlī*.[51] *Maǧāz* thus appears in Faḫr ad-dīn ar-Rāzī's system both in the manner of signification of congruence and in that of implication.[52]

2.3 *Constative and Performative Utterances* [*ad § 23*]

Following the logical and legal-theoretical sub-classification, which focuses on simple linguistic expressions, Faḫr ad-dīn turns to the categorization of compound linguistic expressions:[53] Speakers need compound linguistic expressions in order to bring about understanding (*ifhām*). Here Faḫr ad-dīn distinguishes several types of these word groups or sentence constructions according to what is to be made understood: "Speech (*qawl*), which is what is to be understood (*mufhim*), is either such [1.1.2.1] that it indicates (*an yufīda*) in a primary way (*awwaliyyatan*) the striving for something (*ṭalab aš-šayʾ*) [1.1.2.2] or does not indicate it [*in a primary way*]."[54] The former, i.e. expressing one's demands in a direct manner, can either be such that one strives to know what a thing is—that is inquiry (*istifhām*); or one endeavors to obtain (*taḥṣīl*), accomplish, or effect the cessation (*imtināʿ*) of something, taking into account the various hierarchical relationships in which the interlocutors act with regard to one another: "from a position of superiority (*istiʿlāʾ*), the commandment/imperative (*amr*); from a position of obedience/submissiveness (*ḫuḍūʿ*), the question

48 Cf. Faḫr ad-dīn ar-Rāzī, *al-Maḥṣūl*, vol. 1, pp. 321–322; Bauer also assigns this form of *maǧāz* to the implication reference, see Bauer, "Rhetorik der arabischen Kultur," p. 294.

49 Faḫr ad-dīn ar-Rāzī, *Nihāyat al-īǧāz*, p. 87, line 7–p. 88, line 4.

50 Ibid., pp. 168 ff.

51 Ibid., pp. 173 ff.; cf. Heinrichs, "Contacts between Scriptural Hermeneutics and Literary Theory in Islam," pp. 278 f.

52 Contrary to Bauer, "Rhetorik der arabischen Kultur," p. 295.

53 On this categorization by Faḫr ad-dīn, see Pierre Larcher, "Quand, en arabe, on parlait de l'arabe … (II): Essai sur la catégorie de *ʾinšāʾ* (vs. *ḫabar*)," *Arabica*, vol. 38, no. 2 (July 1991): pp. 246–273, esp. p. 256, fn. 20.

54 Faḫr ad-dīn ar-Rāzī, *al-Maḥṣūl*, vol. 1, p. 231, lines 10–11.

(*su'āl*); and from a position of mutual equality, the request (*iltimās*)."[55] This distinction was usually discussed by legal scholars in chapters on commandment in connection with the question of which word forms and phrase types give rise to the obligation to perform or refrain from an act and in what ways.[56]

If, on the other hand, the striving for a thing is not indicated in a primary way, i.e, if a demand is only expressed in an indirect way with regard to the form of the sentence, Faḫr ad-dīn distinguishes between whether it is a truth-apt statement or not: If belief (*taṣdīq*) or disbelief (*takḏīb*) is possible, it is a declarative sentence (*ḫabar*). If they are not possible, it falls under the category of *tanbīh* (notification), which includes the wish (*tamannin*), the hope/expectation (*taraǧǧin*), the oath (*qasam*), and the address/exclamation (*nidā'*).[57]

FIGURE 19 Classification of the speech act and sentence

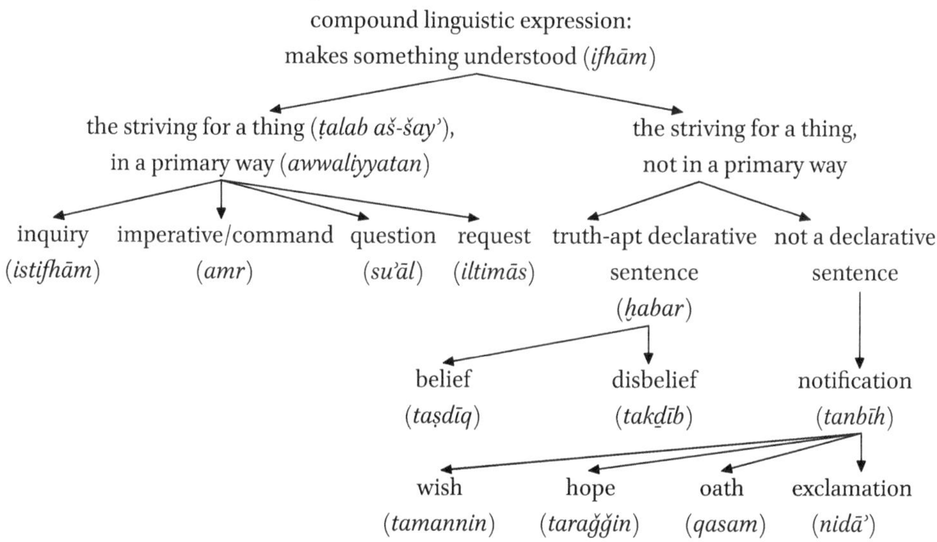

55 Ibid., line 13–p. 232, line 1.

56 Cf. al-Baṣrī, *Kitāb al-Mu'tamad*, vol. 1, pp. 49 ff.; al-Ġazālī, *al-Mustaṣfā*, vol. 3, pp. 119 ff.; as-Saraḫsī, *Uṣūl*, vol. 1, pp. 11 f.; a detailed discussion—even before the beginning of the *amr* chapter—can be found in al-Ǧuwaynī, *al-Burhān*, vol. 1, p. 59, line 14–p. 60; see in this context also Zysow, *The Economy of Certainty*, pp. 60 ff. and Pierre Larcher, "Quand, en arabe, on parlait de l'arabe ... (III): Grammaire, logique, rhétorique dans l'islam postclassique," *Arabica*, vol. 39, no. 3 (Nov. 1992): pp. 358–384, esp. pp. 361 ff.

57 Faḫr ad-dīn ar-Rāzī, *al-Maḥṣūl*, vol. 1, p. 232, lines 3–5; the term is also used in this context by al-Ǧuwaynī, cf. al-Ǧuwaynī, *al-Burhān*, vol. 1, p. 60, lines 12 ff.; on this term, see also Larcher, "Quand, en arabe, on parlait de l'arabe ... (II)," p. 256, fn. 20.

This schema that Faḫr ad-dīn uses therefore has two criteria for differentiation: [1.] direct demand (*ṭalab*)[58]/indirect demand and [2.] truth-apt (corresponds to *ḫabar*)/non-truth-apt (corresponds to *tanbīh*).[59] The two categories *ṭalab* and *tanbīh* are performative utterances, which in the post-classical period are summarized under the superordinate term *inšāʾ*; *ḫabar* comprises constative utterances.[60]

This systematization, as it is presented here by Faḫr ad-dīn, is based on lines of tradition from various disciplines, which will be briefly outlined in order to illustrate how this schema fits into Faḫr ad-dīn's synthesis concept:

[a] The grammarians initially distinguished four types of utterance: [1.] *ḫabar*—here also in the sense of constative utterances; [2.] question/inquiry (*istiḫbār*); [3.] positive command (*amr*); and [4.] negative command (*nahy*).[61] Ibn Fāris (d. 395/1004) already described ten types: [1.] *ḫabar*; [2.] *istiḫbār*; [3.] *amr* and [4.] *nahy*; [5.] request/blessing (*duʿāʾ*); [6.] demand (*ṭalab*); [7.] offer/proposal (*ʿarḍ*); [8.] encouragement (*taḥḍīḍ*); [9.] wish (*tamannin*); [10.]

58 On the term *ṭalab*, see Faḫr ad-dīn ar-Rāzī, *al-Maḥṣūl*, vol. 2, pp. 18 ff.

59 Larcher: "Quand, en arabe, on parlait de l'arabe … (II)," pp. 256–257.

60 On this classification in the post-Rāzian *uṣūl al-fiqh* tradition, see Larcher, "Quand, en arabe, on parlait de l'arabe … (II)," pp. 257 ff. The terms "constative utterance" and "performative utterance" go back to Austin's speech act theory, see John L. Austin, *How to Do Things with Words* (Oxford: Clarendon Press, 1962), pp. 3–7.

61 A very good overview of these categorizations within the framework of Arabic speech act theories—also in relation to the modern approaches of Austin and Searle—is provided by Daniela Rodica Firanescu, "Speech Acts", *EALL*, vol. 4, pp. 328–334; for a detailed account of the different types of utterance in Greek philosophy, rhetoric, and Arabic grammar, see Cornelis Versteegh, "Meanings of Speech: The Category of Sentential Mood in Arabic Grammar," in *Le voyage et la langue: Mélanges en l'honneur d'Anouar Louca et d'André Roman*, ed. by Joseph Dichy and Hassan Hamzé (Damascus: Institut Français du Proche-Orient, 2004), pp. 269–287; on the categorization in early grammarians, Daniela R. Buburuzan, "Exclamation et actes de langage chez Sībawayhi," *Revue Roumaine de Linguistique*, vol. 38, no. 5 (1993): pp. 421–437, as well as Frank, "Meanings Are Spoken of in Many Ways," pp. 269–271; see also Ahmed Moutaouakil, *Réflexions sur la Theorie de la Signification dans la Pensée Linguistique Arabe* (Rabat: Faculté des Lettres et des Sciences Humaines, 1982), pp. 162 ff.; as well as all of Pierre Larcher's writings, such as Pierre Larcher, "Quand, en arabe, on parlait de l'arabe … (II)," pp. 246–273, 'Quand, en arabe, on parlait de l'arabe … (III),' pp. 358–384, 'Éléments pragmatiques dans la théorie grammaticale arabe post-classique,' in *Studies in the History of Arabic Grammar II. Proceedings of the 2nd Symposium on the History of Arabic Grammar, Nijmegen, 27. April–1. May 1987*, ed. by Kees Versteegh and Michael G. Carter (Amsterdam/Philadelphia: John Benjamins, 1990), pp. 195–214; a brief overview is also given in Versteegh, *The Explanation of Linguistic Causes*, p. 35, note 15; see also Michael G. Carter, "Sentence Types in Grammar, Law and Philosophy," in *Centre and Periphery within the Borders of Islam. Proceedings of the 23rd Congress of L'Union Européenne des Arabisants et Islamisants*, ed. by Giuseppe Contu (Leuven [et al.]: Peeters, 2012), pp. 313–325.

astonishment/wonder (*taʿağğub*).[62] Utterances that correspond to truth-apt, constative utterances can deviate from this in a variety of ways in terms of their meaning and can take on a performative character. Similarly, the question can also fulfill functions other than mere inquiry, and the same applies to the other types of utterance.[63]

[b] The aforementioned fourfold division (*ḫabar*, *istiḫbār*, *amr*, and *nahy*) was also used in legal theory—for example by al-Ġazālī.[64] Extensions and alternative models are also discussed here, for example by al-Ǧuwaynī, who proposes an expanded fourfold division: [1.] demand (*ṭalab*), consisting of positive and negative commandment (*amr/nahy*) and request (*duʿāʾ*); [2.] *ḫabar*, including astonishment/wonder (*taʿağğub*) and oath (*qasam*); [3.] question/inquiry (*istiḫbār*), including inquiry (*istifhām*) and offer/suggestion (*ʿarḍ*); [4.] *tanbīh*, including wish (*tamannin*), hope/expectation (*tarağğin*), and address/exclamation (*nidāʾ*).[65] In contrast to Ibn Fāris's distinction, *ḫabar* utterances in al-Ǧuwaynī are apparently not truth-apt utterances. In legal practice, it can be of considerable legal significance whether a statement is categorized as performative or declarative, for example with regard to the *ṭalāq* divorce: If the claim *ṭallaqtuki* is meant performatively, its utterance represents the act of divorce; but it could equally be the description of an act that has already been performed.[66]

[c] In logic, on the other hand, based on Aristotle's *De Int.* 17a2–4, a distinction is made between truth-apt and non-truth-apt statements in order to relegate the latter to other disciplines, such as rhetoric or poetics.[67] Ibn Sīnā nevertheless devotes a few lines in his writings on logic to utterances in the latter category, which—such as "inquiry (*istifhām*), request (*iltimās*), wish (*tamannin*), hope/expectation (*tarağğin*), and astonishment/wonder (*taʿağğub*)"[68]—

---

62 Cf. Aḥmad Ibn Fāris, *aṣ-Ṣāḥibī fī fiqh al-luġa wa-sunan al-ʿarab fī kalāmihā*, ed. by Muṣṭafā al-Chouémi (Beirut: Muʾassasat Badrān li-ṭ-ṭibāʿa wa-našr, 1964 [1383]), p. 179, lines 6–7; see also Versteegh, "Meanings of Speech", pp. 277–278.

63 Ibn Fāris, *aṣ-Ṣāḥibī*, p. 179, lines 9ff. and on the question, p. 181, lines 12ff.; see also Frank, "Meanings Are Spoken of in Many Ways," p. 271, and Buburuzan, "Exclamation et actes de langage chez Sībawayhi." The grammarians' reflections on the different levels of meaning of the various sentence types show quite clearly that the assertion that grammar only deals with linguistic expressions and not with meanings is unfounded.

64 Al-Ġazālī, *al-Mustaṣfā*, vol. 3, p. 119, lines 4–5.

65 Al-Ǧuwaynī, *al-Burhān*, vol. 1, p. 60, lines 8–12.

66 Cf. Versteegh, "Meanings of Speech," p. 280.

67 Cf. Weidemann, "Anmerkungen," p. 191; also Shukri B. Abed, *Aristotelian Logic and the Arabic Language in Alfārābī* (New York: State University Press, 1991), p. 41.

68 Ibn Sīnā, *al-Išārāt wa-t-tanbīhāt*, p. 71, line 5; on the categorization in the Arabic logical tradition, see also Versteegh, "Meanings of Speech," pp. 276–277.

cannot be true or false. And, like Faḫr ad-dīn, he treats the relationship between the interlocutors.[69]

Consequently, various disciplines have dealt with the distinction between constative and performative utterances,[70] although each discipline had a different objective. What is special about Faḫr ad-dīn's schema is that it presents a tableau, as it were, of the different types of word groups and sentences, without the focus being on any of the categories, for example on the commandment—which is "the demanding of an action from a position of superiority (*ṭalab al-fiʿl ʿalā sabīl al-istiʿlāʾ*)"[71]—as would have been expected in a work of legal theory. With the same discipline-neutral orientation, the schema can also be found—almost word for word—in his logical compendium the *Manṭiq al-Mulaḫḫaṣ*.[72]

---

69 Cf. Ibn Sīnā, *Kitāb aš-Šifāʾ, al-Manṭiq, al-ʿIbāra*, p. 31, lines 13–15.

70 This categorization plays a particularly important role in the post-Rāzian rhetorical tradition, see for example as-Sakkākī, *Miftāḥ al-ʿulūm*, pp. 414 ff.; cf. *inter alia* Ahmed Moutaouakil, "La notion d'actes de langage dans la pensée linguistique arabe ancienne," in *Studies in the History of Arabic Grammar II. Proceedings of the 2nd Symposium on the History of Arabic Grammar, Nijmegen, 27. April–1. May 1987*, ed. by Kees Versteegh and Michael G. Carter (Amsterdam/Philadelphia: John Benjamins, 1990), pp. 229–237.

71 Faḫr ad-dīn ar-Rāzī, *al-Maʿālim fī uṣūl al-fiqh*, p. 20, line 4.

72 Cf. Faḫr ad-dīn ar-Rāzī, *Manṭiq al-Mulaḫḫaṣ*, p. 18, lines 4–10; for further passages in which the distinction between truth-apt and non-truth-apt sentences is discussed, see Faḫr ad-dīn ar-Rāzī, *Šarḥ al-Išārāt*, pp. 130 f., Faḫr ad-dīn ar-Rāzī, *Šarḥ ʿUyūn al-ḥikma*, vol. 1, p. 120, lines 1–9.

CHAPTER 4

Analysis of Implication in Legal Theory and the Further Development of the Tripartition in *uṣūl al-fiqh*

1 Analysis of the Legal-Theoretical Sub-Classification [ad § 25]

Up until this point in this work, I have presented and analyzed the Tripartition of Signification's logical-philosophical origins. On the one hand, this work has illuminated the Avicennian *Madḫal* background of the Tripartition of Signification; on the other hand, it has shown how the structural aspects of the *Maḥṣūl*'s logical classification have been transferred to its grammatical-theoretical classification. The logical and legal-theoretical classification also clearly shows the synthesis between theorems from *Cat.* 1 and classical legal hermeneutical instruments. At the same time, these various classification schemes and terms, each of which represents a facet of the understanding of the relationship between word and signification, are all assigned to the category of *muṭābaqa*. And so, having discussed the background of the *muṭābaqa* manner of signification and its usefulness for the hermeneutical foundations of legal theory, this present chapter will focus on implication (*iltizām*) and its relevance in legal theory. In doing so, it will work out the historical background of the types of implication as defined from a legal-theoretical perspective and their effects on the establishment of legal principles.

According to the results of the study in Chapter 2, we can distinguish the following levels of *iltizām*:

[a] *iltizām* for the logical and ontological determination of the specific difference (later also the proprium and ultimately the species) and of its relationship to other predicables; this is relevant in the study of definitions and conclusions for avoiding redundancy, omissions, and false conclusions;

[b] *iltizām* in the general linguistic sense as one of the three manners of signification, which—now freed from its exclusive relevance to predicables and universal linguistic expressions and extended to all linguistic expressions—is set up as corresponding to the basic linguistic-theoretical classification of linguistic expressions into *ism*, *fiʿl*, and *ḥarf*;

[c] *iltizām* as a generic term for the types of implication as defined in the field of legal theory. It is this level that is now the focus of our investigation.

1.1 *Faḫr ad-dīn's Concept of* dalālat al-iltizām *as a Generic Term for the Types of Implication in the Field of Legal Theory*

In the classification that Faḫr ad-dīn now makes in §25, the concept of *iltizām* is embedded within a genuine legal-theoretical context. This was familiar enough to his readers that he need only generally allude to the individual concepts subsumed under *iltizām*. Accordingly, the aim of this present study is to contextualize these allusions and make them intelligible to the extent that we will ultimately be able to understand (and justify) which types of Šāfiʿite legal-theoretical implication Faḫr ad-dīn subsumes under *iltizām* and which he does not. 'Implied meanings' are defined in Islamic legal theory as those meanings that "cannot be inferred from the linguistic expressions with regard to their (linguistic) form (*ṣīġa*), but rather only with regard to their import (*faḥwā*) and their allusion (*išāra*)".[1] The meanings are arrived at by means of a relationship of implication—through, *inter alia*, contextual clues and other indicators that go beyond the mere relationship of imposition between the linguistic expression and its meaning. This relationship is understood as a dichotomy, usually expressed in the Šāfiʿite tradition with the terms *manṭūq* ("that which is spoken") and *mafhūm* ("that which is understood").[2] According to the 'classical' Šāfiʿite understanding,[3] implication (*mafhūm*) in legal theory comprises the following five types, which will be discussed in more detail:

[1.] *dalālat al-iqtiḍāʾ*—translated somewhat awkwardly as 'signification by requirement' or 'required meaning,' often synonymous with the ellipsis (*iḍmār*) of a word;

[2.] *dalālat al-išāra*—'signification by allusion';

1 Al-Ġazālī, *al-Mustaṣfā*, vol. 3, p. 402.

2 The term *mafhūm* is ambiguous: On the one hand, it is the generic term for the various types legal-theoretical implication (contrasted with *manṭūq*); at the same time, it is used to encompass the two concepts *mafhūm al-muwāfaqa* and *mafhūm al-muḫālafa*; moreover, it can also be used to specifically refer to *mafhūm al-muḫālafa*; see also Weiss, *The Search*, p. 477. Al-Āmidī calls the pair *manẓūm/ġayr manẓūm*, cf. al-Āmidī, *al-Iḥkām*, vol. 3, pp. 81ff. and Weiss, *The Search*, pp. 322f. and pp. 473ff.

3 Represented here by al-Ġazālī's categorization of these hermeneutical techniques, cf. al-Ġazālī, *al-Mustaṣfā*, vol. 3, pp. 402–434; see also Gleave, *Islam and Literalism*, pp. 53–54—as Gleave combines the two *mafhūm* concepts into *dalālat al-mafhūm*, he lists a total of four types. On this classification, see also Yunis Ali, *Medieval Islamic Pragmatics*, pp. 175–176; Weiss, *The Search*, pp. 473ff.; Ramić, *Language and the Interpretation of Islamic Law*, pp. 42–60—here, however, a later Šāfiʿite classification is tacitly presented, the development of which is examined in Chapter 4, Section 2.2 of this study; on the Ḥanafite classification, see Yunis Ali, *Medieval Islamic Pragmatics*, pp. 159–175, Kamali, *Principles of Islamic Jurisprudence*, pp. 167–175; Ramić, *Language and the Interpretation of Islamic Law*, pp. 3–40.

[3.] *dalālat at-taʿlīl/īmāʾ wa-išāra*—the implication of that which has elicited a specific legal ruling;

[4.] *mafhūm al-muwāfaqa* or 'import of the linguistic expression' (*faḥwā l-lafẓ*)—often synonymous with an *argumentum a minori ad maius* (*at-tanbīh bi-l-adnā ʿalā l-aʿlā*);

[5.] *argumentum e contrario* (*dalīl al-ḫiṭāb/mafhūm al-muḫālafa*)—this controversial type is in turn categorized into various subtypes.

Roughly speaking, Faḫr ad-dīn subsumes the concept of *manṭūq* under *dalālat al-muṭābaqa* and that of *mafhūm* under *dalālat al-iltizām*. In what follows, my aim is to analyze the actual overlaps between the two concepts of legal-theoretical implication—*mafhūm* and *iltizām*. Due to the abundance of research literature on the topic of legal-theoretical implication, I will however refrain from presenting the concepts themselves in excessive detail.[4]

Faḫr ad-dīn begins his categorization of *dalālat al-iltizām* as usual with the distinction between simple and compound linguistic expressions: It is either [1.3.1] the meaning of a simple linguistic expression that implies a further meaning or [1.3.2] it is the meaning of compound linguistic expressions that implies a further meaning. Faḫr ad-dīn then differentiates the function of implication for understanding the statement: The implied meaning is either a condition (*šarṭ*) for being able to understand the statement in a meaningful way, or it results from the meaning of the statement as a consequence or additional meaning.[5]

The following outline provides an overview of the relevant section of the *Maḥṣūl* and will be considered in more detail in the following subsections:

FIGURE 20 *Outline of the Legal-Theoretical Sub-Classification* [§25][6]

[*ad* 1.3] The categorization of signification by implication (*iltizām*):

[1.3.1] The meaning (*maʿnā*) is obtained either from the meanings of simple linguistic expressions (*min maʿānī l-alfāẓi l-mufrada*) or

[1.3.2] from compound linguistic expressions;

[*ad* 1.3.1] The implied meaning represents either a condition (*šarṭ*) for the meaning signified by congruence

[*ad* 1.3.2] or the implied meaning follows (*tābiʿ*) [*from the meaning signified by congruence*].

4 See p. 170, fn. 3 and the information on the respective types of implication.

5 Faḫr ad-dīn ar-Rāzī, *al-Maḥṣūl*, vol. 1, p. 232, lines 13–14.

6 Faḫr ad-dīn ar-Rāzī, *al-Maḥṣūl*, vol. 1, p. 232, line 9–p. 234, last line; cf. the translation of this section, pp. 59 ff. of this work.

[*ad* I.3.1] If it is the first, it is called *dalālat al-iqtiḍāʾ* ('signification by requirement'). Additionally, this condition can occur

[I.3.1.1] by an inference based purely on reasoning, or

[I.3.1.2] by means of a legal derivation.

[*ad* I.3.2] The implied meaning that follows compound linguistic expressions:

[I.3.2.1] completes the meaning

[I.3.2.2] or it does not.

[*ad* I.3.2.1] e.g. *a fortiori qiyās* [*in Ġazālī: reference by means of context* (siyāq) *and intention* (maqṣūd), *also subsumed under* mafhūm al-muwāfaqa].

[*ad* I.3.2.2] In the second case, what is signified by implication is either

[I.3.2.2.1] affirmed [*corresponds in Šāfiʿite and Ḥanafite terminology to 'allusion by means of the linguistic expression'* (išārat al-lafẓ)]

[I.3.2.2.2] or negated [*corresponds to* mafhūm al-muḫālafa].[7]

1.1.1 Implied Meaning as a Condition for Understanding: *dalālat al-iqtiḍāʾ*

Faḫr ad-dīn provides—in contrast to the subsequent types of implication—a term for the type of implication that he regards as a 'condition' for understanding the statement in a meaningful way: He calls it *dalālat al-iqtiḍāʾ* ('signification by requirement'):

> [*ad* I.3.1] If it is the first [*i.e. a condition* (šarṭ)], then it is called 'signification by requirement' (*dalālat al-iqtiḍāʾ*).
> [p. 233] Furthermore, the nature of that condition can [*be such that it*]
> [I.3.1.1] is based on reasoning (*ʿaqliyyatan*), as in [*Muḥammad's*] words "Error (*ḫaṭaʾ*) and forgetfulness (*nisyān*) have been removed from my *umma*": For reason shows us that the meaning can only be correct if we find the legal ruling (*al-ḥukm aš-šarʿī*) concealed within it.
> [I.3.1.2] The condition can also occur based on legal (*šarʿiyyatan*) considerations, as when one says "By God, I will certainly manumit this slave"; for this implies having acquired possession (*taḥṣīl al-milk*), because the ful-

7 See also the summary given by Sirāǧ ad-dīn al-Urmawī in his *Maḥṣūl* commentary, Sirāǧ ad-dīn al-Urmawī, *at-Taḥṣīl min al-Maḥṣūl*, vol. 1, p. 203, lines 4–9.

> filment (*wafāʾ*) of this speech [*i.e. this promise*] in a legal manner is only possible afterwards [*i.e. after the acquisition of the slave by the speaker*].[8]

Faḫr ad-dīn divides *dalālat al-iqtiḍāʾ* into two types, namely (1.) rational and (2.) legal signification by requirement. This—referring back to al-Ġazālī's detailed discussion of the topic[9]—is to be understood as follows: In general, *dalālat al-iqtiḍāʾ* is that form of signification "in which the linguistic expression [*itself*] does not signify it [*i.e. the meaning*] and [*in which*] it is not pronounced (*lā yakūnu manṭūqan bihī*)";[10] instead, in order to grasp the correct meaning, it is necessary to assume the ellipsis (*iḍmār*) of a particular word.[11]

According to al-Ġazālī, three factors can lead the jurist to assume this: Either (i) the credibility of the speaker (*ṣidq al-mutakallim*) cannot otherwise be maintained,[12] or (ii) an impermissible meaning would result from a legal point of view, or (iii) a nonsensical meaning would result from a purely rational point of view. As to the first case of preserving the credibility of the speaker, legal scholars discuss, among other things, the *ḥadīṯ* quoted above: "Error (*ḫaṭaʾ*) and forgetfulness (*nisyān*) have been removed from my *umma*." Since error and forgetfulness do in fact befall Muslims in reality, the statement would have to be considered false—and as a consequence, the credibility of the speaker, in this case Muḥammad, would be damaged.[13] In order to view this sentence as true and meaningful and to maintain its speaker's credibility, it must be assumed that the meaning cannot be gleaned exclusively from the existing words—rather, there has been an ellipsis of the legal ruling (*al-ḥukm aš-šarʿī*),[14] such that what is meant and should be understood is: "The ruling (*ḥukm*) on error (*ḫaṭaʾ*) has been removed from my *umma*."[15] According to this understanding,

---

8 Faḫr ad-dīn ar-Rāzī, *al-Maḥṣūl*, vol. 1, p. 232, last line–p. 233, line 5.

9 Al-Ġazālī, *al-Mustaṣfā*, vol. 3, pp. 403–405.

10 Ibid., p. 403, line 3.

11 For a discussion of the equation of or differentiation between *iqtiḍāʾ* and *iḍmār*, see al-Ġazālī, *al-Mustaṣfā*, vol. 3, p. 405, lines 9–10 as well as Faḫr ad-dīn ar-Rāzī, *al-Maḥṣūl*, vol. 1, p. 351 and al-Qarāfī, *Nafāʾis al-uṣūl*, vol. 1, p. 302, line 23–p. 304, line 1.

12 Al-Ġazālī, *al-Mustaṣfā*, vol. 3, p. 403, line 5 and lines 8 ff.

13 On the concept of *dalālat al-iqtiḍāʾ* in general, see most extensively and comprehensively Ramić, *Language and the Interpretation of Islamic Law*, pp. 29–38; as well as Yunis Ali, *Medieval Islamic Pragmatics*, pp. 170–175, Weiss, *The Search*, p. 475, and Kamali, *Principles of Islamic Jurisprudence*, p. 179; and on this example in particular: Ramić, *Language and the Interpretation of Islamic Law*, p. 30 and pp. 33 f., Yunis Ali, *Medieval Islamic Pragmatics*, pp. 172 f.

14 Faḫr ad-dīn ar-Rāzī, *al-Maḥṣūl*, vol. 1, p. 233, lines 2–3.

15 Faḫr ad-dīn ar-Rāzī, *al-Maḥṣūl*, vol. 2, p. 382, line 11.

God did not remove error itself, but only its judgement—some scholars specify 'blame' (*mu'āḫaḏa*) and 'punishment' (*'iqāb*) for error—from the Muslim community.[16]

Faḫr ad-dīn—in contrast to al-Ġazālī—counts this case among those that require the assumption of ellipsis from a rational point of view. The aspect of the speaker's credibility does not play a role here: It is through reasoning alone that one can see that this sentence does not make sense unless one assumes an ellipsis.

Among the examples of such genuinely rational arguments, cited by other scholars, are the sentences, also cited frequently in the research literature, "And ask the village" (*wa-s'ali l-qaryata*) [Qur'ān 12:82], i.e. "And ask the inhabitants of the village" (*wa-s'ali ahla l-qaryati*)—this is a figurative expression (*maǧāz*)[17] called *metonymy* in Western rhetoric—and "Forbidden to you are your mothers" (*ḥurrimat 'alaykum ummahātukum*) [Qur'ān 4:23], i.e. "Forbidden to you is sexual intercourse (*waṭ'*)/marriage with your mothers."[18]

As an example of a case whereby it is legal considerations that give rise to the assumption of an ellipsis, Faḫr ad-dīn cites the example of "By God, I will certainly manumit this slave" (*wa-Llāhi la-u'tiqanna hāḏā l-'abda*). Al-Ġazālī describes a situation in order to show why this is relevant: "[…] if someone were to point to someone else's slave and say: 'By God, I will certainly manumit this slave,'"[19] then an issue with this statement would arise from the fact that the prerequisite for manumission is ownership (*milk*): Only one's own slave, and not one owned by another, can be set free—consequently, this example implies a legal act in the form of a transaction.[20]

1.1.2 Implied Meaning as a Consequence of What Is Understood

Thus, *dalālat al-iqtiḍā'*, a sub-type of legal-theoretical implication, is subsumed under the concept of *iltizām* and is understood there as a condition for being able to understand a statement as meaningful. Faḫr ad-dīn then turns to the kind of implication that can follow as a consequence of a statement, and in doing so, he makes a further distinction: Implication belongs "either [1.3.2.1]

---

16 Al-Ġazālī, *al-Mustaṣfā*, vol. 3, p. 404; al-Āmidī, *al-Iḥkām*, vol. 3, p. 82, line 5.

17 See, for example, Faḫr ad-dīn ar-Rāzī, *at-Tafsīr al-kabīr*, vol. 18, p. 152, line 13; for this example, see al-Bāqillānī, *at-Taqrīb*, vol. 1, p. 352, lines 16 ff.; cf. e.g. Gleave, *Islam and Literalism*, p. 9.

18 Al-Ġazālī, *al-Mustaṣfā*, vol. 3, p. 405, line 1 and Faḫr ad-dīn ar-Rāzī, *al-Maḥṣūl*, vol. 3, p. 163; Kamali, *Principles of Islamic Jurisprudence*, p. 172.

19 Al-Ġazālī, *al-Mustaṣfā*, vol. 3, p. 404, lines 11–12.

20 Cf. ibid., lines 7–13.

to that which completes this meaning (*min mukammilāt ḏālika l-maʿnā*) or [1.3.2.2] which does not [*complete*] it."[21]

1.1.2.1 Mafhūm al-muwāfaqa

In keeping with his concise style in this chapter, the explanation of the first case consists merely of the following sentence: "[ad 1.3.2.1] The first is like how the prohibition against saying 'Fie!' [*i.e. verbally abusing*] (*taḥrīm at-taʾfīf*) signifies the prohibition against beating (*taḥrīm aḍ-ḍarb*) for the one who does not establish the [*legal ruling*] by a *qiyās* (*ʿinda man lā yuṯbituhū bi-l-qiyās*)."[22]

Faḫr ad-dīn alludes here to the controversy surrounding the interpretation of Sura 17, verse 23: "Your Lord has commanded that you should worship none but Him, and show kindness to your parents. If either or both of them attain old age with you, say not 'Fie' to them [*fa-lā taqul la-humā uff*] and do not rebuke them, but always speak gently to them."[23] Legal scholars agree that it can be deduced from this verse that not only saying 'Fie' to (*taʾfīf*), i.e. verbally abusing, one's parents is forbidden, but also beating (*ḍarb*) them. But the method used to arrive at this legal ruling is controversial: Is it a literal signification (*dalāla lafẓiyya*)—and if not literal, at least an immediate signification through the linguistic expressions themselves—or does it require analogy (*qiyās*)?[24] In his Qurʾanic commentary on this verse, Faḫr ad-dīn does not content himself with cursory remarks like he does in the *Maḥṣūl*. According to him, neither does the

---

21 Faḫr ad-dīn ar-Rāzī, *al-Maḥṣūl*, vol. 1, p. 233, lines 6–7.

22 Ibid., p. 234, lines 1–2.

23 *The Quran: Translation and Commentary by Wahiduddin Khan*, ed. by Farida Khanam (New Delhi: Goodword Books, 2011).

24 Faḫr ad-dīn ar-Rāzī, *at-Tafsīr al-kabīr*, vol. 20, p. 151, lines 21ff.; cf. al-Baṣrī, *Kitāb al-Muʿtamad*, vol. 2, p. 780.

For an overview of the arguments and positions in this debate, see, for example, al-Ġazālī, *Šifāʾ al-ġalīl fī bayān aš-šubah wa-l-muḫīl wa masālik at-taʿlīl*, ed. by Ḥamd al-Kabīsī (Baghdad: al-Maṭbaʿa l-iršād, 1971), p. 53, line 4–p. 58 or al-Ǧuwaynī, *al-Burhān*, vol. 1, pp. 166–167; cf. Hallaq, *A History of Islamic Legal Theories*, pp. 97–99, id., "Non-Analogical Arguments in Sunni Juridical *Qiyās*," *Arabica*, vol. 36 (1989): pp. 289–296, Yunis Ali, *Medieval Islamic Pragmatics*, pp. 168f. and p. 191.

On the concept of *mafhūm al-muwāfaqa* in general, see Yunis Ali, *Medieval Islamic Pragmatics*, pp. 188ff.; Ramić, *Language and the Interpretation of Islamic Law*, pp. 49ff.; Weiss, *The Search*, pp. 477ff.; Kamali, *Principles of Islamic Jurisprudence*, pp. 171–172; and Marie Bernand, "Controverses Médiévales sur le *Dalīl al-Ḫiṭāb*," *Arabica*, vol. 33, no. 3 (Nov. 1986): pp. 269–294; cf. Ǧamāl ad-dīn, *al-Baḥṯ an-naḥwī ʿinda l-uṣūliyyīn*, pp. 276ff.; on *mafhūm al-muwāfaqa* in aš-Šāfiʿī, see Vishanoff, *The Formation of Islamic Hermeneutics*, p. 60. A summary of the Ḥanafite position can be found in, *inter alia*, Niẓām ad-dīn al-Anṣārī al-Laknawī, *Fawātiḥ ar-raḥamūt bi-šarḥ Musallam aṯ-ṯubūt*, ed. by ʿAbdallah Maḥmūd Muḥammad ʿUmar (Beirut: Dār al-Kutub al-ʿilmiyya, 2002), vol. 1, p. 446, lines 19ff.

linguistic expression 'saying "Fie"' signify the linguistic expression 'beating,' nor does the meaning of the former imply that of the latter:

> An indicator [*that it is a conclusion by analogy*] is that the saying of 'Fie' (*taʾfīf*) is not beating (*ḍarb*), such that the forbidding of the saying of 'Fie' (*al-manʿ mina t-taʾfīf*) is not the forbidding of beating. Moreover, the prohibition of saying 'Fie' does not rationally (*ʿaqlan*) necessitate (*lā yastalzimu*) the prohibition of beating.[25]

Rather, it is a *qiyās*: The situation is not only such "that the revelation (*šarʿ*) provides a ruling (*ḥukm*) in one case and is silent about the ruling of another case,"[26] but that this legal ruling is even more obviously appropriate for the case from which a ruling is withheld than it is for the case for which it was explicitly stated; "for the linguistic expression signifies only the prohibition of saying 'Fie,' but to [*prohibit*] beating is more appropriate than to prohibit saying 'Fie.'"[27] The *ʿilla* in both cases is to require the honoring (*taʿẓīm*) and prevent the harming (*aḏīya*) of parents.[28] This is quite clearly a conclusion by analogy (*qiyās ǧalī*), according to Faḫr ad-dīn, which belongs to the category of *argumentum a minori ad maius* (*al-istidlāl bi-l-adnā ʿalā l-aʿlā*).[29]

In the *Maḥṣūl*, however, he provides this case as an example of a type of legal ruling that does not have to be arrived at by means of *qiyās*—i.e. Faḫr ad-dīn assigns this kind of signification, which is understood by some to be purely linguistic and require no deduction, to the realm of implication, even though he himself is of the opinion that it is not a type of implication but rather of a form of analogy.

---

25 Faḫr ad-dīn ar-Rāzī, *at-Tafsīr al-kabīr*, vol. 20, p. 152, lines 4–5.

26 Ibid., p. 151, line 27.

27 Ibid., lines 29–30.

28 Ibid., p. 152, lines 8–9.

29 Ibid., lines 3–4; on the *qiyās ǧalī*, cf. Faḫr ad-dīn ar-Rāzī, *al-Maḥṣūl*, vol. 5, pp. 121 ff.; on *a fortiori* arguments in Islamic legal theory and the debate regarding to what extent they can be subsumed under the *qiyāsāt* at all (a subsumption already made by aš-Šāfiʿī), see Hallaq, "Non-Analogical Arguments," pp. 289–296, as well as id., *A History of Islamic Legal Theories*, pp. 96–97 and p. 29; see also Zysow, *The Economy of Certainty*, pp. 96–100 and Weiss, *The Search*, pp. 478–480; for an overview of the use of this form of conclusion in various Islamic disciplines, see Rosalind Gwynne, "The *A Fortiori* Argument in *Fiqh*, *Naḥw* and *Kalām*," in *Studies in the History of Arabic Grammar II. Proceedings of the 2nd Symposium on the History of Arabic Grammar, Nijmegen, 27. April–1. May 1987*, ed. by Kees Versteegh and Michael G. Carter (Amsterdam/Philadelphia: John Benjamins, 1990), pp. 165–177.

Šihāb ad-dīn al-Qarāfī also comes to the conclusion that this classification does not correspond to Faḫr ad-dīn's own hermeneutical understanding:

> He [*i.e. Faḫr ad-dīn*] says "for the one who does not establish this [*i.e. the legal ruling*] through a *qiyās*" (*ʿinda man lā yuṯbituhū bi-l-qiyās*). Because he [*i.e. Faḫr ad-dīn himself*] arrives at the prohibition against beating through a *qiyās* by saying: The linguistic expression does not signify [*the legal ruling*] at all.—Consequently, the signification is not confirmed by implication, so we only speak about it (*fa-lā tataḥaqqaqu dalālatu l-iltizāmi fa-naḥnu innamā natakallamu fīhi*), [*without confirming its classification*].[30]

Thus we see that Faḫr ad-dīn classifies as implication a hermeneutical position that he himself does not hold and which is generally more commonly held by Ḥanafite jurists.[31] One of the reasons he does this is that the reasoning of those who consider a *qiyās* unnecessary here is actually consistent with Faḫr ad-dīn's conceptualization of *iltizām*: It is the meaning of the explicit linguistic expressions that signifies the implied meaning "prohibition against beating," not the linguistic expressions themselves.[32]

In classical Šāfiʿite legal theory—it can be briefly noted—several terms are used for this type of implication.[33] Al-Ġazālī, who takes the position in this case that the intention (*maqṣūd*) and the context (*siyāq*) of the Qurʾanic verse lead to an immediate understanding of the legal ruling, and who rejects the assumption of an *argumentum a minori ad maius* here due to this directness of understanding,[34] lists the various terms:

> This is sometimes called *mafhūm al-muwāfaqa* ("congruent implication") or *faḥwā l-lafẓ* ("import of the linguistic expression"). Each school (*farīq*)

30 Al-Qarāfī, *Nafāʾis al-uṣūl*, vol. 1, p. 306, lines 3–4.

31 See in particular the summary of the Ḥanafite positions in al-Laknawī, *Fawātiḥ ar-raḥamūt*, vol. 1, p. 446, lines 19 ff.

32 Hallaq, "Non-Analogical Arguments," p. 291 with reference to the work of the Ḥanafite scholar Šams ad-dīn as-Saraḫsī, *Uṣūl*, vol. 1, p. 242, line 17.

33 On the terminology and its differentiations, see, *inter alia*, Zysow, *The Economy of Certainty*, p. 97, fn. 209; Ramić, *Language and the Interpretation of Islamic Law*, pp. 49–50 as well as Kamali, *Principles of Islamic Jurisprudence*, p. 179 and Yunis Ali, *Medieval Islamic Pragmatics*, p. 189.

34 See al-Ġazālī, *al-Mustaṣfā*, vol. 3, pp. 411–412, see also al-Bāqillānī, *at-Taqrīb*, vol. 1, pp. 342–343.

> uses different language—so do not concern yourself with the linguistic expressions [*i.e. the technical terms*] and endeavour to grasp what is essential in this genre.[35]

Faḫr ad-dīn adds another term to the collection:[36] *dalālat al-iltizām*. This manner of signification is the generic term for the types of implication discussed so far, provided that they are actually held to be types of implication—which, according to my research, Faḫr ad-dīn does not do. The type of implication discussed here is described by Faḫr ad-dīn within the *iltizām* type of signification as one in which the implied meaning follows as a consequence of the meaning of the statement and thereby completes the meaning of the statement or corresponds to its legal ruling.

1.1.2.2 *Positive and Negative Implication*

While the type of implication categorized as *mafhūm al-muwāfaqa* corresponds to the meaning of the statement or receives the same legal ruling as the original statement, the following types of implication are incidental consequences of the statement that are not identical to its main intention. Here Faḫr ad-dīn differentiates between a positive and negative type of implication:

> [*ad* I.3.2.2] In the second case [*i.e. in the second type of implication that arises as a consequence of a statement*], what is signified by the implication is either
> [I.3.2.2.1] affirmative (*ṯubūtiyyan*)[37] or
> [I.3.2.2.2] negative (*ʿadamiyyan*).[38]

In Šāfiʿite and Ḥanafite terminology, the first corresponds to 'allusion by means of the linguistic expression' (*išārat al-lafẓ*); the second is the controversial *argumentum e contrario* (*dalīl al-ḫiṭāb/mafhūm al-muḫālafa*)—although the concept of positive and negative implication according to the classical understanding was actually equated with *mafhūm al-muwāfaqa* and *mafhūm al-muḫālafa*.[39] But it is not these two types of implication that Faḫr ad-dīn places

---

35 Al-Ġazālī, *al-Mustaṣfā*, vol. 3, p. 412, line 14–last line.

36 In other places, Faḫr ad-dīn ar-Rāzī also labels this conclusion with the common Šāfiʿite term *mafhūm al-muwāfaqa*, cf. e.g. Faḫr ad-dīn ar-Rāzī, *al-Maḥṣūl*, vol. 3, p. 11, lines 8–11.

37 In a *Maḥṣūl* commentary, the term *wuǧūdī* is found for *ṯubūtī* at this location, cf. Tāǧ ad-dīn al-Urmawī, *al-Ḥāṣil min al-Maḥṣūl fī uṣūl al-fiqh*, vol. 2, p. 98, line 4.

38 Faḫr ad-dīn ar-Rāzī, *al-Maḥṣūl*, vol. 1, p. 234, line 3.

39 Cf. Vishanoff, *The Formation of Islamic Hermeneutics*, p. 7.

as parallel to one another; instead it is *mafhūm al-muḫālafa* and *dalālat al-išāra*. The main reason for this is, according to his own systematization, that the essential difference between *mafhūm al-muwāfaqa* on the one hand and *mafhūm al-muḫālafa* and *dalālat al-išāra* on the other is whether it is the intended main meaning that is implied or an incidental secondary meaning.

1.1.2.3 *Allusion* (išāra)

Faḫr ad-dīn himself provides detailed information about positive implication:

> [*ad* 1.3.2.2.1] The first corresponds to the words of God [Qur'ān 2:187] 'Now have relations with them' (*fa-l-āna bāširūhunna*). This extends to the moment at which the white thread (*al-ḫayṭ al-abyaḍ*) can be discerned; so it follows with regard to one who enters the state of great ritual impurity (*aṣbaḥa ǧunuban*) that his fasting is not impaired. Otherwise, it would necessarily follow that coitus (*waṭ'*) would be forbidden in another part of the night to the extent that ablution could take place.[40]

Qur'ān 2:187 permits eating, drinking, and sexual intercourse during the nights of Ramaḍān until dawn. In this context, scholars discussed the question of when the ritual ablution to end the state of impurity must be performed in order for the fast to be valid. According to one opinion, the ablution must be performed before dawn, meaning that the activities must already have ceased before dawn. According to the majority opinion, however, this verse should be understood to mean that the ablution can be performed at daybreak, i.e. after dawn—the implication is therefore that the state of impurity that persists until this moment does not affect the fast, which would have already begun at daybreak.[41] The unintended but nevertheless implied meaning is therefore that the state of impurity does not affect the fast; the meaning of the statement and its legal ruling are confirmed by implication.

40 Faḫr ad-dīn ar-Rāzī, *al-Maḥṣūl*, vol. 1, p. 234, lines 4–6.

41 Faḫr ad-dīn ar-Rāzī, *at-Tafsīr al-kabīr*, vol. 5, p. 94, lines 23–25, al-Ġazālī, *al-Mustaṣfār*, vol. 3, p. 408; see also Ramić, *Language and the Interpretation of Islamic Law*, p. 12. On the concept of *dalālat al-išāra* in general, see al-Ġazālī, *al-Mustaṣfā*, vol. 3, pp. 406–408; Ramić, *Language and the Interpretation of Islamic Law*, pp. 11–17, Yunis Ali, *Medieval Islamic Pragmatics*, pp. 161–166, Gleave, *Islam and Literalism*, pp. 53–54, Weiss, *The Search*, p. 476, and Kamali, *Principles of Islamic Jurisprudence*, pp. 169–171.

1.1.2.4 *The* Argumentum e Contrario (mafhūm al-muḫālafa/dalīl al-ḫiṭāb)

If in the previous type of implication a meaning is implied that relates affirmatively to the statement or to the legal ruling contained therein, negative implication, on the other hand, refers to the negation of the statement or the legal ruling contained therein for all unmentioned circumstances. It will have to be determined, however, whether Faḫr ad-dīn actually considers it permissible to classify this as implication: "[*ad* 1.3.2.2.2] As for the second, it is [*the question of*] whether something being explicitly mentioned allows one to assume the negation [*of the legal ruling*] that is omitted from [*the statement*] (*anna taḫṣīṣa š-šay'i bi-d-dikri hal yadullu ʿalā nafyihi ʿammā ʿadāhu*)—God knows ..."[42] This corresponds to the definition of the *argumentum e contrario* (*mafhūm al-muḫālafa/dalīl al-ḫiṭāb*)[43] as we find it, for example, in al-Ġazālī's *Mustaṣfā*: "The meaning of this [*i.e. of* mafhūm (al-muḫālafa) *or* dalīl al-ḫiṭāb] is: One infers from the fact that something is explicitly mentioned that the legal ruling does not apply to that which is excluded from [*the statement*] (*al-istidlāl bi-taḫṣīṣi š-šay'i bi-d-dikri ʿalā nafyi l-ḥukmi ʿammā ʿadāhu*)."[44] Positively formulated, this means that "only the facts [*or circumstances*] expressly mentioned by a legal provision are covered by it," because it was deduced by *argumentum e contrario* that all other circumstances not mentioned are excluded from the legal provision.[45]

The various subtypes of *argumentum e contrario* that are distinguished in Islamic legal methodology depend on the element qualifying the statement: If a statement is qualified, for example, by a certain name (*laqab/ism*), a number (*ʿadad*), a condition (*šarṭ*), or by a certain attribute (*ṣifa*), it can be concluded—according to the proponents—that the legal ruling does not apply if the qual-

---

42 Faḫr ad-dīn ar-Rāzī, *al-Maḥṣūl*, vol. 1, p. 234, lines 7–8.

43 Cf., for example, al-Qarāfī's remarks on this passage in his *Maḥṣūl* commentary, al-Qarāfī, *Nafāʾis al-uṣūl*, vol. 1, p. 306, lines 7 ff.; for a detailed discussion of the *argumentum e contrario* and an argument against this form of conclusion, see, *inter alia*, al-Ġazālī, *al-Mustaṣfā*, vol. 3, pp. 413–449 as well as al-Bāqillānī, *at-Taqrīb*, vol. 3, pp. 331 ff. and Imām al-Ḥaramayn al-Ǧuwaynī, *at-Talḫīṣ fī uṣūl al-fiqh*, ed. by Muḥammad Ḥasan Ismaʿīl (Beirut: Dār al-Kutub al-ʿilmiyya, 2003 [1424]), pp. 225 ff.; for detailed presentations of the *argumentum e contrario* in Islamic legal theory, see the very good summary and explanation in Zysow's *The Economy of Certainty*, pp. 100–109 as well as Bernand, "Controverses Médiévales sur le *Dalīl al-Ḫiṭāb*," pp. 269–294; Weiss, *The Search*, pp. 482–493; Yunis Ali, *Medieval Islamic Pragmatics*, pp. 192–224; Kamali, *Principles of Islamic Jurisprudence*, pp. 179–185; Ramić, *Language and the Interpretation of Islamic Law*, pp. 55–60.

44 Al-Ġazālī, *al-Mustaṣfā*, vol. 3, p. 413, lines 3–4.

45 Michael Potacs, *Auslegung im öffentlichen Recht* (Baden-Baden: Nomos, 1994), p. 157.

ification does not apply.[46] The *ḥadīṯ* "*zakāt* is [*to be paid*] for free-grazing sheep" (*fī sāʾimati l-ġanami z-zakātu*) therefore implies that no *zakāt* is to be paid for sheep that are stall-fed (*maʿlūfa*).[47] Those in favor of the *argumentum e contrario* argue, among other things, that the attribute "free-grazing" corresponds to the *ratio legis* (*ʿilla*) for the obligation, so that when the legal basis ceases to apply, so too does the legal ruling.[48] Opponents, on the other hand, argue, among other things, that such a conclusion cannot be drawn without the specific context (*qarīna*);[49] for one can image a case in which it was fed and stabled sheep that were to be taxed, whereupon there was a question to Muḥammad about whether the tax also applied to free-grazing sheep. This *ḥadīṯ* would then have arisen from his response specifying that it did.[50]

This form of reasoning caused much controversy within the Šāfiʿite school of law and between the different schools of law, with the Šāfiʿites being more in favor of the *argumentum e contrario* than the Ḥanafites, who rejected any form of *argumentum e contrario* in the determination of law.[51]

---

46 Al-Qarāfī does specify that in this form of reasoning, the "contradictory opposite of what is explicitly stated" (*naqīḍ al-manṭūq*) can be inferred from a certain statement (al-Qarāfī, *Nafāʾis al-uṣūl*, vol. 1, p. 306, line 11); this would correspond to a logical contraposition and would mean that the affirmation of a legal ruling of the statement "S is P" would imply the negation of the legal ruling for the statement "not-P is not-S." From the statement "Zayd is wise" (S is P) the contraposition would be "One who is not wise is not Zayd," but no such statement is made that someone who is not Zayd cannot be wise. However, the legally relevant *argumentum e contrario* discussed here is not of the type of a logical contraposition and instead corresponds to the schema "not-S is not-P." Al-Ġazālī states, among other things, that this conclusion would lead to heretical statements. A sentence such as "Zayd is wise" would negate the wisdom of God; "Jesus is the prophet of God" would deny the prophethood of Muḥammad and all other prophets (al-Ġazālī, *al-Mustaṣfā*, vol. 3, p. 417, lines 7–10). The *argumentum e contrario* is also discussed in contemporary, non-religious legal hermeneutics and understood as "Only S is P," see Egon Schneider and Friedrich E. Schnapp, *Logik für Juristen: Die Grundlagen der Denklehre und der Rechtsanwendung* (Munich: Franz Vahlen, 2006 [6th ed.]), p. 156.

47 Al-Ġazālī, *al-Mustaṣfā*, vol. 3, p. 413, line 11.

48 Al-Ġazālī cites this argument, see ibid. p. 432, lines 5–6.

49 Ibid., p. 426, last line–p. 427, first line.

50 Weiss, *The Search*, p. 489.

51 See, among others, Zysow, *The Economy of Certainty*, p. 101; Kamali, *Principles of Islamic Jurisprudence*, p. 182; Ramić, *Language and the Interpretation of Islamic Law*, p. 55; on aš-Šāfiʿī's own position on this question, see Vishanoff, *The Formation of Islamic Hermeneutics*, p. 60. We find such an opposing position, open to the *argumentum e contrario*, above all in later, post-Rāzian Šāfiʿites, see Chapter 4, Section 2.2.2 of this work.

Prominent Šāfiʿites such as al-Ġazālī[52] and al-Āmidī, however, did reject the *argumentum e contrario*, as did Abu l-Ḥusayn al-Baṣrī, whom Faḫr ad-dīn follows in many aspects. Faḫr ad-dīn also agrees with him on this matter, although at first glance his position appears to be less dismissive and more deliberative: In certain circumstances it may be sensible and permissible to understand the opposite of what is explicitly stated—as in the case of the *argumentum e contrario*,

> for it [*i.e. the* argumentum e contrario] indicates that the mentioned legal ruling does not apply to that which is not mentioned—although it is conceivable that the signification of the existence of the mentioned legal ruling remains in force for some of the cases which are not mentioned.[53]

Faḫr ad-dīn points out first of all that all possibilities must be taken into consideration when making legal rulings for unmentioned circumstances. It may be that this legal ruling does not apply; however, it may also be that by means of (a) other textual evidence or (b) a *qiyās*, it can be shown that the legal ruling applies even if the specified circumstances are lacking: The prohibition 'Do not kill your children out of fear of impoverishment' [Qurʾān 17:31] does not turn into the permission to kill your children in the case of wealth. Instead, the prohibition remains because there are other indicators and instructions regarding this matter.[54]

While the *argumentum e contrario* assumes that, "since a and b are expressly regulated by the law, but c is not, the law does not wish c to be treated in the same manner as a and b,"[55] (b) analogy (*qiyās*) follows exactly the opposite train of thought: Case c falls, on the basis of similarity, under the purview of the same legal ruling that has been explicitly determined for both cases a and b.[56] A misapplication of the two types of reasoning or a misidentification of the *ratio legis*

---

52 On the development of al-Ġazālī's position from favorable in the *Manḫūl* to dismissive in the *Mustaṣfā*, see Zysow, *The Economy of Certainty*, p. 107.

53 Faḫr ad-dīn ar-Rāzī, *al-Maḥṣūl*, vol. 3, p. 11, lines 13–15; al-Qarāfī, *Nafāʾis al-uṣūl*, vol. 2, p. 561, line 7; Sirāǧ ad-dīn al-Urmawī, *at-Taḥṣīl min l-Maḥṣūl*, vol. 1, p. 367, lines 9–12.

54 Faḫr ad-dīn ar-Rāzī, *al-Maḥūl*, vol. 2, p. 138, line 10–p. 139, line 3; see also Faḫr ad-dīn ar-Rāzī, *at-Tafsīr al-kabīr*, vol. 10, p. 48, lines 6 ff. and id., *al-Maʿālim fī uṣūl al-fiqh*, p. 30, lines 4 ff.

55 Zysow, *The Economy of Certainty*, p. 103.

56 On the contrast between these two forms of conclusion, see for example Ǧamāl ad-dīn al-Isnawī, *Nihāyat as-sūl fī šarḥ Minhāǧ al-wuṣūl ilā ʿilm al-uṣūl li-l-qāḍī Nāṣir ad-dīn al-Bayḍāwī*, ed. s.n. (Beirut: ʿĀlam al-Kutub, s.d.), vol. 2, pp. 207–208; cf. Bernand, "Controverses Médiévales sur le *Dalīl al-Ḫiṭāb*," pp. 275 ff.

could, for example, lead to the drinking of grape wine being prohibited while date wine remains permitted.[57]

I will now analyze Faḫr ad-dīn's core argument against the *argumentum e contrario*. For, as will be shown, the argument proves to have been influential on the camp of the opponents of the *argumentum e contrario*, allowing them to deny the legitimacy of the *argumentum e contrario* on the basis of the Tripartition of Signification.[58] In his chapter on linguistic structure and the nature of commandments, Faḫr ad-dīn deals, among other things, with the "commandment/imperative (*amr*) that is qualified by an attribute (*ṣifa*),"[59] and in this context with the question of whether the aforementioned *ḥadīṯ* concerning *zakāt*

> [§1] signifies the fact that no *zakāt* is to be paid for [*sheep*] not grazing freely.
> [§1.1] The truth (*ḥaqq*) is that it does not signify [*this, i.e. the negation of the legal ruling for sheep that do not graze freely*]. This is the speech of Abū Ḥanīfa; and this was held by Ibn Surayǧ, al-Qāḍī Abū Bakr, Imām al-Ḥaramayn, and the majority of the Muʿtazila (*ǧumhūr al-muʿtazila*).
> [§1.2] Aš-Šāfiʿī and al-Ašʿarī [...] and most of those legal scholars who belong to us are, on the contrary, of the opinion that it does signify [*this, i.e. the negation of the legal ruling for sheep that do not graze freely*].
> [§2] For us there are [*the following*] aspects [*to consider*]:
> [1.] The first is:
> [*Antecendent*] If speech (*ḫiṭāb*), which is qualified by an attribute, were to signify that which is excluded from it and opposed to it, it would have to signify it either
> [1.1] by its linguistic expression (*bi-lafẓihī*) or
> [1.2] by its meaning (*bi-maʿnāhu*).
> [*Consequent*] However, it does not signify it in either of these two ways; so it follows necessarily that it does not signify it at all.
> [§2.1.1] [*ad* 1.1] We only say that it [*i.e. the speech*] does not signify [*the negation*] by its linguistic expression, because the linguistic expression

57 Al-Ġazālī, *al-Mustaṣfā*, vol. 3, p. 432, lines 14ff. On the debate between the supporters of analogy who reject the *argumentum e contrario* and those who favor it, see Zysow, *The Economy of Certainty*, pp. 103ff. Zysow sees the cause of the Ḥanafite rejection of the *argumentum e contrario* in their "unrelenting attachment to analogy."

58 See Chapter 4, Section 2.2.2.

59 Faḫr ad-dīn ar-Rāzī, *al-Maḥṣūl*, vol. 2, p. 136, line 3.

> signifies the existence of the legal ruling in one of the two categories [*i.e. with regard to commandment or prohibition*]:
> [1.1.1] If the negation of the legal ruling in the second category has not been based on it [*i.e. the linguistic expression*] together [*with the affirmation of the legal ruling*], then this is not a literal signification (*dalāla lafẓiyya*) [*for the negation*].
> [1.1.2] If this [*the negation of the legal ruling*] has been based on it [*i.e. the linguistic expression*], then that linguistic expression is taken as a basis for the entire existence of the legal ruling in one of the two categories and negates the other category [*i.e. the existence of a commandment for this very case negates the prohibition*]. There is no conflict that, for example, such a linguistic expression [*upon which negation has been based*] signifies negation.
> [§ 2.1.2] [*ad* 1.2] The explanation (*bayān*) for why it [*i.e. the speech*] does not signify [*negation*] by its meaning is that the signification by means of the meaning (*dalāla maʿnawiyya*) is such that what is named makes something necessary, so that the mind turns from what is named to that which adheres to it [*i.e. what is named*].[60]

Faḫr ad-dīn's answer to the question of whether a statement qualified by an attribute and signifying a legal ruling also signifies the opposite legal ruling in the absence of the qualifying circumstance is now clearly that it does not.[61] According to his argumentation, in which he follows Abū l-Ḥusayn al-Baṣrī,[62] the contrary legal ruling would have to be indicated either by the wording itself or else by the meaning of the wording. According to Faḫr ad-dīn, neither the wording nor the meaning signified in any way an opposite legal ruling for the other circumstance, so there is no relationship of signification at all; and the

60 Ibid., line 5–p. 137, line 14.

61 The situation is different in the *Maʿālim*, where it is stated that this manner of signification can occur in general language usage (*ʿurf ʿāmm*), see Faḫr ad-dīn ar-Rāzī, *al-Maʿālim fī uṣūl al-fiqh*, pp. 29–30; with regard to the different nuances of Faḫr ad-dīns' positions, cf. al-Isnawī, *Nihāyat as-sūl*, vol. 2, p. 209, lines 10–11. For the present debate in connection with the Tripartition of Signification, it is not the argumentation in the *Maʿālim* but that in the *Maḥṣūl* that is relevant and influential, especially since only it is based on the legally relevant rulings and goes beyond the question of the understanding of proverbs and idiomatic expressions—hence it is the subject of investigation here.

62 Cf. al-Baṣrī, *Kitāb al-Muʿtamad*, vol. 1, p. 162, lines 5–7; cf. also al-Bāqillānī, *at-Taqrīb*, vol. 2, p. 199, lines 19f. and the wording of al-Ġazālī, *al-Mustaṣfā*, vol. 1, p. 273; on this debate, which in the *uṣūl al-fiqh* works occurs mainly in the chapter on commandment (*amr*), see Weiss, *The Search*, pp. 371–373.

existence of the legal ruling in one of two circumstances does not in any way imply a legal ruling for the opposite circumstance[63]—if an oppositional relationship can even be assumed at all.[64]

Faḫr ad-dīn emphasizes [*ad* § 2.1.1] that the statement does, however, signify the opposite legal ruling—corresponding to the opposition of positive commandment (*amr*) and negative commandment (*nahy*)—for the same circumstance, and that this question is not at all at issue in the dispute about the *argumentum e contrario*: A certain positive commandment may well signify in a literal way the fact that there is no negative commandment for the same circumstance.[65]

While a statement can also signify the opposite legal ruling for the same circumstance by means of implication because "what is named makes something necessary, so that the mind turns from what is named to that which adheres to it [*i.e. what is named*]," [*ad* § 2.1.2] this manner of signification is excluded when it comes to signifying the opposite legal ruling of the other of two circumstances. In other words, a positive command applying to a specific circumstance neither means nor even implies that the corresponding negative command applies to the opposite circumstance.[66]

This means that Faḫr ad-dīn sees no form of implication in the case of the *argumentum e contrario*. He thus refutes the kind implication (*luzūm/iltizām*) that proponents saw as operating in such cases when they assumed that the omission of the applicability of the attribute is followed by the omission of

63 Faḫr ad-dīn ar-Rāzī, *al-Maḥṣūl*, vol. 2, p. 141, lines 8–9. This conclusion corresponds to the *modus tollendo tollens*: if *p*, then *q*; not *q*, therefore not *p*, cf. William Kneale and Martha Kneale, *The Development of Logic* (Oxford: Clarendon Press, 1962 [reprint 2008]), p. 163 and pp. 219–220.

64 In the case of sheep, the two specifications "free-grazing/stall-fed" are understood as oppositional, even if they are merely linguistically contrary and do not actually exclude a third option, cf. al-Isnawī, *Nihāyat as-sūl*, vol. 2, p. 208, line 10.

65 On the transmission of *amr* and *nahy* with "positive" and "negative commandment" and the relationship of these two categories to the five legal rulings, see Weiss, *The Search*, pp. 326 f., see also Harald Löschner, *Die dogmatischen Grundlagen des šīʿitischen Rechts: Eine Untersuchung zur modernen imāmitischen Rechtsquellenlehre* (Cologne [et al.]: Carl Heymanns Verlag, 1971), pp. 49 ff.

66 This topic, which had not been discussed in direct connection with the *argumentum e contrario* in earlier texts, will not be discussed in any further detail here. A detailed presentation can be found in al-Bāqillānī, who also makes the distinction made by Abū l-Ḥusayn al-Baṣrī and Faḫr ad-dīn ar-Rāzī in this context, cf. al-Bāqillānī, *at-Taqrīb*, vol. 2, p. 198 ff.

the applicability of the legal ruling.[67] Faḫr ad-dīn takes the position "that the existence of a legal ruling in one of two circumstances is not followed by a legal ruling on the other circumstance—either affirmatively or negatively";[68] whether two circumstances are related to each other must first be determined and cannot be postulated in a general way. It must first be examined on a case-by-case basis whether a particular attribute actually represents the *ratio legis* for the legal ruling. As has already been explained, it may turn out that this is indeed the case and the legal ruling can be negated. However, it may also turn out that the cause is not to be found in the attribute and therefore, even if the attribute in question is not present, it can be concluded by means of analogy that the same legal ruling is required as in the original case.

It can be noted that Faḫr ad-dīn—after the case of the legal-theoretical implication type *mafhūm al-muwāfaqa*—again classifies as a type of implication (*iltizām*) a hermeneutical position that he himself does not hold, or at least he mentions it in his schema without evaluation. In contrast to the previous case, he this time espouses a critical view of the methodology itself—not just its classification and naming. Due to this critical stance that he takes towards the *argumentum e contrario*, and due to the fact that Faḫr ad-dīn argues elsewhere against the *argumentum e contrario* as a type of implication, Tāǧ ad-dīn al-Urmawī reformulates the argument cited above in his commentary on the *Maḥṣūl*:

> [*ad* § 2] [1.] If [*the legal ruling on that speech* (ḫiṭāb) *which is qualified by an attribute*] were to signify the inapplicability of the legal ruling for the other attribute, it would either signify it
> [1.1] by congruence (*bi-l-muṭābaqa*)—and this is incorrect because the absence of the legal ruling for one of two attributes is not the same as the presence [*of the legal ruling*] for the other [*attribute*];
> [1.2] or by implication (*bi-l-iltizām*)—and this is also incorrect—due to the fact that the presence [*of the legal ruling*] for one of two attributes does not necessitate the omission [*of the legal ruling*] for the other [*attribute*].[69]

67 Cf. Faḫr ad-dīn ar-Rāzī, *al-Maḥṣūl*, vol. 2, p. 144, lines 11–14, who quotes the proponents here.

68 Ibid., p. 141, lines 8–9.

69 Tāǧ ad-dīn al-Urmawī, *al-Ḥāṣil min al-Maḥṣūl fī uṣūl al-fiqh*, vol. 2, p. 239, line 4–p. 240, line 3.

In his summary of the first argument, Tāǧ ad-dīn al-Urmawī replaces Faḫr ad-dīn's formulation "[1.1] by its linguistic expression (*bi-lafẓihī*)" with signification by congruence and the formulation "[1.2] by its meaning (*bi-maʿnāhu*)" with the manner of signification of implication. On the one hand, this reformulation suggests itself readily because Faḫr ad-dīn chooses the same formulations in the description of 1.1 and 1.2 as in the description of these two manners of signification: In the case of literal signification or signification by congruence, the linguistic expression is based on a meaning (*mawḍūʿ*), whereas in the case of signification by meaning or by implication, "the mind turns from what is named to that which adheres to it [*i.e. what is named*]." On the other hand, Faḫr ad-dīn himself states elsewhere in his *Maḥṣūl* that signification by meaning is a *dalāla iltizāmiyya*.[70]

As will be shown, this line of reasoning would continue to be used in the coming generations with this wording—and with the addition of the manner of signification of inclusion (*taḍammun*)—as an argument by the opponents of the *argumentum e conrario*. However, the positions of the legal schools on this question would shift. This became a Ḥanafite argument against the position of the Šāfiʿites, who had in turn turned against it.

1.2 *Summary*

This chapter identified and outlined the various legal-theoretical types of implication that Faḫr ad-dīn counted under *iltizām* in his *Maḥṣūl*, our source text.

It shows, firstly, that Faḫr ad-dīn includes all the types of implication that we also find elaborated upon by al-Ġazālī and which correspond to the classical Šāfiʿite scheme—all except one (namely the implication of that which elicits the legal judgement: *taʿlīl/īmāʾ wa-išāra/tanbīh wa-l-īmāʾ*), which he treats separately in the chapter on *qiyās*, in the context of tracing the *ratio legis* (*ʿilla*).[71]

In the following table, these types of implication are compared with the legal-theoretical types of implication as presented in al-Ġazālī's *Mustaṣfā*:

70 Faḫr ad-dīn ar-Rāzī, *al-Maḥṣūl*, vol. 1, pp. 409–410, esp. p. 410, line 6.

71 See Faḫr ad-dīn ar-Rāzī, *al-Maḥṣūl*, vol. 5, pp. 143 ff. For details on the methodology, see Ahmad Hasan, "Finding the Cause of a Legal Injunction in Islamic Jurisprudence," *Islamic Studies*, vol. 25, no. 1 (1986): pp. 15 ff.

TABLE 7 The legal-theoretical types of implication in Faḫr ad-dīn ar-Rāzī's MAḤṢŪL and al-Ġazālī's MUSTAṢFĀ

Faḫr ad-dīn ar-Rāzī: *al-Maḥṣūl*, vol. 1, p. 232, line 9–p. 234, last line	**Al-Ġazālī: *al-Mustaṣfā*, vol. 3, pp. 402–434**
Signification by implication (*dalālat al-iltizām*)	Al-Ġazālī's categorization of these hermeneutical techniques can be found in his chapter "On that which is taken from linguistic expressions not in terms of their (external) form (*ṣīġa*), but in terms of their import (*faḥwā*) and their allusion (*išāra*)" This includes five types:
The ellipsis (*iḍmār*) of a simple linguistic expression is assumed to be the condition (*šarṭ*) for understanding a sentence: [1.3.1] Signification by requirement (*dalālat al-iqtiḍā'*) [1.3.1.1] Implication is inferred based on reasoning [*Example: "Error* (ḫaṭa') *and forgetfulness* (nisyān) *have been removed from my* umma*"*] [1.3.1.2] Implication is legally derived [corresponds to 1.2 in al-Ġazālī] [*Example: manumission of the slave*]	[1.] Signification by requirement (*iqtiḍā'*) [1.1] To preserve the credibility of the speaker (*ṣidq al-mutakallim*), an ellipsis must be assumed [*Example: "There is no fasting"*] [1.2] In order to understand the sentence as meaningful, an implied legal ruling must be assumed [*Example: manumission of the slave*] [1.3] In order to consider the sentence meaningful, an ellipsis must be assumed, which is derived on the basis of reasoning [*Examples: e.g. "Ask the village"/"Forbidden to you are your mothers"*]
[1.3.2.2.1] Unintended consequence of a compound linguistic expression [*Example: nights of Ramaḍān*] [*No technical term is used.*]	[2.] *Allusion* (*išāra*) [*Example: e.g. nights of Ramaḍān*] [*Al-Ġazālī also calls the meaning implied here an unintended consequence, cf. al-Ġazālī*: al-Mustaṣfā, *vol. 3*, p. *406*, lines *5–6*]

TABLE 7 The legal-theoretical implications (*cont.*)

Faḫr ad-dīn ar-Rāzī: *al-Maḥṣūl*, vol. 1, p. 232, line 9–p. 234, last line	**Al-Ġazālī: *al-Mustaṣfā*, vol. 3, pp. 402–434**
– [*īmāʾ* is mentioned by Faḫr ad-dīn in the *qiyās* chapter as one of the ways of comprehending the *ratio legis*]	[3.] The implication of the *ratio legis* (*ʿilla*) with the technical terms *taʿlīl* ("causation") and *īmāʾ wa-išāra* ("indication/sign and allusion")
[1.3.2.1] Consequence of a compound linguistic expression in which the intended meaning is taken further [Example: *argumentum a minori ad maius* (*at-tanbīh bi-l-adnā ʿalā l-aʿlā*)] [*No technical term is used.*]	[4.] Indication by context (*siyāq*) and intention (*maqṣūd*) [Various technical terms: congruent implication (*mafhūm al-muwāfaqa*)/ 'import of the linguistic expression' (*faḥwā l-lafẓ*)]
[1.3.2.2.2] *Argumentum e contrario* [*Not provided with a name, example, or assessment of its permissibility*]	[5.] *Argumentum e contrario* (*mafhūm* or *mafhūm al-muḫālafa*) [*Not permissible*]

Secondly, the high degree of systematization in Faḫr ad-dīn's description is striking: He does not content himself with simply listing the types of implication. Instead he brings them into a relationship with each other that partly contradicts previous understandings of them. And he works out, or at least systematically groups, the patterns and principles underlying these techniques.

Based on the distinction between simple and compound linguistic expressions, the types of implication are differentiated according to whether they represent the condition for an intelligible meaning or follow from the understood meaning as a consequence. This shows that *mafhūm al-muwāfaqa* and *mafhūm al-muḫālafa* are not contrasted with each other as positive and negative implication, but instead 'allusion' (*išāra*) is contrasted with the implication type of *mafhūm al-muḫālafa* as a positive type of implication, because in both cases—in contrast to the *a fortiori* argument *mafhūm al-muwāfaqa*—the implied meanings do not correspond to the intended meaning.

Thirdly, it can be stated that *iltizām* takes over the role of *mafhūm* as a generic term for legal-theoretical types of implication—even if Faḫr ad-dīn himself does not acknowledge the respective manner of signification to be a type of implication (as in the case of *mafhūm al-muwāfaqa*), or if he questions whether

FIGURE 21 Outline of the Legal-Theoretical Types of Implication in Faḫr ad-dīn's MAḤṢŪL

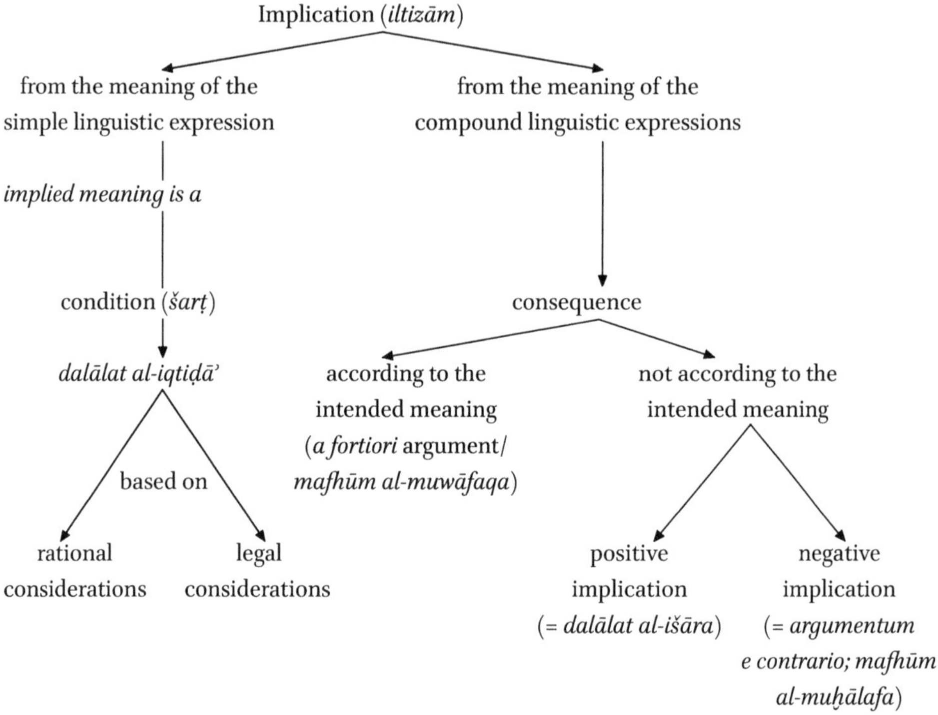

it is even valid legal methodology at all (as in the case of *mafhūm al-muḫālafa*). This means that the signification relationships now categorized under *iltizām* remain types of implication and are opposed to the category *muṭābaqa/manṭūq*.[72]

2 The Adaptation and Further Development of the Tripartition of Signification in Post-Rāzian *uṣūl al-fiqh* Works

Having shown how Faḫr ad-dīn links the concept of *iltizām*, derived from the field of logic, with the legal-theoretical types of implication, we will now examine on the one hand how this synthesis was received in the *uṣūl al-fiqh* works, and on the other hand how the Tripartition of Signification was treated in the general introductory chapters of these works. It is in these two sections of the *uṣūl al-fiqh* works—their comments on the synthesis and on the Tripartition

72 For *muṭābaqa/manṭūq*, see Chapter 3, Section 2.

itself—where a canonical treatment of the Tripartition of Signification can be discerned.

In order to gain an impression of the development of the historical reception of the Tripartition in Islamic legal methodology, I will give a brief, by no means exhaustive overview of the various influential and much commented upon texts. The selection of these texts largely corresponds to Ibn Ḫaldūn's brief overview of *uṣūl al-fiqh* works that are significant with regard to reception history[73]—supplemented by later works from the period after Ibn Ḫaldūn; i.e, the following works in particular: (1.) the work *al-Iḥkām fī uṣūl al-aḥkām* by the Šāfiʿite Sayf ad-dīn al-Āmidī (d. 631/1233) as well as his work *al-Muntahā*; (2.) the writings of the Mālikite Šihāb ad-dīn al-Qarāfī (d. 684/1285) that engage with Faḫr ad-dīn's *Maḥṣūl*, i.e. the *Nafāʾis al-uṣūl fī šarḥ al-Maḥṣūl*, *Šarḥ Tanqīḥ al-fuṣūl fī iḫtiṣār al-Maḥṣūl fī l-uṣūl*, and *Muḫtaṣar at-Tanqīḥ al-fuṣūl fī l-uṣūl*;[74] (3.) the work *Minhāǧ al-wuṣūl ilā ʿilm al-uṣūl* by the Šāfiʿite ʿAbdallāh b. ʿUmar al-Bayḍāwī (d. 685/1286)[75]—this work and the *Šarḥ at-Tanqīḥ* are, as Ibn Ḫaldūn confirms, two much commented upon compendia that have played a central role in the doctrinal tradition for centuries;[76] (4.) furthermore the likewise much commented upon work the *Muḫtaṣar al-Muntahā* by the Mālikite Ibn al-Ḥāǧib (d. 646/1249), which is an abridged version of his *Muntahā al-wuṣūl wa-l-amal fī ʿilmay al-uṣūl wa-l-ǧadal*, a summary of Āmidī's *Iḥkām*;[77] and (5.) the

---

73 Ibn Ḫaldūn, *al-Muqaddima*, vol. 3, p. 22, line 6–p. 23, line 12.

74 Al-Qarāfī, *Šarḥ Tanqīḥ al-fuṣūl*; id., *Muḫtaṣar at-Tanqīḥ al-fuṣūl fī l-uṣūl*, ed. by Aḥmad Muḥammad Walīd an-Naššār (Damascus: Dār al-farfūr, 2007 [1428]). On this scholar in general, see in particular Jackson, *Islamic Law and the State*, pp. 1–32 and pp. 7–8 on the relationship of these writings to the *Maḥṣūl*: "[…] it is clear that he had a genuine admiration for al-Rāzī. In fact, he repeatedly refers to the latter as 'al-Imām,' so much so that he has to alert his reader on occasion that he is using this title to refer to Mālik! This attachment to al-Rāzī may appear at first blush a tad anomalous. But this may be a result of our failure to appreciate the significance of al-Rāzī in later, i.e. post 7th/13th century, *uṣūl al-fiqh* overall."

75 This is the date of death given by as-Suyūṭī, see Ǧalāl ad-dīn as-Suyūṭī, *Kitāb Buġyat al-wuʿāt*, ed. by Muḥammad Amīn Ḫānǧī and Aḥmad ibn al-Amīn Šinqīṭī (Cairo: Maṭbaʿat as-Saʿāda, 1908 [1326]), vol. 1, p. 286, line 5; on the controversy surrounding al-Bayḍāwī's date of death, see J. Robson, "al-Bayḍāwī," EI2 and as-Suyūṭī, *Kitāb Buġyat al-wuʿāt*, vol. 1, p. 286, line 6, see also Walid Saleh, "al-Bayḍāwī," EI3.

76 Ibn Ḫaldūn, *al-Muqaddima*, vol. 3, p. 22, line 17; cf. (in relation to al-Baḍāwī's *Minhāǧ*) Monique C. Cardinal, "Islamic Legal Theory Curriculum: Are the Classics Taught Today?," *Islamic Law and Society*, vol. 12, no. 2 (2005): pp. 241 f. and (in relation to al-Qarāfī) Jackson, *Islamic Law and the State*, pp. 3–4.

77 Cf. Ibn Ḫaldūn, *al-Muqaddima*, vol. 3, pp. 22, lines 18–20, who refers to the summary of Āmidī's *Iḥkām* as *al-Muḫtaṣar al-kabīr*; see also Jackson, *Islamic Law and the State*, p. 8, fn. 49.

Kitāb al-Badīʿ by the Ḥanafite Aḥmad b. ʿAlī Ibn as-Sāʿātī (d. 694/1295), which, according to Ibn Ḫaldūn, is a compilation of Āmidi's *Iḥkām* and Bazdawī's (d. 482/1089) *uṣūl al-fiqh* work the *Kanz al-wuṣūl*.[78] In addition to the works mentioned by Ibn Ḫaldūn, some of the commentaries on the *Muḫtaṣar* and the *Minhāǧ* as well as the much later Ḥanafite legal work the *Musallam aṯ-ṯubūt* by Muḥibb Allāh al-Bihārī (d. 1119/1707)[79] and the associated commentary *Fawātiḥ ar-raḥmūt bi-šarḥ Musallam aṯ-ṯubūt* by Niẓām ad-dīn al-Anṣārī al-Laknawī (d. 1225/1810) are also taken into account in the investigation of the kinds of implication in Chapter 4, Section 2.2. The last two deal critically and meaningfully with the lines of tradition going back to Ibn al-Ḥāǧib's *Muḫtaṣar* and al-Bayḍāwī's *Minhāǧ*; in them, the course of the further development of the Tripartition of Signification—especially with regard to the questioning of the legitimacy of the *argumentum e contrario*—can be clearly traced.

2.1 *Remarks on the History of Reception*

As has already been shown,[80] Faḫr ad-dīn raises the three-part categorization of *muṭābaqa*, *taḍammun*, and *iltizām* to a more fundamental status, which exceeds the function it had under Ibn Sīnā where it specified the mutual relationships of signification of the predicables. In fact, this function of the Tripartition is retained at a specific level, but two additional functions are added to it: On the one hand, the Tripartition of Signification is set parallel to the classification of linguistic expressions into name (*ism*), verb (*fiʿl*), and particle (*ḥarf*) as a fundamental, general principle of linguistic classification. On the other hand, the Tripartition is used as the starting point for further categorizations, whereby the classification into *ism*, *fiʿl*, and *ḥarf* is subsumed under the congruent linguistic expression.

---

78 Ibn Ḫaldūn, *al-Muqaddima*, vol. 3, p. 23, lines 6–8; on this scholar, see Robert Brunschvig, "*Théorie générale de la capacité chez les Hanafites médiévaux*," *Revue Internationale des Droits de l'Antiquité*, vol. 1,2 (1949): pp. 157–172, on the distinction between Faḫr ad-dīn al-Bazdawī, the author of the *Kanz al-wuṣūl* (usually referred to with the title *Uṣūl al-Bazdawī*), and his brother Ṣadr al-Islām Abū l-Yusr Muḥammad b. Muḥammad b. al-Ḥusayn b. ʿAbd al-Karīm al-Bazdawī, see Marie Bernand and Éric Chaumont, introduction to *Al-Bazdawī: Livre où repose la connaissance des preuves légales*, ed. by Marie Bernand and Éric Chaumont (Cairo: Institut français d'archéologie orientale, 2003), pp. 5–11, here: p. 5.

79 On this scholar, see (in addition to the *EI*² article by A.S. Bazmee Ansari) Asad Q. Ahmed's article "The *Sullam al-ʿulūm* of (d. 1707) Muḥibballāh al-Bihārī," in *The Oxford Handbook of Islamic Philosophy*, ed. by Khaled El-Rouayheb and Sabine Schmidtke (Oxford: Oxford University Press, 2017), pp. 488–508.

80 See Chapter 2, Section 3.1.

At this point, I will give a cursory overview of whether and how the Tripartition of Signification is treated in the chapters on language theory of those legal-theoretical compendia that are significant for its further history of reception.

2.1.1 Classificatory Principle of Linguistic Expressions or Basic Linguistic Principle?

2.1.1.1 *The Writings of al-Āmidī and Ibn al-Ḥāǧib*

Both al-Āmidī's *Iḥkām fī uṣūl al-aḥkām* and his own summary of the *Iḥkām*, the *Muntahā as-sūl fī ʿilm al-uṣūl*, contain an overview of the three-part classification of signification already at the beginning of their treatises on the fundamentals of language, together with the further categorizations that are subsumed under this classification by Faḫr ad-dīn:

> [§ 1] We say: The linguistic expression has either [1.] not been imposed for a meaning—and then it is unusual (*muhmal*). Or [2.] it has been imposed for a meaning. Then it signifies either [2.1] the whole [*meaning*] for which it has been imposed—this signification is called signification by congruence (*dalālat al-muṭābaqa*), like the linguistic term 'man' for 'rational being'; or [2.2] [*it signifies*] a part [*of the meaning*] [...] and is called signification by containment (*dalālat at-taḍammun*); or [2.3] [*it signifies*] an external thing and is called signification by implication (*dalālat al-iltizām*) [...].
> [§ 2] The first two significations are literal (*lafẓiyya*) [*significations*], the third is a mental (*ḏihniyya*) [*signification*] [...].
> [§ 3] The linguistic expression is either simple (*mufrad*)—that is the one of which no part signifies anything—like [*the simple linguistic expression*] 'man'; or [*it is*] compound (*murakkab*)—that is the one of which one part signifies the part of its meaning, like 'man is an animal.'
> [§ 4] The simple is either suitable for forming a nominal statement (*qaḍiyya ḫabariyya*) from its genus—this is the name (*ism*), or it is not suitable, [...] this is the verb (*fiʿl*) or [...] the particle (*ḥarf*).[81]

As already explained in Chapter 2, Section 3.2.1, Sayf ad-dīn al-Āmidī further develops Faḫr ad-dīn's complex distinction between *dalāla waḍʿiyya* and *dalāla ʿaqliyya,* which is related to the question of the immediacy or mediacy of the manners of signification, and comes to a different conclusion both with regard

81 Al-Āmidī, *Muntahā*, p. 10, lines 4–12.

to terminology and content. Faḫr ad-dīn had regarded congruent signification as a signification based on imposition (*dalāla waḍʿiyya*) and *taḍammun* and *iltizām* as significations based on reasoning (*dalāla ʿaqliyya*). Al-Āmidī, on the other hand—basing himself on the terminology of ʿUmar b. Sahlān as-Sāwī (fl. 540/1145)—considers the signification of congruence and containment as literal signification and implication as non-literal signification (*dalāla ġayr lafẓiyya*) or as mental (*ḏihnī*) signification.[82] Al-Āmidī bases this classification—which is opposed to both Faḫr ad-dīn's classification before him and the one that would be established after him[83]—on one of Ibn Sīnā's comments on the Tripartition of Signification: "Signification by congruence and signification by containment have in common that neither of them is a signification for something outside of the [*signified*] thing."[84] Faḫr ad-dīn had based his own categorization on Ibn Sīnā's second note, according to which containment and implication have in common "that each of them requires the first signification [*i.e. signification by congruence*]."[85] Al-Āmidī's classification results in the epistemological valorization of *taḍammun*.

As for the way in which the Tripartition of Signification is presented, it can be seen that Sayf ad-dīn al-Āmidī focuses on the second function of the Tripartition as the structuring principle for the other subsequent classifications.[86]

At this general introductory level, al-Āmidi's adaptation of the Tripartition of Signification makes perfect sense. It remains to be seen whether it works well when applied to the more specific use of the Tripartition in al-Āmidī's writings in the context of the types of implication.[87]

The introductory chapter of Ibn al-Ḥāǧadal's *Muḫtaṣar al-Muntahā fī s-sūl wa-l-amal fī ʿilmay al-uṣūl wa-l-ǧadal*, a much commented upon work that takes influence from al-Āmidī, also represents a reception of the Tripartition of Signification that goes beyond the simple mention of the Tripartition as such:[88]

---

82 See Chapter 2, Section 3.2.1.

83 Namely, the classification according to which all three significations are regarded as imposed linguistic significations (*ad-dalāla al-lafẓiyya al-waḍʿiyya*), see Chapter 2, Section 3.2.1.

84 Ibn Sīnā, *Manṭiq al-Mašriqiyyīn*, p. 15, lines 3–4.

85 Ibid., lines 5–6.

86 See Chapter 2, Section 3.2.1.

87 See Chapter 4, Section 2.2.1.

88 On the significance and commentary tradition of this work, see Kātib Çelebī, *Kašf aẓ-ẓunūn*, vol. 2, pp. 1615–1616; see also Stewart, *Islamic Legal Orthodoxy*, pp. 97 ff., see also Josef van Ess, *Die Träume der Schulweisheit. Leben und Werk des ʿAlī b. Muḥammad al-Ǧurǧānī (d. 816/1413)* (Wiesbaden: Harrassowitz Verlag, 2013), p. 64. It should be noted that

> [§1] To the goodness of God (*min luṭfi Llāh*) belongs the creation of the linguistic impositions/fundamentals (*iḥdāṯu l-mawḍūʿāti l-luġawiyya*). So let us talk about their definition and categorization. We will begin with their imposition and the method of recognizing them [*i.e. the linguistic impositions/fundamentals*].
> 1. [*Definition*] Each linguistic expression was imposed for a meaning.
> 2. Their categories: [2.1] simple and [2.2] compound.
> [*ad* 2.1] The simple is a linguistic expression [*consisting of*] a single word (*bi-kalimatin wāḥidatin*). It is said [*namely by the logicians, see the* Kitāb al-Muntahā[89]] that it is that which is imposed for a meaning, whereby no part of it signifies within it.
> [*ad* 2.2] In the compound [*linguistic expression*] there are two [*signifying parts*] […].
> [*ad* 2.1] The simple [*linguistic expression*] is divided into *ism*, *fiʿl*, and *ḥarf*, and its literal signification (*dalālatuhu l-lafẓiyyatu*) is signfication by congruence in relation to its complete meaning (*fī kamāli maʿnāhā*), [*or*] signification by containment in relation to a part [*of the meaning*]; the non-literal (*ġayr lafẓiyya*) [*signification*] is implication, which is said [*to be the case only*] if (*iḏā*) it is a mental [*implication*].[90]

Compared to al-Āmidī's *Muntahā*, there is a different emphasis here in the presentation of the linguistic fundamentals. Ibn al-Ḥāǧib uses the Tripartition not in its second, but rather in its first function: The classifications *ism/fiʿl/ḥarf* on the one hand and *muṭābaqa/taḍammun/iltizām* on the other are considered, as they are in Faḫr ad-dīn's *Šarḥ al-Išārāt*, as two sides of the simple linguistic expression that behave parallel to one other.

On the other hand, Ibn al-Ḥāǧib's assignment of congruence and containment to the literal manner of signification and of implication to the non-literal manner is taken over from al-Āmidī.

2.1.1.2 *Al-Bayḍāwī's* Minhāǧ al-wuṣūl ilā ʿilm al-uṣūl

This work, which according to Ibn Ḫaldūn came about as an extract from the *Maḥṣūl* commentaries *at-Taḥṣīl min al-Maḥṣūl* by Sirāǧ ad-dīn al-Urmawī and *al-Ḥāṣil min al-Maḥṣūl fī uṣūl al-fiqh* by Tāǧ ad-dīn al-Urmawī, begins, after its

---

Ibn al-Ḥaǧib wrote an introduction to scientific theory and logic, which is in part strongly oriented toward the wording of the *Maḥṣūl*, cf. e.g. Ibn al-Ḥāǧib, *Muḫtaṣar al-muntahā*, p. 209.

89 Ibn al-Ḥāǧib, *Muntahā al-wuṣūl*, p. 16, last line.

90 Id., *Muḫtaṣar al-muntahā*, pp. 220–221.

introductory section, with a brief introduction to linguistic theory. It lists the Tripartition of Signification in its second chapter entitled "The Categories of the Linguistic Expression" (*aqsām al-lafẓ*):

> On the categorization (*taqsīm*) of linguistic expressions (*alfāẓ*): If the linguistic expression signifies the entirety (*tamām*) of that which is named by it (*musammāhu*), that is congruence; [*if it signifies*] a part of it, that is containment; [*if it signifies*] that which is mentally adhered to it [*i.e. what is named by the linguistic expression*], that is implication.
>
> If a part of the linguistic expression signifies a part of the meaning, then it is compound (*murakkab*); if not, then it is simple (*mufrad*).
>
> The simple [*linguistic expression*] is either such that it does not possess its meaning independently—and this is the particle (*ḥarf*); or it possesses it independently—and these are the verb (*fiʿl*) […] [*and*] the name (*ism*).[91]

In this presentation—as in al-Āmidī's *Muntahā* and in contrast to Ibn al-Ḥāğib's *Muḫtaṣar*—we find the second function, according to which the Tripartition is used as a structuring principle, subsuming under it the classifications that follow it (such as *mufrad/murakkab*, *ism/fiʿl/ḥarf*, and *kullī/ǧuzʾī*). This is followed by the grammatical-theoretical classification and a brief outline of the classification from the perspective of logic and legal theory, in which a distinction is made between polyonymy, heteronymy, Aristotelian synonymy, and homonymy as well as between the legal-theoretical technical terms *muǧmal*, *ẓāhir*, *muʾawwal*, etc.[92]

2.1.2 Šihāb ad-dīn al-Qarāfī: Fundamental Questions about Signification from the Perspective of Communication Theory

The well-received scholar Šihāb ad-dīn al-Qarāfī, also cited by Ibn Ḫaldūn, deals intensively with the Tripartition of Signification in several of his writings on legal theory—in his *Nafāʾis al-uṣūl fī šarḥ al-Maḥṣūl*, the commentary on this complex of topics alone comprises 59 pages in the Beirut edition, linking topics from various disciplines.[93] A brief sampling of these topics can then also be found in his other works, such as his *Šarḥ Tanqīḥ al-fuṣūl fī iḫtiṣār al-Maḥṣūl fī l-uṣūl*, a commentary on his own work intended as an aid for those

---

91 Al-Bayḍāwī, *Minhāǧ*, p. 56, lines 12–15.

92 Ibid., line 14–p. 57, line 4; on the grammatical-theoretical classification in Faḫr ad-dīn, see Chapter 3, Section 1 and for the logical and legal-theoretical one, see Chapter 3, Section 2.

93 Al-Qarāfī, *Nafāʾis al-uṣūl*, vol. 1, pp. 253–312.

struggling to comprehend his *Tanqīḥ*.[94] The *Tanqīḥ* is a work that is in turn an extract, namely of the *Maḥṣūl* commentaries of the two Urmawīs, i.e. Sirāǧ ad-dīn al-Urmawī's *at-Taḥṣīl min al-Maḥṣūl* and Tāǧ ad-dīn al-Urmawī's *al-Ḥāṣil min al-Maḥṣūl fī uṣūl al-fiqh*.[95]

After a chapter on logic modeled in terms of structure and references, though not in terms of length, on the *Mustaṣfā*'s introduction to logic,[96] the *Šarḥ Tanqīḥ al-fuṣūl* contains an extensive passage on the Tripartition of Signification, beginning as follows:

> On signification and its categories.
> [§1] Singification of the linguistic expression (*dalālatu l-lafẓ*) is when the listener (*sāmiʿ*) understands from the speech (*kalām*) of the speaker (*mutakallim*) the complete named thing (*kamāl al-musammā*) or a part of it or what follows from it.
> Ibn Sīnā states that there are two views (*maḏhabān*) on this:
> 1. The first of the two is this one [*already mentioned above*].
> 2. According to the second, it [*i.e. signification*] is such that the linguistic expression, whenever it is uttered (*iḏā uṭliqa*), signifies.[97]

Šihāb ad-dīn introduces the commentary on Faḫr ad-dīn's discussion of the Tripartition with a reference to Ibn Sīnā and the fundamental question of the bearer of the signification. The question, as posed by Šihāb ad-dīn, focuses on the process of signification including its actors: Does the linguistic expression exist as such or do the human actors of the communication process stand at the center of the signification process? What does it mean to say "the signification of a linguistic expression" (*dalālatu l-lafẓ*)?

The passage in Ibn Sīnā's *Kitāb aš-Šifāʾ* referred to here reads:

> This [*i.e. the fact that Ibn Sīnā considers a certain addition to the definition of the simple linguistic expression to be superfluous*] is because a linguistic expression does not *per se* signify anything (*anna l-lafẓa bi-nafsihī lā yadullu l-battata*). If this were not so, then every linguistic expression

94 Id., *Šarḥ Tanqīḥ al-fuṣūl*, p. 10, lines 4–11.

95 Ibn Ḫaldūn, *al-Muqaddima*, vol. 3, p. 22, lines 14–16.

96 Al-Qarāfī, *Šarḥ Tanqīḥ*, pp. 11–20.

97 Ibid., p. 25, lines 22–25. On this discussion, see also al-Iṣfahānī, *al-Kāšif ʿan al-Maḥṣūl*, vol. 2, p. 3 as well as Badr ad-dīn Muḥammad az-Zarkašī, *al-Baḥr al-Muḥīṭ fīṣūl al-fiqh*, ed. by ʿAbd al-Qādir ʿAbd Allāh ʿĀnī (Kuwait: Wizārat al-awqāf wa-š-šuʾūn al-Islāmiyya, 1992), vol. 2, pp. 36 ff.

> would have an incontrovertible claim to the meaning. Instead, it [*i.e. the linguistic expression*] signifies only by the will of the speaker (*al-lāfiẓ*), just as the speaker can use it [*i.e. the linguistic expression*] to signify a particular meaning, like how [*he uses the expression*] *ʿayn* for a spring (*yanbūʿ al-māʾ*), such that this is its signification; and how he may thereafter use it to signify another meaning, such as [*the expression*] *ʿayn* for *dīnār*, such that this is its signification.
>
> In the same way, if he [*i.e. the speaker*], in using it [*i.e. the linguistic expression*], were to rid it of its signification, it would not signify at all.
>
> In the opinion of many theorists, this [*i.e. the non-signifying sound*] is not a linguistic expression; for a letter (*ḥarf*) or a sound (*ṣawt*)—as I think—is, according to the agreement of the opinion of many logicians (*bi-ḥasabi t-taʿāruf*), not a linguistic expression if it does not contain a signification (*aw yaštamilu ʿalā dalālatin*).[98]

In this passage, Ibn Sīnā makes a small digression in order to justify why, in the definition of the simple linguistic expression, the addition of "a group of theorists" (*farīq min ahl an-naẓar*), according to whom the parts of the simple linguistic expression "signify nothing of the whole meaning (*maʿnā l-kulli*),"[99] is unnecessary. The background concerns the question of whether a linguistic expression signifies *per se*. Ibn Sīnā is of the opinion that it is not the linguistic expression that signifies, but the speaker, who signifies something by means of the linguistic expression in a concrete communication process. Contrary to al-Fārābī's view, for whom a non-signifying sound cannot be a linguistic expression,[100] for Ibn Sīnā a linguistic expression remains a linguistic expression even if the speaker has deprived it of any meaning or if it is merely a string of letters, such as the nonsense word *šanqanqatayn*.[101] According to Ibn Sīnā, in order to be considered a linguistic expression, the following criterion must be met: "Something is a linguistic expression precisely because it consists of letters that are articulated individually by sounds (*huwa lafẓun li-annahū muʾaṭṭalafun min ḥurūfin muqaṭṭaʿatin ʿan aṣwātin*). The fact that this is the case, however, does not additionally require them to signify or not signify."[102] This discussion became relevant, for example, in the context of the question of the adequate

98 Ibn Sīnā, *Kitāb aš-Šifāʾ, al-Manṭiq, al-Madḫal* I.5, p. 25, line 15–p. 26, line 2.

99 Ibid., line 12.

100 See Abū Naṣr al-Fārābī, "Šarḥ al-ʿIbāra," p. 15, line 13.

101 Ibn Sīnā, *Kitāb aš-Šifāʾ, al-Manṭiq, al-ʿIbāra*, p. 9, lines 6–8.

102 Ibid., p. 10, lines 3–4.

translation of φωνή (*ṣawt* or *lafẓ*) in the Aristotelian definition of the name and the question of the justification of the word 'convention' (*tawāṭu'*) in it.[103]

Šihāb ad-dīn al-Qarāfī identifies the thesis that signification arises in the process of communication as a view of unspecified "later" scholars. While Ibn Sīnā—just like the Aš'arite position in connection with the question of the status of divine speech, in particular the meaning of the commandment[104]—focuses on the speaker, according to Šihāb ad-dīn's presentation of the first thesis, the speaker's speech and the listener's understanding stand at the center of the signification process:

> Later [*scholars*] (*al-muta'aḫḫirūna*) favored the first definition, and they conclude the correctness of what they advocated from the fact that the linguistic expression is as follows: Whenever (*iḏā*) it circulates between the two interlocutors (*dāra bayna l-mutaḫāṭibayni*) and understanding (*fahm*) occurs by means of it in the listener, then it is said, 'this is a signifying linguistic expression' (*wa-huwa lafẓun dāllun*). And if (*wa-in*) it does not occur: 'It is not signifying' (*laysa bi-dāllin*).[105]

This alludes, for example, to Abū l-Barakāt al-Baġdādī, who in his *Kitāb al-Mu'tabar fī l-ḥikma*, in the introduction to the Tripartition of Signification,

103 On the question of the translation of φωνή in the Aristotelian definition of the name, see al-Fārābī, "Šarḥ al-'Ibāra," p. 15, line 7–p. 16, line 7; Ibn Sīnā, *Kitāb aš-Šifā', al-Manṭiq, al-'Ibāra*, p. 8, line 13–p. 10, line 5, see also Zimmermann's "Einleitung" (introduction) to *Al-Farabi's Commentary*, p. lxxiv.

According to Ibn Sīnā, the expression *fa-l-ismu huwa lafẓatun dāllatun bi-tawāṭu'* is tautological, since a linguistic expression always signifies on the basis of convention (Ibn Sīnā, *Kitāb aš-Šifā', al-Manṭiq, al-'Ibāra*, p. 8, lines 13–14). Al-Fārābī, on the other hand, tries to justify the word 'convention' in this Arabic translation of Aristotle's definition by arguing that, according to Aristotle, there can also be linguistic expressions that do not signify based on convention: "But we see that Aristotle says in the *Kitāb al-Ḥayawān* that many of the birds and the rest of the animals sometimes make a sound that can be composed of letters (*qad tuṣawwitu bi-ašyā'in murakkabatin min ḥurūfin*). And if the linguistic expression (*lafẓ*) is composed of letters, then these animals emit something that is a linguistic expression, even if they are letters that we do not know. [...] These [*sounds*] are linguistic expressions, although they do not [*come about*] by convention. I think that he [*i.e. Aristotle*] made the expression 'on the basis of convention' a condition only because of the linguistic expressions heard from these animals," al-Fārābī, *Šarḥ al-'Ibāra*, p. 18, line 22–p. 19, line 7.

104 An overview of one of the theological dimensions of the debate can be found e.g. in Bāqillānī, see id., *at-Taqrīb*, vol. 2, pp. 10–16, pp. 25–27, and pp. 88–92, as well as in Āmidī, see id., *al-Iḥkām*, vol. 2, pp. 160 ff.; cf. Vishanoff, *The Formation of Islamic Hermeneutics*, p. 165, and Weiss, *The Search*, pp. 64 ff.

105 Al-Qarāfī, *Nafā'is al-uṣūl*, vol. 1, p. 253, lines 14–16.

takes both the communication situation in which the process of signification is embedded as well as the interlocutors involved in it into account:

> Every linguistic expression that circulates between people in their discussions and in their dialogues (*fī mufāwaḍātihim wa-muḥāwarātihim*) has [a] a meaning in the mind of its speaker (*fī ḏihni qāʾilihī*), who signifies it [*i.e. the meaning*] by means of it [*i.e. by means of the linguistic expression*], and [b] something that is understood in the mind of its hearer—who derives it [*i.e. the meaning*] from it [*i.e. from the linguistic expression*].[106]

The process of signification is thus initiated by the speaker with a linguistic expression, which—according to Aristotle's *De Interpretatione* 16a3–8—is a sign for the meaning present in the mind and which conveys this meaning to the listener such that it sets in in his thinking.

In addition, the "later" scholars here, alongside Ibn Sīnā and al-Baġdādī, may primarily refer to grammarians and language theorists such as ʿAbd al-Qāhir al-Ǧurǧānī, who emphasize the relevance of the syntactic composition of the word for the decipherment of the lexical meaning and for the transmission of information.[107] This is opposed—according to al-Qarāfī—by the position that "signification is a property (*ṣifa*) of the linguistic expression"[108]—and not, as in the first position, a property of the listener (*ṣifa li-s-sāmiʿ*).[109] According to this second view, signification is like carpentry: The linguistic expression is just as much an actor as the carpenter who acts on the wood; the wood, in turn, is compared to the listener:

> [...] Signification [*is*] like tailoring (*ḫiyāṭa*), carpentry, and goldsmithing (*ṣiyāġa*) and like carpentry (*niǧāra*) in relation to wood, goldsmithing in relation to jewelery (*ḥaly*), and tailoring in relation to the dress; and just as the carpenter or the goldsmith is the actor (*fāʿil*), so it is with signification in relation to the listener, because he [*i.e. the listener*] is the place (*mawḍiʿ*) where the linguistic expression acts (*taʾṯīru l-lafẓi*), because the linguistic expression is the actor (*wa-l-lafẓ huwa fāʿil*).[110]

---

106 Al-Baġdādī, *Kitāb al-Muʿtabar*, vol. 1, p. 56, lines 6–7.

107 Cf. Antonella Ghersetti, "'Word' in the Linguistic Thinking of Jurjānī," in *The Word in Arabic*, ed. by Giuliano Lancioni and Lidia Bettini (Leiden [et al.]: Brill, 2011), p. 97 and pp. 101–102.

108 Al-Qarāfī, *Šarḥ Tanqīḥ*, p. 26, line 5.

109 Id., *Nafāʾis al-uṣūl*, vol. 1, p. 253, last line.

110 Ibid., p. 254, lines 3–5.

According to this view, signification is something that is brought about by the linguistic expression and produces understanding in the listener. Through Šihāb ad-dīn's answer to the question of what "signification of the linguistic expression" (*dalālatu l-lafẓ*) is, the question of the relationship between the linguistic expression and the listener comes into focus:

According to the first position, it is the speaker who produces understanding in the listener by means of the linguistic expression; according to the second position, the ability of signification is inherent to the linguistic expression, while the listener has the ability to understand.[111] In the first position, 'signification' is synonymous with 'understanding,' while in the second position it is synonymous with the ability of the linguistic expression; the first position thus refers to the actually existing understanding, the second to the potentially existing signification of the linguistic expression, in which the relationship of imposition takes the foreground and the intention of the speaker is negligible.

Šihāb ad-dīn then formulates a reificatory middle position from these two, according to which "signification of the linguistic expression" (*dalālatu l-lafẓ*) means "getting the listener to understand/creating understanding (*ifhām*)":[112]

> Know that the discussion of the two schools of thought is superfluous by [*saying*]: The signification of the linguistic expression is getting the listener to understand/producing understanding (*ifhām*). [...] Getting one to understand is thus a property of the linguistic expression (*ṣifatu l-lafẓ*). Understanding (*fahm*) is its effect (*aṯar*)—and this is a property of the listener (*ṣifatu s-sāmiʿ*). In this way, there is an amalgamation of the fundamentals (*qawāʿid*) mentioned by both sides, such that the ambiguities (*iškālāt*) are eliminated.[113]

Šihāb ad-dīn agrees with the second position to the effect that signification is a property of the linguistic expression; however, he understands signification—in a modification of the first position—as getting one to understand, as the production of understanding in the listener. Understanding is therefore the result of signification and a property of the listener, whereas the signification itself is the process of bringing about understanding. According to this synthesis, the role of the speaker and his intention are considered irrelevant for the signification process; instead, it concentrates on the linguistic expression as a code that is decoded by the speaker.

111 Ibid., p. 254, lines 6–9.
112 Ibid., line 16.
113 Ibid., lines 18–21.

After clarifying what is meant by signification, Šihāb ad-dīn continues in his *Šarḥ at-Tanqīḥ* with the enumeration of the Tripartition of Signification already outlined at the beginning:

> It [*i.e. signification*] has three types:
> [1.] Signification by congruence; this means that the listener (*sāmiʿ*) understands the entirey of what is named (*kamāl al-musammā*) from the speech (*kalām*) of the speaker (*mutakallim*).
> [2.] Signification by containment; this means that the listener understands a part of what is named from the speech of the speaker.
> [3.] Signification by implication; this means that the listener understands the obvious implication of what is named (*lāzim al-musammā al-bayyin*) from the speech of the speaker.[114]

Šihāb ad-dīn's discussion of the Tripartition of Signification thus goes beyond the basic subdivision of linguistic expressions and is embedded in fundamental contexts of linguistic and communication theory. At the same time, Šihāb ad-dīn al-Qarāfī's treatment of the Tripartition of Signification allows us to observe a modification in the approach to the process of signification as such: The discussion of the Tripartition in its previously canonized form was based purely on the relationship of imposition between linguistic expression and meaning, i.e. apparently on "what the vocable means in and of itself (that is, through *waḍʿ*)";[115] the context-based communication relationship between listener and speaker was generally ignored—at least in the context of the Tripartition of Signification. Both perspectives are now merged by al-Qarāfī and made useful for the explanation of the signification process.

2.1.3 Cursory Overview of the Further Reception

The following is a cursory overview of the post-Rāzīan *uṣūl al-fiqh* works that enumerate or discuss the Tripartition and that are considered important in the tradition of the four Sunnī schools of law and in the Šiʿīte tradition.[116]

---

114 Al-Qarāfī, *Šarḥ Tanqīḥ*, p. 26, lines 15–19.

115 Gleave, *Islam and Literalism*, p. 33.

116 The discussions of the Tripartition in connection with the types of implication relationships and in particular with the *argumentum e contrario* are excluded from this overview.

2.1.3.1 Uṣūl al-fiqh *Texts in the Ḥanafite Tradition*[117]

The Ḥanafite Aḥmad b. ʿAlī Ibn as-Sāʿātī (d. 694/1295) refers to the Tripartition of Signification in his work the *Kitāb al-Badīʿ*, which is based on both Āmidi's *Iḥkām* and Bazdawī's *uṣūl al-fiqh* work and thus combines two different traditions. He refers to it not in the function of a structuring principle, but by juxtaposing it with the threefold classification of linguistic expressions.[118]

Furthermore, the Tripartition of Signification is discussed in the *Taḥrīr* by Ibn al-Humām (d. 861/1457) and in the commentary on it, the *Taqrīr* by Ibn Amīr al-Ḥāǧǧ (d. 879/1474),[119] as well as in Niẓām ad-dīn al-Anṣārī al-Laknawī's (d. 1225/1810) commentary on Muḥibb Allāh al-Bihārī's (d. 1119/1707) *Musallam aṯ-ṯubūt*.[120] On the other hand, there is no discussion in Abū l-Barakāt an-Nasafī's (d. 710/1310) *Manār al-anwār*, in al-Maḥbūbī's (d. 747/1346) *Tawḍīḥ*, or in al-Buḫārī's (d. 730/1329) *Kašf al-asrār*.[121]

2.1.3.2 Uṣūl al-fiqh *Texts in the Ḥanbalite Tradition*

Ibn Qudāma al-Maqdisī (d. 620/1223) devotes himself in his work the *Rawḍat an-nāẓir wa-ǧunnat al-munāẓir fī uṣūl al-fiqh* to the Tripartition of Signification—this passage is obviously closely modeled on al-Ġazālī's *Mustaṣfā* and is not in the tradition of Faḫr ad-dīn ar-Rāzī's *Maḥṣūl*.[122] In addition, an enumeration of the Tripartition—in a much later work belonging to the commentary

117 With regard to the works that stand outside the line of tradition dealt with so far, I orient myself using the list that is given for this tradition in Wilhelm Heffening and Joseph Schacht, "Ḥanafiyya," *EI*².

118 Aḥmad b. ʿAlī Ibn as-Sāʿātī, *Kitāb al-Badīʿ*, ed. by Muṣṭafā Maḥmūd al-Azharī and Muḥammad Ḥusayn ad-Dimyāṭī (Riyāḍ/Cairo: Dār Ibn al-Qayyim/Dārn Ibn ʿAffān, 2014 [1435]), vol. 1, pp. 152–153. On the significance of Ibn as-Sāʿātī, see Norman Calder "Uṣūl al-Fiḳh," *EI*²: "Towards the end of the 7th/13th century, Aḥmad b. ʿAlī Ibn al-Sāʿātī (d. 694/1295), author of the famous *Madjmaʿ al-baḥrayn*, a work of *furūʿ*, combined, in his *K. al-Badīʿ*, the Ḥanafī (jurists') tradition with the tradition derived from al-Āmidī, thereby ensuring considerable convergence of the two traditions in the subsequent period."

119 Muḥammad b. Muḥammad b. Amīr al-Ḥāǧǧ, *at-Taqrīr wa-t-taḥbīr*, ed. by ʿAbd Allāh Maḥmūd Muḥammad ʿUmar (Beirut: Dār al-Kutub al-ʿilmiyya, 1999 [1419]), vol. 1, pp. 130 ff.

120 Al-Laknawī, *Fawātiḥ ar-raḥamūt*, vol. 1, p. 143.

121 Cf. Abū l-Barakāt an-Nasafī, *Matn al-Manār fī uṣūl al-fiqh*, ed. by Aḥmad ʿAbd al-Malik ʿAbd ar-Raḥmān as-Saʿdī (Damascus: Dār Saʿd ad-dīn, 2010); Saʿd ad-dīn at-Taftāzānī, *Šarḥ at-Talwīḥ ʿalā t-Tawḍīḥ*, ed. s.n. (Beirut: Dār al-Kutub al-ʿilmiyya, 1996); ʿAbd al-ʿAzīz al-Buḫārī, *Kašf al-asrār*, ed. by Aḥmad Ḫulūṣī and Muṣṭafā Darwīš (Istanbul, 1890–1891 [1308]).

122 Cf. ʿAbd Allāh b. Aḥmad b. Qudāma al-Maqdisī, *Rawḍat an-nāẓir wa-ǧunnat al-munāẓir fī uṣūl al-fiqh*, ed. by ʿAbd al-Karīm b. ʿAlī b. Muḥammad an-Namla (Riyāḍ: Maktabat ar-rušd, 1993 [1413]), vol. 1, pp. 94–95, cf. al-Ġazālī, *al-Mustaṣfā*, vol. 1, pp. 92–93. On the relation of this work to al-Ġazālī's *Mustaṣfā*, see the editors' introduction to Ibn as-Sāʿātī, *Kitāb al-Badīʿ*, vol. 1, p. 32.

tradition of Ibn al-Ḥāǧib's *Muḫtaṣar* and al-Bayḍāwī's *Minhāǧ*—is found in Ibn al-Laḥḥām's (d. 803/1401) *al-Muḫtasar fī uṣūl al-fiqh ʿalā maḏhab al-imām Aḥmad ibn Ḥanbal.*[123]

2.1.3.3 Uṣūl al-fiqh *Texts in the Mālikite Tradition*

In addition to the aforementioned Mālikite scholars Šihāb ad-dīn al-Qarāfī and Ibn al-Ḥāǧib, a discussion of the Tripartition of Signification is undertaken in the *Taqrīb al-wuṣūl ilā ʿilm al-uṣūl* by Abū l-Qāsim Ibn Ǧuzayy (d. 741/1340). Here the engagement with Faḫr ad-dīn's account is not only obvious from the wording, but is also explicitly mentioned.[124] To my knowledge, there is no mention in the *Miftāḥ al-wuṣūl* by Šarīf at-Tilimsānī (d. 771/1370) or in aš-Šāṭibī's (d. 790/1388) *al-Muwāfaqāt.*[125] The passages on the philosophy of language in the work the *Šarḥ Marāqī as-suʿūd* by Muḥammad al-Amīn aš-Šinqīṭī (d. 1373/1973), which also derive, *inter alia*, from an intensive explicit and implicit engagement with Ibn al-Ḥāǧib's *Muḫtaṣar* and Faḫr ad-dīn's *Maḥṣūl*, deserve a separate study which should work out, among other things, the adaptations and further developments as well as the critical points of friction.[126]

2.1.3.4 Uṣūl al-fiqh *Texts in the Šāfiʿite Tradition*

In addition to the aforementioned *uṣūl al-fiqh* works of al-Āmidī and al-Bayḍāwī and their commentaries, a very detailed discussion of the Tripartition of Signification can be found in Badr ad-Dīn Muḥammad az-Zarkašī's

---

123 Cf. Ibn al-Laḥḥām, *al-Muḫtasar fī uṣūl al-fiqh ʿalā maḏhab al-imām Aḥmad ibn Ḥanbal*, ed. by Muḥammad Ḥasan Ismāʿīl (Beirut: Dār al-Kutub al-ʿilmiyya, 2000 [1421]), p. 26.
At the same time, it is not mentioned in the following texts that are considered important in the Ḥanbalite school of law: Āl ibn Taymiyya, *al-Muswadda fī uṣūl al-fiqh*; Muḥammad b. Qayyim al-Ǧawziyya, *Iʿlām al-Muwaqqiʿīn ʿan rabb al-ʿālamīn*, ed. by Abū ʿUbayda Āl Salmān (Dammām: Dār Ibn al-Ǧawzī, 2002 [1423]).

124 Cf. Abū l-Qāsim Ibn Ǧuzayy, *Taqrīb al-wuṣūl ilā ʿilm al-uṣūl*, ed. by Muḥammad al-Muḫtār b. Šayḫ Muḥammad al-Amīn aš-Šanqīṭī (Medina, 2002 [1423]), pp. 106–107. Ibn Rušd (d. 595/1198) does not deal with the Tripartition in his *Mustaṣfā* commentary—he skips the logic section in its entirety, cf. Ziad Bou Akl, *Averroès: Le philosophe et la Loi: Édition, Traduction et Commentaire de l'Abrégé du Mustasfa* (Boston: De Gruyter, 2015), p. 122, lines 14–17.

125 Cf. Muḥammad ibn Aḥmad at-Tilimsānī, *Miftāḥ al-wuṣūl ilā bināʾ al-furūʿ ʿalā l-uṣūl* (Beirut [et al.]: Muʾassasat ar-rayyān, 1998 [1419]); Abū Isḥāq Ibrāhīm b. Mūsa aš-Šāṭibī, *al-Muwāfaqāt*, ed. by Abū ʿUbayda Āl Salmān, with a foreword by ʿAllāma Bakr b. ʿAbdallāh Abū Zayd (Ḫubar: Dār Ibn ʿAffān, 1997).

126 Muḥammad al-Amīn aš-Šinqīṭī, *Šarḥ Marāqī as-suʿūd: al-musammā Naṯr al-wurūd* (Mecca: Dār ʿālam al-fawāʾid, 2005 [1426]), cf. for example p. 76, where he refers to the *dalālat al-iqtiḍāʾ* as *dalālat al-iltizām*, or pp. 99 f., where he discusses the question of why indeterminate generic names (*asmāʾ al-aǧnās al-munakkara*) were imposed.

(d. 794/1392) *al-Baḥr al-Muḥīṭ fī uṣūl al-fiqh*.[127] An enumeration, presented at this point with the assumption that the concept is self-explanatory to readers, can be found in Tāǧ ad-dīn as-Subkī's (d. 771/1369) *Ǧamʿ al-ǧawāmiʿ fī uṣūl al-fiqh*.[128]

2.1.3.5 Uṣūl al-fiqh *Texts in the Šiʿīte Tradition*

As Devin Stewart has shown, (Twelver) Šiʿīte *uṣūl al-fiqh* scholarship is characterized by the same line of tradition that was formative for the Šāfiʿite tradition—namely, above all, the one which developed on the basis of Ibn al-Ḥāǧib's *Muḫtasar* and al-Īǧī's commentary on it—so that "for a lengthy period the standard *uṣūl al-fiqh* works studied in the Shiite curriculum were al-ʿAllāmah al-Ḥillī's *Tahdhīb al-wuṣūl*, followed by the *Mukhtaṣar* of Ibn al-Ḥājib and *al-Sharḥ al-ʿAḍudī*."[129] The latter remained a favorite subject of Šiʿīte commentary for centuries.[130] The Tripartition of Signification is not only dealt with in Ibn al-Ḥāǧib and al-Īǧī, but also in Ḥillī's *Tahḏīb al-wuṣūl*.[131]

These works were superseded by Ḥasan b. Zayd ad-dīn al-ʿĀmilī's *Maʿālim ad-dīn*, by Mīrzā Abū l-Qāsim al-Qummī's (1231/1816) *Qawānīn al-uṣūl*, and by Mullā Kāẓim al-Ḫurāsānī's *Kifāyat al-uṣūl*[132]—as far as I know, none of these three deals with the Tripartition.[133] In some important Šiʿīte works of the 19th and 20th centuries, on the other hand—in the line of tradition of al-Ḥillī—the Tripartition of Signification is treated, such as in Muḥammad ibn ʿAlī Muǧāhid's (1242/1826?) *Mafātiḥ al-uṣūl* and Fāḍil Ardakānī's (1305/1887) *Ġāyat al-masʾūl*, as well as in the work the *Badāʾiʿ al-afkār* by Mīrzā Ḥabīb Allāh Raštī (d. 1312/1894), in Ḍiyāʾ ad-dīn al-ʿIrāqī's (d. 1361/1942) *Maqālāt al-uṣūl*, and in Ḥusayn Ṭabāṭabāʾī Burūǧirdī's (d. 1380/1961) *Nihāyat al-uṣūl*.[134]

---

127 Az-Zarkašī, *al-Baḥr al-Muḥīṭ*, vol. 2, pp. 37 ff.

128 Tāǧ ad-dīn as-Subkī, *Ǧamʿ al-ǧawāmiʿ fī uṣūl al-fiqh*, ed. by ʿAbd al-Munʿim Ḫalīl Ibrāhīm (Beirut: Dār al-Kutub al-ʿilmiyya, 2003 [1424]), p. 22, lines 8 f. The Tripartition is also discussed in contemporary textbooks, see, for example, Wahba az-Zuhaylī, *al-Uṣūl al-fiqh al-islamī* (Damascus: Dār al-fikr, 1986), vol. 1, p. 360.

129 Stewart, *Islamic Legal Orthodoxy*, p. 97.

130 Ibid., pp. 98–99.

131 Ǧamāl ad-dīn al-Ḥillī, *Tahḏīb al-wuṣūl ilā ʿilm al-wuṣūl*, ed. by Muḥammad Ḥusayn al-Kašmīrī (London: Muʾassasat al-Imām ʿAlī, 2001 [1421]), p. 65.

132 Stewart, *Islamic Legal Orthodoxy*, pp. 97–98.

133 Cf. al-Ḥasan b. Zayn ad-dīn b. aš-Šahīd aṯ-Ṯānī, *Maʿālim ad-dīn fī l-uṣūl* (Tehran: Lith. 1890, reprint, ca. 1970); Muḥammad Kāẓim Ibn Ḥusayn al-Ḫurāsānī, *al-Kifāya fī bayān al-imārāt wa-l-uṣūl* (Tehran, 1906).

134 Cf. Muḥammad b. ʿAlī Muǧāhid, *Mafātiḥ al-uṣūl*, ed. s.n. (Qom: Muʾassasat Āl al-Bayt, s.d.), p. 5; Fāḍil Ardakānī, *Ġāyat al-masʾūl*, ed. s.n. (Qom: Muʾassasat Āl al-Bayt, s.d.), pp. 331 ff.; Mīrzā Ḥabīb Allāh Raštī, *Badāʾiʿ al-afkār*, ed. s.n. (Qom: Muʾassasat Āl al-Bayt, 1896 [1313]),

This cursory overview gives a first impression of the fact that the Tripartition of Signification has achieved canonical status in the commentary traditions of all Sunnī schools of law treating this subject as well as in Šiʿīte works of the same lineage. In a next step, which cannot be undertaken in the present work, it would be necessary to work out whether and how the chapters on language philosophy of the modern and contemporary works of the various schools of law have developed and differentiated over time and whether a fundamental change in approach can be recognized.

2.2 *The Transmission and Modification of* iltizām *as a Generic Term for Legal-Theoretical Types of Implication*

Now that we have seen how the treatment of the Tripartition of Signification in the post-Rāzian *uṣūl al-fiqh* compendia's general introductory chapters on linguistic theory came to achieve canonical status in a particular line of tradition, we will now examine whether and how Faḫr ad-dīn's concept of *iltizām* was received and handed down as a generic term for certain legal-theoretical types of implication. The focus here is on the discussion of the historical development of its reception and modification, i.e. I aim to examine the group of concrete, hermeneutical discussion points in which the *iltizām* debate is located and has been used as well as the extent to which approaches specific to individual legal schools can be recognized in within it.

2.2.1 *Iltizām* and Legal-Theoretical Types of Implication: From the Šāfiʿite to the Ḥanafite Paradigm

Faḫr ad-dīn associated the *iltizām* category with several gradations and subdivisions of legal-theoretical types of implication: (1.) *dalālat al-iqtiḍāʾ*, (2.) *dalālat al-išāra*, (3.) *mafhūm al-muwāfaqa*, and (4.) *mafhūm al-muḫālafa*.[135] Subsequent Šāfiʿite and Mālikite scholars, who referred directly or indirectly to the *Maḥṣūl*, adopted this classification in increments and formed something new from it over time, as will be shown below.

The Šāfiʿite ʿAbdallāh b. ʿUmar al-Bayḍāwī summarizes the distinction between explicit and implicit types of signification along with their subtypes in his *Minhāǧ* as follows:

---

pp. 188 ff.; Ḍiyāʾ ad-dīn al-ʿIrāqī, *Maqālāt al-uṣūl*, ed. s.n. (Qom: Maǧmaʿ al-fikr al-islāmī, 1993–1994 [1414]), pp. 121 ff.; Ḥosayn Ṭabāṭabāʾī Borūǧerdī (1380/1961), *Nihāyat al-uṣūl*, ed. s.n. (Qom: Našr tafakkur, 1994 [1415]), pp. 290 ff.

135 See Chapter 4, Section 1.

> [*Divine*] speech (*al-ḫiṭāb*) signifies the legal judgement (*ḥukm*) either
> [1.] in an explicit way (*bi-manṭūqihī*), so that it is traced back to the legal (*šarʿī*) [*speech/way of speaking*], then to that of the conventional usage (*ʿurfī*), then to the linguistic/lexicographical (*luġawī*), then to the figurative (*maǧāzī*) [*speech/way of speaking*];
> [2.] or in an implicit way (*bi-mafhūmihī*). This is either [2.1] that [*meaning*] which adheres to the [*meaning of the*] simple [*linguistic expression*] which is dependent on it in a rational or legal way—such as […] 'Freed is your slave by me'; this is called 'requirement' (*iqtiḍāʾ*); or
> [2.2.1] it is [*that meaning*] which [*adheres to*] [*the meaning of the*] compound [*linguistic expression*] and agrees with it; this is *faḥwā al-ḫiṭāb*, just like the prohibition against verbal abuse signifies the prohibition against beating, and
> [2.2.2] [*this includes* dalālat al-išāra] just like the permission of sexual intercourse (*ǧawāz al-mubāšara*) into the morning signifies the permission to fast in a state of great ritual impurity (*ǧunuban*); or
> [2.2.3] [*the implied meaning*] is the opposite (*muḫālafa*)—just like the legal ruling implies the negation of what is omitted from what is mentioned—this is called *dalīl al-ḫiṭāb*.[136]

Here al-Bayḍāwī uses the distinction between *manṭūq*—all types of signification that are based on a primary or secondary imposition[137]—and *mafhūm*, to summarize the corresponding section on legal-theoretical implication in the *Maḥṣūl*. Consequently, it is under *mafhūm* that we find here, after the subdivision into those meanings that are implied by the meanings of the simple or compound linguistic expressions, the types of implication that Faḫr ad-dīn subsumed under the concept of *iltizām*: namely (1.) *dalālat al-iqtiḍāʾ*, (2.) *dalālat al-išāra*, (3.) *mafhūm al-muwāfaqa*, and (4.) *mafhūm al-muḫālafa*. Al-Bayḍāwī, like Faḫr ad-dīn, does not count *taʿlīl* or *īmāʾ wa-išāra*.

However, he adopts neither the further differentiations of the categorization scheme (condition/consequence/intention/positive-negative implication) nor—for the time being—the reference to the Tripartition of Signification. In this classification, implications are subsumed under the generic term *mafhūm*, not *iltizām*. The reference to the Tripartition is established a few lines later, as will be shown in Chapter 4, Section 2.2.2—namely in connection with the *argumentum e contrario*.[138]

136 Al-Bayḍāwī, *Minhāǧ*, p. 68, lines 11–16.
137 See Chapter 3, Section 2, e.g. pp. 162 ff.
138 See Chapter 4, Section 2.2.2, p. 219.

FIGURE 22 The Legal-Theoretical Types of Signification in al-Bayḍāwī's *Minhāǧ al-wuṣūl*

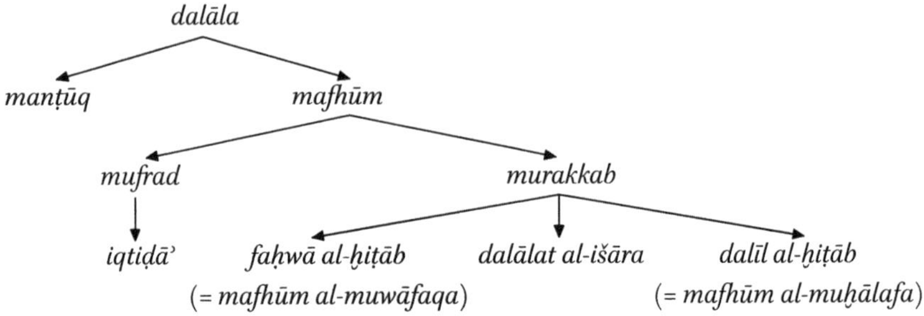

In the works on legal theory of the Šāfiʿite Sayf ad-dīn al-Āmidī, the approach in the *Maḥṣūl* is not adopted;[139] instead, we find al-Ġazālī's classification, presented in a somewhat more systematic fashion and with different terminology. This classification will be briefly presented below because it will become relevant in the subsequent history of reception with regard to the question I am focusing on here. Al-Āmidī assigns implications to those types of signification that are not based on the arrangement and form of the linguistic expressions, as they in some way transcend what is explicitly articulated:

> The second part: About signification by the non-arranged (*ġayr al-manẓūm*). This is that which does not signify by its plain (external) form and imposition (*bi-ṣarīḥ ṣīġatihī wa-waḍʿihī*). This is either such that what is signified
> [1.] is intended (*maqṣūd*) by the speaker or [2.] is not intended (*ġayr maq ṣūd*).
> [*ad* 1] If it is intended, then it is either such that
> [1.1] the credibility of the speaker (*ṣidq al-mutakallim*) or the correctness of what is said depends on it [*i.e. on the implied signified thing*], or
> [1.2] is does not dependent on it.
> [*ad* 1.1] If it [*i.e. if the speaker's credibility or the correctness of what is said*] depends on it [*i.e. the implied meaning*], then this signification of the linguistic expression is called *dalālat al-iqtiḍāʾ*.
> [*ad* 1.2] And if it [*i.e. if the speaker's credibility or the correctness of what is said*] does not depend on it [*i.e. the implied meaning*], then it is either such that

139 Yunis Ali makes it seem as if al-Āmidī incorporates the three-fold classification of *muṭābaqa*, *taḍammun*, and *iltizām* into the *manṭūq/mafhūm* classification. But this is a back-projection through the later history of reception, which is why Yunis Ali does not cite any textual evidence for this statement, cf. Yunis Ali, *Medieval Islamic Pragmatics*, pp. 180–181.

> [1.2.1] that which is implied (*mafhūm*) [*lit.: 'that which is understood'*] lies within the realm to which the linguistic expression extends in the manner of articulated speech (*nuṭq*) or
> [1.2.2] it does not.
> [*ad* 1.2.1] If it is the first, then the signification is called *dalālat at-tanbīh wa-l-īmāʾ*.
> [*ad* 1.2.2] If it is the second, then the signification is called *dalālat al-mafhūm.*
> [*ad* 2] If the signification is not intended by the speaker, then this signification of the linguistic expression is called *dalālat al-išāra*.[140]

Like al-Ġazālī, al-Āmidī here describes those meanings that are not signified by the linguistic expressions themselves, i.e. not by the word form (*ṣīġa*) itself, but instead by something that transcends the mere arrangement (*manẓūm*) of the words. The meaning is implied between the lines and is not carried by the linguistic expressions themselves.[141] Like al-Ġazālī and Faḫr ad-dīn ar-Rāzī, he then makes a distinction between intended and unintended meaning, whereby the unintended meaning is a kind of secondary meaning that results from the main meaning of the statement.[142] Al-Āmidī considers the type *dalālat at-tanbīh wa-l-īmāʾ* or *taʿlīl* to be a special case amongst the types of implication, because here the implied meaning still lies to a certain extent within the realm of articulated speech; for this reason, this type of implication was not even treated by Faḫr ad-dīn under the category of implication, and al-Āmidī refers the reader to the section on *qiyās* for a detailed discussion.[143]

The classification of the legal-theoretical types of implication as elaborated in Faḫr ad-dīn ar-Rāzī's *Maḥṣūl* seems not to have been of much value to al-Āmidī's *Iḥkām*: The focus is rather on the question of whether the implication is intended or not. The question of whether the implied meaning is also a condition for maintaining the credibility of the speaker or the accuracy of the statement is also mentioned. On the other hand, the counterpart to this—namely the implied meaning as a consequence of the statement and the question of whether the meaning of a word or a sentence is implied—is not considered.

---

140 Al-Āmidī, *al-Iḥkām*, vol. 3, p. 81, lines 1–12; see also al-Āmidī, *Muntahā*, p. 165, lines 6–10; cf. Weiss, *The Search*, p. 474; for a detailed discussion and paraphrase of the legal-theoretical types of implication in al-Āmidī's *Iḥkām*, see Weiss, *The Search*, pp. 473–493.

141 Cf. ibid., p. 473.

142 On the distinction between intended and unintended meaning, see ibid., p. 474.

143 Al-Āmidī, *al-Iḥkām*, vol. 3, p. 82, line 14. Elsewhere, al-Āmidī explains that all five types of implication in the dichotomy *manṭūq/ġayr manṭūq* belong to the realm of *ġayr manṭūq*, cf. al-Āmidī, *Muntahā*, p. 264, lines 1–2.

The dichotomous relationship between explicit and implied types of signification remains intact in spite of it all, and all kinds previously categorized as types of implication are still regarded as such.

FIGURE 23 The Legal-Theoretical Types of Signification in al-Āmidī's *Iḥkām*

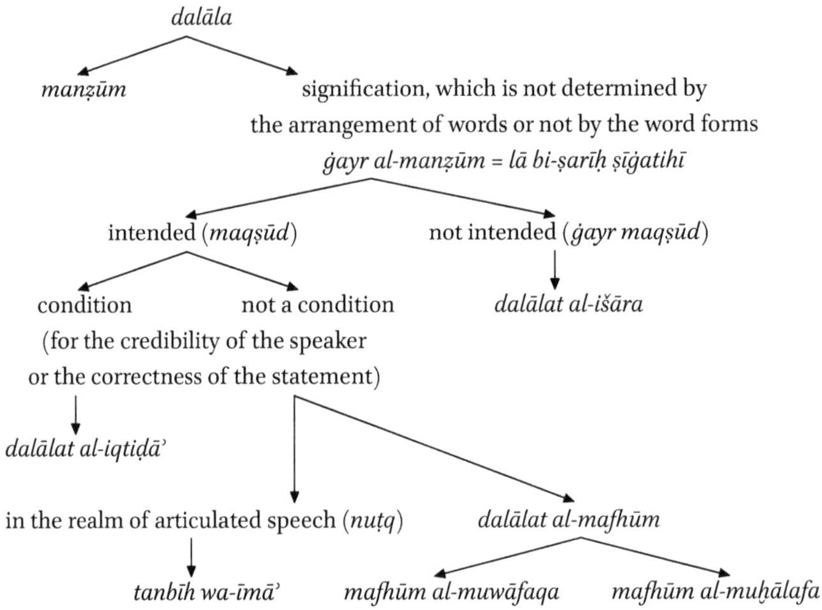

Al-Āmidī's classification in turn influenced subsequent generations of scholars from various schools of law. In his *Muḫtaṣar al-Muntahā*, Ibn al-Ḥāǧib adopts al-Āmidī's classification, albeit with significant modifications:

> The explicitly spoken and the implied (*al-manṭūq wa-l-mafhūm*):
> [1.] The signification is explicitly spoken (*manṭūq*); this [*i.e. what is explicitly spoken*] is that which the linguistic expression signifies in the realm of articulated speech (*nuṭq*).
> [2.] That which is implied (*mafhūm*) [*lit.: 'that which is understood'*] is in contrast to it, i.e. it is not in the realm of articulated speech (*maḥall an-nuṭq*).
>
> [*ad* 1] The first [*i.e. al-manṭūq*] is
> [1.1] *ṣarīḥ* ('plain')—it is that for which the linguistic expression has been imposed;
> [1.2] *ġayr aṣ-ṣarīḥ* ('not plain') stands in contrast to this; it is that which adheres (*mā yalzamu ʿanhu*) to that [*'for which the linguistic expression has been imposed'*].

> [*ad* 1.2] If it [*i.e. the adhering meaning*]
> [1.2.1] is intended and upon it the
> [1.2.1.1] credibility (*ṣidq*) [*of the speaker*] or the correctness [*of what is said*] in rational or legal terms is dependent, then it is the *dalālat iqtiḍā᾽* […]; if
> [1.2.1.2] it is not dependent on it, […] then it is *tanbīh wa-imā᾽* […].
> If it [*i.e. the adhering meaning*]
> [1.2.2] is not intended, then it is the *dalālat išāra* […].
> [*ad* 2] The implied (*mafhūm*) is *mafhūm muwāfaqa* and *mafhūm muḫālafa*.[144]

Ibn al-Ḥāǧib adopts al-Āmidī's subdivision into those significations that are and are not based on the plain word form. However, he does not classify the latter as a genuine type of implication, but instead as a type of explicit speech.[145] This means that the following subtypes *dalālat iqtiḍā᾽*, *tanbīh wa-īmā᾽*, and *dalālat išāra*—which are again differentiated according to Āmidī's criteria—do not belong to the *mafhūm* category, but instead still belong to the *manṭūq* category. It is only *mafhūm al-muwāfaqa* and *mafhūm al-muḫālafa* that are subsumed under the *mafḥūm* category.

FIGURE 24 Legal-Theoretical Types of Signification in Ibn al-Ḥāǧib's *Muḫtaṣar al-Muntahā*

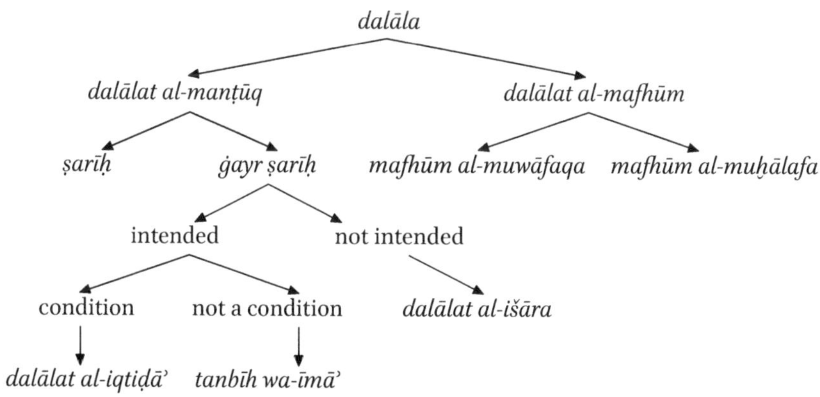

144 Ibn al-Ḥāǧib, *Muḫtaṣar al-Muntahā*, pp. 924–934, cf. Ibn al-Ḥāǧib, *Kitāb Muntahā*, pp. 147–148 and al-Āmidī, *Muntahā*, p. 165, lines 6–10.

145 Gleave's presentation of Ibn al-Ḥāǧib's classification assigns the not plain (*ġayr aṣ-ṣarīḥ*) signification to *mafhūm*. Although one is easily inclined to understand this in accordance with al-Āmidī's classification, this presentation is not accurate on closer examination, cf. Gleave, *Islam and Literalism*, p. 53.

Ibn al-Ḥāǧib thus considerably restricts the realm of genuine types of implication while expanding the realm of explicit signification. One can therefore by no means claim that Ibn al-Ḥāǧib has simply reproduced al-Āmidī's scheme. Instead, this represents a significant paradigm shift.[146] Before going into the question of which assumptions underlie this shift, another aspect of this debate should be mentioned: In his commentary on Ibn al-Ḥāǧib's *Muḫtaṣar*, the Šāfiʿite ʿAḍud ad-dīn al-Īǧī (d. 756/1355) links this classification with the Tripartition of Signification:

> I say:
> [1.] The explicitly spoken (*manṭūq*) is divided into
> [1.1] *ṣarīḥ* ('plain') and
> [1.2] *ġayr aṣ-ṣarīḥ* ('not plain');
> [*ad* 1.1] *ṣarīḥ* is that for which the linguistic expression has been imposed, such that it signifies it by congruence (*muṭābaqa*) or by containment (*taḍammun*).
> [*ad* 1.2] *Ġayr aṣ-ṣarīḥ* stands in contrast to this and is not that for which the linguistic expression has been imposed, but instead what adheres to that for which it has been imposed, such that it signifies it by implication (*iltizām*).
> *Ġayr aṣ-ṣarīḥ* is divided into [1.2.1] *dalālat al-iqtiḍāʾ* and [1.2.2] *īmāʾ* and [1.2.3] *išāra*, because it is either intended by the speaker or not.[147]

In his commentary, ʿAḍud ad-dīn al-Īǧī adopts Ibn al-Ḥāǧib's classification and links it to the Tripartition of Signification: The significations by congruence (*muṭābaqa*), containment (*taḍammun*), and implication (*iltizām*) are now explicitly situated in the *manṭūq* category. *Iltizām* is no longer an umbrella term for legal-theoretical types of implication in general, but only for *dalālat al-*

---

146 Yunis Ali recognizes that *manṭūq* is used "in a very broad sense," but firstly finds this incomprehensible and secondly attributes it to al-Ǧuwaynī, see Yunis Ali, *Medieval Islamic Pragmatics*, pp. 185–186. His assertion that Ibn al-Ḥāǧib follows al-Ǧuwaynī in this classification with the broad understanding of *manṭūq* is not substantiated; apparently it stems from the fact that Ibn al-Ḥāǧib's and al-Ǧuwaynī's understanding of *mafhūm* are equivalent inasmuch as they only include *mafhūm muwāfaqa* and *mafhūm muḫālafa* (cf. al-Ǧuwaynī, *al-Burhān*, vol. 1, pp. 165–166); but such a reference to al-Ǧuwaynī falls short.

147 ʿAḍud ad-dīn al-Īǧī, *Šarḥ Muḫtaṣar al-Muntahā*, ed. by Fādī Naṣīf and Ṭāriq Yaḥyā (Beirut: Dār al-Kutub al-ʿilmiyya, 2000 [1421]), p. 254, lines 1–4. On the significance of this work, see for example Stewart, *Islamic Legal Orthodoxy*, pp. 97 ff.; van Ess, *Die Träume der Schulweisheit*, pp. 64 f.

iqtiḍāʾ, *dalālat al-išāra*, and *al-tanbīh wa-l-īmāʾ*; Faḫr ad-dīn had not counted the latter as *iltizām*.[148] The two types of implication *mafhūm al-muḥāfaqa* and *mafhūm al-muḫālafa*—in contrast to Faḫr ad-dīn's original classification—fall outside the Tripartition of Signification. This arrangement, as will be shown, is particularly relevant with regard to the legitimization or delegitimization of the *argumentum e contrario*.[149]

FIGURE 25 Legal-Theoretical Types of Signification in al-Īǧī's *Šarḥ Muḫtaṣar al-Muntahā*

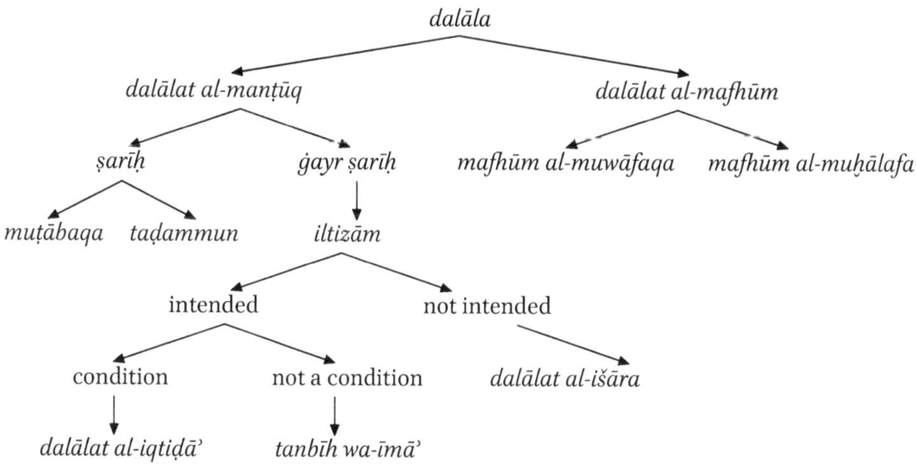

The Ḥanafite Akmal ad-dīn Muḥammad b. Maḥmūd al-Bābartī (d. 786/1384) defends this classification against Šāfiʿite objections in his meta-commentary *ar-Rudūd wa-n-nuqūd: Šarḥ Muḫtaṣar Ibn al-Ḥāǧib*, which is based on Iṣfahānī's *Bayān al-Muḫtaṣar*.[150] To this end, he cites the objection—raised by the Šāfiʿite scholar ʿAlāʾ ad-dīn al-Qūnawī (d. 729/1329)[151]—according to whom *ġayr ṣarīḥ* cannot be categorized as explicitly spoken (*manṭūq*):

148 See also Tāǧ ad-dīn as-Subkī, *Rafʿ al-ḥāǧib ʿan Muḫtaṣar Ibn al-Ḥāǧib*, ed. by ʿAlī Muḥammad Muʿawwaḍ and ʿĀdil Aḥmad ʿAbd al-Mawǧūd (Beirut: ʿĀlam al-kutub, 1999), vol. 3, p. 485.

149 See Chapter 4, Section 2.2.2.

150 Cf. the editor's introduction in Šams ad-dīn al-Iṣfahānī, *Bayān al-Muḫtaṣar: Šarḥ Muḫtaṣar Ibn al-Ḥāǧib*, ed. by Muḥammad Maẓhar Baqā (Mecca: Ǧāmiʿat Umm al-Qurā, 1986 [1406]), p. 25; in a weakened formulation, cf. the editor's introduction to Akmal ad-dīn Muḥammad b. Maḥmūd al-Bābartī's *ar-Rudūd wa-n-nuqūd: Šarḥ Muḫtaṣar Ibn al-Ḥāǧib*, vol. 1, ed. by Ṣāliḥ b. ʿAwn al-ʿUmarī (Riyāḍ: Maktabat ar-Rušd Nāširūn, 2005), p. 63 On the person of al-Bābartī himself, see also the introduction to al-Bābartī, *ar-Rudūd wa-n-nuqūd*, vol. 1, pp. 37 ff.

151 For more detail on his person, see Livnat Holtzmann, "The Dhimmi's Question on Predetermination and the Ulama's Six Responses: The Dynamics of Composing Polemical

> Šayḫ ʿAlāʾ ad-dīn al-Qūnawī doubted that *ġayr ṣarīḥ* belongs to *manṭūq* […]; for he said: "The first is *ṣarīḥ*; it is that for which the linguistic expression has been imposed. *Ġayr ṣarīḥ* stands in contrast to it." […] The fact that he says "*ġayr ṣarīḥ* stands in contrast to it" indicates that it must be a category other than *manṭūq*. Accordingly, the signification of the linguistic expression is divided into three parts: [1.] *manṭūq*, which is *ṣarīḥ*, and [2.] *mafhūm*, which is the opposite of *manṭūq*, and [3.] *ġayr ṣarīḥ*, which is the opposite of each one of the two [*i.e. manṭūq and mafhūm*].
>
> There is no difference (*wa-lā tafriqa*) between the parts of *ġayr ṣarīḥ* (namely *iqtiḍāʾ*, *tanbīh*, and *išāra*) and *mafhūm* (namely [*deriving*] beating from verbally abusing)—with regard to the fact that the signification of the linguistic expression is such that something external to the [*meaning*] for which the linguistic expression has been imposed is signified.[152]

Based on the assumption that the category of *manṭūq* is more or less equivalent with that of *ṣarīḥ*—in which signification is plainly and explicitly borne by the linguistic expression itself, this objection to Ibn al-Ḥāǧib's classification criticizes its further dichotomization of *manṭūq* into *ṣarīḥ* and *ġayr ṣarīḥ*. The category that is opposed to *ṣarīḥ* cannot be a subcategory of *manṭūq*: firstly, because it must be contrary to the category of *manṭūq*, and secondly, because it fulfills the same conditions as the category of *mafhūm*, i.e. the opposite of *manṭūq*; for here something is signified that is external with relation to the original meaning. On the basis of these premises, it can then be argued that *ġayr ṣarīḥ* should be equated with *mafhūm*, such that all four or five types of implication are subsumed under it, just as al-Āmidī had done.[153]—However, the assumption that these types of signification should actually be regarded as types of implication and that they belong to the category in which the meanings are not taken from the linguistic expressions themselves is Šāfiʿite and is obviously not shared by Ibn al-Ḥāǧib. In the dichotomous—and also Šāfiʿite—distinction between *manṭūq* and *mafhūm*, the former category is assigned a greater epistemological significance than the latter.[154] The Šāfiʿite schema is contrasted with the Ḥanafite schema, in which this dichotomy does not exist. Instead, it

---

Didactic Poems in Mamluk Cairo and Damascus," *Mamluk Studies Review*, vol. 16 (2012): pp. 36–37.

152 Akmal ad-dīn Muḥammad b. Maḥmūd al-Bābartī, *ar-Rudūd wa-n-nuqūd: Šarḥ Muḫtaṣar Ibn al-Ḥāǧib*, vol. 2, ed. by Tarḥīb b. Rabīʿān ad-Dawsarī (Riyāḍ: Maktabat ar-Rušd Nāširūn, 2005), p. 355, lines 12–20.

153 And as Gleave also (incorrectly) attributes it to Ibn al-Ḥāǧib, see Gleave, *Islam and Literalism*, p. 53.

154 Cf. al-Āmidī, *Muntahā*, p. 149, line 7.

differentiates between *ʿibārat an-naṣṣ* (corresponding in the broadest sense to the *manṭūq* category in the Šāfiʿite tradition), *išārat an-naṣṣ* (corresponding to *dalālat al-išāra*), *dalālat an-naṣṣ* (corresponding to *mafhūm al-muwāfaqa*), and *iqtiḍāʾ an-naṣṣ* (corresponding to *dalālat al-iqtiḍāʾ*) in hierarchical gradation.[155] In the Ḥanafite explanation of these hermeneutical techniques, there is a tendency to see certain meanings as immediately understood by all those who are proficient in Arabic. Consequently, rules for deriving certain meanings and epistemological concerns raised by Šāfiʿite scholars become superfluous: With regard to *mafhūm al-muwāfaqa* or *dalālat an-naṣṣ*, the Ḥanafite Niẓām ad-dīn al-Anṣārī al-Laknawī, for example, writes that here the meaning or the legal ruling "can be understood intuitively (*badīhī*) by those who have mastered the language (*li-l-ʿārif bi-l-luġa*),"[156] while "the one who considers this to be an analogy claims that the signification for it [*i.e. for the meaning or for the legal ruling*] does not occur in a linguistic way (*luġatan*) or according to linguistic usage (*ʿurfan*), but instead that the legal ruling (*ḥukm*) follows from the existence of the *ʿilla*."[157]

On the one hand, there is a tendency to locate certain meanings more in the broad semantic realm, where they can be understood with an "ordinary linguistic competence"[158] and considered legitimate and capable of producing certain knowledge in the hermeneutical process. On the other hand, there is a tendency to understand certain meanings as being derived in some respect and as having a lower epistemological status. In legal hermeneutical practice, the former means an expansion of the scope of exegesis, while the latter reduces it.[159] To put it cautiously, the former could be called the Ḥanafite hermeneutical paradigm and the latter the Šāfiʿite paradigm.

The Mālikite Ibn al-Ḥāǧib proposed in his *Muḫtaṣar al-Muntahā* an approach that merges two different schemata together and in which a large part of what was subordinated under the category *mafhūm* in the Šāfiʿite schema is integrated into the category *manṭūq*. It thus corresponds more to the Ḥanafite

155 See, for example, ʿAlī ibn Muhammad al-Bazdawī (together with al-Buḫārī's commentary), *Kašf al-asrār*, ed. by Aḥmad Ḫulūṣī and Muṣṭafā Darwīš (Istanbul, 1890 [1308]), vol. 1, p. 67; Ibn as-Sāʿātī, *Kitāb al-Badīʿ*, vol. 3, pp. 113 ff.; see also the entry *dalāla* in Šarīf al-Ǧurǧānī, *Kitāb at-Taʿrīfāt*, p. 46; cf. Ramić, *Language and the Interpretation of Islamic Law*, p. 4, pp. 6–40 (on the Ḥanafite classification) and pp. 41–64 (on the Šāfiʿite classification); Yunis Ali, *Medieval Islamic Pragmatics*, p. 159.

156 Al-Laknawī, *Fawātiḥ ar-raḥamūt*, vol. 1, p. 446, lines 22–23.

157 Ibid., p. 447, lines 21–22.

158 Zysow, *The Economy of Certainty*, p. 50, cf. Ramić, *Language and the Interpretation of Islamic Law*, p. 18.

159 Cf. Weiss, *The Search*, p. 481.

paradigm—even if Ibn al-Ḥāǧib's classification, in the expanded version of al-Īǧī, proved to be very influential to the Šāfiʿite *uṣūl al-fiqh* tradition. Therefore the Ḥanafite Niẓām ad-dīn al-Anṣārī al-Laknawī (1225/1810) cites this schema as the Šāfiʿite schema:

> [§1] As for the Šāfiʿite school of law (*aš-šāfiʿiyya*), it divides signification (*dalāla*) into
> [1.] *manṭūq* ('that which is explicitly spoken')—it is that in which the linguistic expression signifies the presence (*ṯubūt*) of the mentioned legal ruling (*ḥukm*) in the manner of congruence (*muṭābaqa*), containment (*taḍammun*), or implication (*iltizām*); and into
> [2.] *mafhūm* ('that which is understood/implied') on the contrary, i.e. that the signification does not occur in the way of being named (*maḏkūr*), but in the way of being concealed (*maskūt*).
> [§2] Consequently, *manṭūq* and *mafhūm* are two parts of the signification (*qismā d-dalāla*) [...].
> [§3] *Manṭūq* is [*either*]
> [1.1] plain (*ṣarīḥ*), it is that which is signified by congruence or containment, or it is the opposite of this
> [1.2] not plain (*ġayr ṣarīḥ*), i.e. that which is not signified by congruence or containment, such that it is signified by implication (*iltizām*).
> Accordingly, implication belongs to [1.] the explicitly spoken (*manṭūq*).
> [§4] Some from the Šāfiʿite school of law, including the author of the *Minhāǧ* [*i.e. al-Bayḍāwī*], categorize it [*i.e. implication* (iltizām)] [*however*] under [2.] *mafhūm*.[160]

Niẓām ad-dīn al-Anṣārī al-Laknawī cites this schema, introduced by Ibn al-Ḥāǧib and expanded by al-Īǧī, as the *Šāfiʿite* scheme in order to, anachronistically, refer to al-Bayḍāwī's *Minhāǧ al-wuṣūl ilā ʿilm al-uṣūl* (in which, as already shown, Faḫr ad-dīn's classification is still predominant).[161] Al-Bayḍāwī's *Minhāǧ* and Ibn al-Ḥāǧib's *Muḫtaṣar* generated two parallel commentary traditions, whereby in some cases the same author even wrote a commentary on each of the works.[162] This led to divergent approaches with regard to the classification problem at hand, since, roughly speaking, only each individual

160 Al-Laknawī, *Fawātiḥ ar-raḥamūt*, vol. 1, p. 449, lines 19–24.
161 See pp. 203f.
162 See, for example, Šams ad-dīn al-Iṣfahānī, *Bayān al-Muḫtaṣar*; id., *Šarḥ al-Minhāǧ li-l-Bayḍāwī fī ʿilm al-uṣūl*, ed. by ʿAbd al-Karīm b. ʿAlī b. Muḥammad an-Namla (Riyāḍ: Maktabat ar-rušd, 1999 [14.20]); Tāǧ ad-dīn as-Subkī, *Rafʿ al-ḥāǧib ʿan Muḫtaṣar Ibn al-*

work's approach was described in its respective commentary. In Subkī's *Minhāǧ* commentary, the two approaches are then finally harmonized in favor of the one advocated by Ibn al-Ḥāǧib, which then becomes established as the Šāfiʿite approach.[163]

Both Šāfiʿite classifications—the old one, i.e. that of al-Bayḍāwī, which is rejected in the end, as well as the new one—are contested by Niẓām ad-dīn. The old one could not be correct anyway because all three types of signification, i.e. congruence (*muṭābaqa*), containment (*taḍammun*), and implication (*iltizām*), must belong under *manṭūq*. The new one is to be criticized on the grounds that it classifies *dalālat al-iqtiḍāʾ* under *al-manṭūq al-ġayr aṣ-ṣarīḥ*. According to Niẓām ad-dīn, this is instead a plain, congruent signification.[164] The Ḥanafite paradigm seen here can again can be considered, in Zysow's words, as a kind of "optimism as to the workings of language".[165]

ʿAḍud ad-dīn al-Īǧī's classification, which combines Ibn al-Ḥaǧib's legal-theoretical classification with the Tripartition of Signification, orients itself within the Šāfiʿite system of signification towards the Ḥanafite paradigm. It also corresponds to the logical classification scheme developed in the commentaries on Naǧm ad-dīn al-Kātibī's (d. 657/1276) *ar-Risāla aš-šamsiyya* and was ultimately canonized by Šarīf al-Ǧurǧānī's (d. 816/1413) lexicon the *Kitāb at-Taʿrīfāt*.[166] Faḫr ad-dīn ar-Rāzī had previously distinguished between the congruent type of signification based on imposition and the type of signification based on reasoning, which includes containment and implication. The former corresponds to the 'meaning' (*al-maʿnā*) of a linguistic expression, the latter to the 'meaning of the meaning' (*maʿnā l-maʿnā*), which must first be derived through thought. As has already been explained, the correct classification of this distinction was the subject of intense debate in the subsequent logical tradition, resulting in a not insignificant modification:[167] While [a] some scholars shared Faḫr ad-dīn ar-Rāzī's assumption that only the congruent manner of signification is to be called *dalāla waḍʿiyya*, [b] others regarded both congruence and containment as *dalāla waḍʿiyya*. In the end, through e.g. the *Šamsiyya* commentaries of Quṭb ad-dīn ar-Rāzī at-Taḥtānī (d. 766/1365) and Šarīf al-Ǧurǧānī,

---

Ḥāǧib; id. and Taqī ad-dīn as-Subkī, *Ibhāǧ fī Šarḥ al-Minhāǧ*, ed. by Šaʿbān Muḥammad Ismāʿīl (Cairo: Maktabat al-Kullīyāt al-Azharīyah, 1981 [1401]).

163 As-Subkī, *Ibhāǧ fī Šarḥ al-Minhāǧ*, vol. 1, p. 368, lines 3–4.

164 See al-Laknawī, *Fawātiḥ ar-raḥamūt*, vol. 1, p. 449, line 31–p. 450, line 2.

165 Zysow, *The Economy of Certainty*, p. 109.

166 See Chapter 2, Section 3.2.1.

167 This debate is also occasionally carried over into the *uṣūl al-fiqh* works, see for example as-Subkī, *Ibhāǧ fī Šarḥ al-Minhāǧ*, vol. 1, pp. 203f.

position [c] prevailed, whereby all three manners of signification are assigned to *dalāla waḍʿiyya* and whereby *dalāla ʿaqliyya*, which had previously been regarded as a catch-all for transferred meanings, receives a different definition.[168] The understanding that *iltizām* signifies the 'meaning of the meaning' did not change as a result, for the new categorization still considers the meaning of the meaning to be mediately based on the relationship of imposition. Just as, in the writings on logic, the classification scheme in which all three manners of signification are subsumed under "signification by imposition" (*dalāla waḍʿiyya*) came to prevail, in the legal-theoretical classification of signification, all three manners of signification came to be subsumed under the category *dalālat al-manṭūq*—and with the same justification, namely that everything that is signified by means of these three manners of signification is immediately or mediately based on what is explicitly spoken.[169]

2.2.2 Not a Manner of Signification: Questioning the Legitimacy of the *Argumentum e Contrario* on the Basis of the Tripartition of Signification

From schema outlined here, in which a majority of the manners of signification defined from a legal-theoretical perspective are subsumed under the category *dalālat al-manṭūq*, we can quite easily argue as follows: There are only the three manners of signification (, all three of which belong to the category *manṭūq*); the *argumentum e contrario* (*mafhūm al-muḫālafa*), which is the opposite of *manṭūq*, is not one of them; therefore, it is not valid. Because *mafhūm al-muwāfaqa* has a different name (namely *dalālat an-naṣṣ*) in the Ḥanafite legal-theoretical system of signification and is therefore not assigned to the category of *mafhūm* but instead also to the three manners of signification, this argument for illegitimacy would only apply to the *argumentum e contrario* and would not affect the admissibility of *mafhūm al-muwāfaqa*. The situation would be different in the Šāfiʿite system of signification, where this argument would affect both types of *mafhūm* signification.

In the *Musallam aṯ-ṯubūt* of the Ḥanafite scholar Muḥibb Allāh al-Bihārī (d. 1119/1707), the following quite concise formulation is also found among the arguments against the *argumentum e contrario*: "Fourthly: [*signification by the*

168 See Chapter 2, Section 3.2.1, pp. 134 ff.

169 It should be noted here that, within this comparison with the logical classification of signification, there are some incongruencies in Īǧī's legal-theoretical classification of signification that can be explained by the fact that the latter is based on Ibn al-Ḥāǧib's schema, which in turn corresponds to the tradition of position [b]. Meanwhile the logical signification schema originates from the tradition of position [c].

argumentum e contrario] is not one of the three manners of signification (*wa-rābiʿan laysat bi-iḥdā d-dalālāt aṯ-ṯalāṯ*)."[170] Niẓām ad-dīn al-Anṣārī al-Laknawī (d. 1225/1810) comments on this as follows: "[*The fact that the* argumentum e contrario *is not valid*] is concluded fourthly from the fact that if the *argumentum e contrario* [*were valid*], it would have to be one of them, namely congruence, containment, and implication. 'It [*i.e. signification by the* argumentum e contrario] is not one of the three manners of signification'";[171] therefore it is invalid.

In this terminology, this argument in these two Ḥanafite texts goes back to the Šāfiʿite Tāǧ ad-dīn al-Urmawī, who reformulated Faḫr ad-dīn's argument in his commentary on the *Maḥṣūl*, as already shown in Chapter 4, Section 1.1.2, p. 186. In Faḫr ad-dīn and Abū l-Ḥusayn al-Baṣrī, the argument reads as follows:

[*Antecedent*] If the *argumentum e contrario* (or a subtype of it) were valid, the legal ruling of the mentioned circumstance would signify the legal ruling of the unmentioned circumstance either
[a] by the wording (*bi-lafẓihī*) of the statement or
[b] by its meaning (*bi-maʿnāhu*)
[*Consequent*] However, it does not signify it in either of these ways; therefore, it is necessary that it does not signify it [*i.e. the legal ruling of the unmentioned circumstance*] at all.
Tāǧ ad-dīn al-Urmawī on the other hand replaces [a] wording and [b] meaning with
[a] by congruence (*bi-l-muṭābaqa*)
[b] or by implication (*bi-l-iltizām*).

He comes to the same conclusion as Faḫr ad-dīn before him, namely that the statement does not signify in either of these ways what it does not mention, and therefore does not signify it at all. Unlike Tāǧ ad-dīn al-Urmawī in his *Maḥṣūl* commentary, al-Bayḍāwī in his *Minhāǧ al-wuṣūl ilā ʿilm al-uṣūl*, a work based on the *Maḥṣūl* commentaries of the two Urmawīs, advocates for the implication thesis:

> It is said: If it were to signify it [*i.e. if the legal ruling of the original case were to signify the negation of the legal ruling on the circumstance qualified by*

---

170 Muḥibb Allāh ibn ʿAbd aš-Šakūr al-Bihārī, *Musallam aṯ-ṯubūt*, Ms. Maktabat Ǧāmiʿat al-Malik Saʿūd 8144, fol. 93ᵛ, last line or the quotation in al-Laknawī, *Fawātiḥ ar-raḥamūt*, vol. 1, p. 454, line 10.

171 Ibid., lines 9–10.

the other unmentioned attribute], then it would signify [*it*] either by congruence (*muṭābaqatan*) or by implication (*iltizāman*). We say that it [*i.e. the legal ruling on the original case*] signifies by implication, since it has been established that the sequence (*tartīb*) signifes causation (*ʿilliyya*), whereby the elimination of the cause (*ʿilla*) in turn necessitates the elimination of the thing caused by it.[172]

The fact that the circumstance is qualified by a certain attribute must be for a good reason and cannot be superfluous; therefore, the proponents of this form of *argumentum e contrario* assume that the presence of the attribute in this circumstance elicits the legal ruling. If the circumstance were to occur without this specific attribute, this legal ruling would in turn be omitted.

In his commentary on Bayḍāwī's *Minhāǧ al-wuṣūl ilā ʿilm al-uṣūl*, Šams ad-dīn al-Iṣfahānī (d. 749/1348) quotes the counter-thesis and ultimately justifies Bayḍāwī's position, according to which implication is to be assumed in this case. This reasoning deserves closer consideration; al-Iṣfahānī firstly cites the opposing position—advocated by Faḫr ad-dīn, among others:

[§1] It is said:

"[§1.1] If attaching (*taʿlīq*) the legal ruling (*al-ḥukm*) to one of two essential attributes would signify the negation of that which is omitted from the legal ruling, then it [*i.e. the legal ruling of the initial case*] signifies [*the negation of the legal ruling on that circumstance, which is qualified by the other, unmentioned attribute*]
either in the way
[a] of congruence (*muṭābaqatan*),
[b] of inclusion (*taḍammunan*),
[c] or of implication (*iltizāman*).
[§1.2] But what adheres (*lāzim*) [*i.e. here: the consequent of this conditional sentence*] is false, so that to which it adheres (*malzūm*) [*i.e. the antecedent of this conditional sentence*] is also [*false*].
[§1.3] As concerns the entailment (*mulāzama*) [*i.e. here: the conditional sentence in question*], it is clear that the linguistic signification based on imposition (*ad-dalāla al-lafẓiyya bi-l-waḍʿiyya*)[173] can be divided into these three [*manners of signification*].

172 Al-Bayḍāwī, *Minhāǧ*, p. 69, lines 6–8.

173 The editor indicates a different placement of the diacritics, such that the edition reads *waṣfiyya* instead of *waḍʿiyya*; it must however read *waḍʿiyya*. The translation of *lafẓiyya* as

[§1.4] As concerns the falseness of what adheres (*lāzim*) [*i.e. here: the consequent of this conditional sentence*], [*it, the consequent, is false*], since it is evident that congruence and inclusion do not apply [*i.e. the* argumentum e contrario *does not occur by means of these two manners of signification*]; for the negation of the legal ruling of that [*attribute*] which is excluded from what is mentioned is not equivalent to the existence of the mentioned legal ruling or its part.

[§1.5] The [*manner of*] implication [*also does*] not [*apply*], because the condition for implication is that the mind (*ḏihn*) turns from the named thing (*al-musammā*) to the thing signified by implication (*ilā l-madlūli l-iltizāmī*). Here [*i.e. in the case of the* argumentum e contrario] the mind does not turn to it, for whoever conceptualizes what is signified by congruence by his saying "*zakāt* is [*to be paid*] for free-grazing sheep" (*fī sā'imati l-ġanami zakātun*) does not think whatsoever about stall-fed [*sheep*] (*ma'lūfa*) or the fact that the obligation of *zakāt* does not exist for them."

[§2] The author [*of the Minhāǧ, i.e. al-Bayḍāwī*] responds [*to this argument against the* argumentum e contrario] that it [*i.e. the legal ruling of the original case*] indeed signifies [*the negation of the legal ruling for the unmentioned attribute*] in the manner of implication (*iltizāman*), since it has been established that the resulting of the legal ruling from the attribute (*waṣf*) indicates the causality (*'illiyya*) of the attribute with regard to the legal ruling. The absence of the cause (*'illa*) necessitates the absense of that which is caused by it with certainty (!).

[§3] As for his words "here the mind does not turn to it," this is ruled out and is rejected. For amongst the Uṣūlīs, it is sufficient for the signification of implication that certainty about that which is adhered to (*ǧazm bi-l-malzūm*) is obtained by conceptualizing simultaneously both the adhering thing and that which is adhered to; [*implication to the Uṣūlīs*] is not dependent on the mind turning (involuntarily) from that which is adhered to that which adheres.[174]

The type of *argumentum e contrario* called *mafhūm aṣ-ṣifa* refers to the situation in which a statement qualified by a certain attribute entails a certain legal

"linguistic" emerges from the classification itself, as has been worked out and justified in Chapter 2, Section 3.2.1, p. 136.

174 Šams ad-dīn al-Iṣfahānī, *Šarḥ al-Minhāǧ*, vol. 1, p. 292, line 10–p. 293, line 5; see also Ǧamāl ad-dīn al-Isnawī, *Nihāyat as-sūl*, vol. 2, p. 215, lines 3ff.

ruling where this qualification has the purpose of excluding from this legal ruling all other circumstances not specified by this attribute.

[*ad* § 1.1] The opponent of the *argumentum e contrario*, or at least this type of it, who is quoted here by Šams ad-dīn al-Iṣfahānī argues that the original case would have to signify the negation of the legal ruling on the unmentioned attribute in one of the three manners of signification—otherwise there is no signification occurring.[175] Linking this type of signification with the three manners of signification in the form of a conditional—"if such a signification is present, then it is one of the three manners of signification"—is [*ad* § 1.3] obvious, it is said, since ultimately all spoken or written linguistic significations can be traced back to one of these three manners. The quoted scholar here uses the terminology that—as shown in Chapter 2, Section 3.2.1—became established in the later logical tradition, and classifies each of the three manners of signification as a "linguistic signification based on imposition" (*ad-dalāla l-lafẓiyya bi-l-waḍʿiyya*).[176]

The opponent then goes on to show that none of the three manners of signification is connected with the *argumentum e contrario*: [*ad* § 1.4] That which is not mentioned cannot be signified by either of the first two manners of signification because there is obviously no relationship of imposition: there are no linguistic expressions directly designating the negation of the legal ruling or any parts of it. In other words, the commandment to perform a certain act is not tantamount to saying that the opposite of this act or another unmentioned act should not be performed.

[*ad* § 1.5] Implication is also excluded because the condition for the *iltizām* manner of signification is not fulfilled, namely that "the mind (*ḏihn*) turns from what is named (*al-musammā*) to that which is signified by implication (*ilā l-madlūli l-iltizāmī*)."

[*ad* § 1.2] The consequent, according to which the negation is signified in one of these three ways, is false according to the quoted position; therefore the antecedent proposition, according to which the negation is signified, cannot be true either. This argument corresponds to a *modus tollendo tollens*: if p, then q; not q, therefore not p.[177]

---

175 See Chapter 4, Section 1.1.2, pp. 197 ff., especially p. 202 and p. 205. Cf. Ǧamāl ad-dīn Ibn al-Ḥāǧib, *Muḫtaṣar al-Muntahā*, vol. 2, pp. 668 ff.; cf. al-Bābartī, *ar-Rudūd wa-n-nuqūd*, vol. 2, pp. 58 ff.; al-Īǧī, *Šarḥ Muḫtaṣar al-Muntahā*, pp. 170–172 and pp. 256 ff., and as-Subkī, *Ibhāǧ fī Šarḥ al-Minhāǧ*, vol. 1, pp. 374–376.

176 See Chapter 2, Section 3.2.1, pp. 121 ff.

177 Cf. Kneale, *The Development of Logic*, p. 163 and pp. 219–220; see Chapter 4, Section 1.1.2.

[*ad* § 2] Iṣfahānī next presents al-Bayḍāwī's reasoning as an answer to this objection: This type of *argumentum e contrario* indeed represents a case of implication because the specific attribute is regarded as the cause of the legal ruling; if this cause ceases to exist, the legal ruling also ceases to exist.

[*ad* § 3] The objection that the condition for the *iltizām* manner of signification is not fulfilled because the mind does not turn to the negation of legal judgement is refuted by means of an internal differentiation of this manner of signification: It is true that in this case there is no mental or essential implication (*luzūm ḏihnī*), so the argumentation claims; but we do not actually need this in legal methodology. Instead, it is entirely sufficient to obtain an external implication (*luzūm ḫāriǧī*). In another work, Šams ad-dīn al-Iṣfahānī discusses this differentiation in more detail:

> [§ 1] The Uṣūlīs did not make mental implication (*luzūm ḏihnī*) a condition for the signification of implication (*dalālat al-iltizām*), but instead used the term [*implication* (iltizām)] for 'that which adheres to what is named' (*lāzim al-musammā*)—regardless of whether what adheres is external (*ḫāriǧ*) or essential (*ḏihnī*).
> [§ 2] The logicians did make mental implication (*luzūm ḏihnī*) a condition, i.e. that an external meaning is in the state that the conceptualization of it follows the conceptualization of what is named. Otherwise, no understanding occurs, because understanding only occurs if the linguistic expression has been imposed for that meaning or [*if*] the conceptualization of it [*i.e. the conceptualization of the meaning for which the linguistic expression has not been imposed*] follows the conceptualization of what is named.[178]

The distinction between *luzūm ḏihnī* and *luzūm ḫāriǧī* recurs, as has already been noted,[179] in the description of different relationships of necessity in the logical texts. External implication is as follows: "Things are necessary according to implication (*luzūm*), without one of them being necessary for the other according to substance (*ǧawhar*) or nature (*ṭabīʿa*)—these are the externally adhering things (*lawāzim ḫāriǧa*)."[180] Extrinsic attributes in this case adhere to the quiddity as a quiddity or to the realized quiddity; despite the simultaneity of occurrence, the necessity is not grounded in the substance or nature

178 Šams ad-dīn al-Iṣfahānī, *Bayān al-Muḫtaṣar*, vol. 1, p. 155, lines 10–15.
179 For a detailed discussion of this topic, see Chapter 2, Section 3.2.3, pp. 142 f.
180 Ibn Sīnā, *Kitāb aš-Šifāʾ*, *Kitāb al-Burhān*, II.5, p. 150, lines 6–7.

of the thing; no certain knowledge (*ʿilm yaqīnī*) is generated in this type of implication.[181]

Faḫr ad-dīn coined the term *luzūm ḏihnī* in reference to Ibn Sīnā's description of this implication as a type of signification in which the mind (*ḏihn*) turns from the primary, congruent meaning to the implied meaning: "this [*primary*] meaning is accompanied by another (*wa-yakūnu ḏālika l-maʿnā yaṣḥabuhū maʿnan āḫar*), such that the mind also turns to this second meaning (*fa-yantaqilu ḏ-ḏihnu ayḍan ilā ḏālika l-maʿnā ṯ-ṯānī*),"[182]—i.e., we are dealing in this case with a relationship of necessity that is established in the essence, even if the linguistic expressions themselves have not been imposed for the meaning. A frequently cited example to illustrate this type of implication is that the meaning of the word 'rational' (*nāṭiq*) is "'a thing that is endowed with reason' (*šayʾ lahū nuṭq*) and 'a thing that has a soul endowed with reason.'" The word does not say anything about "whether this thing is a substance or not a substance; however, adhering [*to it*] (*illā annahū yalzamu*) is the fact that this thing can be nothing other than a substance, a body, and sentient."[183] Another example is that "evenness/being even" (*zawǧiyya*) adheres to the conceptualization of the number "four."

The intent to refute the argument that the *argumentum e contrario* is not a type of implication by illustrating the distinction between these two types of implication (essential and external) goes back to Šihāb ad-dīn al-Qarāfī: According to al-Qarāfī, a distinction must be made between [a] implication (*mulāzama*) that generates certain knowledge, and [b] that which does not generate certain knowledge, but instead merely presumption (*ẓann*). The first is like evenness in relation to four and the second is like "impurity (*naǧāsa*) in relation to the cup of the barber (*kaʾs al-ḥaǧǧām*)."[184] It is the second type of implication to which the type of *argumentum e contrario* in question belongs.[185]

Lowering the requirements with regard to certainty of knowledge might seem logical in view of the fact that the epistemological requirements in jurisprudence and legal hermeneutics are generally not as strict as in theology or logic.[186] And Faḫr ad-dīn cited such an argument by the proponents of

181 Ibid., line 7; see Chapter 2, Section 3.2.3.
182 Ibn Sīnā, *Manṭiq al-Mašriqiyyīn*, p. 15, lines 1–2.
183 Ibn Sīnā, *Kitāb aš-Šifāʾ, al-Ilāhiyyāt*, v.6, p. 233, lines 1–4.
184 Al-Qarāfī, *Nafāʾis al-uṣūl*, vol. 2, p. 218, line 14.
185 Cf. ibid., lines 10–14.
186 Cf. for example van Ess, *Die Erkenntnislehre*, p. 382: "[I]n legal *ictihād*, convincing probability was sufficient, in kalām one strived for unquestionable certainty."

the *argumentum e contrario* with regard to "signification by meaning" that distinguishes two epistemological statuses (namely *qaṭʿiyya* and *ẓanniyya*).[187] However, he rejects it because, due to the methodological weakness of this form of inference and all the other objections to the *argumentum e contrario*, it does not lead to any gain in knowledge.[188] His remarks in § 4 of the *Maḥṣūl* as presented in Chapter 1 also directly related to this question: Here Faḫr ad-dīn had worked out, among other things, that implication is understood to mean only mental or essential implication, and not external implication.[189]

It can be noted that both the proponents and opponents of the *argumentum e contrario* refer to the Tripartition of Signification and its associated concepts and distinctions in their arguments. Moreover, Faḫr ad-dīn's argument develops into a standard argument of the Ḥanafite scholars against the Šāfiʿites' arguments in favor of the *argumentum e contrario*. The debate about it shows the general and practical relevance that has been attributed to the Tripartition of Signification. Furthermore, the detailed foray through the commentaries has given us insight into the productive transformation and further development of the content of his *Maḥṣūl*.[190]

3 Summary

The manner of signification of implication given the technical term *dalālat al-iltizām*—after being established in the theory of the logical writings—undergoes an extension of its application and receives a practical relevance in Faḫr ad-dīn ar-Rāzī's legal methodology. It comes to function as a generic term for the classical Šāfiʿite view of the types of implication (1.) *dalālat al-iqtiḍāʾ*, (2.) *dalālat al-išāra*, (3.) *mafhūm al-muwāfaqa*, and (4.) *mafhūm al-muḫālafa*, which are set in relation to one another in a new way from a systematic point of view. This happens quite independently of whether Faḫr ad-dīn himself rejects the respective manner of signification as implication (as in the case of *mafhūm al-muwāfaqa*) or whether he considers it illegitimate as a method of making law

187 Faḫr ad-dīn ar-Rāzī, *al-Maḥṣūl*, vol. 2, p. 139, line 13–p. 140, line 6.
188 Ibid., p. 140, lines 7–10.
189 Faḫr ad-dīn ar-Rāzī, *al-Maḥṣūl*, vol. 1, p. 220, lines 4 ff.; see Chapter 1, Section 3.2, p. 50 and Chapter 2, Section 3.2.3, p. 142.
190 See in detail (in relation to philosophical commentaries), Asad Q. Ahmed, "Post-Classical Philosophical Commentaries/Glosses: Innovations in the Margins," *Oriens*, vol. 41, no. 3–4 (2013): pp. 317–348.

(as in the case of *mafhūm al-muḫālafa*); it is sufficient if certain scholars in the *uṣūl al-fiqh* debates had voted in favor of implication using sound arguments. Thus, the *dalālat al-iltizām* becomes a comprehensive hermeneutical toolbox that sorts and unifies competing approaches according to their similarities.

By making *iltizām*, among other things, the generic term for legal-theoretical types of implication, it replaces *mafhūm*, which had previously held this role in the *manṭūq/mafhūm* dichotomy. This hermeneutical toolbox is not adopted in this form, but is developed further in very interesting ways: Al-Bayḍāwī, for example, adopts Faḫr ad-dīn's systematization of implication relationships to a certain extent in his *Minhāǧ*, but retains *mafhūm* as a generic term for it. The *manṭūq/mafhūm* dichotomy thus continues to be handed down. But in Ibn al-Ḥāǧib's *Muḫtaṣar al-Muntahā* a paradigm shift takes place that has not yet been recognized as such. Instead, scholars and commentators of the past and present have either instated a strange classification (such as the Šāfiʿite scholar ʿAlāʾ ad-dīn al-Qūnawī, d. 729/1329, or the Islamic scholar Yunis Ali); adopted the changed classification tacitly (such as the Šāfiʿite ʿAḍud ad-dīn al-Īǧī, d. 756/1355) or loudly (Ḥanafite Akmal ad-dīn Muḥammad b. Maḥmūd al-Bābartī, d. 786/1384); or perceived no change at all in comparison to al-Āmidī's schema. Ibn al-Ḥāǧib does label the types of implication "not plain" (*ġayr aṣ-ṣarīḥ*) in order to signal, like al-Āmidī, that the implied meanings and legal rulings are not signified by the plain word form itself (*lā bi-ṣarīḥ ṣīġatihī*) or by the establishments between word and meaning. But unlike al-Āmidī, who equated this category with *mafhūm* and included all relationships of implication under it, for the Mālikite Ibn al-Ḥağib, *ġayr aṣ-ṣarīḥ* is now an area of *manṭūq*, i.e. explicit speech, and no longer counts as a genuine type of implication.

Ibn al-Ḥāǧib empties out the toolbox and reorganizes it: The dichotomy of "explicitly spoken" (*manṭūq* = *ṣarīḥ*) vs. "implied" (*mafhūm* = *ġayr aṣ-ṣarīḥ*) shifts its center of gravity and becomes "explicitly spoken" (*manṭūq* = *ṣarīḥ* and *ġayr aṣ-ṣarīḥ*) vs. "implied" (*mafhūm* = almost empty), whereby the latter only includes the two implication types *mafhūm al-muwāfaqa* and *mafhūm al-muḫālafa* because the others have been shifted into the *manṭūq* realm. Even if this synthesis finally prevails in the Šāfiʿite school of law, it must be recognized that it is an accomplishment of synthesis that did *not* previously correspond to the Šāfiʿite approach—one should not be deceived by the decidedly Šāfiʿite terminology. This change is not merely a quibble; rather, in the Šāfiʿite-Mālikite legal methodology, the distinction between *manṭūq* and *mafhūm* came to assign greater epistemological significance to the former category than to the latter. Shifting types of implication into the realm of 'explicit speech' means—even if an internal differentiation is made—first of all a valorization of implications in the process of law-making. As has been shown, this approach, which Ibn al-Ḥāǧib makes effective here by including more in the realm of explicit speech than the Šāfiʿites were previously inclined to do, could be described as a Ḥanafite hermeneutical paradigm. This is characterized by the fact that meanings, which Šāfiʿite scholars tend to arrive at by means of fixed rules of deduction, are situated in a broad semantic area that can still be accessed with ordinary linguistic competence. These different approaches entail different epistemological evaluations and a greater or lesser scope for exegesis. The fact that such different approaches can be crystallized, allowing us to call them Šāfiʿite or Ḥanafite, shows that, despite a Mālikite scholar's work becoming style-forming for Šāfiʿite legal hermeneutics by incorporating fundamental Ḥanafite principles into the Šāfiʿite-Mālikite approach, there are still certain legal school-specific approaches and positions in the *uṣūl al-fiqh* literature.[191] Moreover, this again points to the insignificance of Ibn Ḫaldūn's topos of the theologically vs. the legally orientated *uṣūl al-fiqh*.

In the commentary literature on the *Muḫtaṣar al-Muntahā*, namely with ʿAḍud ad-dīn al-Īǧī, Ibn al-Ḥāǧib's new classification is finally harmonized with the Tripartition of Signification. While the congruent manner of signification (*dalālat al-muṭābaqa*) and that of containment (*dalālat at-taḍammun*) are labeled as *ṣarīḥ*, the signification of implication (*dalālat al-iltizām*) is considered *ġayr ṣarīḥ*; all three manners of signification remain in the realm of explicit speech (*manṭūq*). This classification is identical to the approach that developed at the same time in the tradition of logic, in which, based on Quṭb ad-dīn ar-Rāzī at-Taḥtānī's (d. 766/1365) and Šarīf al-Ǧurǧānī's commentaries on Kātibī's *ar-Risāla aš-šamsiyya*, the position prevails according to which each of the three manners of signification (i.e. *muṭābaqa*, *taḍammun*, and *iltizām*) is regarded as a signification based on the imposition between word and meaning, *dalāla waḍʿiyya*. Thus no longer, as in Faḫr ad-dīn, is only the first signification accorded this status, with containment and implication being regarded as derived significations based on reasoning (*dalāla ʿaqliyya*).

However, Īǧī's harmonization leads to a decoupling of the two types of implication *mafhūm al-muwāfaqa* and *mafhūm al-muḫālafa* from the manner of signification of implication (*iltizām*). In contrast to Faḫr ad-dīn, *iltizām* thus only summarizes part of the types of implication—on this basis, Ḥanafite

---

191 I am referring to the question posed by Jackson: "Is there, in fact, such a thing as Mālikī *uṣūl* that is as distinct from Ḥanbalī or Ḥanafī *uṣūl* as Mālikī *furūʿ* is from Ḥanbalī or Ḥanafī *furūʿ*?" Sherman A. Jackson, "Fiction and Formalism: Towards a Functional Analysis of *Uṣūl al-Fiqh*," in *Studies in Islamic Legal Theory*, ed. by Bernard G. Weiss (Leiden [et al.]: Brill, 2002), pp. 179–180.

scholars who reject the *argumentum e contrario* can easily argue against it: There are only the three types of signification in the linguistic system (namely *muṭābaqa, taḍammun,* and *iltizām,* all three of which belong to the *manṭūq* category); the *argumentum e contrario* (*mafhūm al-muḫālafa,* which is opposite to *manṭūq*) is not one of them; thus, it is not valid. Since the other implication, *mafhūm al-muwāfaqa,* is named and situated differently in the Ḥanafi system of signification, it is not affected by this argument. As has been shown, this argument against the validity of the *argumentum e contrario* is Tāǧ ad-dīn al-Urmawī's modification of an argument of Faḫr ad-dīn and Abū l-Ḥusayn al-Baṣrī against the *argumentum e contrario*—thus completing the circle.

Summary and Outlook: Faḫr ad-dīn's Interdisciplinary Hermeneutical Toolkit

The aim of this work was to contribute to research into the influence that the Avicennian philosophy of language and logic had on Islamic compendia of legal theory. On the one hand, the study focused textually on the *uṣūl al-fiqh* compendium by Faḫr ad-dīn ar-Rāzī as well as on subsequent works and works that were influenced by it—compendia, abridged versions, and commentaries; on the other hand, the focus of the content was on the analysis of the Tripartition of Signification into congruence (*muṭābaqa*), containment (*taḍammun*), and implication (*iltizām*) and on the reconstruction of its historical development—prompted by the observation that this is a classification that would become an integral part of the introductory chapters of post-Avicennian works on logic, legal theory, and rhetoric.

The origin of this classification can be located in the discipline of logic. Based on the synthesizing presentation of this classification of signification in Faḫr ad-dīn's *Maḥṣūl*, the first task was to trace the development of the classification in the logical writings of al-Fārābī and Ibn Sīnā and to sift out the functions that this classification assumed in the various logical writings. In a second step, the development of this classification in the writings of Faḫr ad-dīn ar-Rāzī was traced, whereby the presentation in the *Maḥṣūl* was analyzed in particular. Finally, the function assigned to the classification, especially implication (*iltizām*), in the legal theory of Faḫr ad-dīn and subsequent scholars was analyzed.

[1.] It turns out that the Tripartition was preceded by a dichotomy: In a passage based on *De Int.* 11 of his guide the "*Book of Circumstances that Lead to Errors*" (*Kitāb al-Amkina al-Muġliṭa*), al-Fārābī distinguishes between two different types of implication in order to explain the extent to which predicates that apply to a thing independently of each other may also be stated in conjunction with each other. These two types of implication are called *luzūm* by al-Fārābī and are not yet terminologically differentiated from one another. Based on various logical and ontological themes—for example, Ibn Sīnā uses these two types of implication to answer the question of whether the specific difference in turn belongs to a genus, which would result in the aporia of the infinite regress of the specific difference—Ibn Sīnā consolidates the discussion of the two manners of signification in the *Madḫal* treatises of his works. While in earlier works we still encounter the dichotomy—albeit now terminologically differentiated—Ibn Sīnā finally makes a distinction in *Madḫal* 1.8 of his *Kitāb aš-Šifāʾ*, between a primary, secondary, and extrinsic type of signification using the terms *dalālat muṭābaqa*, *dalālat taḍammun*, and *dalālat luzūm*. Among other things, he is thus able to show the difference between the signification of whatness/quiddity (*māhiyya*) and howness (*ayyiyya*) and to assign different significations to the various predicables, thus making a significant contribution to the theory of definition. In Ibn Sīnā's later writings—especially in the *Išārāt wa-t-tanbīhāt*—an ever higher degree of systematization can be seen in the presentation of the three manners of signification, which is accompanied, among other things, by the fact that they are no longer offered as solutions in the context of specific problems, but are instead combined with other topics at the beginning of the logic treatises to form a package of linguistic fundamentals. Last but not least, the enormous amount of commentary literature generated by the *Išārāt*—a process in which Faḫr ad-dīn ar-Rāzī played a decisive role—led to the classification of signification becoming increasingly generalized and finally embedded in the foundations of what logicians had to learn from the start of their careers.

[2.] The degree of systematization and abstraction outlined by Ibn Sīnā reaches a climax in Faḫr ad-dīn ar-Rāzī's logical writings: Whereas Ibn Sīnā had e.g. previously attempted to grasp the relationships between predicables by classifying the manners of signification, Faḫr ad-dīn extends these three manners of signification to all linguistic expressions. In addition, he sets the Tripartition, whose position in the language system he regards as fundemental, on parallel with the three-part classification of linguistic expressions into *ism*, *fiʿl*, and *ḥarf*. All linguistic expressions can be categorized as either name (*ism*), verb (*fiʿl*), or particle (*ḥarf*), and their significations as either congruence (*muṭābaqa*), containment (*taḍammun*), or implication (*iltizām*).

In addition, the classification of signification in the *Maḥṣūl*, *Maʿālim*, and *Mulaḫḫaṣ* serves as a starting point for further classifications that characterize the linguistic expression from different points of view. The line of tradition of the relevant passage of the *Maḥṣūl*—the focus of this work—which I have labelled the "logical sub-classification," is particularly noteworthy. For this work is not a logical one, but a work on legal theory that contains no introduction or references to logic that it declares as such. The passage shows that Faḫr ad-dīn directly engages with Ibn Sīnā's logic and philosophy of language—and here in particular with the genre of *Madḫal*, a genre of logical propaedeutics—in the context of his theory of law. As we have seen, the structure of the logical subclassification (with the differentiation criteria of simpleness vs. compoundness, particularity vs. universality, and up to the various predicables) is made useful for other language-related content, for example for the differentiation of name (*ism*), verb (*fiʿl*), and particle (*ḥarf*) and the further sub-classification of the name. On the one hand, the (simple, universal) generic name of the grammarians is set as a parallel to the genus of the logicians; on the other hand, the paronym (*ism muštaqq*), i.e. the simple, universal derived name, is compared with the specific difference in the function of the attribute. The discussion of the scope of signification of the specific difference originating from the logical writings is transferred to the discussion of the derived name, such that the stand-alone paronymous name signifies the substance or the generic name by the manner of implication.

These structural principles can also be found in the logical and legal-theoretical sub-classification, in which Faḫr ad-dīn combines logical and legal-theoretical concepts in order to classify the semantic unambiguity/ambiguity of linguistic expressions—for example, polyonymy, heteronymy, Aristotelian synonymy, and homonymy from *Cat.* 1 which are linked with the legal-theoretical technical terms *muǧmal, ẓāhir, mu'awwal, ḥaqīqa*, and *maǧāz*. The same applies to the distinction between constative and performative sentence types; here, too, the structural principles are applied, and here, too, there is a linking of logical, grammatical-theoretical, and legal-theoretical topics.

[3.] Also based on the structural principles outlined in the logical sub-classification, Faḫr ad-dīn groups the classical Šāfiʿite relationships of implication (1.) *dalālat al-iqtiḍā'*, (2.) *dalālat al-išāra*, (3.) *mafhūm al-muwāfaqa*, and (4.) *mafhūm al-muḫālafa*, using *iltizām* as a generic term—this instead of *mafhūm*, which previously held this role in the *manṭūq/mafhūm* dichotomy. Through this new grouping, Faḫr ad-dīn can work out patterns and principles—and is thus able to explain the modes of action of the various relationships of implication and structure them in relation to one another. What is remarkable about this regrouping is that Faḫr ad-dīn classifies relationships as *iltizām* even when he himself does not regard the relevant singification relationship to be one of implication (but instead, for example, analogy) or questions its methodological legitimacy in other writings.

By aligning the hermeneutical toolkit of the various disciplines (legal theory, logic, grammar theory) with a structural guideline based on the classification of the manners of signification, Faḫr ad-dīn creates a *general* hermeneutical toolbox that—in the disciplines where this applies—attempts to end the state of the "multitude of simultaneous yet independent inquiries into the hermeneutic structure underlying each discipline."[1] This concerns the field of reflections on language and methodological investigations concerning language. On the one hand, he thus standardizes the propaedeutic linguistic knowledge of

1 Schwarb: "Capturing the Meaning of God's Speech," pp. 111–112.

the various disciplines, and on the other, he transforms the classification of the three manners of signification, which occupies a prominent position in this interdisciplinary toolbox, into a theory of signification that can be derived both empirically and purely rationally. This theory of signification, with its basic assumptions, its specific terminology, and the various remarks and limitations that Faḫr ad-dīn adds to it, has been the subject of discussion, commentary, and explanation for centuries. The fruitfulness of these debates has been pointed out at various points in this work. It is expressed (with regard to the post-Rāzian *uṣūl al-fiqh* compendia and commentaries), for example, in the authoritative paradigm shift of the Mālikite Ibn al-Ḥāǧib: His re-systematization of the legal-theoretical types of implication according to the Ḥanafite paradigm was to develop into the Šāfiʿite legal-theoretical classification par excellence. Another discipline in which an intensive examination of Faḫr ad-dīn's theory of signification has also taken place has so far been largely ignored and must be the focus of a separate work: This is the *ʿilm al-balāġa* and the key work of that discipline, namely Sīrāǧ ad-dīn as-Sakkākī's *Miftāḥ al-ʿulūm*.

This study has made clear the natural and uncontroversial way in which Avicennian logic and philosophy of language were received and adapted in the Islamic sciences using the example of *uṣūl al-fiqh*.

Bibliography

Primary literature

Alexander of Aphrodisias. "Risāla fī l-faṣli ḫāṣṣatan wa-mā huwa." In *Die arabische Version einer unbekannten Schrift des Alexander von Aphrodisias über die Differentia specifica*, ed. by Albert Dietrich, pp. 122–128. Göttingen: Vandenhoeck and Ruprecht, 1964.

al-Āmidī, Sayf ad-dīn. *al-Iḥkām fī uṣūl al-aḥkām*. Ed. by ʿAbd ar-Razzāq ʿAfīfī. Riyāḍ: Dār aṣ-Ṣumayʿī, 2003.

al Āmidī, Sayf ad-dīn. *Kašf at-tamwīhāt fī Šarḥ at-Tanbīhāt*. Ms. Berlin Petermann II 596.

al-Āmidī, Sayf ad-dīn. *Kašf at-tamwīhāt fī Šarḥ ar-Rāzī ʿalā l-Išārāt wa-tanbīhāt*. Ed. by Aḥmad Farīd al-Mazīdī. Beirut: Dār al-Kutub al-ʿilmiyya, 2013 [1434].

al-Āmidī, Sayf ad-dīn. *Muntahā as-sūl fī ʿilm al-uṣūl*. Ed. by Aḥmad Farīd al-Mazīdī. Beirut: Dār al-Kutub al-ʿilmiyya, 2003 [1424].

Ardakānī, Fāḍil. *Ġāyat al-masʾūl*. Ed. s.n. Qom: Muʾassasat Āl al-Bayt, s.d.

Aristotle. *Aristotelis Categoriae et Liber de Interpretatione* [Greek]. Ed. by Lorenzo Minio-Paluello. Oxford: Clarendon Press, 1949 [cited as *Cat.* and *De int.*].

Aristotle. *Aristotle's Prior and Posterior Analytics. A revised Text with Introduction and Commentary* [Greek]. Ed. by William D. Ross. Oxford: Clarendon Press, 2001 [reprint of the 1949 edition].

Aristotle. *Aristotelis Topica et Sophistici Elenchi* [Greek]. Ed. by William D. Ross. Oxford: Clarendon Press, 1958.

Aristotle. *De Interpretatione* [English]. In *The Complete Works of Aristotle: The Revised Oxford Tranlsation*, vol. 1, ed. by Jonathan Barnes. Princeton, NJ: University Press, 1984.

Aristotle. *De Interpretatione* [English]. Translated with notes by J.L. Ackrill. In *Atristotle. Categories and De Interpretatione*, pp. 43–68. Oxford: Clarendon Press, 1963 [reprint 2002].

Aristotle. *Manṭiq Arisṭū*. Ed. by ʿAbd ar-Raḥmān Badawī. al-Kuwayt: Wikālat al-Maṭbūʿāt, 1980 [reprint of the 1947 edition].

Aristotle. *Metaphysics* [English]. In *The Complete Works of Aristotle: The Revised Oxford Tranlsation*, vol. 2, ed. by Jonathan Barnes. Princeton, NJ: University Press, 1984.

Aristotle. *an-Naṣṣ al-kāmil li-Manṭiq Arisṭū* [Arabic]. Ed. by Farīd Ǧabr. Beirut: Dār al-Fikr al-Lubnānī, 1999.

Aristotle. *Posterior Analytics* [English]. *Translated with a Commentary by Jonathan Barnes*. Oxford: Clarendon Press, 2002.

al-Bābartī, Akmal ad-dīn Muḥammad b. Maḥmūd. *ar-Rudūd wa-n-nuqūd: Šarḥ*

Muḫtaṣar Ibn al-Ḥāǧib. Vol. 1, ed. by Ṣāliḥ b. ʿAwn al-ʿUmarī; Vol. 2, ed. by Tarḥīb b. Rabīʿān ad-Dawsarī. Riyāḍ: Maktabat al-Rušd Nāširūn, 2005.

al-Baġdādī, Abū l-Barakāt. *Kitāb al-Muʿtabar fī l-ḥikma*. Ed. by Zayn al-ʿAbidīn al-Musāwī. Haydarābād 1938–1939 [Reprint Ǧubayl: Dār wa-maktabat bībliyūn, 2012].

al-Bāqillānī, Qāḍī Abū Bakr. *Kitāb at-Tamhīd*. Ed. by Richard J. McCarthy. Beirut: Librairie Orientale, 1957.

al-Bāqillānī, Qāḍī Abū Bakr. *at-Taqrīb wa-l-iršād*. Ed. by ʿAbd al-Ḥamīd b. ʿAlī Abū Zunayd. Beirut: Muʾassasat ar-Risāla, 1998 [1418].

al-Baṣrī, Abū l-Ḥusayn. *Kitāb al-Muʿtamad fī uṣūl al-fiqh*. Ed. by Muḥammad Ḥamīd Allāh. Damascus: al-Maʿhad al-ʿilmī l-faransī li-d-dirāsāt al-ʿarabiyya, 1964–1965 [1384–1385].

al-Bayḍāwī, ʿAbdallāh b. ʿUmar. *Minhāǧ al-wuṣūl ilā ʿilm al-uṣūl*. Ed. by Salīm Šabʿānīya. Damascus: Dār Dāniya, 1989.

al-Bazdawī, ʿAlī ibn Muḥammad. *Kanz al-wuṣūl ilā maʿrifat al-uṣūl* (together with al-Buḫārī's commentary *Kašf al-asrār*). Ed. by Aḥmad Ḫulūṣī and Muṣṭafā Darwīš. Istanbul, 1890–1891 [1308].

al-Bihārī, Muḥibb Allāh ibn ʿAbd aš-Šakūr. *Musallam aṯ-ṯubūt*. Ms. Maktabat Ǧāmiʾat al-Malik Saʿūd 8144.

Borūǧerdī, Ḥosayn Ṭabāṭabāʾī. *Nihāyat al-uṣūl*. Ed. s.n. Qom: Našr tafakkur, 1994 [1415].

al-Buḫārī, ʿAbd al-ʿAzīz. *Kašf al-asrār*. Ed. by Aḥmad Ḫulūṣī and Muṣṭafā Darwīš. Istanbul, 1890–1891 [1308].

al-Fārābī, Abū Naṣr. *Kitāb al-alfāẓ al-mustaʿmala fī l-manṭiq*. Ed. by Muḥsin Mahdī. Beirut: Dār al-Mašriq, 1986.

al-Fārābī, Abū Naṣr. "Kitāb al-Amkina al-Muġliṭa." In *al-Manṭiq ʿinda l-Fārābī*. Ed. by Rafīq al-ʿAǧam. Beirut: Dār al-Mašriq, 1985–1986. Vol. 2, pp. 131–164; or in: *al-Manṭiqiyyāt li-l-Fārābī*. Ed. by Moḥammad Taqī Dānešpažūh. Qom: Maktabat-e Āyatollāh al-ʿAẓmī al-Marʿašī an-Naǧafī, 1988–1989/90 [1408–1410 h.š.]. Vol. 1: *an-Nuṣūṣ al-manṭiqiyya*, pp. 195–228.

al-Fārābī, Abū Naṣr. "Kitāb al-Burhān." In *al-Manṭiq ʿinda l-Fārābī*. Ed. by Māǧid Faḫrī. Beirut: Dār al-Mašriq, 1987, pp. 17–96; or in *al-Manṭiqiyyāt li-l-Fārābī, vol. 1, an-Nuṣūṣ al-manṭiqiyya*, pp. 265–349.

al-Fārābī, Abū Naṣr. *Al-Farabi's Commentary and Short Treatise on Aristotle's* De Interpretatione. Translation with introduction and commentaries by F.W. Zimmermann. New York: Oxford University Press, 1981.

al-Fārābī, Abū Naṣr. "Fuṣūl." In *al-Manṭiqiyyāt li-l-Fārābī, vol. 1, an-Nuṣūṣ al-manṭiqiyya*, pp. 18–27.

al-Fārābī, Abū Naṣr. *Kitāb al-Ḥurūf*. Ed. by Muḥsin Mahdī. Beirut: Dār al-Mašriq, 1970.

al-Fārābī, Abū Naṣr. "Šarḥ al-ʿIbāra." In *al-Manṭiqiyyāt li-l-Fārābī*. Ed. by Moḥammad Taqī Dānešpažūh. Qom: Maktabat-e Āyatollāh al-ʿAẓmī al-Marʿašī an-Naǧafī, 1988–1989/90 [1408–1410 h.š.]. Vol. 2: *aš-Šurūḥ al-manṭiqiyya*, pp. 1–259.

al-Fārābī, Abū Naṣr. *Iḥṣā' al-'ulūm*. Ed. by 'Alī Abū Mulḥim. Beirut: Dār wa-maktabat al-hilāl, 1996.

al-Fārābī, Abū Naṣr. "Kitāb Īsāġūǧī ay al-Madḫal." Ed. by D.M. Dunlop. In *The Islamic Quarterly*, vol. 3 (1956–1957): pp. 117–138.

al-Ġazālī, Abū Ḥāmid Muḥammad. *Kitāb Miḥakk an-naẓar*. Ed. by Rafīq al-'Aǧam. Beirut: Dār al-fikr al-lubnānī, 1994.

al-Ġazālī, Abū Ḥāmid Muḥammad. *Mi'yār al-'ilm*. Ed. by Sulaymān Dunyā. Cairo, 1961.

al-Ġazālī, Abū Ḥāmid Muḥammad. *al-Mustaṣfā min 'ilm al-uṣūl*. Ed. by Ḥamza b. Zuhayr Ḥāfiẓ. Medina: Šarikat al-Madīna al-munawwara li-ṭ-ṭibā'a wa-n-našr, 1993 [1413].

al-Ġazālī, Abū Ḥāmid Muḥammad. *Šifā' al-ġalīl fī bayān aš-šubah wa-l-muḫīl wa masālik at ta'līl*. Ed. by Ḥamd al-Kabīsī. Baghdad: al-Maṭba'a l-iršād, 1971.

al-Ǧurǧānī, 'Abd al-Qāhir. *Asrār al-balāġa*. Ed. by Hellmut Ritter. Istanbul: Government Press, 1954.

al-Ǧurǧānī, 'Abd al-Qāhir. *Dalā'il al-i'ǧāz*. Ed. by Muḥammad 'Abd al-Mun'im Ḫafāǧī. Cairo: Maktabat al-Qāhira, 1969 [1389].

al-Ǧurǧānī, 'Alī b. Muḥammad aš-Šarīf. *Kitāb al-Ta'rīfāt*. Ed. s.n. Cairo: al-Maṭba'a al-Ḫayriyya, 1888.

al-Ǧurǧānī, 'Alī b. Muḥammad aš-Šarīf. *al-Ḥawāšī 'alā Šarḥ al-Išārāt li-ṭ-Ṭūsī*. Ms. Leiden or. 190.

al-Ǧurǧānī, 'Alī b. Muḥammad aš-Šarīf. See al-Īǧī.

al-Ǧurǧānī, 'Alī b. Muḥammad aš-Šarīf. See at-Taḥtānī.

al-Ǧuwaynī, Imām al-Ḥaramayn. *al-Burhān fī uṣūl al-fiqh*. Ed. by Ṣāliḥ b. Muḥammad b. 'Uwayḍa. Beirut: Dār al-Kutub al-'ilmiyya, 1997 [1418].

al-Ǧuwaynī, Imām al-Ḥaramayn. *at-Talḫīṣ fī uṣūl al-fiqh*. Ed. by Muḥammad Ḥasan Isma'īl. Beirut: Dār al-Kutub al-'ilmiyya, 2003 [1424].

al-Ḥillī, Ǧamāl ad-dīn. *al-Ǧawhar an-naḍīd fī manṭiq at-taǧrīd*. Ed. by Muḥsin Bīdārfar. Qom: Intišārāt-i Bīdār, 1984 [1363].

al-Ḥillī, Ǧamāl ad-dīn. *al-Qawā'id al-ǧaliyya fī šarḥ ar-Risāla aš-šamsiyya*. Ed. by Fāris Ḥassūn Tabrīziyān. Qom: Mu'assasat an-našr al-islāmī, 1992 [1412].

al-Ḥillī, Ǧamāl ad-dīn. *Mabādi' al-wuṣūl ilā 'ilm al-uṣūl*. Ed. by 'Abd al-Ḥusayn Muḥammad 'Alī al-Baqqāl. Naǧaf: al-Adab, 1970 [1390].

al-Ḥillī, Ǧamāl ad-dīn. *Nihāyat al-wuṣūl ilā 'ilm al-uṣūl*. Ed. by Ibrāhīm Bahādurī. Qom, 2004/5 [1425].

al-Ḥillī, Ǧamāl ad-dīn. *Tahḏīb al-wuṣūl ilā 'ilm al-wuṣūl*. Ed. by Muḥammad Ḥusayn al-Kašmīrī. London: Mu'assasat al-Imām 'Alī, 2001 [1421].

al-Ḫūnaǧī, Afḍal ad-dīn. *Kašf al-asrār 'an ġawāmiḍ al-afkār*. Ed. by Khaled El-Rouayheb. Tehran: Iranian Institute of Philosophy and Institute of Islamic Studies, Free University of Berlin, 2010.

al-Ḫurāsānī, Muḥammad Kāẓim Ibn Ḥusayn. *al-Kifāya fī bayān al-imārāt wa-l-uṣūl*. Ed. s.n. Tehran, 1906.

Ibn Amīr al-Ḥāǧǧ, Muḥammad ibn Muḥammad. *at-Taqrīr wa-t-taḥbīr*. Ed. by ʿAbd Allāh Maḥmūd Muḥammad ʿUmar. Beirut: Dār al-Kutub al-ʿilmiyya, 1999 [1419].

Ibn Fāris, Aḥmad. *aṣ-Ṣāḥibī fī fiqh al-luġa wa-sunan al-ʿarab fī kalāmihā*. Ed. by Muṣṭafā al-Chouémi. Beirut: Muʾassasat Badrān li-ṭ-ṭibāʿa wa-našr, 1964 [1383].

Ibn Ǧinnī, Abū l-Fatḥ ʿUṯmān. *al-Ḫaṣāʾiṣ*. Vols. 1–3. Ed. by Muḥammad ʿAlī an-Naǧǧār. Beirut: Dār al-Kitāb al-ʿArabī [2nd edition; reprint of the Cairo edition, 1952–1957].

Ibn Ǧuzayy, Abū l-Qāsim. *Taqrīb al-wuṣūl ilā ʿilm al-uṣūl*. Ed. by Muḥammad al-Muḫtār b. Šayḫ Muḥammad al-Amīn aš-Šanqīṭī. Medina, 2002 [1423].

Ibn al-Ḥāǧib, Ǧamāl ad-dīn. *Kitāb Muntahā al-wuṣūl wa-l-amal fī ʿilmay al-uṣūl wa-l-ǧadal*. Ed. s.n. Beirut: Dār al-Kutub al-ʿilmiyya, 1985 [1405].

Ibn al-Ḥāǧib, Ǧamāl ad-dīn. *Muḫtaṣar al-muntahā fī s-sūl wa-l-amal fī ʿilmay al-uṣūl wa-l-ǧadal*. Ed. by Naẓīr Ḥamādū. Algiers: Dār Ibn Ḥazm, 2006.

Ibn an-Nadīm. *Kitāb al-Fihrist*, 2 vols. Ed. by Gustav Flügel. Leipzig: F.C.W. Vogel, 1871–1872.

Ibn an-Nadīm. *The Fihrist of al-Nadīm* [English], 2 vols. Edited and translated by Bayard Dodge. New York: Columbia University Press, 1970.

Ibn Ḫaldūn, ʿAbd ar-Raḥmān b. Muḥammad. *al-Muqaddima*. Beirut: Maktabat Lubnān, 1970 [reprint of the edition by Benjamin Duprat, Paris, 1858].

Ibn Ḫallikān, Aḥmad b. Muḥammad. *Wafayāt al-aʿyān wa-anbāʾ abnāʾ az-zamān*. Ed. by Iḥsān ʿAbbās. Beirut: Dār aṯ-ṯaqāfa, 1968–1972.

Ibn al-Laḥḥām. *al-Muḫtaṣar fī uṣūl al-fiqh ʿalā maḏhab al-imām Aḥmad ibn Ḥanbal*. Ed. by Muḥammad Ḥasan Ismāʿīl. Beirut: Dār al-Kutub al-ʿilmiyya, 2000 [1421].

Ibn Manẓūr. *Lisān al-ʿArab*. Būlāq: Al-maṭbaʿa al-amīriyya, 1883–1890 [1300–1308].

Ibn al-Marzubān, Abū l-Ḥasan Bahmanyār. *Kitāb at-Taḥṣīl*. Ed. by Mortaḍā Moṭahharī. Tehran: Entešārāt-e dānešgāh, 1997 [1375].

Ibn Qayyim al-Ǧawziyya, Muḥammad. *Iʿlām al-Muwaqqaʿīn ʿan rabb al-ʿālamīn*. Ed. by Abū ʿUbayda Āl Salmān. Dammām: Dār Ibn al-Ǧawzī, 2002 [1423].

Ibn Qudāma al-Maqdisī, ʿAbd Allāh b. Aḥmad. *Rawḍat an-nāẓir wa-ǧannat al-munāẓir fī uṣūl al-fiqh*. Ed. by ʿAbd al-Karīm b. ʿAlī b. Muḥammad an-Namla. Riyāḍ: Maktabat ar-rušd, 1993 [1413].

Ibn Sāʿātī, Aḥmad b. ʿAlī. *Kitāb al-Badīʿ*. Ed. by Muṣṭafā Maḥmūd al-Azharī and Muḥammad Ḥusayn ad-Dimyāṭī. Riyāḍ/Cairo: Dār Ibn al-Qayyim/Dār Ibn ʿAffān, 2014 [1435].

Ibn aš-Šahīd aṯ-Ṯānī, al-Ḥasan b. Zayn ad-dīn. *Maʿālim ad-dīn fī l-uṣūl*. Tehran: Lith. 1890 [reprint, ca. 1970].

Ibn Sīnā, Abū ʿAlī al-Ḥusayn b. ʿAlī. "İbn Sīnā'nın 'el-Mūcez fi'l Mantıq' Risālesi." Ed. by Mehmet Fatih Demirci. In *M.Ü. İlāhiyat Fakültesi Dergisi*, vol. 36, no. 1 (2009), pp. 151–206.

Ibn Sīnā, Abū ʿAlī al-Ḥusayn b. ʿAlī. *al-Išārāt wa-t-tanbīhāt*. Ed. by Muǧtabā az-Zarʿī. Qom: Būstān-e Ketāb 2008 [1387].

Ibn Sīnā, Abū ʿAlī al-Ḥusayn b. ʿAlī. "Logyca." In *Avicennae perhypatetici philosophi ac medicorum facili primi opera in lucem redacta ac nuper quantum ars niti potuit emendata.* Venice: Scotus 1508 [Reprint: Frankfurt a. M.: Minerva, 1961].

Ibn Sīnā, Abū ʿAlī al-Ḥusayn b. ʿAlī. *Kitāb al-Maǧmūʿ aw al-Ḥikma al-ʿArūḍiyya.* Ed. by Muḥsin Ṣāliḥ. Beirut, 2007.

Ibn Sīnā, Abū ʿAlī al-Ḥusayn b. ʿAlī. *Manṭiq al-Mašriqiyyīn.* Ed. s.n. Cairo: al-Maktaba as-Salafiyya, 1910.

Ibn Sīnā, Abū ʿAlī al-Ḥusayn b. ʿAlī. *al-Muḫtaṣar al-awsaṭ fī l-manṭiq.* Ms. Nuruosmaniye 2763 and ms. Turhan Valide Sultan 213 (Istanbul).

Ibn Sīnā, Abū ʿAlī al-Ḥusayn b. ʿAlī. *Kitāb an-Naǧāt.* Ed. by Moḥammad Taqī Dānešpažū, Tehran, 1985.

Ibn Sīnā, Abū ʿAlī al-Ḥusayn b. ʿAlī. *Risāla Asbāb hudūṯ al-ḥurūf. A Treatise on Arabic Phonetics. Translation, Notes and Comments.* Ed. by Solomon I. Sara. Munich: Lincom, 2009.

Ibn Sīnā, Abū ʿAlī al-Ḥusayn b. ʿAlī. *Kitāb aš-Šifāʾ, al-Ilāhiyyāt.* (1: maqāla 1–5) Ed. by Ǧurǧ Qanawātī and Saʿīd Zāyid (2: maqāla 6–10) Ed. by Muḥammad Yūsuf Mūsā, Sulaymān Dunya, and Saʿīd Zāyid. Cairo: al-Hayʾa al-ʿĀmma li-Šuʾūn al-Maṭābiʿ al-Amīriyya, 1960.

Ibn Sīnā, Abū ʿAlī al-Ḥusayn b. ʿAlī. *Kitāb aš-Šifāʾ, al-Ilāhiyyāt, The Metaphysics of the Healing.* [Reprint of the Georges Anawati et al. edition (Cairo 1960), translation and revision of the Anawati edition of Michael Marmura. Provo (UT), 2005].

Ibn Sīnā, Abū ʿAlī al-Ḥusayn b. ʿAlī. *Kitāb aš-Šifāʾ, al-Manṭiq, Kitāb al-Burhān.* Ed. by Abū l-ʿAlā ʿAfīfī. Cairo: al-Hayʾa al-ʿĀmma li-Šuʾūn al-Maṭābiʿ al-Amīriyya, 1956.

Ibn Sīnā, Abū ʿAlī al-Ḥusayn b. ʿAlī. *Kitāb aš-Šifāʾ, al-Manṭiq, al-ʿIbārā.* Ed. by Maḥmūd al-Ḫuḍayrī. Cairo: Dār al-kātib al-ʿarabī li-ṭ-ṭibāʿa wa-n-našr, 1970.

Ibn Sīnā, Abū ʿAlī al-Ḥusayn b. ʿAlī. *Kitāb aš-Šifāʾ, al-Manṭiq, al-Madḫal.* Ed. by Ibrāhīm Madkūr and Ǧurǧ Qanawātī et al. Cairo: al-Hayʾa al-ʿĀmma li-Šuʾūn al-maṭābiʿ al-Amīriyya, 1952.

Ibn Sīnā, Abū ʿAlī al-Ḥusayn b. ʿAlī. *Kitāb aš-Šifāʾ, al-Manṭiq, al-Maqūlāt.* Ed. by Ibrāhīm Madkūr. Cairo: al-Hayʾa al-ʿāmma li-šuʾūn al-maṭābiʿ al-amīriyya, 1959.

Ibn Sīnā, Abū ʿAlī al-Ḥusayn b. ʿAlī. *Kitāb aš-Šifāʾ, al-Manṭiq, Kitāb al-Qiyās.* Ed. by Saʿīd Zāyid. Cairo: al-Hayʾa al-ʿĀmma li-Šuʾūn al-Maṭābiʿ al-Amīriyya, 1964.

Ibn Sīnā, Abū ʿAlī al-Ḥusayn b. ʿAlī. *ʿUyūn al-ḥikma.* Ed. by ʿAbd ar-Raḥmān Badawī. Cairo: Manšūrāt al-maʿhad al-ʿilmī al-faransī li-l-āṯār aš-šarqiyya, 1954.

Ibn Yaʿīš. *Šarḥ al-Mufaṣṣal li-z-Zamaḫšarī.* Ed. s.n., s.l., 1876–1886.

al-Īǧī, ʿAḍud ad-dīn. *Risālat al-waḍʿ.* Ed. by ʿUmar Aḥmad ar-Rāwī (together with the *Šarḥ* and *Ḥāšiya*). Beirut: Dār al-Kutub al-ʿilmiyya, 2010.

al-Īǧī, ʿAḍud ad-dīn. *Šarḥ Muḫtaṣar al-Muntahā* (together with the glosses of Taftazānī, Ǧurǧānī, and others). Ed. by Fādī Naṣīf and Ṭāriq Yaḥyā. Beirut: Dār al-Kutub al-ʿilmiyya, 2000 [1421].

al-ʿIrāqī, Ḍiyāʾ ad-dīn. *Maqālāt al-uṣūl.* Ed. s.n. Qom: Maǧmaʿ al-fikr al-islāmī, 1993–1994 [1414].

al-Iṣfahānī, Šams ad-dīn. *Bayān al-Muḫtaṣar: Šarḥ Muḫtaṣar Ibn al-Ḥāǧib*. Ed. by Muḥammad Maẓhar Baqā. Makkah: Ǧāmiʿat Umm al-Qurā, 1986 [1406].

al-Iṣfahānī, Abū ʿAbd Allāḥ. *al-Kāšif ʿan al-Maḥṣūl fī ʿilm al-uṣūl*. Ed. by ʿĀdil Aḥmad ʿAbd al-Mawǧūd and ʿAlī Muḥammad Muʿawwaḍ. Beirut: Dār al-Kutub al-ʿilmiyya, 1998.

al-Iṣfahānī, Šams ad-dīn. *Šarḥ al-Minhāǧ li-l-Bayḍāwī fī ʿilm al-uṣūl*. Ed. by ʿAbd al-Karīm b. ʿAlī b. Muḥammad an-Namla. Riyāḍ: Maktabat ar-rušd, 1999 [1420].

al-Isnawī, Ǧamāl ad-dīn. *Nihāyat as-sūʾl fī šarḥ Minhāǧ al-wuṣūl ilā ʿilm al-uṣūl li-l-qāḍī Nāṣir ad-dīn al-Bayḍāwī*. Ed. s.n. Beirut: ʿĀlam al-Kutub, s.d.

Kātib Çelebī. *Kašf aẓ-ẓunūn ʿan asāmī l-kutub wa-l-funūn*. Istanbul: Maarif Matbaasi, 1941–1943.

al-Kātibī, Naǧm ad-dīn. *As'ilat Naǧm ad-dīn al-Kātibī ʿan Kitāb al-Maʿālim li-Faḫr ad-dīn ar-Rāzī*. Ed. by Sabine Schmidtke and Reza Pourjavady. Tehran: Iranian Institute of Philosophy and Institute of Islamic Studies, Free University of Berlin, 2007.

al-Kātibī, Naǧm ad-dīn. "ar-Risāla aš-šamsiyya." Ed. by Aloys Sprenger. In *Bibliotheca Indica: A Collection of Oriental Works. No. 88. First Appendix to the Dictionary of the Technical Terms used in the Sciences of the Mussulmans, Containing the Logic of the Arabians*. Calcutta: Carbery, 1854.

al-Laknawī, Niẓām ad-dīn al-Anṣārī. *Fawātiḥ ar-raḥamūt bi-šarḥ Musallam aṯ-ṯubūt*. Ed. by ʿAbdallah Maḥmūd Muḥammad ʿUmar. Beirut: Dār al-Kutub al-ʿilmiyya, 2002 [1423].

al-Lawkarī, Abū l-ʿAbbās al-Faḍl ibn Muḥammad. *Bayān al-ḥaqq bi-ḍimān aṣ-ṣidq, al-Manṭiq, al-Madḫal*. Ed. by Ibrāhīm Dibāǧī. Tehran: Moʾassase-ye entešārāt-e Amīr Kabīr 1986 [1364].

al-Maḥbūbī. *Tawḍīḥ*. *See* at-Taftāzānī, Saʿd ad-dīn. *Šarḥ at-Talwīḥ ʿalā t-Tawḍīḥ*.

Muǧāhid, Muḥammad b. ʿAlī. *Mafātiḥ al-uṣūl*. Ed. s.n. Qom: Muʾassasat Āl al-Bayt, s.d.

an-Nasafī, Abū l-Barakāt. *Matn al-Manār fī uṣūl al-fiqh*. Ed. by Aḥmad ʿAbd al-Malik ʿAbd ar-Raḥmān as-Saʿdī. Damascus: Dār Saʿd ad-dīn, 2010.

al-Qarāfī, Šihāb ad-dīn. *Nafāʾis al-uṣūl fī šarḥ al-Maḥṣūl*. Ed. by Muḥammad ʿAbd al-Qādir ʿAṭā. Beirut: Dār al-kutub al-ʿilmiyya, 2000 [1421].

al-Qarāfī, Šihāb ad-dīn. *Muḫtaṣar at-tanqīḥ al-fuṣūl fī l-uṣūl*. Ed. by Aḥmad Muḥammad Walīd an-Naššār. Damascus: Dār al-farfūr, 2007 [1428].

al-Qarāfī, Šihāb ad-dīn. *Šarḥ Tanqīḥ al-fuṣūl fī iḫtiṣār fī l-Maḥṣūl al-uṣūl*. Ed. by Ṣidqī Ǧamīl al-ʿAṭṭār. Beirut: Dār al-fikr, 2004 [1424].

al-Qifṭī, Ǧamāl ad-dīn. *Tāʾrīḫ al-ḥukamāʾ*. Ed. by Julius Lippert. Leipzig: Dietrich'sche Verlagsbuchhandlung, 1903.

Raštī, Mīrzā Ḥabīb Allāh. *Badāʾiʿ al-afkār*. Ed. s.n. Qom: Muʾassasat Āl al-Bayt, 1896 [1313].

ar-Rāzī, Faḫr ad-dīn. *Lubāb al-Išārāt wa-t-tanbīhāt*. Ed. by Aḥmad Ḥiǧāzī Saqqā. Cairo: Maktabat al-kulliyyāt al-Azhariyya, 1986.

ar-Rāzī, Faḫr ad-dīn. *al-Maʿālim fī uṣūl al-fiqh*. Ed. by Muḥammad Ḥasan Ismaʿīl. Beirut: Dār al-Kutub al-ʿilmiyya, 2007.

ar-Rāzī, Faḫr ad-dīn. *al-Maḥṣūl fī ʿilm uṣūl al-fiqh*. Ed. by Ṭaha Ǧābir Fayyāḍ al-ʿAlwānī. Riyāḍ: Ǧāmiʿat al-Imām Muḥammad b. Suʿūd al-Islāmiyya, 1979 [or *Maḥṣūl fī ʿilm al-uṣūl*. Ed. by Muḥammad ʿAbd al-Qādir ʿAṭā. Beirut: Dār al-Kutub al-ʿilmiyya, 1999].

ar-Rāzī, Faḫr ad-dīn. *Manṭiq al-Mulaḫḫaṣ*. Ed. by Aḥad Farāmarz Qarāmalekī and Ādīne Aṣġarī-Nežād. Tehran: Dānešgāh-e Emām Ṣādeq 2002/3 [1381].

ar-Rāzī, Faḫr ad-dīn. *Muḥaṣṣal afkār al-mutaqaddimīn wa-l-mutaʾaḫḫirīn min al-ʿulamāʾ wa-l-ḥukamāʾ wa-l-mutakallimīn*. Ed. by Ṭaha ʿAbd ar-Raʾūf Saʿīd. Beirut: Dār al-Kitāb al-ʿarabī, 1984.

ar Rāzī, Faḫr ad-dīn. *Munāẓarāt Faḫr ad-dīn ar-Rāzī*. Ed. by Fathalla Kholeif. Beirut: Dār al-Mašriq, 1966.

ar-Rāzī, Faḫr ad-dīn. *Nihāyat al-īǧāz fī dirāyat al-iʿǧāz*. Ed. by Bakrī Šayḫ Amīn. Beirut: Dār al-ʿilm li-l-malāyīn, 1985.

ar-Rāzī, Faḫr ad-dīn. *Sāḥirat aṭ-ṭarf*. Ed. by Muḥammad Muḥammad Fahmī ʿUmar. Madinah: Dār az-Zamān, 2006 [1427].

ar-Rāzī, Faḫr ad-dīn. *Šarḥ al-Išārāt wa-t-tanbīhāt*. Ms. Staatsbibliothek Berlin or. oct. 1802.

ar-Rāzī, Faḫr ad-dīn. *Šarḥ al-Išārāt wa-t-tanbīhāt, al-Manṭiq*. Ed. by ʿAlī Reẓā Naǧafzādeh. Tehran: Anǧomān-e Āṯār va-Mofāḫer Farhangī, 2005 [1426 h.q./1384 h.š.].

ar-Rāzī, Faḫr ad-dīn. *Šarḥ ʿUyūn al-ḥikma*. Ed. by Aḥmad Ḥiǧāzī Aḥmad as-Saqqā. Cairo: Maktabat al-Anǧilū al-Miṣriyya, 1986.

ar-Rāzī, Faḫr ad-dīn. *at-Tafsīr al-kabīr aw Mafātīḥ al-ġayb*, vols. 1–33. Ed. by Ibrāhīm Šams ad-dīn and Aḥmad Šams ad-din. Beirut: Dār al-Kutub al-ʿilmiyya, 2013.

ar-Rummānī, Abū l-Ḥasan. "an-Nukat fī iʿǧāz al-Qurʾān." In *Ṯalāṯ rasāʾil fī iʿǧāz al-Qurʾān*. Ed. by M. Ḫalaf Allāh and M. Zaġlūl Sallām. Cairo: Dār al-Maʿārif, 2012, pp. 75–113 [6th edition].

as-Sakkākī, Sīrāǧ ad-dīn. *Miftāḥ al-ʿulūm*. Ed. by ʿAbdul Ḥamīd Hindāwī. Beirut: Dār al-Kutub al-ʿilmiyya, 2011.

as-Saraḫsī, Šams ad-dīn. *Uṣūl*. Ed. By Abū l-Wafāʾ al-Afġānī. Beirut: Dār al-Kutub al-ʿilmiyya, 1993 [1414].

aš-Šāṭibī, Abū Isḥāq Ibrāhīm b. Mūsa. *al-Muwāfaqāt*. Ed. by Abū ʿUbayda Āl Salmān, with a foreword by ʿAllāma Bakr b. ʿAbdallāh Abū Zayd. Ḫubar: Dār Ibn ʿAffān, 1997.

as-Sāwī, ʿUmar b. Sahlān. *al-Baṣāʾir an-naṣīriyya fī ʿilm al-manṭiq*. Ed. by Rafīq al-ʿAǧam. Beirut: Dār al-fikr al-lubnānī, 1993.

Sībawayh, Abū Bišr ʿAmr b. Uṯmān. *al-Kitāb*. Ed. by ʿAbd as-Salām Muḥammad Hārūn. Cairo: Dār al-Qalam, 1966–1977.

aš-Šinqīṭī, Muḥammad al-Amīn. *Šarḥ Marāqī as-suʿūd: al-musammā Naṯr al-wurūd*. Mecca: Dār ʿālam al-fawāʾid, 2005 [1426].

aš-Širāzī, Abū Isḥāq. *al-Lumaʿ fī uṣūl al-fiqh*. Ed. by Muḥyī ad-dīn Dīb Mistū and Yūsuf ʿAlī Badawī. Beirut: Dār Ibn Kaṯīr, 2002.

Stephanus. *In Aristotelis librum de interpretatione commentarium*. In *'Philoponus': On Aristotle On the Soul 3.9–13, with Stephanus: On Aristotle On Interpretation*, translated by William Charlton. London: Duckworth, 2000.

as-Subkī, Tāǧ ad-dīn. *Ǧamʿ al-ǧawāmiʿ fī uṣūl al-fiqh*. Ed. by ʿAbd al-Munʿim Ḫalīl Ibrāhīm. Beirut: Dār al-Kutub al-ʿilmiyya, 2003 [1424].

as-Subkī, Tāǧ ad-dīn and Taqī ad-dīn. *Ibhāǧ fī Šarḥ al-Minhāǧ*. Ed. by Šaʿbān Muḥammad Ismāʿīl. Cairo: Maktabat al-Kullīyāt al-Azharīyah, 1981 [1401].

as-Subkī, Tāǧ ad-dīn. *Rafʿ al-ḥāǧib ʿan Muḫtaṣar Ibn al-Ḥāǧib*. Ed. by ʿAlī Muḥammad Muʿawwaḍ and ʿĀdil Aḥmad ʿAbd al-Mawǧūd. Beirut: ʿĀlam al-kutub, 1999.

as-Subkī, Tāǧ ad-dīn. *Ṭabaqāt aš-Šāfiʿiyya al-kubrā*. Ed. by Maḥmūd M. Ṭanāḥī and ʿAbd al-Fatāḥ M. al-Ḥulw. Cairo: ʿĪsā l-Bābī l-Ḥalabī, 1964–1976 [1324].

as-Suyūṭī, Ǧalāl ad-dīn. *Kitāb Buġyat al-wuʿāt*. Ed. by Muḥammad Amīn Ḥānǧī and Aḥmad b. al-Amīn Šinqīṭī. Cairo: Maṭbaʿat as-Saʿāda, 1908 [1326].

at-Tabrīzī, Ismāʿīl al-Wārānī. *Tanqīḥ Maḥṣūl Ibn al-Ḫaṭīb fī uṣūl al-fiqh*. Ed. By Ḥamza Zuhayr Ḥāfiẓ. Mecca: Umm al-Qurā University, s.d.

at-Taftāzānī, Saʿd ad-dīn. *Ḥāšiya ʿalā Šarḥ al-Muḫtaṣar*. Ed. by Muḥammad Ḥasan Ismāʿīl. Beirut: Dār al-Kutub al-ʿilmiyya, 2004 [1424].

at-Taftāzānī, Saʿd ad-dīn. *Šarḥ at-Talwīḥ ʿalā t-Tawḍīḥ*. Ed. s.n. Beirut: Dār al-Kutub al-ʿilmiyya, 1996.

at-Taḥtānī, Quṭb ad-dīn ar-Rāzī. *al-Muḥākamāt bayna l-Imām wa-n-Naṣīr fī Šarḥ al-Išārāt*. Ms. Berlin Petermann I 549.

at-Taḥtānī, Quṭb ad-dīn ar-Rāzī. *Lawāmiʾ al-asrār fī šarḥ Maṭāliʿ al-anwār*. Ed. s.n., 1885 [1303].

at-Taḥtānī, Quṭb ad-dīn ar-Rāzī. *Taḥrīr al-qawāʿid al-manṭiqiyya: Šarḥ ar-Risāla aš-šamsiyya, wa-bi-asfal ṣaḥāʾifihī Ḥāšiya ʿalā Taḥrīr al-qawāʿid al-manṭiqiyya* (together with Ǧurǧānī's glosses). Ed. by Aḥmad Amīn ʿUmrān. Cairo: Muṣṭafā al-Bābī l-Ḥalabī wa-awlāduhū, 1948.

The Quran: Translation and Commentary by Wahiduddin Khan. Ed. by Farida Khanam. New Delhi: Goodword Books, 2011.

at-Tilimsānī, Muḥammad ibn Aḥmad. *Miftāḥ al-wuṣūl ilā bināʾ al-furūʿ ʿalā l-uṣūl*. Beirut [et al.]: Muʾassasat ar-raʾyān, 1998 [1419].

aṭ-Ṭūsī, Naṣīr ad-dīn. *Ḥall muškilāt al-Išārāt*. In Ibn Sīnā. *Išārāt wa-t-tanbīhāt*. Ed. by Sulaymān Dunyā. Cairo: Dār al-Maʿārif, 1983–1994.

aṭ-Ṭūsī, Naṣīr ad-dīn. *Taǧrīd al-Manṭiq*. Ed. s.n. Beirut: Manšūrāt muʾassasat al-aʿlamī li-l-maṭbūʿāt, 1988 [1408].

al-Urmawī, Sirāǧ ad-dīn. *at-Taḥṣīl min al-Maḥṣūl*. Vol. 2. Ed. by ʿAbd al-Ḥamīd ʿAlī Abū Zunayd. Beirut: Muʾassasat ar-risāla, 1988 [1408].

al-Urmawī, Tāǧ ad-dīn. *al-Ḥāṣil min al-Maḥṣūl fī uṣūl al-fiqh*. Vol. 3. Ed. by ʿAbd as-Salām Maḥmūd Abū Nāǧī. Beirut: Dār al-Madār al-Islamī, 2006.

az-Zaǧǧāǧī, Abū l-Qāsim. *al-Īḍāḥ fī ʿilal an-naḥw*. Ed. by Māzin al-Mubārak. Beirut: Dār an-Nafāʾis, 1979 [1399].
az-Zamaḫšarī, Abū l-Qāsim. *al-Mufaṣṣal*. Ed. by J.P. Broch, 1859.
az-Zarkašī, Badr al-Dīn Muḥammad. *Baḥr al-Muḥīṭ fī uṣūl al-fiqh*. Ed. by ʿAbd al-Qādir ʿAbd Allāh ʿĀnī. Kuwait: Wizārat al-awqāf wa-š-šuʾūn al-Islāmiyya, 1992.
az-Zuhaylī, Wahba. *al-Uṣūl al-fiqh al-islamī*. Damascus: Dār al-fikr, 1986.

Secondary literature

ʿAbd ar-Raḥmān, Ǧalāl ad-dīn. *Ġāyat al-wuṣūl ilā daqāʾiq ʿilm al-uṣūl*. Cairo: s.n., 1990.
Abdel Haleem, Muhammad. "Qurʾān." *Encyclopedia of Arabic Language and Linguistics*, vol. 4, pp. 21–31.
Abdul-Raof, Hussein. *Arabic Rhetoric: A Pragmatic Analysis*. London [et al.]: Routledge, 2006.
Abed, Shukri B. *Aristotelian Logic and the Arabic Language in Alfārābī*. New York: State University Press, 1991.
Abrahamov, Binyamin. "Necessary Knowledge in Islamic Theology." *British Journal of Middle Eastern Studies*, vol. 20, no. 1 (1993): pp. 20–31.
Abu Deeb, Kamal. *Al-Jurjānī's Theory of Poetic Imagery*. Warminster: Aris and Phillips, 1979.
Adamson, Peter and Alexander Key. "Philosophy of Language in the Medieval Arabic Tradition." In *Linguistic Content: New Essays on the History of the Philosophy of Language*, ed. by Margaret Cameron and Robert Stainton, pp. 74–99. Oxford: Oxford University Press, 2015.
Ahmad, Ahmad Atif. *Structural Interrelations of Theory and Practice in Islamic Law. A Study of Six Works of Medieval Islamic Jurisprudence*. Leiden: Brill, 2006.
Ahmed, Asad Q. "Interpreting Avicenna: Urmawī/Taḥtānī and the Later Logical Tradition on Propositions." *Documenti e studi sulla tradizione filosofica medievale*, vol. 21 (2010): pp. 313–342.
Ahmed, Asad Q. "Systematic Growth in Sustained Error: A Case Study in the Dynamism of Post-Classical Islamic Scholasticism." In *The Islamic Scholarly Tradition*, ed. by Asad Q. Ahmed, Behnam Sadeghi, and Michael Bonner, pp. 343–378. Leiden [et al.]: Brill, 2011.
Ahmed, Asad Q. "The *Shifāʾ* in India I: Reflections on the Evidence of the Manuscripts." *Oriens*, vol. 40, no. 2 (2012): pp. 199–222.
Ahmed, Asad Q. "Logic in the Khayrābādī School of India: A Preliminary Exploration." In *Law and Tradition in Classical Islamic Thought*, ed. by Michael Cook, Najam Haider, Intinsar Rabb, and Asma Sayeed, pp. 227–243. New York: Palgrave McMillan, 2013.

Ahmed, Asad Q. "Post-Classical Philosophical Commentaries/Glosses: Innovations in the Margins." *Oriens*, vol. 41, no. 3–4 (2013): pp. 317–348.

Ahmed, Asad Q. "The *Sullam al-ʿulūm* of (d. 1707) Muḥib Allāh al-Bihārī." In *The Oxford Handbook of Islamic Philosophy*, ed. by Khaled El-Rouayheb and Sabine Schmidtke, pp. 488–508. Oxford: Oxford University Press, 2017.

Altaş, Eşref. *Fahreddin er-Rāzī'nin İbn Sīnā Yorumu ve Eleştirisi*. Istanbul: İz Yayıncılık, 2009.

al-ʿAlwānī, Ṭahā Ǧābir. Preface to *Maḥṣūl fī ʿilm uṣūl al-fiqh* by Faḫr ad-dīn ar-Rāzī, ed. by Ṭaha Ǧābir Fayāḍ al-ʿAlwānī, pp. 27–73. Riyāḍ: Ǧāmiʿat al-Imām Muḥammad b. Suʿūd al-Islāmiyya, 1979.

al-ʿAlwānī, Ṭahā Ǧābir. *Uṣūl al-fiqh al-Islāmī. Source Methodology in Islamic Jurisprudence: Methodology for Research and Knowledge*. Herndon, VA: The International Institute of Islamic Thought, 1990.

al-ʿAlwānī, Ṭahā Ǧābir. *al-Imām Faḫr ad-dīn ar-Rāzī wa-muṣannafātuhū*. Cairo: Dār al-Islām, 2010.

Anawati, Georges. *Fakhr al-Dīn al-Rāzī: tamhīd li-dirāsat ḥayātihī wa-muʾallafātihī*. In *Mélanges Taha Hussein*, ed. by ʿAbd ar-Raḥmān al-Badawī, pp. 193–234. Cairo: Dār al-Maʿārif, 1962.

Anawati, Georges (= Ǧurǧ Qanawātī). Fakhr al-Dīn al-Rāzī. *EI*², http://dx.doi.org/10.1163/1573-3912_islam_COM_0206, last accessed 14 October 2017.

Ansari, Hassan and Schmidtke, Sabine. "The Muʿtazilī and Zaydī-Reception of Abū l-Ḥusayn al-Baṣrī's *Kitāb al-Muʿtamad fī Uṣūl al-fiqh*: A Bibliographical Note." *Islamic Law and Society*, vol. 20, no. 1–2 (2013): pp. 90–109.

Arnaldez, Roger. *Fakhr al-Dîn al-Râzî: Commentateur du Coran et philosophe*. Paris: Vrin, 2002.

Austin, John L. *How to Do Things with Words*. Oxford: Clarendon Press, 1962.

Barnes, Jonathan. "Commentary." In *Aristotle. Posterior Analytics. Translated with a Commentary by Jonathan Barnes*, pp. 79–271. Oxford: Clarendon Press, 2002.

Bauer, Thomas. "Rhetorik der arabischen Kultur." In *Rhetorik: Begriff, Geschichte, Internationalität*, ed. by Gert Ueding, pp. 283–300. Tübingen: Niemeyer, 2005.

Bauer, Thomas. *Die Kultur der Ambiguität. Eine andere Geschichte des Islams*. Berlin: Verlag der Weltreligionen, 2011.

Berg, Herbert. *The Development of Exegesis in Early Islam*. Richmond, Surrey: Curzon Press, 2000.

Berg, Herbert. "Polysemy in the Qurʾān." *Encyclopaedia of the Qurʾān*, vol. 4, pp. 155–158.

Bernand, Marie. *L'accord unanime de la communauté comme fondement des statuts légaux de l'Islam d'après Abū l-Ḥusayn al-Baṣrī*. Paris: J. Vrin, 1970.

Bernand, Marie. "Controverses Médiévales sur le *Dalīl al-Ḫiṭāb*." *Arabica*, vol. 33, no. 3 (Nov. 1986): pp. 269–294.

Bernand, Marie and Éric Chaumont. Introduction to *al-Bazdawī: Livre où repose la con-*

naissance des preuves légales, ed. by Marie Bernand and Éric Chaumont, pp. 5–11. Cairo: Institut français d'archéologie orientale, 2003.

Bertolacci, Amos. *The Reception of Aristotle's Metaphysics in Avicenna's Kitāb al-Šifāʾ. A Milestone of Western Metaphysical Thought.* Leiden: Brill, 2006.

Bertolacci, Amos. "The 'Ontologization' of Logic. Metaphysical Themes in Avicenna's Reworking of the Organon." In *Methods and Methodologies. Aristotelian Logic East and West 500–1500*, ed. by Margaret Cameron and John Marenbon, pp. 27–51. Leiden [et al.]: Brill, 2011.

Bertolacci, Amos. "A Hidden *Hapax Legomenon* in Avicenna's Metaphysics: Considerations on the Use of *Anniyya* and *Ayyiyya* in the *Ilāhiyyāt* of the *Kitāb al-Šifāʾ*." In *The Letter before the Spirit. The Importance of Text Editions for the Study of the Reception of Aristotle*, ed. by Aafke M.I. van Oppenraay and Resianne Fontaine-van-Gelder, pp. 289–310. Leiden [et al.]: Brill, 2012.

Black, Deborah L. *Logic and Aristotle's Rhetoric and Poetics in Medieval Arabic Philosophy*. Leiden [et al.]: Brill, 1990.

Black, Deborah L. "Aristotle's 'Peri hermeneias' in Medieval Latin and Arabic Philosophy: Logic and the Linguistic Arts." *Canadian Journal of Philosophy*, Suppl. vol. 17 (1991): pp. 25–83.

Black, Deborah L. "Knowledge (*ʿilm*) and Certitude (*yakīn*) in al-Fārābī's Epistemology." *Arabic Sciences and Philosophy*, vol. 16 (2006): pp. 11–45.

Bohas, Georges, Jean-Patrick Guillaume, and Djamel E. Kouloughli. *The Arabic Linguistic Tradition*. London: Routledge, 1990.

Bonebakker, Seeger A. "Luzūm mā lā yalzam." In *EI*², http://dx.doi.org/10.1163/1573-3912_islam_SIM_4707, last accessed 14 October 2017.

Bou Akl, Ziad. *Averroès: Le Philosophe et la Loi: Édition, Traduction et Commentaire de l'Abrégé du Mustasfa*. Boston: De Gruyter, 2015.

Brockopp, Jonathan E. "Early Islamic Jurisprudence in Egypt: Two Scholars and their Mukhtasars." *International Journal of Middle East Studies*, vol. 30, no. 2 (1998): pp. 176–182.

Brockopp, Jonathan E. "Re-Reading the History of Early Mālikī Jurisprudence." *Journal of the American Oriental Society*, vol. 118, no. 2 (1998): pp. 233–238.

Brodeur, Patrice C. "Religion." In *Encyclopaedia of the Qurʾān*, vol. 4, pp. 395–398.

Brunschvig, Robert. "Théorie générale de la capacité chez les Hanafites médiévaux." *Revue Internationale des Droits de l'Antiquité*, vol. 1,2 (1949): pp. 157–172.

Brunschvig, Robert. "Valeur et fondement du raisonnement juridique par analogie d'après al-Ġazālī." *Studia Islamica*, vol. 34 (1971): pp. 57–88.

Brunschvig, Robert. "Logic and Law in classical Islam." In *Logic in Classical Islamic Culture*, ed. by Gustav E. von Grunebaum, pp. 9–20. Wiesbaden: Harrassowitz, 1970.

Buburuzan, Daniela R. "Exclamation et actes de langage chez Sībawayhi." *Revue Roumaine de Linguistique*, vol. 38, no. 5 (Sept./Oct. 1993): pp. 421–437.

Buburuzan, Daniela R. "Significations des énoncés et actes de langage chez Ibn Fāris." In *Proceedings of the Colloquium on Arabic Linguistics, Bucharest, 29 August to 2 September 1994*, ed. by Nadia Anghelescu and Andrei Avram, vol. I, pp. 103–114. Bucharest: University of Bucharest, Center of Arab Studies, 1995.

Burton, John. "The Qur'ān and the Islamic Practice of wuḍū'." *Bulletin of the School of Oriental and African Studies*, vol. 51, no. 1 (1988): pp. 21–58.

Calder, Norman. *Studies in Early Muslim Jurisprudence*. Oxford: Clarendon Press, 1993.

Calder, Norman. "Uṣūl al-Fiḳh." In *EI*², http://dx.doi.org/10.1163/1573-3912_islam_SIM_7761, last accessed 14 October 2017.

Cardinal, Monique C. "Islamic Legal Theory Curriculum: Are the Classics Taught Today?" *Islamic Law and Society*, vol. 12, no. 2 (2005): pp. 224–272.

Carter, Michael G. "Les origines de la grammaire arabe." *Revue des Études Islamiques*, vol. 40 (1972): pp. 69–97.

Carter, Michael G. "Linguistic Science and Orthodoxy in Conflict: The Case of al-Rummānī." *Zeitschrift für Geschichte der Arabisch-Islamischen Wissenschaften*, vol. 1 (1984): pp. 212–232.

Carter, Michael G. "Language and Law in the *Ṣāḥibī* of Ibn Fāris." *Zeitschrift für arabische Linguistik*, vol. 25 (1993): pp. 138–147.

Carter, Michael G. "A Missing Link between Law and Grammar: The *Intiṣār* of Ibn Wallād." *Arabica*, vol. 48, no. 1 (2001): pp. 51–65.

Carter, Michael G. "Parts of Speech." In *EALL*, vol. 3, pp. 546–552.

Carter, Michael G. "Sentence Types in Grammar, Law and Philosophy." In *Centre and Periphery within the Borders of Islam. Proceedings of the 23rd Congress of L'Union Européenne des Arabisants et Islamisants*, ed. by Giuseppe Contu, pp. 313–325. Leuven [et al.]: Peeters, 2012.

Ceylan, Hadi Ensar. "Ghazali's Account of Signification." *Journal of Islamic Research*, vol. 3, no. 2 (Dec. 2010): pp. 98–114.

Chejne, Anwar G. "Ibn Ḥazm of Cordova on Logic." *Journal of the American Oriental Society*, vol. 104, no. 1 (Jan.–March 1984): pp. 57–72.

Copi, Irving M. *Einführung in die Logik*. Munich: Fink, 1998.

Coseriu, Eugenio. *Geschichte der Sprachphilosophie*. Tübingen: Francke Verlag, 2003.

Czapkiewicz, Andrzej. *The Views of the Medieval Arab Philologists on Language and its Origin in the Light of as-Suyūṭī's "al-Muzhir"*. Krakow: Nakł. Uniwersytetu Jagiellońskiego, 1988.

Darwīš ʿAlī, ʿAbd al-ʿAzīẓ Mūsā and Muḥammad ʿAlī Salīm al-Hawwārī. "Qirāʾatun luġawiyyatun fiqhiyyatun fī āyati l-wuḍūʾ." *Journal of Qur'anic Studies*, vol. 12 (2010): pp. 282–313.

Dichy, Joseph. "Kinâya, a Tropic Device from Medieval Arabic Rhetoric, and Its Tmpact on Discourse Theory." In *Proceedings of the 5th Conference of the International Society for the Study of Argumentation (ISSA), University of Amsterdam, 25–28 June 2002*, ed.

by Frans van Eemeren, J. Anthony Blair, Charles A. Willard, and A. Francisca Snoeck Nenkemans, pp. 237–241. Amsterdam: *Sic* Sat, 2003.

Diem, Werner. "Nomen, Substantiv und Adjektiv bei den arabischen Grammatikern." *Oriens*, vol. 23–24 (1974): pp. 312–332.

Dietrich, Albert. *Die arabische Version einer unbekannten Schrift des Alexander von Aphrodisias über die Differentia specifica*. Göttingen: Vandenhoeck and Ruprecht, 1964.

DiVincenzo, Sylvia. "Avicenna Against Porphyry's Definition of Differentia Specifica." *Documenti e studi sulla tradizione filosofica medievale*, vol. 26 (2015): pp. 129–183.

Duġaym, Samīḥ. *Mawsūʿāt Muṣṭalaḥāt al-imām Faḫr ad-dīn ar-Rāzī*. Beirut: Maktabat Lubnān Nāširūn, 2001.

Dutton, Yasin. *The Origins of Islamic Law. The Qurʾan, the Muwaṭṭaʾ and Madinan ʿAmal*. Richmond, Surrey: Curzon Press, 2002.

Eichner, Heidrun. "Dissolving the Unity of Metaphysics: From Fakhr al-Dīn al-Rāzī to Mullā Ṣadra al-Shirāzī." *Medioevo*, vol. 32 (2007): pp. 139–197.

Eichner, Heidrun. "Dogma und Jurisprudenz im Wissenschaftssystem von al-Ǧuwaynī und al-Ġazālī." In *The Claim of Truths in Religious Contexts. Results of an Interdisciplinary Workshop of the Graduate School 'Society and Culture in Motion'*, ed. by Johannes Thon, pp. 37–50. Halle/Saale: Zentrum für Interdisziplinäre Regionalstudien, 2009.

Eichner, Heidrun. *The Post-Avicennian Philosophical Tradition and Islamic Orthodoxy: Philosophical and Theological Summae in Context*. Unpublished habilitation thesis. Halle, 2009.

Eichner, Heidrun. "Das avicennische *Corpus Aristotelicum*: Zur Virtualisierung des Aristotelestextes in der postavicennischen Tradition." In *Entre Orient et Occident: La philosophie et la science gréco-romaines dans le monde arabe*, ed. by Richard Goulet, pp. 197–239. Geneva: Droz, 2010.

Ellis, John. "Alexander's Defence of Aristotle's Categories". *Phronesis*, vol. 39, no. 1 (1994): pp. 69–89.

EALL = *Encyclopaedia of Arabic Language and Linguistics*, ed. by Cornelis Versteegh et al. Leiden [et al.]: Brill, 2006.

EI^2 = *Encyclopaedia of Islam, Second Edition*, ed. by Pery J. Bearman and Thierry Bianquis et al. Leiden [et al.]: Brill, 1960–2006.

EI^3 = *Encyclopaedia of Islam, three*, ed. by Gudrun Krämer et al. Leiden [et al.]: Brill, 2007–.

EQ = *Encyclopaedia of the Qurʾan*, ed. by Jane Dammen McAuliffe et al. Leiden [et al.]: Brill, 2001–2006.

Endreß, Gerhard. "Grammatik und Logik. Arabische Philologie und griechische Philosophie im Widerstreit." In *Sprachphilosophie in Antike und Mittelalter*, ed. by Burkhard Mojsisch, pp. 163–299. Amsterdam: Gründer, 1986.

Endreß, Gerhard. "Die wissenschaftliche Literatur." In *Grundriß der arabischen Philo-*

logie. Vol. II. Literaturwissenschaft, ed. by Helmut Gätje, pp. 400–530. Wiesbaden: Reichert, 1987.

Endreß, Gerhard. "Die dreifache Ancilla. Hermeneutik und Logik im Werk des Sayfaddīn al-Āmidī." In *Logik und Theologie. Das Organon im arabischen und im lateinischen Mittelalter*, ed. by Dominik Perler and Ulrich Rudolph, pp. 117–145. Leiden: Brill, 2005.

Endreß, Gerhard. "Reading Avicenna in the *Madrasa*: Intellectual Genealogies and Chains of Transmission of Philosophy and the Sciences in the Islamic East." In *Arabic Theology, Arabic Philosophy. From the Many to the One: Essays in Celebration of Richard M. Frank*, ed. by James E. Montgomery, pp. 371–422. Leuven: Peeters, 2006.

Endreß, Gerhard. "Ibn al-Ḫammār." In *Grundriss der Geschichte der Philosophie. Philosophie in der islamischen Welt. Vol. 1: 8.–10. Jh.*, ed. by Ulrich Rudolph, pp. 333–341. Basel: Schwabe Verlag, 2012.

Endreß, Gerhard. "'This is Clear Arabic Speech': God's Speech and Prophetic Language in Early Islamic Hermeneutics, Theology and Philosophy." In *Transcending Words: The Language of Religious Contact Between Buddhists, Christians, Jews and Muslims in Premodern Times*, ed. by Görge K. Hasselhoff and Knut Martin Stünkel, pp. 27–42. Bochum: Winkler, 2015.

van Ess, Joseph. *Die Erkenntnislehre des ʿAḍudaddīn al-Īcī. Übersetzung und Kommentar des ersten Buches seiner Mawāqif*. Wiesbaden: Harrassowitz, 1966.

van Ess, Josef. "The Logical Structure of Islamic Theology." In *Logic in Classical Islamic Culture*, ed. by Gustav E. von Grunebaum, pp. 21–50. Wiesbaden: Harrassowitz, 1970.

van Ess, Josef. *Theologie und Gesellschaft im 2. und 3. Jahrhundert Hidschra. Eine Geschichte des religiösen Denkens im frühen Islam*. Volumes 1–6. Berlin [et al.]: De Gruyter, 1991–1997.

van Ess, Josef. *Der Eine und das Andere: Beobachtungen an islamischen häresiographischen Texten*. Berlin [et al.]: De Gruyter, 2011.

van Ess, Josef. *Die Träume der Schulweisheit. Leben und Werk des ʿAlī b. Muḥammad al-Ǧurǧānī (gest. 816/1413)*. Wiesbaden: Harrassowitz Verlag, 2013.

Fadel, Mohammad. "The Social Logic of *Taqlīd* and the Rise of the *Mukhtaṣar*." *Islamic Law and Society*, vol. 3, no. 2 (1996): pp. 193–233.

Fahd, Toufic. "Khaṭṭ (*bi-raml*)." In *EI*².

Ferejohn, Michael. *The Origins of Aristotelian Science*. New Haven: Yale University Press, 1991.

Firanescu, Daniela Rodica. "Speech Acts." In *EALL*, vol. 4, pp. 328–334.

Frank, Richard M. *Beings and Their Attributes: The Teaching of the Basrian School of the Muʿtazila in the Classical Period*. Albany: State University of New York Press, 1978.

Frank, Richard M. "Meanings Are Spoken of in Many Ways: The Earlier Arab Grammarians." *Le Muséon*, vol. 94 (1981): pp. 259–319.

Frank, Richard M. "Al-Ghazâlî's Use of Avicenna's Philosophy." *Revue des Études Islamiques*, No. 55–57 (1987–1989), pp. 271–285.

Fudge, Bruce. "Taḍmīn: The Notion of 'Implication' According to al-Rummānī." In *Classical Arabic Humanities in Their Own Terms: Festschrift for Wolfhart Heinrichs on his 65th Birthday Presented by His Students and Colleagues*, ed. by Beatrice Gruendler, pp. 468–492. Leiden [et al.]: Brill, 2008.

Ǧabr, Farīd and Rafīq al-ʿAǧam [eds.]. *Mawsūʿat muṣṭalaḥāt ʿilm al-manṭiq ʿinda l-ʿarab*. Beirut: Maktabat Lubnān Nāširūn, 1996.

Gadamer, Hans-Georg. *Wahrheit und Methode: Grundzüge einer philosophischen Hermeneutik*. In *Gesammelte Werke, vols. 1–2*, Tübingen: J.C.B. Mohr, 1999.

Ǧamāl ad-dīn, Muṣṭafā. *al-Baḥṯ an-naḥwī ʿinda l-uṣūliyyīn*. Baghdad: Dār ar-Rašīd li-n-našr, 1980.

Gardet, Louis. "kalām." In EI², http://dx.doi.org/10.1163/1573-3912_islam_COM_0421, last accessed 14 October 2017.

Gätje, Helmut. "Zur Lehre von den Voraussetzungsschlüssen bei Avicenna." *Zeitschrift für Geschichte der Arabisch-Islamischen Wissenschaften*, vol. 2 (1985): pp. 140–204.

Ghersetti, Antonella. "'Word' in the Linguistic Thinking of Jurjānī." In *The Word in Arabic*, ed. by Giuliano Lancioni and Lidia Bettini, pp. 85–108. Leiden [et al.]: Brill, 2011.

Ǧihāmī, Ǧirār [ed.]. *Mawsūʿat muṣṭalaḥāt Ibn-Sīnā (aš-Šayḫ ar-raʾīs)*. Beirut: Maktabat Lubnān Nāširūn, 2004.

Gimaret, Daniel. "Taklīf." In EI², http://dx.doi.org/10.1163/1573-3912_islam_SIM_7344, last accessed 14 October 2017.

Gleave, Robert. *Islam and Literalism: Literal Meaning and Interpretation in Islamic Legal Theory*. Edinburgh: Edinburgh University Press, 2013.

Griffel, Frank. *Apostasie und Toleranz im Islam. Die Entwicklung zu al-Ġazālīs Urteil gegen die Philosophie und die Reaktionen der Philosophen*. Leiden: Brill, 2000.

Griffel, Frank. "Al-Ghazālī's Concept of Prophecy: The Introduction of Avicennan Psychology into Ašʿarite Theology." *Arabic Sciences and Philosophy*, vol. 14 (2004): pp. 101–144.

Griffel, Frank. "On Fakhr al-Dīn al-Rāzī's Life and the Patronage He Received." *Journal of Islamic Studies*, vol. 18, no. 3 (2007): pp. 313–344.

Griffel, Frank. "Al-Ghazālī or al-Ghazzālī? On a Lively Debate Among Ayyubid and Mamluk Historians in Damascus." In *Islamic Thought in the Middle Ages: Studies in Transmission and Translation in Honour of Hans Daiber*, ed. by Anna Akasoy and Wim Raven, pp. 101–112, Leiden: Brill Academic Publishing, 2008.

Griffel, Frank. *Al-Ghazālī's Philosophical Theology*. New York: Oxford University Press, 2009.

Griffel, Frank. "Between al-Ghazālī and Abū l-Barakāt al-Baghdādī: The Dialectical Turn in the Philosophy of Iraq and Iran During the Sixth/Twelfth Century." In *In the Age of Averroes: Arabic Philosophy in the Sixth/Twelfth Century*, ed. by Peter Adamson, pp. 45–75. London: The Warburg Institute, 2011.

Guillaume, Jean-Patrick. "'Le discours tout entier est nom, verbe et particule.' Élaboration et constitution de la théorie des parties du discours dans la tradition grammaticale arabe." *Langages*, vol. 23, no. 92 (1988): pp. 25–36.

Guillaume, Jean-Patrick. "Defining the Word Within the Arabic Grammatical Tradition: ʾAstarābāḏī's Predicament." In *The Word in Arabic*, ed. by Giuliano Lancioni and Lidia Bettini, pp. 49–68. Leiden [et al.]: Brill, 2011.

Gully, Adrian. "*Taḍmīn*: 'Implication of Meaning' in Medieval Arabic." *Journal of the American Oriental Society*, vol. 117, no. 3 (1997): pp. 466–480.

Gutas, Dimitri. *Avicenna and the Aristotelian Tradition: Introduction to Reading Avicenna's Philosophical Works. Second, Revised and Enlarged Edition, Including an Inventory of Avicenna's Authentic Works*. Leiden [et al.]: Brill, 2014 [1st edition: 1988].

Gutas, Dimitri. "Aspects of Literary Form and Genre in Arabic Logical Works." In *Glosses and Commentaries on Aristotelian Logical Texts. The Syriac, Arabic and Medieval Latin Traditions*, ed. by Charles Burnett, pp. 29–76. London: Warburg Institute, 1993.

Gutas, Dimitri. "Avicenna's Eastern ('Oriental') Philosophy: Nature, Contents, Transmission." *Arabic Sciences and Philosophy*, vol. 10 (2000): pp. 159–180.

Gutas, Dimitri. "The Heritage of Avicenna: The Golden Age of Arabic Philosophy, 1000–ca. 1350." In *Avicenna and his Heritage*, ed. by Jules Janssens and Daniel De Smet, pp. 81–97. Leuven: University Press, 2002.

Gutas, Dimitri. "Certainty, Doubt, Error: Comments on the Epistemological Foundations of Medieval Arabic Science." *Early Science and Medicine*, vol. 7, no. 3 (2002): pp. 276–289.

Gutas, Dimitri. "Avicenna's Philosophical Project." In *Interpreting Avicenna: Critical Essays*, ed. by Peter Adamson, pp. 28–47. Cambridge: Cambridge University Press, 2013.

Gwynne, Rosalind. "The *A Fortiori* Argument in *Fiqh*, *Naḥw* and *Kalām*." In *Studies in the History of Arabic Grammar II. Proceedings of the 2nd Symposium on the History of Arabic Grammar, Nijmegen, 27. April–1. May 1987*, ed. by Kees Versteegh and Michael G. Carter, pp. 165–177. Amsterdam/Philadelphia: John Benjamins Publishing Company, 1990.

Gyekye, Kwame. "The Terms *Prima Intentio* and *Secunda Intentio* in Arabic Logic." *Speculum*, vol. 46, no. 1 (Jan. 1971): pp. 32–38.

Haarmann, Ulrich. "Religiöses Recht und Grammatik im klassischen Islam." *Zeitschrift der Deutschen Morgenländischen Gesellschaft*, suppl. 2 (1974): pp. 149–169.

Hallaq, Wael B. "Considerations on the Function and Character of Sunnī Legal Theory." *Journal of the American Oriental Society*, vol. 104, no. 4 (Oct.–Dec. 1984): pp. 679–689.

Hallaq, Wael B. "The Logic of Legal Reasoning in Religious and Non-Religious Cultures:

The Case of Islamic and the Common Law." *Cleveland State Review*, vol. 34 (1985–1986): pp. 79–96.

Hallaq, Wael B. "A Tenth-Eleventh Century Treatise on Juridical Dialectic." *Muslim World*, vol. 77, no. 2–3 (1987): pp. 198–227.

Hallaq, Wael B. "Non-Analogical Arguments in Sunni Juridical *Qiyās*." *Arabica*, vol. 36 (1989): pp. 286–306.

Hallaq, Wael B. "Logic, Formal Arguments and Formalisation of Arguments in Sunnī Jurisprudence." *Arabica*, vol. 37 (1990): pp. 315–358.

Hallaq, Wael B. "On Inductive Corrobation, Probability and Certainty in Sunnī Legal Thought." In *Islamic Law and Jurisprudence*, ed. by Nicholas Heer, pp. 3–31. Seattle [et al.]: University of Washington Press, 1990.

Hallaq, Wael B. "The Primacy of the Qur'ān in Shāṭibī's Legal Theory." In *Islamic Studies Presented to Charles J. Adams*, ed. by Wael B. Hallaq and Donald P. Little, pp. 69–90, Leiden [et al.]: Brill, 1991.

Hallaq, Wael B. "Was al-Shafi'i the Master Architect of Islamic Jurisprudence?" *International Journal of Middle East Studies*, vol. 25, no. 4 (Nov. 1993): pp. 587–605.

Hallaq, Wael B. *A History of Islamic Legal Theories: An Introduction to Sunnī uṣūl al-fiqh*. Cambridge: Cambridge University Press, 1997.

Hallaq, Wael B. "From Regional to Personal Schools of Law? A Reevaluation." *Islamic Law and Society*, vol. 8, no. 1 (2001): pp. 1–26.

Hallaq, Wael B. *The Origins and Evolution of Islamic Law*. Cambridge: Cambridge University Press, 2005.

Hallaq, Wael B. *An Introduction to Islamic Law*. Cambridge: Cambridge University Press, 2009.

Halm, Heinz. *Die Ausbreitung der šāfiʿitischen Rechtsschule von den Anfängen bis zum 8./14. Jahrhundert*. Wiesbaden: Reichert, 1974.

Hanafi, Hassan. *Les Méthodes d'Exégèse: Essai sur la Science des Fondements de la Compréhension 'Ilm Uṣul al-Fiqh'*. Cairo: Le Conseil des Arts, des Lettres et des Sciences Sociales, 1965.

Hasan, Ahmad. "Finding the Cause of a Legal Injunction in Islamic Jurisprudence." *Islamic Studies*, vol. 25, no. 1 (1986): pp. 11–44.

Heinrichs, Wolfhart. *Arabische Dichtung und griechische Poetik: Ḥāzim al-Qarṭāǧannīs Grundlegung der Poetik mit Hilfe aristotelischer Begriffe*. Beirut: Orient-Institut, 1969.

Heinrichs, Wolfhart. *The Hand of the Northwind. Opinions on Metaphor and the early Meaning of Istiʿāra in Arabic Poetics*. Wiesbaden: Franz Steiner, 1977.

Heinrichs, Wolfhart. "Naḳd". In EI², http://dx.doi.org/10.1163/1573-3912_islam_COM_1438, last accessed 14 October 2017.

Heinrichs, Wolfhart. "Contacts Between Scriptural Hermeneutics and Literary Theory in Islam: The Case of Majāz." *Zeitschrift für Geschichte der Arabisch-Islamischen Wissenschaften*, vol. 7 (1991–1992): pp. 253–284.

Heinrichs, Wolfhart. "The Classification of the Sciences and the Consolidation of Philology in Classical Islam." In *Centres of Learning: Learning and Location in Pre-Modern Europe and the Near East*, ed. by Jan Willem Drijvers and A.A. MacDonald, pp. 119–139, Leiden: Brill, 1995.

Heffening, Wilhelm and Joseph Schacht. "Ḥanafiyya". In *EI*², http://dx.doi.org/10.1163/1573-3912_islam_SIM_2703, last accessed 14 October 2017.

Hintikka, Jaakko. "Aristotle's Different Possibilities." In *Time and Necessity: Studies in Aristotle's Theory of Modality*, ed. by Jaakko Hintikka, pp. 27–40. Oxford: Clarendon Press, 1973.

Holtzmann, Livnat. "The Dhimmi's Question on Predetermination and the Ulama's Six Responses: The Dynamics of Composing Polemical Didactic Poems in Mamluk Cairo and Damascus." *Mamluk Studies Review*, vol. 16 (2012): pp. 1–54.

Holtzmann, Livnat. "Debating the Doctrine of *jabr* (Compulsion): Ibn Qayyim al-Jawziyya Reads Fakhr al-Dīn al-Rāzī." In *Islamic Theology, Philosophy and Law: Debating Ibn Taymiyya and Ibn Qayyim al-Jawziyya*, ed. by Birgit Krawietz and Georges Tamer, pp. 61–93. Berlin [et al.]: De Gruyter, 2013.

Horn, Christoph and Christof Rapp [eds.]. *Wörterbuch der antiken Philosophie*. Munich: C.H. Beck, 2002.

Hugonnard-Roche, Henri: *La logique d'Aristote du grec au syriaque: Études sur la transmission des textes de l'*Organon *et leur interprétation philosophique*. Paris: Vrin, 2004.

Hurvitz, Nimrod. "Schools of Law and Historical Context: Re-Examining the Formation of the Ḥanbalī Madhhab." *Islamic Law and Society*, vol. 7, no. 1 (2000): pp. 37–64.

Hurvitz, Nimrod. *The Formation of Ḥanbalism: Piety into Power*. London [et al.]: Routledge, 2002.

Ibrahim, Bilal. *Freeing Philosophy from Metaphysics: Fakhr al-Dīn al-Rāzī's Philosophical Approach to the Study of Natural Phenomena*. Unpublished doctoral thesis. Montreal: McGill University, 2013.

Ibrahim, Bilal. "Faḫr ad-Dīn ar-Rāzī, Ibn al-Hayṯam and Aristotelian Science: Essentialism versus Phenomenalism in Post-Classical Islamic Thought." *Oriens*, vol. 41 (2013): pp. 379–431.

Inati, Shams C. *Ibn Sīnā: Remarks and Admonitions. Part One: Logic*. Toronto: Pontifical Institute of Mediaeval Studies, 1984.

Inati, Shams C. "Ibn Sina on Single Expressions." In *Islamic Theology and Philosophy: Studies in Honor of George F. Hourani*, ed. by Michael E. Marmura, pp. 148–159. Albany: State University of New York Press, 1984.

Iványi, Tamás. "Luġa." In *EALL*, vol. 3, pp. 88–95.

Jackson, Sherman A. "From Prophetic Actions to Constitutional Theory: A Novel Chapter in Medieval Muslim Jurisprudence." *International Journal of Middle East Studies*, vol. 25, no. 1 (1993): pp. 71–90.

Jackson, Sherman A. *Islamic Law and the State: The Constitutional Jurisprudence of Shihāb Al-Dīn al-Qarāfī*. Leiden [et al.]: Brill, 1996.

Jackson, Sherman A. "*Taqlīd*, Legal Scaffolding and the Scope of Legal Injunctions in Post-Formative Theory *Muṭlaq* and *ʿĀmm* in the Jurisprudence of Shihāb al-Dīn al-Qarāfī." *Islamic Law and Society*, vol. 3, no. 2 (1996): pp. 165–192.

Jackson, Sherman A. "Fiction and Formalism: Towards a Functional Analysis of *Uṣūl al-Fiqh*." In *Studies in Islamic Legal Theory*, ed. by Bernard G. Weiss, pp. 177–201. Leiden [et al.]: Brill, 2002.

Jaffer, Tariq. "Muʿtazilite Aspects of Faḫr ad-dīn al-Rāzī's Thought." *Arabica*, vol. 59 (2012): pp. 510–535.

Jaffer, Tariq. *Rāzī: Master of Qurʾānic Interpretation and Theological Reasoning*. Oxford: Oxford University Press, 2014.

Janssens, Jules. "Al-Ghazzālī's *Miʿyār al-ʿilm fī fann al-manṭiq*. Sources Avicenniennes et Farabiennes." *Archives d'histoire doctrinale et littéraire du Moyen Âge*, vol. 69 (2002): pp. 39–66.

Janssens, Jules. "Review: Frank Griffel: Apostasie und Toleranz im Islam." *Journal of Islamic Studies*, vol. 14, no. 1 (2003): pp. 69–72.

Janssens, Jules. "Al-Ghazālī: The Introduction of Peripatetic Syllogistic in Islamic Law (and Kalām)." *Mélanges de l'Institut Dominicain d'Études Orientales du Caire* (MIDEO), vol. 28 (2010): pp. 219–233.

Janssens, Jules. "Ibn Sīnā's Impact on Faḫr ad-dīn ar-Rāzī's *Mabāḥiṯ al-Mašriqiyya*, with Particular Regard to the Section Entitled *al-Ilāhiyyāt al-maḥḍa*: An Essay of Critical Evaluation." *Documenti e studi sulla tradizione filosofica medievale*, vol. 21 (2010): pp. 259–285.

Janssens, Jules. "Al-Lawkarī's Reception of Ibn Sīnā's Ilāhiyyāt." In *The Arabic, Hebrew and Latin Reception of Avicenna's 'Metaphysics'*, ed. by Dag Nikolaus Hasse and Amos Bertolacci, pp. 7–26. Berlin/Boston: De Gruyter, 2011.

Johansen, Baber. *Contingency in a Sacred Law: Legal and Ethical Norms in the Muslim Fiqh*. Leiden [et al.]: Brill, 1999.

Jomier, Jacques. "Les Mafātiḥ al-ghayb de l'Imām Fakhr al-din al-Rāzī: quelques dates, lieux, manuscrits." *Mélanges de l'Institut Dominicain d'Études Orientales du Caire* (MIDEO), vol. 13 (1977): pp. 253–290.

Jomier, Jacques. "The Qurʾanic Commentary of Imām Fakhr al-din al-Rāzī: Its Sources and its Originality." In *International Congress for the Study of the Qurʾan*, pp. 93–111. Canberra: Australian National University, 1980.

Jomier, Jacques. "L'autorité de la révélation et la raison dans le commentaire du Coran de Faḫr al-Dīn al-Rāzī." In *La notion d'autorité au Moyen Age: Islam, Byzance, Occident*, ed. by George Makdisi and Dominique Sourdel, pp. 245–261. Paris: Presses Universitaires de France, 1982.

Jomier, Jacques. "Fakhr al-dīn al-Rāzī (m. 606 H./1210) et les Commentaires du Coran plus anciens." *MIDEO*, vol. 15 (1982): pp. 145–172.

Kalbarczyk, Alexander. "*The Kitāb al-Maqūlāt of the Muḫtaṣar al-awsaṭ fī l-manṭiq*: A Hitherto Unknown Source for Studying Ibn Sīnā's Reception of Aristotle's *Categories*." *Oriens*, vol. 40, no. 2 (2012): pp. 305–354.

Kalbarczyk, Alexander. *Predication and Ontology: Studies and Texts on Avicennian and Post-Avicennian Readings of Aristotle's* Categories. Berlin: De Gruyter, 2018.

Kamali, Mohammad H. *Principles of Islamic Jurisprudence*. Cambridge: Islamic Texts Society, 2013 [reprint of the 3rd modified edition, 2003].

Karimullah, Kamran I. *Avicenna (d. 1037), Logical Theory, and the Aristotelian Tradition*. Montreal: McGill University, 2014 [retrieved October 2015, http://digitool.library.mcgill.ca/R/?func=dbin-jump-full&object_id=123019&local_base=GEN01-MCG02].

Karimullah, Kamran I. "Unusual Syllogisms: Avicenna and Najm al-Dīn al-Kātibī on *per impossibile* Syllogisms and Implication (*luzūm*)." *Oriens*, vol. 43, no. 1–2 (2015): pp. 223–271.

Katz, Marion Holmes. *Body of Text: The Emergence of the Sunnī Law of Ritual Purity*. Albany: State University of New York Press, 2002.

Katz, Marion Holmes. *Prayer in Islamic Thought and Practice*. New York [et al.]: Cambridge University Press, 2013.

Kholeif, Fathalla. *A Study on Fakhr al-Dīn al-Rāzī and his Controversies in Transoxiana*. Beirut: Dar el-Machreq, 1966.

Kneale, William and Martha Kneale. *The Development of Logic*. Oxford: Clarendon Press, 1962 [reprint 2008].

Knobel, Franziska. "Faḫraddīn ar-Rāzī, Al-Manṭiq al-kabīr (MS Aḥmad III, no. 3401, Jahr 1268 n. Chr.): Über den Nutzen der Dialektik." *Oriens*, vol. 43, no. 3–4 (2015): pp. 414–432.

Koutzarova, Tiana. *Das Transzendentale bei Ibn Sīnā*. Leiden [et al.]: Brill, 2009.

Krawietz, Birgit. "Zum Verhältnis von Sprache, Recht und Theologie in der islamischen Rechtstheorie von Sayf al-Dīn al-Āmidī." *Der Islam*, vol. 72 (1995): pp. 137–147.

Krawietz, Birgit. *Hierarchie der Rechtsquellen im tradierten sunnitischen Islam*. Berlin: Duncker and Humblot, 2002.

Krawietz, Birgit and Georges Tamer [eds.]. *Islamic Theology, Philosophy and Law: Debating Ibn Taymiyya and Ibn Qayyim al-Jawziyya*. Berlin [et al.]: De Gruyter, 2013.

Kukkonen, Taneli. "Al-Ghazālī on the Signification of Names." *Vivarium*, vol. 48 (2010): pp. 55–74.

Lagarde, Michel. *Index du Grand commentaire de Faḫr al-Dīn al-Rāzī*. Leiden [et al.]: Brill, 1996.

Lagarde, Michel. *Les Secrets de l'invisible. Essai sur le Grand Commentaire de Faḫr al-Dīn al-Rāzī*. Beirut: Dar al-Bouraq, 2008.

Lameer, Joep. "The Organon of Aristotle in the Medieval Oriental and Occidental Traditions." *Journal of the American Oriental Society*, vol. 116, no. 1 (1996): pp. 90–98.

Lameer, Joep. *Conception and Belief in Ṣadr al-Dīn Shīrāzī (ca. 1571–1635)*: Al-Risāla fī l-taṣawwur wa-l-taṣdīq. Tehran: Iranian Institute of Philosophy, 2006.

Lameer, Joep. "Towards a New Edition of Avicenna's *Kitāb al-Ishārāt wa-l-tanbīhāt*." *Journal of Islamic Manuscripts*, vol. 4 (2013): pp. 199–248.

Lane, Edward W. *An Arabic-English Lexicon*. 8 vols. New Delhi: Asian Educational Services, 2003 [2nd reprint; first publication 1863–1893].

Larkin, Margaret. *The Theology of Meaning: 'Abd al-Qāhir al-Jurjānī's Theory of Discourse*. New Haven, CT: American Oriental Society, 1995.

Larcher, Pierre. "Quand, en arabe, on parlait de l'arabe … (I): Essai sur la méthodologie de l'histoire de 'Metalangages Arabes.'" *Arabica*, vol. 35, no. 2 (July 1988): pp. 117–142.

Larcher, Pierre. "Éléments pragmatiques dans la théorie grammaticale arabe postclassique." In *Studies in the History of Arabic Grammar II. Proceedings of the 2nd Symposium on the History of Arabic Grammar, Nijmegen, 27. April–1. May 1987*, ed. by Kees Versteegh and Michael G. Carter, pp. 195–214. Amsterdam/Philadelphia: John Benjamins Publishing Company, 1990.

Larcher, Pierre. "Quand, en arabe, on parlait de l'arabe … (II): Essai sur la catégorie de *ʾinšāʾ* (vs. *ḫabar*)." *Arabica*, vol. 38, no. 2 (July 1991): pp. 246–273.

Larcher, Pierre. "Quand, en arabe, on parlait de l'arabe … (III): Grammaire, logique, rhétorique dans l'islam postclassique." *Arabica*, vol. 39, no. 3 (Nov. 1992): pp. 358–384.

Larcher, Pierre. "Les *ʾAmālī* d'Ibn al-Ḥāǧib ou les *Annales* d'un grammairien." *Arabica*, vol. 41, no. 2 (1994): pp. 273–280.

Larcher, Pierre. "Coran et théorie linguistique de l'enociation." *Arabica*, vol. 47, no. 3 (2000): pp. 441–456.

Larcher, Pierre. "ʾinšāʾ." In EALL.

Larcher, Pierre. "Arabic Linguistic Tradition II: Pragmatics." In *The Oxford Handbook of Arabic Linguistics*, ed. by Jonathan Owens, pp. 185–212. New York: Oxford University Press, 2013.

Löbner, Sebastian. *Semantik: Eine Einführung*. Berlin [et al.]: De Gruyter, 2003.

Löschner, Harald. *Die dogmatischen Grundlagen des šīʿitischen Rechts: Eine Untersuchung zur modernen imāmitischen Rechtsquellenlehre*. Cologne [et al.]: Carl Heymanns Verlag, 1971.

Loucel, Henri. "L'origine du langage d'après les grammairiens arabes I–IV." *Arabica*, vol. 10, (1963): pp. 188–208, pp. 253–281 and vol. 11 (1964): pp. 57–72, pp. 151–187.

Lowry, Joseph E. "Does Shāfiʿī have a Theory of 'Four Sources' of Law?" In *Studies in Islamic Legal Theory*, ed. by Bernard G. Weiss, pp. 23–50, Leiden: Brill, 2002.

Lowry, Joseph E. *Early Islamic Legal Theory: The Risāla of Muḥammad ibn Idrīs al-Šāfiʿī*. Leiden [et al.]: Brill, 2007.

Lowry, Joseph E. "The first Islamic Legal Theory: Ibn al-Muqaffaʿ on Interpretation,

Authority, and the Structure of Law." *Journal of the American Oriental Society*, vol. 128, no. 1 (2008): pp. 25–40.

Lowry, Joseph E. "Some Preliminary Observations on al-Šāfiʿī and Later *Uṣūl al-fiqh*: The Case of the Term *bayān*." *Arabica*, vol. 55 (2008): pp. 505–527.

Madelung, Wilferd F. "Abū l-Ḥusayn al-Baṣrī." In *EI*², http://dx.doi.org/10.1163/1573-3912_islam_SIM_8253, last accessed 14 October 2017.

Madkūr, Ibrāhīm. Introduction to Ibn Sīnā's *Kitāb aš-Šifāʾ, al-Manṭiq, al-Madḫal*, ed. by Ibrāhīm Madkūr, pp. 1–77. Cairo: al-Hayʾa al-ʿĀmma li-Šuʾūn al-Maṭābiʿ al-Amīriyya, 1952.

Madkūr, Ibrāhīm. *L'Organon d'Aristote dans le monde arabe*. Paris: Vrin, 1969.

Mahdavī, Yaḥyā. *Fehrest-e nosḫehā-ye moṣannafāt-e Ebn-e Sīnā/Bibliographie d'Ibn Sina*. Tehran: Entešārāt-e Dānešgāh-e Tehrān, 1954 [1333].

Makdisi, George. "Ashʿarī and the Ashʿarites in Islamic Religious History II." *Studia Islamica*, vol. 18 (1963): pp. 19–39.

Makdisi, George. *The Rise of Colleges. Institutions of Learning in Islam and the West.* Edinburgh: Edinburgh University Press, 1981.

Makdisi, George. "The Juridical Theology of Shāfiʿī: Origins and Significance of *Uṣūl al-Fiqh*." *Studia Islamica*, vol. 59 (1984): pp. 5–47.

Marmura, Michael E. "Avicenna's Chapter on Universals in the Isagoge of His Shifāʾ." In *Islam, Past Influence and Present Challenge*, ed. by Alford T. Welch and Pierre Cachia, pp. 34–56. Edinburgh: Edinburgh University Press, 1979.

Marmura, Michael E. "Avicenna on the Division of the Sciences in the *Isagoge* of His *Shifāʾ*." *Journal of the History of the Arabic Science*, vol. 4, no. 2 (1980): pp. 239–251.

Marmura, Michael E. "Quiddity and Universality in Avicenna." In *Neoplatonism and Islamic Thought*, ed. by Parviz Morewedge, pp. 77–87. Albany, NY: State University of New York Press, 1992.

Marmura, Michael E. "Fakhr al-Dīn al-Rāzī's Critique of an Avicennan *Tanbīh*." In *Historia Philosophiae Medii Aevi: Studien zur Geschichte der Philosophie des Mittelalters*, ed. by Burkhard Mojsisch and Olaf Pluta, vol. 2, pp. 627–641. Amsterdam: John Benjamins, 1991.

Marogy, Amal E. "Zayd, ʿAmr and ʿAbdullāhi: Theory of Proper Names and Reference in Early Arabic Grammatical Tradition." In *The Foundations of Arabic Linguistics: Sībawayhi and Early Arabic Grammatical Theory*, ed. by Amal E. Marogy, pp. 119–134. Leiden [et al.]: Brill, 2002.

Maróth, Miklos. *Ibn Sīnā und die peripatetische 'Aussagenlogik'*. Leiden [et al.]: Brill, 1989.

Maróth, Miklos. "The Changes of Metaphor in Arabic Literature." *Arabic Sciences and Philosophy*, vol. 12, no. 2 (2002): pp. 241–255.

McGinnis, Jon. "Logic and Science: The Role of Genus and Difference in Avicenna's

Logic, Science and Natural Philosophy." *Documenti e Studi sulla Tradizione filosofica medievale*, vol. 18 (2007): pp. 165–187.

Mehren, August F. *Die Rhetorik der Araber*. Copenhagen: Otto Schwartz, 1853.

Meisami, Julie Scott. *Structure and Meaning in Medieval Arabic and Persian Poetry*. London: Routledge, 2006.

Mosel, Ulrike. *Die syntaktische Terminologie bei Sibawaih*. 2 vols. Munich, 1975.

Moutaouakil, Ahmed. *Réflexions sur la Theorie de la Signification dans la Pensée Linguistique Arabe*. Rabat: Faculté des Lettres et des Sciences Humaines, 1982.

Moutaouakil, Ahmed. "La notion d'actes de langage dans la pensée linguistique arabe ancienne." In *Studies in the History of Arabic Grammar II. Proceedings of the 2nd Symposium on the History of Arabic Grammar, Nijmegen, 27. April–1. May 1987*, ed. by Kees Versteegh and Michael G. Carter, pp. 229–237. Amsterdam/Philadelphia: John Benjamins, 1990.

Muḥassab, Muḥyī ad-dīn. *ʿIlm ad-dalāla ʿinda l-ʿarab: Faḫr ad-dīn ar-Rāzī namūḏağan*. Beirut: Dār al-kitāb al-ğadīd al-muttaḥida, 2008.

Muranyi, Miklos. "Religiöse Literatur in arabischer Sprache. Fiqh." In *Grundriß der arabischen Philologie. Vol. II. Literaturwissenschaft*, ed. by Helmut Gätje, pp. 299–325. Wiesbaden: Reichert, 1987.

Muranyi, Miklos. *Beiträge zur Geschichte der Ḥadīṯ- und Rechtsgelehrsamkeit der Mālikiyya in Nordafrika bis zum 5. Jh. d.H.: Bio-bibliographische Notizen aus der Moscheebibliothek von Qairawān*. Wiesbaden: Harrassowitz, 1997.

Nagel, Tilman. *Das islamische Recht: Eine Einführung*. Westhoven: WVA-Verlag Skulima, 2001.

Oberauer, Nobert. *Religiöse Verpflichtung im Islam. Ein ethischer Grundbegriff und seine theologische, rechtliche und sozialgeschichtliche Dimension*. Würzburg: Ergon, 2004.

Oertmann, Paul. *Interesse und Begriff in der Rechtswissenschaft*. Leipzig: A. Deichertsche Verlagsbuchhandlung, 1931.

Owens, Jonathan. *The Foundations of Grammar: An Introduction to Medieval Arabic Grammatical Theory*. Amsterdam [et al.]: John Benjamins, 1988.

Owens, Jonathan. "The Syntactic Basis of Arabic Word Classification." *Arabica*, vol. 36, no. 2 (July 1989): pp. 211–234.

Owens, Jonathan [ed.]. *The Oxford Handbook of Arabic Linguistics*. New York: Oxford University Press, 2013.

Pakatchi, Ahmad. "Alfāẓ." In *Encyclopaedia Islamica*, vol. 3, pp. 461–469.

Potacs, Michael. *Auslegung im öffentlichen Recht*. Baden-Baden: Nomos, 1994.

al-Rahim, Ahmed H. "Avicenna's Immediate Disciples: Their Lives and Works." In *Avicenna and his Legacy. A Golden Age of Science and Philosophy*, ed. by Tzvi Y. Langermann, pp. 1–25. Turnhout: Brepols, 2009.

Ramić, Šukrija H. *Language and the Interpretation of Islamic Law*. Cambridge: The Islamic Texts Society, 2003.

Reinhart, Kevin A. "'Like the Difference between Heaven and Earth.' Ḥanafī and Shāfiʿī Discussions of *Farḍ* and *Wājib* in Theology and Uṣūl." In *Studies in Islamic Legal Theory*, ed. by Bernard G. Weiss, pp. 205–234. Leiden [et al.]: Brill, 2002.

Reisman, David C. "Bahmanyār b. al-Marzubān." In *EI*³, http://dx.doi.org/10.1163/1573-3912_ei3_COM_22743, last accessed 14 October 2017.

Reisman, David C. *The Making of the Avicennan Tradition. The Transmission, Contents, and Structure of Ibn Sīnā's* al-Mubāḥāṯāt (*The Discussions*). Leiden: Brill, 2002.

Rescher, Nicholas. *The Development of Arabic Logic*. Pittsburgh: University of Pittsburgh Press, 1964.

Robson, J. "al-Bayḍāwī." In *EI*², http://dx.doi.org/10.1163/1573-3912_islam_SIM_1310, last accessed 14 October 2017.

Rohe, Mathias. *Das islamische Recht: Geschichte und Gegenwart*. Munich: C.H. Beck, 2009.

El-Rouayheb, Khaled. "Post-Avicennan Logicians on the Subject Matter of Logic: Some Thirteenth- and Fourteenth-Century Discussions." *Arabic Sciences and Philosophy*, vol. 22 (2012): pp. 69–90.

El-Rouayheb, Khaled. *See* al-Ḫūnaǧī, Afḍal ad-dīn.

Rudolph, Ulrich. "Die Neubewertung der Logik durch al-Ġazālī." In *Logik und Theologie. Das Organon im Arabischen und im Lateinischen Mittelalter*, ed. by Dominik Perler and Ulrich Rudolph, pp. 73–97. Leiden [et al.]: Brill, 2005.

Sabra, A.I. "Avicenna on the Subject Matter of Logic." *The Journal of Philosophy*, vol. 77, no. 11 (Nov. 1980): pp. 746–764.

Saleh, Walid. "al-Bayḍāwī." In *EI*³, http://dx.doi.org/10.1163/1573-3912_ei3_COM_25267, last accessed 14 October 2017.

Sanni, Amidu. "On *Taḍmīn* (Enjambment) and Structural Coherence in Classical Arabic Poetry." *Bulletin of the School of Oriental and African Studies*, vol. 52, no. 3 (1989): pp. 463–466.

Sanni, Amidu. "Again on *taḍmīn* in Arabic Theoretical Discourse." *Bulletin of the School of Oriental and African Studies*, vol. 61, no. 1 (1998): pp. 1–19.

Sarrió Cucarella, Diego R. *Muslim-Christian Polemics Across the Mediterranean: The Splendid Replies of Shihāb al-Dīn al-Qarāfī (d. 684/1285)*. Leiden [et al.]: Brill, 2015.

Schacht, Joseph. *An Introduction to Islamic Law*. Oxford: Clarendon Press, 1982 [1st edition 1964].

Schmidtke, Sabine. *The Theology of ʿAllāma al-Ḥillī (d. 726/1325)*. Berlin: Klaus Schwarz Verlag, 1991.

Schmidtke, Sabine. "Two Commentaries on Najm al-Dīn al-Kātibī's *al-Shamsiyya*, Copied in the Hand of David b. Joshua Maimonides (fl. ca. 1335–1410 CE)." In *Law and Tradition in Classical Islamic Thought*, ed. by Michael Cook, Najam Haider, Intinsar Rabb, and Asma Sayeed, pp. 203–225. New York: Palgrave McMillan, 2013.

Schneider, Egon and Friedrich E. Schnapp. *Logik für Juristen: Die Grundlagen der Denklehre und der Rechtsanwendung*. Munich: Franz Vahlen, 2006 [6th edition].

Scholz, Oliver R. *Verstehen und Rationalität. Untersuchungen zu den Grundlagen von Hermeneutik und Sprachphilosophie*. Frankfurt a. M.: Vittorio Klostermann, 2001.

Schöck, Cornelia. "Aussagenquantifizierung und -modalisierung in der frühen islamischen Theologie." In *Logik und Theologie. Das Organon im Arabischen und im Lateinischen Mittelalter*, ed. by Dominik Perler and Ulrich Rudolph, pp. 19–43. Leiden [et al.]: Brill, 2005.

Schöck, Cornelia. *Koranexegese, Grammatik und Logik. Zum Verhältnis von arabischer und aristotelischer Urteils-, Konsequenz- und Schlusslehre*. Leiden [et al.]: Brill, 2006.

Schöck, Cornelia. "Discussions on Conditional Sentences from the Year AH 17/AD 638 to Avicenna." In *Classical Arabic Philosophy: Sources and Reception*, ed. by Peter Adamson, pp. 55–73. London [et al.]: The Warburg Institute, 2007.

Schöck, Cornelia. "Name (*ism*), Derived Name (*ism mushtaqq*) and Description (*waṣf*) in Arabic Grammar, Muslim Dialectical Theology and Arabic Logic." In *The Unity of Science in the Arabic Tradition. Science, Logic, Epistemology and their Interactions*, ed. by Shahid Rahman, Tony Street and Hassan Tahiri, pp. 329–360. Dordrecht: Springer, 2008.

Schwarb, Gregor. "Capturing the Meaning of God's Speech: The Relevance of *uṣūl al-fiqh* to an Understanding of *uṣūl al-tafsīr* in Jewish and Muslim Kalām." In *A Word Fitly Spoken: Studies in Medieval Exegesis of the Hebrew Bible and the Qur'ān Presented to Haggai Ben-Shammai*, ed. by Meir M. Bar-Asher, Simon Hopkins, Sarah Stroumsa, and Buno Chiesa, pp. 111–156. Jerusalem: Ben-Zvi Institute, 2007.

Shah, Mustafa. "Classical Islamic Discourse on the Origins of Language: Cultural Memory and the Defence of Orthodoxy." *Numen*, vol. 58 (2011): pp. 314–343.

Shehaby, Nabil. *The Propositional Logic of Avicenna. A Translation from al-Shifā': al-Qiyās with Introduction, Commentary and Glossary*. Boston [et al.]: D. Reidel, 1973.

Shihadeh, Ayman. "From al-Ghazālī to al-Rāzī: 6th/12th Century Developments in Muslim Philosophical Theology." *Arabic Sciences and Philosophy*, vol. 15 (2005): pp. 141–179.

Shihadeh, Ayman. *The Teleological Ethics of Fakhr al-Dīn al-Rāzī*. Leiden [et al.]: Brill, 2006.

Shihadeh, Ayman. "Al-Razı's (d. 1210) Commentary on Avicenna's Pointers. The Confluence of Exegesis and Aporetics." In *The Oxford Handbook of Islamic Philosophy*, ed. by Khaled El-Rouayheb and Sabine Schmidtke, pp. 296–325. Oxford: Oxford University Press, 2017.

Simon, Udo Gerald. *Mittelalterliche arabische Sprachbetrachtung zwischen Grammatik und Rhetorik*: ʿilm al-maʿānī *bei as-Sakkākī*. Heidelberg: Heidelberger Orientverlag, 1993.

Simon, Udo Gerald. "Majāz." In *EALL*, vol. 3, pp. 116–123.

Sinnū, Ahyaf and Ǧirār Ǧihāmī [eds.]. *Mawsūʿat muṣṭalaḥāt al-ʿulūm an-naḥwiyya.*

Silsilat mawsūʿāt al-muṣṭalaḥāt al-ʿarabiyya wa-l-islamiyya. Beirut: Maktabat Lubnān Nāširūn, 2010.

Smith, Wilfred C. *The Meaning and End of Religion*. Minneapolis: Fortress Press, 1963 [reprint 1991].

Smyth, William. "Criticism in the Post-Classical Period: A Survey." In *Arabic Literature in the Post-Classical Period*, ed. by Roger Allen, pp. 387–417. Cambridge [et al.]: Cambridge University Press, 2006.

Stewart, Devin J. *Islamic Legal Orthodoxy: Twelver Shiite Responses to the Sunni Legal System*. Salt Lake City: University of Utah Press, 1998.

Street, Tony. "Ṭūsī on Avicenna's Logical Connectives." *History and Philosophy of Logic*, vol. 16 (1995): pp. 257–268.

Street, Tony, "Concerning the Life and Works of Fakhr al-Dīn al-Rāzī." In *Islam: Essays on Scripture, Thought and Society. A Festschrift in Honour of Anthony H. Johns*, ed. by Peter G. Riddel and Tony Street, pp. 135–146. Leiden [et al.]: Brill, 1997.

Street, Tony, "An Outline of Avicenna's Syllogistics." *Archiv für Geschichte der Philosophie*, vol. 84 (2002): pp. 129–160.

Street, Tony. "Arabic Logic." In *Handbook of the History of Logic. Volume 1: Greek, Indian and Arabic Logic*, ed. by Dov M. Gabbay and John Woods, pp. 523–596. Amsterdam [et al.]: Elsevier North Holland, 2004.

Street, Tony. "Faḫraddīn ar-Rāzī's Critique of Avicennan Logic." In *Logik und Theologie. Das Organon im Arabischen und im Lateinischen Mittelalter*, ed. by Dominik Perler and Ulrich Rudolph, pp. 99–116. Leiden [et al.]: Brill, 2005.

Street, Tony, "Arabic and Islamic Philosophy of Language and Logic." *Stanford Encyclopedia of Philosophy*, 2008, http://plato.stanford.edu/archives/spr2009/entries/arabic-islamic-language/, last accessed 12 September 2017.

Street, Tony, "Avicenna on the Syllogism." In *Interpreting Avicenna: Critical Essays*, edited by Peter Adamson, pp. 48–70. Cambridge: Cambridge University Press, 2013.

Street, Tony, "Afḍal al-Dīn al-Khūnajī (d. 1248) on the Conversion of Modal Propositions." *Oriens*, vol. 42 (2014): pp. 454–513.

Street, Tony. "Al-ʿAlāma al-Ḥillī (d. 1325) and the Early Reception of Kātibī's *Shamsīya*: Notes Towards a Study of the Dynamics of Post-Avicennan Logical Commentary." *Oriens*, vol. 44 (2016): pp. 267–300.

Strobino, Riccardo. "Avicenna on the Indemonstrability of Definition." *Documenti e studi sulla tradizione filosofica medievale*, vol. 21 (2010): pp. 113–163.

Strobino, Riccardo. "Per Se, Inseparability, Containment and Implication. Bridging the Gap between Avicenna's Theory of Demonstration and Logic of the Predicables." *Oriens*, vol. 44 (2016): pp. 181–266.

Suleiman, Yasir. "Sībawaihi's 'Parts of Speech' according to Zajjājī: A New Interpretation." *Journal of Semitic Studies*, vol. 35, no. 2 (Autumn 1990): pp. 245–263.

Szlezák, Thomas A. *Pseudo-Archytas über die Kategorien*. Berlin [et al.]: De Gruyter, 1972.

Talmon, Rafael. "'Al-kalām mā kāna muktafiyan bi-nafsihī wa-huwa l-ǧumla': A Study in the History of Sentence-Concept and the Sībawaihian Legacy in Arabic Grammar." *Zeitschrift der Deutschen Morgenländischen Gesellschaft*, vol. 138 (1988): pp. 74–98.

Treiger, Alexander. "Avicenna's Notion of Transcendental Modulation of Existence (*taškīk al-wuǧūd, analogia entis*) and its Greek and Arabic Sources." In *Islamic Philosophy, Science, Culture and Religion: Studies in Honor of Dimitri Gutas*, ed. by Felicitas Opwis and David Reisman, pp. 327–363. Leiden [et al.]: Brill, 2012.

Trumpp, Ernst: "Beiträge zur Erklärung des Mufaṣṣal." *Sitzungsberichte der philosophisch-philologischen und historischen Classe der k.b. Akademie der Wissenschaften*, vol. III, Munich: F. Straub, 1878.

Versteegh, Cornelis H.M. (or Kees). *Greek Elements in Arabic Linguistic Thinking*. Leiden [et al.]: Brill, 1977.

Versteegh, Cornelis H.M. *Arabic Grammar and Qur'ānic Exegesis in Early Islam*. Leiden [et al.]: Brill, 1993.

Versteegh, Cornelis H.M. *The Explanation of Linguistic Causes. Az-Zaǧǧāǧī's Theory of Grammar*. Amsterdam: John Benjamins, 1995.

Versteegh, Cornelis H.M. "The Linguistic Introduction to Rāzī's *Tafsīr*." In *Studies in Near Eastern Languages and Literatures. Memorial Volume of Karel Petráček*, ed. by Petr Zemánek, pp. 589–603. Prague: Academy of Sciences of the Czech Republic Oriental Institute, 1996.

Versteegh, Cornelis H.M. "The Arabic Tradition." In *The Emergence of Semantics in four Linguistic Traditions: Hebrew, Sanskrit, Greek, Arabic*, ed. by Wout J. van Bekkum, Jan Houben, Ineke Sluiter, and Kees Versteegh, pp. 225–284. Amsterdam [et al.]: John Benjamins, 1996.

Versteegh, Cornelis H.M. "Linguistic Attitudes and the Origin of Speech in the Arab World." In *Understanding Arabic: Essays in Contemporary Arabic Linguistics in Honor of El-Said Badawi*, ed. by Alaa Elgibali, pp. 15–31. Cairo: The American University in Cairo Press, 1996.

Versteegh, Cornelis H.M. *Landmarks in Linguistic Thought III: The Arabic Linguistic Tradition*. London [et al.]: Routledge, 1997.

Versteegh, Cornelis H.M. "Grammar and Logic in the Arabic grammatical tradition." In *History of the Language Sciences: An International Handbook on the Evolution of the Study of Language from the Beginnings to the Present*, ed. by Sylvain Auroux and Kees Versteegh, pp. 300–306. Berlin [et al.]: De Gruyter, 2000.

Versteegh, Cornelis H.M. "Meanings of Speech: The Category of Sentential Mood in Arabic Grammar." In *Le voyage et la langue: Mélanges en l'honneur d'Anouar Louca et d'André Roman*, ed. by Joseph Dichy and Hassan Hamzé, pp. 269–287. Damascus: Institut Français du Proche-Orient, 2004.

Vishanoff, David R. *The Formation of Islamic Hermeneutics: How Sunni Legal Theorists Imagined a Revealed Law*. New Haven, CT: American Oriental Society, 2011.

WKAS = *Wörterbuch der klassischen arabischen Sprache*. Founded by J. Krämer and H. Gätje. Ed. by M. Ullmann. Wiesbaden: Harrassowitz, 1957 ff.

Walbridge, John. "Logic in the Islamic Intellectual Tradition: The Recent Centuries." *Islamic Studies*, vol. 39, no. 1 (2000): pp. 55–75.

Wansbrough, John. "Arabic Rhetoric and Qur'anic Exegesis." *Bulletin of the School of Oriental and African Studies*, vol. 31, no. 3 (1968): pp. 469–485.

Weidemann, Hermann. "Anmerkungen." In *Aristoteles. Werke in deutscher Übersetzung vol. 1, part II*. Translation and commentary by Hermann Weidemann, pp. 133–477. Berlin: Akademie Verlag, 2002 [1st edition 1994].

Weiss, Bernard G. *Language in Orthodox Muslim Thought: A Study of* Waḍʿ al-Lugha *and Its Development*. Princeton: Princeton University, 1966.

Weiss, Bernard G. "Medieval Muslim Discussions of the Origin of Language." *Zeitschrift der Deutschen Morgenländischen Gesellschaft*, vol. 124 (1974): pp. 33–41.

Weiss, Bernard G. "A Theory of the Parts of Speech in Arabic (Noun, Verb and Particle): A Study in "ilm al-waḍʿ"." *Arabica*, vol. 23, no. 1 (Feb. 1976): pp. 23–36.

Weiss, Bernard G. "Language and Tradition in Medieval Islam: The Question of *al-Ṭarīq ilā maʿrifat al-lugha*." *Der Islam*, vol. 61 (1984): pp. 91–99.

Weiss, Bernard G. "Language and Law: The Linguistic Premises of Islamic Legal Science." In *In Quest of an Islamic Humanism: Arabic and Islamic Studies in Memory of Mohamed al-Nowaihi*, ed. by A.H. Green, pp. 15–21. Cairo: The American University in Cairo Press, 1984.

Weiss, Bernard G. "Exotericism and Objectivity in Islamic Jurisprudence." In *Islamic Law and Jurisprudence*, ed. by Nicholas Heer, pp. 53–71. Seattle [et al.]: University of Washington Press, 1987.

Weiss, Bernard G. "*ʿIlm al-waḍʿ*: An Introductory Account of a Later Muslim Philological Science." *Arabica*, vol. 34 (Nov. 1987): pp. 339–356.

Weiss, Bernard G. *The Search for God's Law. Islamic Jurisprudence in the Writings of Sayf al-Dīn al-Āmidī*. Salt Lake City: University of Utah Press, 2010 [1st edition 1992].

Weiss, Bernard G. *The Spirit of Islamic Law*. London [et al.]: University of Georgia Press, 1998.

Weiss, Bernard G. "Text and Application: Hermeneutical Reflections on Islamic Legal Interpretation." In *The Law Applied. Contextualizing the Islamic Shariʿa*, ed. by Peri Bearman, Wolfhart Heinrichs, and Bernard G. Weiss, pp. 374–396. London [et al.]: I.B. Tauris, 2008.

Wisnovsky, Robert. "One Aspect of the Avicennian Turn in Sunnī Theology." *Arabic Sciences and Philosophy*, vol. 14 (2004): pp. 65–100.

Wisnovsky, Robert. "The Nature and Scope of Arabic Philosophical Commentary in Post-Classical (c. 1100–1900 AD) Islamic Intellectual History: Some Preliminary Observations." In *Philosophy, Science and Exegesis in Greek, Arabic and Latin Commentaries*, ed. by Peter Adamson, Han Baltussen, and Martin W.F. Stone, pp. 149–191. London: Institute of Classical Studies, 2004.

Wisnovsky, Robert. "Avicenna's Islamic Reception." In *Interpreting Avicenna: Critical Essays*, ed. by Peter Adamson, pp. 190–213. Cambridge: Cambridge University Press, 2013.

Wisnovsky, Robert. "Avicennism and Exegetical Practice in the Early Commentaries on the *Ishārāt*." *Oriens*, vol. 41, no. 3–4 (2013): pp. 349–378.

Wisnovsky, Robert. "Towards a Genealogy of Avicennism." *Oriens*, vol. 42, no. 3–4 (2014): pp. 323–363.

Yunis Ali, Mohamed M. *Medieval Islamic Pragmatics: Sunni Legal Theorists' Models of Textual Communication.* Richmond, Surrey: Curzon Press, 2000.

Zimmermann, F.W. Introduction to *Al-Farabi's Commentary and Short Treatise on Aristotle's* De Interpretatione. Translation with introduction and commentaries by F.W. Zimmermann, pp. xxi–cl. New York: Oxford University Press, 1981.

Zysow, Aron. *The Economy of Certainty: An Introduction to the Typology of Islamic Legal Theory*. Atlanta: Lockwood Press, 2013.

Zysow, Aron. "Muʿtazilism and Māturīdism in Ḥanafī Legal Theory." In *Studies in Islamic Legal Theory*, ed. by Berhard G. Weiss, pp. 235–265. Leiden [et al.]: Brill, 2002.

Index of Names

Index of Subjects

Index of Qur'anic Citations

www.ingramcontent.com/pod-product-compliance
Ingram Content Group UK Ltd.
Pitfield, Milton Keynes, MK11 3LW, UK
UKHW022227051026
15624UKWH00002B/394

9 789004 736023